Bt 5.40

the modern
american political novel
1900-1960

the modern american political novel 1900-1960

By Joseph Blotner

university of texas press austin & london

Library of Congress Catalog Card
No. 65–27533
Copyright © 1966, by Joseph Blotner
All rights reserved

Printed by University of Texas Printing Division, Austin
Bound by Universal Bookbindery, Inc., San Antonio

PERMISSIONS TO QUOTE

I wish to give special thanks to John Dos Passos, Upton Sinclair, Karl Schriftgiesser, and Robert Penn Warren for permission to quote from their books and articles, and to Alfred A. Knopf, Inc., for allowing me to quote extensively from the following books:

W. J. Cash, *The Mind of the South*
Chester T. Crowell, *Liquor Loot and Ladies*
Harvey Fergusson, *Capitol Hill: A Novel of Washington Life*
Eric Goldman, *Rendezvous with Destiny: A History of Modern American Reform*
Richard Hofstadter, *The Age of Reform: From Bryan to F. D. R.*
V. O. Key, Jr., *Southern Politics*
Arthur Link, *American Epoch: A History of the United States since the 1890's*
Robert Rylee, *The Ring and the Cross*

The Sewanee Review and Trinity College, Cambridge, too have been kind enough to allow me to use material for which they hold the copyright. Acknowledgment is also due the following publishers.

The University of Chicago Press
Bernard A. Weisberger, *The American Newspaperman*. Copyright 1961 by Bernard A. Weisberger.

Dorrance & Company, Inc.
John Francis Goldsmith, *President Randolph as I Knew Him*

Doubleday & Company, Inc.
Margaret Culkin Banning, *The Spellbinders*. Copyright 1922 by George H. Doran Company. Reprinted by permission of Doubleday & Company, Inc.
Estes Kefauver, *Crime in America*. Copyright 1951 by Estes Kefauver. Reprinted by permission of Doubleday & Company, Inc.

Duke University Press
Harold Zink, *City Bosses in the United States: A Study of Twenty Municipal Bosses*

Farrar, Straus & Giroux, Inc.
Gerald Sykes, *The Children of Light*
Nathanael West, *The Complete Works of Nathanael West*

Victor Gollancz, Ltd.
  Estes Kefauver, *Crime in America*
Harcourt, Brace & World, Inc.
  Daniel Aaron, *Writers on the Left*
  Richard H. Rovere, *Senator Joe McCarthy*
  Robert Penn Warren, *All the King's Men*
Harper & Row, Publishers
  Richard Crossman, *The God That Failed*
Harvard University Press
  Walter Rideout, *The Radical Novel in the United States 1900–1954*
Holt, Rinehart and Winston, Inc.
  May Sarton, *Faithful Are the Wounds*
Houghton Mifflin Company
  James Reichley, *The Burying of Kingsmith*
  Arthur M. Schlesinger, Jr., *The Age of Roosevelt: The Politics of Up-heaval*
The Macmillan Company
  Sir James Frazer, *The Golden Bough: A Study in Magic and Religion.*
  Copyright 1943 by The Macmillan Company
William Morrow and Company, Inc.
  Merle Miller, *The Sure Thing.* Copyright 1949 by Merle Miller.
  Tom Wicker, *The Kingpin.* Copyright 1953 by Tom Wicker.
W. W. Norton Co.
  William Lederer and Eugene Burdick, *The Ugly American*
Random House, Inc.
  Charles Francis Coe, *Ashes*
  Robert Penn Warren, Introduction to Modern Library edition of *All the King's Men*
The Viking Press, Inc.
  Lester Cohen, *Coming Home*
  Arthur Hadley, *The Joy Wagon*
  Lionel Trilling, *The Middle of the Journey*
H. W. Wilson Co.
  Victory: How Women Won It

For
my wife,
Yvonne,
and
my grandmother,
Carrie Jane Wright

ACKNOWLEDGMENTS

It would take several pages for me to thank all the people who helped bring this book to completion. However, to a few I wish to voice my special gratitude. After I had finished an earlier book, Professor Richard C. Snyder, who was editor of the series in which that book appeared, urged me to write this one. Mr. Benjamin F. Houston also encouraged me to go on to a larger study. The Research Committee of the University of Virginia provided two grants, and the Committee's chairman, Professor C. Julian Bishko, always gave a sympathetic hearing to my needs.

A portion of these grants covered the expenses of taking materials with me to Denmark in 1958. There, while I was Fulbright Lecturer in American Literature at the University of Copenhagen, I had the chance to treat my subject in a seminar with intelligent and amiable students. I owe much to the Conference Board of Associated Research Councils for that appointment, during which the lightened teaching load accelerated my work by well over a year, under the most pleasant circumstances. At the term's end, in the spring of 1959, the United States Educational Foundation in Denmark generously provided a research grant which permitted me to travel and to write. A return to Copenhagen on a second Fulbright Lectureship in 1963 gave me the time I needed to make final revisions. During both Danish appointments the Secretary of the Educational Foundation, Mrs. Karin Fennow, did everything she could to help me in my work. Throughout this time span I benefited from the reactions of varied audiences before whom I had lectured on the subject.

The University of Virginia Library helped me in many ways: the late Miss Louise Savage bought the books I needed in the infrequent cases when the library did not already have them; Miss Helena C. Koiner efficiently saw to it that books were sent, transatlantic, when I needed them; Miss Katherine H. Beville helped me when I had to use interlibrary loan facilities; and Mr. Harvey Deal aided me when I encountered reference problems.

Professor Walter B. Rideout, with great generosity, gave my manuscript the most close and helpful critical reading I could have hoped for. The late Professor Frederick L. Gwynn supplied information, comments on style, and editorial advice; Professor Snyder read the manuscript from a political scientist's point of view; and Professor Paul M. Gaston provided very helpful advice in the field of American History.

Mrs. Adele Hall and Mrs. Betty Jean Blincoe typed the manuscript, in both the original and revised versions—laborious work which they did admirably and cheerfully.

To all these friends, and to these institutions, I owe profound thanks and gratitude. They have a large share in any merit this study may have. Its shortcomings are solely my own.

One of the rewards of this work was the chance it afforded me to talk with the makers of literature: William Faulkner, Albert Camus, John Dos Passos, Vasco Pratolini, and Stephen Spender. Now as then, they have my deepest gratitude.

My wife saw me through the whole thing, giving counsel and comfort. Other wives and husbands will know how vital that function was.

Joseph Blotner

TABLE OF CONTENTS

the modern
american political novel
1900-1960

INTRODUCTION

Joyce Cary's *To Be a Pilgrim* (1942) is narrated by Tom Wilcher. Looking back, he recalls the stormy days early in the century "during the last great battle with the Lords," when, he says, "any loud noise at night, a banging door, a roll of thunder, would bring me sitting upright in bed, with sweat on my forehead and the thought, 'The first bomb—it has come at last'."[1] By nature an observer, he has had an inside view through his brother Edward, a prominent M.P. and minister. At one point he tells Tom, "No one has written a real political novel—giving the real feel of politics . . . of people feeling the way: of moles digging frantically about to dodge some unknown noise overhead . . . you don't get the sense of limitation and confusion, of walking on a slack wire over an unseen gulf by a succession of lightning flashes . . ."[2] Cary's novel substantially belies Wilcher's words. His portrayal of the complex politician Chester Nimmo in *Prisoner of Grace* (1952) and *Except the Lord* (1953) gave further evidence of the novelist's unique resources in this area. But the question which Tom Wilcher's assertion raises is not to be dismissed, and it has challenging implications. How much political reality can literature reflect? Are politics and literature so different that relationships are impossibly tenuous and dubious? Is there any importance in trying to show any relation?

These questions can be developed further. One can try to distinguish between politics and other kinds of human experience as material for the novelist's shaping art. One can try to differentiate the methods of the social scientist and the artist in prose fiction when each turns his skills upon political experience. Political scientist Richard Snyder wrote some years ago that, generally speaking, "the novelist is primarily concerned with a coherent story, with a whole fabric of description, and with specific details while the political scientist is concerned with events, processes, and factors, with abstractions from wholes and with classes of general phenomena." He went on to argue that the scientist builds his analyses through the use of extensive "gross data" and repeated behavior

[1] Joyce Cary, *To Be a Pilgrim,* p. 198.
[2] Cary, *Pilgrim,* p. 265.

PUBLICATION DATES OF NOVELS IN THIS STUDY

Classified by Types

	I The Young Knight	II The Boss	III Corruption	IV Novel of the Future	V The Role of Woman	VI The Southern Politician	VII American Fascism	VIII The Far Right and McCarthyism	IX Disillusionment and the Intellectual in Politics	X American Politics Abroad
	1902									
	1903	1903								
			1904							
		1905								
	1907									
	1908			1908*						
	1909									
	1911									
	1912*			1912						
	1914									
					1922	1922				
	1923		1923							
			1926							
	1927	1927	1927		1927					
		1928	1928*					1928		
		1929			1929					
	1930	1930	1930							
	1931		1931							
				1932	1932	1932				
			1933	1933	1933					
	1934		1934	1934			1934			
			1935	1935*						
	1936	1936	1936		1936*	1936	1936			

	1937	1937*	1938	1937*				
				1937*			1939	
1939						1940	1939	
					1941	1941		
1942					1942*			1952
	1944				1943	1943		
						1944*		1954
					1945	1945		1955
1946					1946	1946	1947	
1947*			1948		1947	1947		
			1949				1949	
		1952*			1950	1949*		
	1951	1953	1952				1951	1951
					1953		1952	1952
			1954			1954		
1955	1955		1956				1955**	
	1956**	1957*						
	1957**		1958	1958*			1958	1958*
1959*	1959*	1959*		1959	1959	1959*		
	1960	1960			1960	1960***		

* Additional novel of the same classification published in the same year.

patterns, whereas the novelist works from amassed "individualized data" to create a unique story. His broad generalizing is done at the expense of detail, whereas the reverse is true in the case of the political scientist. "For the novelist," he continued, "Uncle Tom becomes a microcosm, a device for revealing the tragedy of the whole Negro race in America through a portrait of a single character. For the political scientist, Uncle Tom is lost in what can be said of the entire group of which he is a member. Both are limited and both pay a price accordingly."[3]

Both pay a price, and both, conversely, gain an advantage. The political scientist often provides a mass of analyzed data. He may then use it to demonstrate the action of certain processes and theorize about (or perhaps even verify) their causes. The novelist may use a set of "models," as Professor Snyder calls them, which will give the sight, sound, and feel of the political experience with an immediacy the scientist can rarely match. But the novelist can be wrong, with respect to objective reality, to a degree impossible to a bona-fide social scientist no matter how inadequate his data or how misapplied his formulae. The artist is often a special pleader, and he may lavish his eloquence on the side of error as freely as that of truth. But sometimes he experiences that conjunction of form and content, of idea and emotion, which produces enduring art. And the story of his model—whether an Ahab or a Nostromo—will be enriched by truths about monomaniacal absolutism or romantic opportunism which simply cannot emerge with the same force and paradigmatic clarity from scientific data and analyses.

The question of differences between politics and other kinds of experience as material for the novelist is equally complex. One can follow the lead, however, provided by Tom Wilcher as he notes Tolstoy's success in using war for the purposes of fiction. And it is useful to recall von Clausewitz's famous dictum that "War is merely the continuation of Politics by other means." Common elements in these two areas of experience should make the latter quite as much a subject (or at least background) for fiction as the former. Both often involve large issues and the sense of vast forces. Beyond this, individuals emerge from the mass—serving, one supposes, as models of a kind—the emperor preparing for the fateful cast, the grenadier patching the coat soon to be pierced by the shrapnel of Wagram or Waterloo. And, of course, the novelist is not limited to the use of models. Something of the sense of masses of people, intricately

[3] Richard C. Snyder, in Joseph Blotner, *The Political Novel,* pp. vi–viii.

stratified into classes, was conveyed in fiction before the time of the naturalists. And with the interlocked novels of Balzac, the *romans fleuves* of Romains and Dos Passos, the patterns of fiction imitated those of society itself.

The answers to these secondary questions imply answers, if equally tentative, to the primary ones with which I began. Literature can reflect only a limited amount of political reality, but the bridges between experience and art are not so unsure as to be useless. Literature can provide insights into man as political animal as well as martial or amorous animal. As it can treat the individual, so it can treat the group, although it will most often proceed through the few to arrive at the many. The works are rewarding for their intrinsic merits of form and substance, but they also repay study which places them against the background and specific conditions out of which they developed. Comparing "real life" and the "story," while avoiding the pitfalls of the "intentional fallacy," one may learn something more about the way in which the artist's shaping vision imposes form upon the materials of his art.

The principal purpose of this study is to discover the image of American politics presented in American novels over the sixty-year span from 1900 through 1960. There are 138 novels which meet the terms of the definition used in this study. The purpose is actually twofold in that it is concerned with the artist's conception of this aspect of the American experience and also with the nature and quality of the fictional art itself. Put another way, the concern of the study is both cultural and aesthetic.

General conceptions of politics are often formed early in the reader's training process. From the work of historians and social scientists comes acquaintance with phases in the continuum of American political life. The student's earliest views are likely to resemble a series of tableaux: the Pilgrim Fathers in tall hats and the Founding Fathers in white wigs; Washington at Valley Forge and Lincoln at Gettysburg; an ebullient Teddy Roosevelt superseded by a sad-serene Woodrow Wilson; then in quick succession the figures of Roosevelt and Truman, Eisenhower and Kennedy. This view is supplemented by newspaper stories and televised speeches, debates, investigations, and conventions. Personal experience of government in action may further modify or enlarge it. The statistics, analyses, and theories of the social scientist remain available, as do the changing assessments of the historians. But if Carlyle was right in hailing the artist as poet and prophet, the reader may find in the novelist's work another conception of truth in this area of human experience, a view which—Aristotle claimed—goes beyond the particular to the universal. In any case, the best of these artistic distillations will offer some further understanding of the American political experience.

The present study is confined to novels published in this century which deal with this century. Novels set in its early years will usually reflect concerns of earlier periods. Novels written in this century but dealing principally with earlier periods are excluded. In order to keep the study from extending to all outdoors, "political" is here defined in a very literal and functional sense. The subject of these works, apart from a few on the fringe noted as such but illustrating particular themes, is also primarily political. Politics is not merely a secondary interest.[4] These novels deal with the overt, institutionalized politics of the officeholder, the candidate, the party official, or the individual who performs political acts as they are conventionally understood. Sociological novels such as Sinclair's *The Jungle* (1906) and proletarian novels such as Steinbeck's *The Grapes of Wrath* (1939), for example, are excluded. This definition excludes novels which do not deal primarily with political processes and actions, but concentrate instead on the conditions out of which political action may eventually arise. It also omits novels portraying actions and attitudes which can be regarded as political only after being extracted from a matrix of allegory and symbol—a highly subjective process.

Upton Sinclair's *Lanny Budd* novels are not treated here because, though they deal with political events and persons, they are equally concerned with other aspects of the modern scene. Sinclair had for years published what he called "contemporary historical novels," and in the "eleven volumes, 7,364 pages, over four million words," which by his own count constituted the series, he continued to use this technique even more assiduously. These books can be read, he writes, "as history, as politics, art, and science, and a little bit of everything—business, fashion, war and peace and human hope."[5] It is a lively series, and another demonstration that Sinclair has been, as Walter Rideout puts it, "one of the

---

[4] An example of a novel excluded on these grounds is Ilka Chase's *Three Men on the Left Hand* (1960). Although this novel's political theme arises out of the plan whereby an industrial magnate secretly sponsors an ex-senator and has him appointed Secretary of the Interior in order to secure postwar leasing of uranium-bearing government lands, this is clearly subordinate to the novel's romantic theme. The reader is a third of the way into the novel before political affairs assume any real importance, and fifty pages before the novel ends a coroner's inquest signals the demise of the political theme, after which the star-crossed lovers find a happy ending in Rome.

[5] *The Autobiography of Upton Sinclair,* pp. 292, 297.

greatest information centers in American literature."[6] The interested reader may want to go on to these entertaining works, but they lie outside the boundaries of the present study.

A few of the novels included—such as John Dos Passos's *Adventures of a Young Man* (1939), Lionel Trilling's *The Middle of the Journey* (1947), and Norman Mailer's *Barbary Shore* (1951)—stretch these boundaries at some points. Though they do not deal primarily with politicians in the process of directing campaigns, running for office, or performing the duties of elective or appointive posts, these novels are included because they present persons (and phenomena) of intense political seriousness who are prevented from performing most such functions because the avenues to office and power are in the main denied them. Beyond this, they are intensely concerned with both political theory and action. They are distinct from novels such as Steinbeck's *In Dubious Battle* (1936). Though the latter deals with Communist manipulation of a strike for Communist purposes, and though Marxist theory is introduced, the novel's emphasis is upon one particular tactic—the subversion of the strike for partisan aims—and upon the economic and social plight of migrant workers. This emphasis makes the work essentially a strike novel rather than a political novel as defined here.[7]

As to the critic who feels that the political novel should be approached with a wider net, I concede him his view. But to treat all the works in this body of fiction under a broadened definition would require more volumes than one. To broaden the definition and then treat examples would constitute a selective approach rather than the inclusive one I have adopted. This study will, I hope, be taken on its own terms, as one which examines *all* the novels published between 1900 and 1960 which meet the terms of the definition. This task would swell prohibitively, I think, if the floodgates of definition were opened, challenging and exhilarating as that act might seem.

Several studies deal with politics and literature from other viewpoints. Walter Rideout's *The Radical Novel in the United States 1900–1954* distinguishes, within the larger category of the "social-protest novel," between the novel which embodies the views of the reformer and the one which accepts the premises of the radical. The latter calls for "a transformation of the system itself," and demonstrates "either explicitly or im-

[6] Walter B. Rideout, *The Radical Novel in the United States 1900–1954: Some Interrelations of Literature and Society*, p. 38.

[7] Neither is it a proletarian novel in Rideout's terms. See Rideout, *Radical Novel*, p. 325.

plicitly, that its author objects to the human suffering imposed by some socioeconomic system and *advocates that the system be fundamentally changed.*"[8] The reader will note how useful I have found Professor Rideout's work, even though he and I share only seven novels in common.[9] In *Writers on the Left* Daniel Aaron presents "a social chronicle of the Left Wing Writer from 1912 to the early 1940's." His book "describes the response of a selected group of American writers to the idea of Communism and deals with particular issues and events during the first forty years of this century which helped to shape their opinions."[10] Professor Aaron's work provides helpful analyses of the intellectual milieu in which many of the writers whose novels I treat lived and worked. It also supplies much useful information—as does Rideout's book—about the politics of the writers themselves—"extrinsic" but valuable material, whether in the case of novelists, such as John Dos Passos and Upton Sinclair, whose intellectual histories are familiar, or in the case of the relatively obscure writers such as I. K. Friedman and Henry Hart. *Politics and the Novel,* Irving Howe writes, "is meant primarily as a study of the relation between literature and ideas." It was written with an interest "far less in literature as social evidence or testimony than in the literary problem of what happens to the novel when it is subjected to the pressures of politics and political ideology."[11] Professor Howe's book provides examples of perceptive literary criticism. My own briefer study, *The Political Novel,* was an attempt to indicate various aspects of this form in the United States and elsewhere and to show the unique insights it could give as complementary with those of the social science disciplines.[12]

As one would expect, types and themes very soon emerge in a reading of the novels in this study. Some, in their persistence and simplicity, suggest myths and behavior patterns common to many cultures and many times.

It is fortunately no longer necessary to fight the battle to validate the insights into literature provided by myth criticism. Upon the pioneering work of Jung, Freud, Frazer, Bodkin, and others, a number of astute

---

[8] Rideout, *Radical Novel,* p. 12.

[9] Rideout notes that it is unusual to find a political novel in American radical fiction. See p. 120.

[10] Daniel Aaron, *Writers on the Left: Episodes in American Literary Communism,* p. ix.

[11] Irving Howe, *Politics and the Novel,* p. 11.

[12] The earliest full-length study in this area of literature was Morris Edmund Speare's *The Political Novel: Its Development in England and America.* His three chapters on Henry Adams, Winston Churchill, and Paul Leicester Ford occupy something over one-seventh of his book.

critics have erected a method which—when used circumspectly and with the safeguards provided by conventional critical and historical scholarship—permits generalizations and linkages between individual works and the great themes which run through man's attempts to express himself in literary art. In discussing modern interpretations of myth, Campbell writes that it has been seen as

a primitive, fumbling effort to explain the world of nature (Frazer); as a production of poetical fantasy from prehistoric times, misunderstood by succeeding ages (Muller); as a repository of allegorical instruction, to shape the individual to his group (Durkheim); as a group dream, symptomatic of archetypal urges within the depths of the human psyche (Jung); as the traditional vehicle of man's profoundest metaphysical insights (Coomaraswamy); and as God's Revelation to His children (the Church). Mythology is all of these.[13]

For the student of literature, mythology is valuable in that it provides a number of characters and situations which recur in literature and which can help the reader perceive literary patterns. How these patterns get into the works is a vexed question. Whether the mythic character or situation is consciously imposed upon the work by the author, whether he expresses himself in terms to which his culture has given a mythic component, or whether there is in his psyche an autochthonous mythmaking faculty—all these possibilities fortunately need not concern us. All we need do is make use of these mythic patterns. They will provide a means of organizing a large and varied number of works and of better understanding fundamental aspects of the characters and situations which dominate them.

Jung has described a number of archetypal figures: the shadow, the anima, the wise old man, the mother, the child, the Kore or divine maiden, and the trickster.[14] All of these, Jung cautions the reader, have their positive and negative aspects. The anima is a feminine being who is both "the serpent in . . . paradise" and a believer in "the 'beautiful and the good'." She can be embodied in Goethe's Helen of Troy, but she can "appear also as an angel of light, a psychopomp who points the

---

[13] Joseph Campbell, *The Hero with a Thousand Faces*, p. 382.

[14] See C. G. Jung's chapters, "Archetypes of the Collective Unconscious," and "Concerning the Archetypes, with Special Reference to the Anima Concept," in *The Archetypes and the Collective Unconscious*, pp. 3–41 and 54–74. In making use of the concept of the archetype as a device for organizing and understanding aspects of literary materials, I do not thereby employ all Jungian concepts attaching thereto. I am in no way concerned, for example, with the collective unconscious, with racial memories, or with *mandalas*.

way to the highest meaning, as we know from *Faust.*"[15] In these novels she appears in the role which I call that of Woman as Guide. The archetype of the wise old man usually appears in these novels as a counselor of the protagonist, often as a kind of father-figure.

The chief archetypal figure in these novels is, of course, the hero. Frazer and Bodkin both trace his evolution from fertility god to mythic figure. Lord Raglan makes a familiar synthesis when he suggests that "the god is the hero as he appears in ritual, and the hero is the god as he appears in myth; in other words, the hero and the god are two different aspects of the same superhuman being."[16] He also records a pattern of twenty-two typical incidents in the life of the hero, most of which he finds in the stories of heroes of myth and legend of the principal recorded cultures. In dealing with the hero as warrior, Joseph Campbell writes, "From obscurity the hero emerges, but the enemy is great and conspicuous in the seat of power; he is enemy, dragon, tyrant, because he turns to his own advantage the authority of his position . . . With a gesture as simple as the pressing of a button, [the hero] annihilates the impressive configuration."[17] In his theory of myths, Northrup Frye deals with the various embodiments of the hero. Divine in myth, human in romance, he can take on the archetypal form of Perseus slaying Medusa or St. George slaying the Dragon. This second embodiment is most apt for my purposes here, since this figure and situation are the most obvious and recurrent. Of one of the best known uses of this myth, in Spenser's *The Faerie Queene,* Frye comments, "St. George's mission, a repetition of that of Christ, is by killing the dragon to raise Eden in the wilderness and restore England to the status of Eden."[18] Maud Bodkin recalls from poetic drama certain "transfigured hero-images" who may be compared with "the Christ of the Gospel story."[19] R. W. B. Lewis argues that Herman Melville near the end of his life "found a new conviction about the saving strength of the Adamic personality." He was one of several, argues Lewis, to whom "the story implicit in American experience had to do with an Adamic person [before the Fall] . . . who is thrust by circumstances into an actual world and an actual age. American fiction grew out of the attempt to chart the impacts which ensued, both upon

[15] Jung, *Archetypes,* pp. 28–29.
[16] Lord Raglan, *The Hero: A Study in Tradition, Myth, and Drama,* p. 203.
[17] Campbell, *Thousand Faces,* p. 337.
[18] Northrup Frye, *Anatomy of Criticism: Four Essays,* p. 194.
[19] Maud Bodkin, *Archetypal Patterns in Poetry: Psychological Studies of Imagination,* p. 272.

Adam and upon the world he is thrust into." To return to Miss Bodkin's comment and Lewis's observation about Melville, "this conviction became articulate in *Billy Budd*," writes Lewis, and thereupon "the American hero as Adam became the hero as Christ and entered, once and for all into the dimension of myth."[20] It is not my business here to urge Professor Lewis's ingenious and persuasively argued thesis. I cite it, however, as another example of the pervasiveness of the myth of the hero in literature and the kind of permutation which it can undergo.

For my purposes the hero as St. George is more useful than the hero as Adam, although similarities exist between the two. And there are, of course, other aspects in which the hero will appear.

Just as the reader encounters in many different guises the young man who goes forth to battle evil, like St. George seeking his Dragon, so he will see another perennial figure. He is the Boss—the man who conquers only to be conquered in his turn—like the King of the Wood who was priest of Diana in the grove at Nemi. Although he is, in Campbell's phrase, "enemy, dragon, tyrant," he shares some of the hero's attributes, debase them though he may. The wise old man usually appears as counselor to the Knight, although the Boss as young man finds him equally useful. Sometimes the Boss will act as wise old man and counselor to the rising power who will assume his mantle. The trickster appears but seldom as the principal figure of a novel. In the clearest instance, it is the Boss who is seen in this aspect.[21] There is almost always an anima-character to inspire the Young Knight. And although no heroine appears as the Kore or divine maiden of myth, some who play Woman as Guide enjoy some of her attributes.

In general terms, then, characters and situations recur in all literatures which, stripped to their basic characteristics, suggest the identity and simplicity of the great myths and mythic characters. A perception of this helps the reader both to understand aspects of the work in which they appear and to recognize kinship between the individual work and others. And these archetypal patterns serve, at the very least, as useful means of organizing large and often apparently diverse masses of material. And if Professor Lewis is right, the mythic hero enjoys a cardinal place in American literature in his Adamic aspect, appearing in Cooper, Hawthorne, Melville, James, Faulkner, and lesser writers. The mythic hero, in both his pre- and postlapsarian states, dominates many of the

---

[20] R. W. B. Lewis, *The American Adam: Innocence, Tragedy and Tradition in the Nineteenth Century*, pp. 130, 89, and 130.
[21] See Mary Deasy's novel, *O'Shaughnessy's Day* (1957), in Chapter Two.

novels treated here. His foil, the Boss, is another figure. Still other characters and situations operate, if less strikingly, in the same way.

Besides further persistent themes—corruption, the role of the press—there are familiar kinds of novels within this genre, such as the comic novel and the novel set in the future. There are other groups of novels whose subject matter belongs, in an approximate way, to a particular era: groups such as the novel of American Fascism, of disillusionment, or of McCarthyism.

I regard these works as reflections of aspects of American political life as seen by the novelists. In analyzing these reflections I do not use statistical methods. Put simply, this study includes all the political novels I could find. In works important or typical, I try to present and then evaluate the authors' conclusions. I then go on in summary passages to state my own conclusions. Wherever possible, I use key passages or phrases from the books themselves. They convey the differences in the presentations of political experience as summaries cannot do. They are the evidence, the primary materials themselves. But I use both excerpts and summaries wherever they will help to reveal my objective: the fictional depiction of the modern American political experience. Since these novels are works to which critical standards must be applied, I accordingly make such assessments. The best ones—occasionally those most representative—are examined at some length. Walter Rideout aptly describes the writer's situation in attempting this dual function: "The strict literary historian may object to finding some literary analysis and evaluation here, while the formalist critic will surely be unhappy over the very large amount of what he would call 'extrinsic' material. Likewise, if the literary critic may object that the book contains too much talk of politics, the political scientist may feel that it contains too little."[22] The writer is also likely to find himself—to change the metaphor—caught in a crossfire from humanists and social scientists. But benefits may accrue from this method to justify the risk.

This study proceeds both by type and by time, since proceeding by strict chronology alone results in wearisome repetition and excessive cross references. The novel about the young crusader appears first in time and that about American politics abroad appears last. These two bodies of fiction consequently occupy the first and last chapters. There is an overlap in time rather than an exclusive progression because novels of the type treated in Chapter One were still being published in the

[22] Rideout, *Radical Novel*, p. vii.

decade when those of the type in Chapter Ten began to appear. All but two of the types treated in these chapters were represented in the decade of the 1930's, and all but one in the 1950's. With one exception, however, Chapters One through Ten are sequential. The only instance in which I have violated chronology—taking up a type whose first novel appeared later than the first novel in the next chapter—is in discussing American Fascism before treating the Far Right and McCarthyism, to provide more logical continuity. Some nineteenth-century predecessors which are not, strictly speaking, a part of this study, are discussed as new types and themes are introduced. Figure I shows the times of appearance of the various themes and also suggests trends of interest. Another writer would probably put some of these novels in other categories. Several straddle boundaries. I have tried to place each where its basic characteristics pointed.

At the beginning of each chapter I have supplied historical summaries as background for the fiction. These are meant to serve only as introductions for the general reader, not as scholarly analyses for the specialist—which they obviously are not. I first determined on treating these novels on their own, so to speak, without introducing secondary materials. But I learned that these novels could not be treated *in vacuo,* hence the effort to supply relevant information about movements and forces, people and events. My business is not the breaking of new ground in politics or history. But I have made this study in the hope that the literary material it presents on this phase of the American experience will be useful to students and teachers of politics and history as well as to those in literature. Because these novels so often recall historical antecedents—and are so often cast as *romans à clef*—I have suggested models for some of the portraits. Where the novelist's politics seemed particularly relevant, I have briefly indicated them.

A kind of counterpoise to the words of Joyce Cary's Tom Wilcher is provided in James F. Davidson's "Political Science and Political Fiction." This essay contains the best assessment I have found of the similarities and differences between the two approaches as seen from the vantage point of the political scientist. In presenting the last of five main arguments, Professor Davidson writes, "At its best, fiction illuminates politics as it illuminates all of life: by imposing an order sufficient to give meaning and flexible enough to impart the sense of vital confusion. If an attention to political fiction did nothing more than remind us of the extent to which we fictionalize in all analysis, or restore the critical role of the writer, or give greater vitality to the language in which we discuss politics, it would be justified."[23] Some of these novels will, I think, sub-stantiate this view. At the same time, it may be useful if, in a kind of reciprocal gesture, I indicate some gaps in the fictional presentation of American political experience.

Although these novels are set on village, city, state, and national levels, some aspects of politics have failed to interest the novelist. For example, although legislators and lobbyists swarm through these novels, there is no one of the books devoted to a consistent examination of the legisla-tive process on any level. It is probably too much to expect that the ar-tist—primarily interested in people, emotions, and ideas—should devote his three hundred-odd pages to a process. This is why most novels deal with leaders and followers, with governors and senators. These charac-ters become involved with the legislative process, but the focus of interest remains on them and secondarily upon the process. The same thing is true of the judicial function. Judges, good and bad, frequently appear. But though they may contribute crucially to plot and motivation, the reader rarely gets extended fictional treatment of the process by which a judge is selected or extended analysis of his area of the democratic proc-ess. The degree to which these novels faithfully reflect twentieth-cen-tury American political experience is also conditioned by other factors. The focus of these novels has, by and large, accurately reflected the shift whereby the most important decisions are increasingly made at the na-tional center. This seems true in spite of recent novels whose small-town setting may represent a nostalgic reaching back for local control. One clearly cannot say that all these novelists understand the American poli-tical system in terms of "structures and processes of hard choice, con-sensus building, satisfaction of public needs," as Richard Snyder puts it. Instead, a number of them appear to "project onto politics a more gen-erally felt ambivalence in the society—what is prescribed or valued vs. what is done, aspiration vs. achievement . . ."[24] Novelists such as the former diplomat writing under a non de plume will have a good work-ing knowledge of the realities of modern American politics, but this level of competence is likely to be the exception. As a result, some may base their narratives on overly simple or outdated conceptual models. Although this may not lead to oversimplification of human motive and action, it may produce oversimplification of process and structure. Some-times novelists may be unaware of the extent to which sociological and

[23] James F. Davidson, "Political Science and Political Fiction," *American Poli-tical Science Review,* LV (December, 1961), 860.
[24] Letter to the writer, April 29, 1963.

psychological factors are impinging on politics and exercising a modifying effect. By the early 1960's conflict over civil rights reached a pitch of intensity nowhere anticipated in any of the novels of the Southern Politician. Similarly, the gains of the Republican Party in the South receive scant treatment. Since art usually follows history in this subject area, there will almost always be a time lag. Thus, though American Fascism may be turned to the purposes of fiction almost as soon as it begins to appear, this is by no means the rule, and four or five years may elapse before experience appears as art rather than journalism.

As this study considers American politics in fiction, it will also raise several questions. Why is there such a concentration in these novels upon evil rather than good? What conclusion, if any, can be drawn from the fact that the two figures which have had the most powerful impact upon the imaginations of these writers are those of Abraham Lincoln on one hand and Huey Long on the other? Why are there so few modern American political novels of any excellence? Why are there so many bad ones? Before the end, some answers should emerge, and with them a character—in the old sense of the word—of the American political experience as seen by the artist. There, among the distortions and omissions, some truth should reside.

1. the young knight

A gentle knight was pricking on the plain,
Y-clad in mighty arms and silver shield
Wherein old dents of deep wounds did remain,
The cruel marks of many a bloody field . . .

. . . the dreadful beast drew nigh to hand,
Half flying and half footing in his haste,
That with his largeness measured much land
And made wide shadow under his huge waist . . .

The knight gan fairly couch his steady spear
and fiercely ran at him with rigorous might.

> Edmund Spenser,
> *The Faerie Queene*, Canto I.

The Figure in the Foreground

The novel dominated by the figure of the young hero setting out to fight evil appears more than a score of times in the sixty years spanned by this study. And the similarities in these novels justify this hero's archetypal designation as the Young Knight. There is a variant of this pattern, but the dominant characteristics are quite clear. The hero is physically unmistakable. Usually in his mid-twenties or round about thirty, he is suffused with vigor and strength often embodied in a heroic frame and handsome head. If he is ungainly, his ungainliness is tempered by innate dignity—in a word, he is Lincolnesque. He may be a young hero come out of the West. Like Lochinvar, he is romantic. If he is strong in spiritual rather than physical terms, he may wear the aura of a prophet or even a messiah. Often rising out of poverty and obscurity, he usually enacts his drama on a state or national stage. Rarely is it confined to a city. If he has been born to wealth and position, he has been harmed by neither. If he has been tainted with youthful evil-doing, he atones for it in the struggle his heroic role demands. He advances driven by ambition or idealism or both. Sometimes he goes beyond political idealism to radicalism.

There is always a woman. Though her influence can be sinister, she is usually inspirational. She changes in these novels just as the image of woman has changed in other American literature, but she too has reasonably consistent characteristics. Above all, she is good. She may be the hero's spiritual guide, playing Una to his Red Cross Knight. Sometimes she improves his position as well as his mind. In the few cases where she is wrongheaded, she comes around at last, taking her position at her husband's side. There she adores him in triumph or uplifts him in defeat, rededicating herself with him to work for future victory. The author will sometimes cast her in a familiar way: she will play Capulet to the hero's Montague. And she will be especially steadfast when, as is usually the case, she is rich and he is poor.

The climax comes when the plot has built to the inevitable battle between the Knight and the Dragon of evil. The Dragon may be the creation of any of several progenitors: the corrupt political machine or the Interests of which it is the creature—the railroads, oil, the industrial combine. Preliminary successes precede the climactic battle. But in its throes the hero is more apt to succumb than conquer. Evil is simply too powerful for the lone quester. But defeat does not signify the end of the Quest. He merely retires to rebuild his strength against the day when he will sally forth again. This time, he is convinced (usually with the author's apparent agreement), he will conquer.

In a variant pattern the Knight is not defeated but corrupted. His struggle with the Dragon is a no-decision match, for he comes to terms with him. He shares the spoils of his depredations but ultimately becomes his creature. This Knight's tarnished shield makes that of his uncorrupted brother shine the more brightly. This variant may result from several causes. The Knight may become cynical about politics and decide simply to look out for himself. He may also be subjected to pressures of varying force and subtlety. A woman (the anima in her negative aspect, in Jung's terms) may seduce him from his early dedication to righteousness no matter what the ultimate price. More often, he will be enticed by the pleasures of position, power, and pelf. At a critical moment he will often discover to his surprise and dismay that to retain his eminence he is willing to do anything—to make the deals, to vote the right way, to sell out his constituency. The end of the Quest will reveal not the Grail or even the Chapel Perilous, but instead a Whited Sepulcher.

Backgrounds

Though the figure of the young champion of the right doing battle with the forces of evil is archetypal, it should be seen in other contexts as well for an understanding of the way it operates in the American political novel. The tendency to judge issues in terms of moral absolutes has been called a particularly American predilection. The idea of political action as a direct embodiment of religious conviction has been prominent in the American ethos from the New England theocracies through the Chautauqua circuits to the Prohibition crusade and beyond. But the figure of the Young Knight and the forces he represents are perhaps best seen in the context of the impulse toward reform in American political life.

This impulse, argues Richard Hofstadter, "is endemic in American political culture."[1] Gathering force in the Age of Jackson, it manifested itself in such different forms as the Greenback and Granger movements. With the rising resentment against monopoly which also began to crystallize after the Civil War, it was to receive even greater impetus. It gave expression to the discontents of farmers and small businessmen, of segments of late nineteenth-century America reacting against change which militated not only against their economic welfare but also against their general status in their environment, and appeared to run wholly counter to assumptions on which, it had seemed, the Republic had been based. These manifestations form a kind of continuum in American history, an extended three-phase cycle of reform: "the agrarian uprising that found its most intense expression in the Populism of the 1890's and the Bryan campaign of 1896; the Progressive movement, which extended from about 1900 to 1914; and the New Deal, whose dynamic phase was concentrated in a few years of the 1930's.[2]

These novels also convey broader currents of thought than those which can be circumscribed by dates and terminologies. One sees the effect of socialist doctrine and hears it spoken by characters who subscribe to the principle that the state should own and control the means of production. But there is a body of attitudes and ideas which can only be subsumed under that other word—much more difficult of definition—"liberalism."

---

[1] Richard Hofstadter, *The Age of Reform: From Bryan to F. D. R.*, p. 4.
[2] Hofstadter, *Reform*, p. 3.

The liberal, while wishing to eliminate abuses and inequities, to utilize resources more fully, has remained committed to a society with privately controlled means of production. The successive waves of reform have been generated by a movement which, writes Eric Goldman, "has included both the flexible-minded and the guardians of the previous generation's dogmas, both people who were in the movement to give as much as they could to the community and those who were in it for what they could get out of it for themselves or their group."[3] Motives may be ambiguous in politics, but they are rarely so in the fiction of politics. They may shift like the values on which they are based, but the author will make these shifts as clear as he can. The reader sees the patrician reformer motivated by a sense of duty and a zest for the strife. He sees the naive reformer who may win a skirmish or a campaign but cannot possibly win a war. He sees the dedicated revolutionary—the socialist— and also the earnest reformer who chooses to work within the existing framework—the liberal. There are those too whose dedication and earnestness cannot withstand success. But the reader also follows the fortunes of inheritors of Populism, the farmers' alliances, and the Grange, and he meets Progressives and New Dealers. So these backgrounds are worth sketching in.

Ignatius Donnelly, whose macabre novel of a terrible future, *Caesar's Column* (1890), is discussed in Chapter Four, stood before a convention in Omaha on July 4, 1892. In an excoriating address, he gave the platform of what was to become the Populist Party of America.[4] The delegates in the audience represented organizations as diverse as anarchist groups and the Knights of Labor. Their shared bond was a fear of the encroachments of industrial and financial forces they thought powerful enough to evolve into an oligarchy which could destroy the Republic. In its brief life the party fought for the regulation of the great financial and industrial interests, legislative reform, and free coinage of silver. Its candidate never had a chance for the Presidency, but in Western and Midwestern states it elected more governors, senators, and representatives than any third party had in nearly thirty years.

Spectacular revelations of the growing power of an industrial-financial oligarchy and its baleful influence on the process of government made reform a matter of greatest urgency to many citizens. Although

[3] Eric F. Goldman, *Rendezvous with Destiny: A History of Modern American Reform*, p. x.
[4] In the same year he published a utopian romance called *The Golden Bottle* which illustrated Populist Party principles.

newspaper and magazine exposés had been familiar since the 1870's, graphically documented studies of corruption in business and politics were part of a new and sensational movement in magazine journalism. Miss Ida Tarbell began her "History of the Standard Oil Company" in 1896 and published it serially in *McClure's Magazine* from 1902 through 1904. Parallel studies such as those of Ray Stannard Baker and David Graham Phillips presented spectacular inquiries into American industrial and political life in "muckraking" magazines with a total readership that was enormous. Other novelists who contributed to this genre were Samuel Hopkins Adams, Upton Sinclair, and Winston Churchill.

To an extraordinary degree [writes Hofstadter], the work of the Progressive movement rested upon its journalism. The fundamental critical achievement of American Progressivism was the business of exposure, and journalism was the chief occupational source of its creative writers. It is hardly an exaggeration to say that the Progressive mind was characteristically a journalistic mind, and that its characteristic contribution was that of the socially responsible reporter-reformer. The muckraker was a central figure . . . It was muckraking that brought the diffuse malaise of the public into focus.[5]

These attacks upon powerful interests which *McClure's, Cosmopolitan, Collier's, Hampton's,* and several other magazines published, stand in strong contrast to the role of the newspapers, at least as it is presented in the novels. More dependent on advertisers, more vulnerable to pressure, more often owned by the Interests, the newspapers are not vehicles for truth or reform, but organs of opinion to be played by whoever can afford them. In actual fact, almost all the best-known muckrakers had been trained on newspapers. And a few newspapers allied themselves with reform, as did Joseph Pulitzer's New York *World,* whose "editorial columns crackled with crusades—against aldermen who took bribes for favorable votes on a streetcar franchise that was a bad bargain for the city, against tenement contractors, against the Bell telephone monopoly and the Standard Oil Trust . . ."[6] More common were journalists like the small-town publishers who had taken Boss Tweed's money and forthwith fallen silent about his attempts in Albany to engineer changes in the New York City charter. Tweed told the investigators in 1868 that the bribes ranged anywhere from $500 to $5,000. "It

[5] Hofstadter, *Reform,* p. 185. See further Hofstadter, pp. 185–212, and Goldman, *Rendezvous,* pp. 171–176. See also D. M. Chalmers, *The Social and Political Ideas of the Muckrakers.*
[6] Bernard A. Weisberger, *The American Newspaperman,* p. 140.

was," he complained, "a general dribble all the time."[7] Although the muckraking magazines were more concerned with circulation than crusading, it has been suggested that the movement, which subsided in the decade before the first World War, did not die a natural death, but rather "was choked off at its sources by those who were most affected by its exposures."[8]

When William Jennings Bryan hit the campaign trail in 1896 he had the endorsement of both the Democratic and the Populist parties. He also had the Free Silver issue besides other Populist notions less familiar than that trumpeted in his famous "Cross of Gold" speech. The Populist Party passed from the scene after the Republican juggernaut, ridden by William McKinley and oiled by Mark Hanna, had steamed over the Great Commoner. But less than a decade later, when an assassin's bullet had put Theodore Roosevelt in the White House, the old Populists could point to an impressive list of those once-radical reforms now enacted into law. Direct election of senators, the initiative and referendum, income tax, railroad regulation, and a number of other such measures were now on the statute books. Teddy Roosevelt, intent on reoccupying the White House, had by 1912 adopted so many Populist ideas for his Bull Moose Party that they had, said William Allen White, "caught the Populists in swimming and stole all of their clothing except the frayed underdrawers of free silver."[9]

The reform movement was made more complex by the way diverse reform ideologies tended at times to merge in a process of mutual modification. Sometimes the process was paradoxical. Of the many labels pinned on Teddy Roosevelt, that of "trust buster" gained the widest and longest currency. But his slower and bulkier successor, William Howard Taft, initiated twice as many antitrust actions as did T. R.[10] Then, in attempting to storm back into the White House, T. R. campaigned with a collocation of authoritarian ideas called "the New Nationalism." The winner emerged—no kind of Republican but instead a self-styled Jeffersonian Democrat—with a body of policies subsumed under the name of "the New Freedom." Though Wilson spoke out against the trusts, he disappointed many by his failure to bust more of them. During

---

[7] Quoted in Weisberger, *Newspaperman,* p. 147.

[8] Hofstadter, *Reform,* p. 194. Cited by Hofstadter: C. C. Regier, *The Era of the Muckrakers;* and Louis Filler, *Crusaders for American Liberalism,* pp. 370–373.

[9] William Allen White, *The Autobiography of William Allen White,* pp. 482–483.

[10] See Hofstadter, *Reform,* p. 244.

the Hoover administration, consolidation in many industries went on apace, and trade associations, which wrote codes and set standards, had flourished and grown to the extent that the President proclaimed it "a period of associational activities."[11] Then the eclectic, pragmatic New Deal sailed ahead toward old progressive goals with experimental programs embodying elements of associational activities, the New Nationalism, and the New Freedom.

It is useful to distinguish the original coloration of these diverse strands thus drawn together. The New Nationalism was a kind of systematic progressivism which had been set forth by Herbert Croly in 1909 in *The Promise of American Life*. It advocated "an efficient national organization and . . . exclusive and aggressive devotion to the national welfare," which would regulate commerce and industry, labor and agriculture, for "the distribution of wealth in the national interest." The leaders of the state, given the power necessary for efficiency by willing fellow-citizens, would determine this interest in the light of the national historical mission, providing an "authoritative expression of the Sovereign popular will."[12] When T. R.'s stetson went into the ring in 1912, its owner was completely committed to Croly's ideas.

Woodrow Wilson countered with advocacy of the New Freedom, which emphasized competition and attack on monopoly and special privilege. The New Jersey governor made it clear that he was not against size as such. He did not want to turn back the clock but to insure the survival of free enterprise. His failure to pursue a vigorous trust-busting policy showed how the apparent difference between his position and T. R.'s was greater than the real one. The legislation which went through in the first year of his administration showed, however, just how much he was in the Progressive tradition. The Federal Reserve Act struck at the "money trust," and a tariff cut incensed commercial interests.

With Wilson's ardent encouragement, many another reform bill tumbled through Congress—most notably the La Follette Act, improving the ordinary sailor's well-being . . . millions for farm demonstration work and . . . vocational and agricultural education, a workmen's compensation act for federal employees . . . an eight-hour day on all interstate railroads, and the exclusion from interstate commerce of the products of child labor.[13]

[11] Charles A. Beard: *Jefferson, Corporations and the Constitution*, p. 79; cited in Goldman, *Rendezvous*, p. 309.
[12] Herbert Croly, *The Promise of American Life*, pp. 270, 409, 281.
[13] Goldman, *Rendezvous*, p. 218.

The New Freedom had steered American government once more into the Progressive channels it had navigated when T. R. grasped the helm. The ship of state, it appeared, had swerved from the currents of authoritarianism and industrial-financial influence which generated Ignatius Donnelly's Progressives' nightmare.

The war inevitably diverted the President and his Administration from the New Freedom. Some of the results, militating against reform, were probably predictable. As Hofstadter writes, war "has always been the Nemesis of the liberal tradition in America. From our earliest history as a nation there has been a curiously persistent association between democratic politics and nationalism, jingoism, or war. Periodically war has written the last scene to some drama begun by the popular side of the party struggle."[14] The idea of cooperative control of competition by trade associations and federal regulation had been implicit in the New Nationalism and had been advocated by contemporaries of Croly. Wilson's War Industries Board was run principally by dollar-a-year businessmen who found these ideas in practice a good deal more congenial than they had imagined they could be. Then, in his tenure as Secretary of Commerce in the 1920's, Herbert Hoover encouraged this kind of cooperative regulation. By the time he left the White House, over two thousand trade associations were in operation, many of them promulgating codes which ran counter to the antitrust laws.[15]

The Roosevelt Administration's earliest massive response to the national emergency which had swept Roosevelt into office drew fire from many quarters. The National Recovery Administration's inclusive system of regulatory codes was construed on the left as "a clear imitation of Mussolini's corporate state." On the right it embodied "fascist tendencies in the 'violations' of fundamental liberties with which they regularly charged the architects of the New Deal."[16] In actual fact, the New Deal was deliberately aiming toward the right no more than it was intentionally turning left, for it "never became committed to a categorical 'dissection' of the business order of the sort Wilson had talked of in 1912, nor to the 'demonstration' prosecutions with which T. R. had both excited and reassured the country."[17] The President and his Administration were improvising, exhilaratedly trying and discarding, discovering and

---

[14] Hofstadter, *Reform,* p. 270.
[15] See Goldman, *Rendezvous,* p. 309.
[16] Hofstadter, *Reform,* p. 325.
[17] *Ibid.,* p. 311.

implementing. But these alterations and experiments conformed to a larger pattern, in which the guiding motive of reform was to use

> the power of the federal government to smash concentrated wealth and to re-store free enterprise; use it simultaneously to lift the standard of living of the country's less favored groups; and, by these moves, make opportunity more abundant—in short, the reform program conceived in the depression of 1873, erected into a powerful political force by decades of agitation, given effective-ness and respectability by the early Theodore Roosevelt and by Woodrow Wilson, kept alive even during the complacent Twenties. When Uncle Ted's New Nationalism failed, there was always the Jeffersonian New Freedom of the Chief.[18]

These national currents of reform are often reflected in novels of state and municipal politics. They display many hues of attitude toward re-form. The apotheosis of municipal reform is embodied in men like trac-tion-magnate Tom Johnson who brought a new era to Cleveland politics in the first decade of the twentieth century. Under his program Cleve-land was called the best-run city in the United States. His regime gained credit for "a score of civic improvements, put through more equitable tax laws, came close to ridding the government of all graft, checked the political influence of corporations, and made his office a power for mu-nicipal reform throughout the country."[19] His counterpart on the state level was Robert M. LaFollette, who swept into the governor's chair of Wisconsin in 1900, bringing with him his own brain trust, which put more than one hundred new reform laws on the state's books and set off a progressive reaction in which the "Wisconsin Idea" was being emulated within ten years in states from one end of the continent to the other.[20]

But the novels which present reform in this light are predictably in the minority. The rest ultimately reflect a judgment much like that of Hofstadter. The agitation against the trusts as late as the time of the Wilson administration, he writes, produced results so incomplete as to show that "the men who took a conservative view of the needs of the hour never lost control."[21] The novels most often show the reform lead-ers as men whose final effect, despite their well-known thought and work, had fundamentally been superficial; they had temporarily changed the climate but not the geography. In the words of Thurman Arnold, "Wher-ever the reformers are successful—whenever they see their direct pri-

---

[18] Goldman, *Rendezvous,* p. 361.
[19] *Ibid.,* pp. 167–168.
[20] *Ibid.,* pp. 168–171.
[21] Hofstadter, *Reform,* p. 250.

maries, their antitrust laws, or whatever else they base their hopes on, in actual operation—the great temporal institutions adapt themselves, leaving the older reformers disillusioned, like Lincoln Steffens, and a newer set carrying on the banner."[22] Reform and the reformer—fighting idealist or silk-stocking dilettante—are ephemeral. The machine will go on, operating on a pragmatic knowledge of human nature as it works in political institutions in the immemorial ways.

Nineteenth-Century Predecessors

The figure of the Young Knight had first appeared in the closing decades of the nineteenth century. Although only two of these Knights were successful, none was corrupt. Two of the novels were romances in which a corrupt protagonist would have been unthinkable. F. Marion Crawford's *An American Politician* (1885) had related the career of a wealthy idealist-reformer as it carried him to membership in the Senate and in a secret council which helped rule the nation. Ultimately John Harrington had almost singlehandedly kept the Union together, with the Presidency seemingly the next prize in the triumphal procession of his career. The novel had been impossibly handicapped by a creaky love story done in clichés and purple passages, and by its generally pervasive air of artificiality and unreality. Less trammeled with period-piece romance and closer to life was Paul Leicester Ford's *The Honorable Peter Stirling* (1894). Led into politics, like Harrington, by an Irish machine politician, Stirling was another idealist who made good. A poor man who became an honest political Boss, Stirling at the novel's end contemplated the possibility of the Presidency. Familiar with corruption, he took a Calvinistic view repeatedly encountered in these novels. "The fault is not in politics," he had concluded. "It is in humanity."[23] But like Crawford's novel, this one suffered too much from the clichés of popular fiction: twists and turns, misunderstandings and unitings. And if this were not enough, there were talking horses, wearisome puns, and foreign accents which suggested not so much the melting pot as the vaudeville circuit.

Hamlin Garland had already published *Main-Travelled Roads* when *A Spoil of Office* appeared in 1892. In the novel he drew again on his knowledge of the Midwestern farmers depicted in the earlier book's

---

[22] Thurman Arnold, *The Symbols of Government*, p. 124.
[23] Paul Leicester Ford, *The Honorable Peter Stirling and What People Thought of Him*, p. 311.

stories. He set the career of Bradley Talcott against the Grange farmers' struggle in the 1870's for economic betterment through their People's Party. Carried into the Iowa legislature and then into Congress by victories over the railroads and the organized Republicans, Talcott had returned disillusioned by politics in Washington only to find himself unseated by factionalism at home. But the novel's end showed him girding for another struggle, aided by his bride, Ida, a Grange lecturer and visionary political activist. This Populist novel, writes Hofstadter, "showed how general was the familiarity with state corruption."[24] Artistically the book was little better than its immediate predecessors, replete like them with sentimental clichés and catch phrases, and containing little exploration in depth of character and motivation. But unlike them, this novel of the Young Knight (with subsidiary themes of Woman as Guide, feminism, corruption, and the battle against the Interests) had made use of radical political theory including new concepts of wealth and its production. Beyond this, it had advocated not reform within the old system, but revolution through class warfare.

Ellen Glasgow's *The Voice of the People* (1900) also helped mark the transition from romance to realism. In this novel of the Reconstruction era she dealt with her particular subject matter, life in Virginia, as she did in the whole series of novels that followed. Ironically, her book was the first of this group in which the central character was that most pervasive one in the modern American political novel—the Lincoln figure. A lowborn, self-educated lawyer, Nicholas Burr was a natural leader, "square-jawed, large-featured" with an attractive "uncompromising ugliness."[25] His rise to the governorship and his conflict with the state machine were capped, unsatisfactorily, by an accidental martyrdom. Miss Glasgow's failure to carry the problem through to a more meaningful end in terms of her original framework was counterbalanced by a general artistic advance over her predecessors. Character was more fully explored and enriched by the grafting of the Lincoln-martyr pattern onto that of the Young Knight.

The Early Years

Although most of the Young Knights remain true to the vows underlying their Quests, the first one the reader encounters becomes corrupt. Jerome B. Garwood is Congressional representative of seven Illinois

24 Hofstadter, *Reform*, p. 186.
25 Ellen Glasgow, *The Voice of the People*, p. 186.

counties in Brand Whitlock's *The 13th District* (1902). His figure is familiar; he is an imposing young lawyer who is called "the tall Sycamore of the Sangamon."[26] His initial motives are unexceptionable: "in that enthusiasm for humanity which springs in most men of the liberal professions with the shock of their first impact with a hard, material age, and develops until the age taints them with its sordidness, Garwood had enlisted in the world-old fight for equality and democracy." But Whitlock adds, "he was elected to the Legislature. Thereafter, he dreamed of becoming some day a great commoner, and so was in danger of turning out a demagogue."[27] Garwood's future is implicit in this paragraph. Despite his fiancée, Emily, who provides intellectual guidance, he falls from grace in that great disillusioner of young politicians, the state legislature. He accepts a bribe from the railroad interests. His career thereafter declines into a struggle to stay in office at the cost of whatever duplicity is necessary. Having betrayed his political manager to attain Washington again, Garwood looks back at Grand Prairie, Polk County, Illinois: "it's worth all a fellow has to go through out in that beastly mud hole to be back here where one can really live" (349). The political customs and institutions of Garwood's native mudhole enhance the novel's interest as sociopolitical history. Whitlock recreates them so as to give a vivid sense of a vanished time and place. Nomination is achieved at the tumultuous congressional district convention. Flushed partisans "flung their hats into the air, tore off their coats to wave aloft, brandished chairs, and pounded one another on the back, yelling all the time" (314). The oratory of Civil War veterans from bunting-draped platforms under a blazing summer sun is followed by the crashing brassy rendition of military airs. Three months later spectators watch the election-eve climax: "in the darkness of the November night, far away through the trees, they caught the lick of a torch's flame, then another and another, until they made a river of yellow fire that poured itself down the street from curb to curb, rising and falling as the marchers' feet kept time to the punctuated rolling of the drums" (158). The procession of soldiers with flags and railroad men with transparencies—led by the grand marshal and policemen four abreast—forms a blazing host under the marshal's shouted commands as his aides gallop "wildly up

---

[26] Lincoln had split rails on the Sangamon River in Illinois. See Carl Sandburg, *Abraham Lincoln: The Prairie Years,* I, 106 and 103.

[27] Brand Whitlock, *The 13th District,* p. 35. The first quotation from each novel will be footnoted. Thereafter, page references for quotations from the same novel will be given within parentheses in the text.

and down until at last the torches began to dance in varying directions as the column executed some complex maneuver that wrought a change in its formation"(160). At last the grand cavalcade passes, followed by a rabble of frolicking boys, leaving a trail of burnt-out torches and spent roman candles.

By the time retribution overtakes Garwood, physical deterioration (paralleling moral deterioration) has transformed him into a man with flowing locks, fat white hands, and a distended paunch. His wife Emily is forced to sustain the household as he loses himself in grandiose plans for a return to political life. This is an embodiment of a familiar phenomenon: corruption by place and power. Whitlock makes clear his view, however, as Mark Twain and Charles Dudley Warner had done earlier in *The Gilded Age* (1873), that the age itself has been corrupted by materialism. In the 13th district men campaign by fighting, bribing, deceiving, and coercing to gain office for their own ends. "This condition," writes Whitlock, "prevailed all over the land" (117). By an inevitable process, this Knight, infected by a disease endemic in his society, is too ill to fight any Dragon.

In a foreword to *The Spoilsmen* (1903), Elliott Flower wrote that his Chicago scenes were used "to demonstrate conditions that do exist in some wards in nearly all large cities."[28] Although the author's qualifications were not imposing (he had published *Policeman Flynn,* among other books), his novel came well recommended. "The world of municipal politics is put before the reader in a striking and truthful manner," wrote the Honorable Grover Cleveland in a prefatory statement, "and the sources of evil that afflict the government of our cities are laid bare in a manner that should arrest the attention of every honest man who wishes to purge and cleanse our local governments" (2).

The novel's first paragraph is a jewel of its kind, encapsulating as it does personages, attitudes, and conditions found again and again in these works:

"What the Old Man says goes!"
Billy Ryan banged his fist on the table with such force that Bartender Jim Casey, in the outer room, took his cigar from his mouth, and, pointing with it, remarked casually to the only customer at the bar,
"They're makin' histh'ry in there."(9)

[28] Elliott Flower, *The Spoilsmen,* p. v.

Boss rule, saloon environment, Mr. Dooley brogue—all are there.[29] And the author soon introduces the Citizens' Safety League, the cynical newspaperman, the sweetheart who sends deep red roses to "her knight,"[30] and the villain who tries to usurp her affections (208). Although Flower deals at length with the machinations of the machine and focuses the reader's attention upon its leader with his title, there is actually much more emphasis on the struggles of the two—not one—cooperative Young Knights who came to grips with it. A stalwart hardware merchant and a likeable society swell, they are tolerated by the Democratic machine as they win nomination and election as aldermen. The remainder of the novel relates the struggle in which they remain unintimidated. What emerges from this book, gauche as a dime novel and rudimentary as a morality play, is the author's apparent conclusion that the honest man cannot survive in politics without great resources, and that even then he will be unable to accomplish much good. This situation might be conceivably ameliorated if the Citizens' Safety League were to gain power, but there is no expectation of such a development here, as there is, for instance, in David Graham Phillips's *The Conflict* (1911).

Six Young Knights appeared in the seven years between 1907 and 1912. Their quarries were still the Dragons of the Interests and corruption, but nothing in their vows or vigils compelled them to espouse the old economic and political order. Apart from one fuddled millionaire and one reformer, most of them wanted to do nothing less than sweep the old order away. If there are any devices emblazoned on their banners, they are more likely to be Marxist than heraldic. None becomes corrupted and most achieve some measure of success.

Isaac Kahn Friedman's *The Radical* was published in 1907. The son of wealthy parents, Friedman had turned from the political economy he had studied at the University of Michigan to immerse himself in Chicago settlement-house work. This helped make him a Socialist, and he

---

[29] Mr. Dooley, the most celebrated user of this stage-Irishman dialect, was created by Finley Peter Dunne. In humorous sketches often set in his Chicago saloon, Mr. Dooley discoursed to his friend Hinnisy on political and social matters. The sketches were gathered together in such popular volumes as *Mr. Dooley in Peace and in War* (1898) and *Mr. Dooley in the Hearts of his Countrymen* (1898). See *Mr. Dooley Remembers: The Informal Memoirs of Finley Peter Dunne*, edited by Philip Dunne.

[30] This appellation is not casually used. Earlier the author has said of her, "She pictured ideal conditions—not in Arcady, but in the city where she lived. Her knights were of the modern school, but they were nevertheless knights" (54).

remained one through his career on the foreign staff and the editorial department of the Chicago *Daily News*. Friedman's protagonist is Illinois-born Bruce McAllister. Orphaned at thirteen, he conquers his later problems of drink, gambling, and grafting to become an upright lawyer. His appearance is unequivocally Lincolnian. He has other attributes. "A Siegfried born to overthrow the gods, defying their mandates in the name of the people," he battles the O'Brien machine in Springfield and then the Universal Trust in Washington.[31] Sickened by defeat and chicanery in a time of social upheaval, he resigns from Congress. Returning to Illinois with his bride, he awaits the call of the people. Friedman never demonstrates McAllister's "fantastic radicalism." He is simply an enemy of corruption who urges reform within the existing system. Friedman's apparent intent comes through only in a long passage in his own voice near the end of the novel: "What meant the restlessness and stirring . . . dissatisfaction at the present régime, other than that the ideals of humanity had evolved to higher things . . . that competition must yield to cooperation, even as feudalism and serfdom had given way to a new civilization which now, in its turn, was dropping behind in the march of progress . . ." (362). More damaging to the novel than vague and undramatized principles, however, were the author's inability to write dialogue that might conceivably have issued from a human mouth and his inability to avoid addressing himself indirectly to the reader in passages of insufferable cuteness.[32]

Like Friedman's book, Winston Churchill's *Mr. Crewe's Career* (1908) conveyed a sense of change, of an era passing and a new order emerging. Using a situation and characters developed in *Coniston* (1906), he depicted a conflict between dominant railroad interests and the oppressed farmers.[33] A citizens' coalition is now led by a Young

[31] I. K. Friedman, *The Radical*, p. 294.
[32] For further background material on Friedman, and for an analysis of his other fiction, especially *By Bread Alone* (1901), the strike novel with which the history of the radical novel in this century begins, see Walter B. Rideout, *The Radical Novel in the United States 1900–1954: Some Interrelations of Literature and Society*, pp. 13–18.
[33] For a discussion of this story of a political Boss, apparently set in New Hampshire a quarter of a century earlier, see Chapter Two. With royalties from best-selling romances, Churchill had bought a New Hampshire estate and built a mansion. Running for the legislature on a Progressive platform, he won two terms, serving from 1903 to 1907. His experiences there prompted him to write *Coniston* and *Mr. Crewe's Career*. See Richard and Beatrice Hofstadter, "Winston Churchill: A Study in the Popular Novel," *American Quarterly*, 2 (Spring, 1950), pp. 12–28.

Knight who is also the son of the chief counsel for the Northeastern Railroad and political Boss of the state. But romancer Churchill does not stop there. Young Austen Vane loves Victoria Flint, daughter of Augustus Flint, his father's boss and head of the railroad interests. In a predictable fashion, Austen wins the girl, rebuffs the Interests, and attains the power to defeat their political apparatus. Humphrey Crewe, an unsuccessful millionaire candidate for the governorship, serves as a foil for the Young Knight. A Knight with a long-term view of his task, Vane delays the final blow, withholding his name from the gubernatorial nominating convention out of deference to his infirm father, who is committed to this one last campaign. But as Flint watches the disaffected elder Vane leave his study, he senses the "end of an era of fraud, of self-deception, of conditions that violated every sacred principle of free government which men had shed blood to obtain."[34]

The Quest in David Graham Phillips

In David Graham Phillips the reader encounters the advanced ideas only suggested in the protagonists of Friedman and Churchill. Phillips published three political novels in the years between 1909 and 1912.[35] Their protagonists formed a unique progression. One was a dynamic re-

---

[34] Winston Churchill, *Mr. Crewe's Career*, p. 379. The Hofstadters note that in both these novels the politicians repent and are forgiven, unlike the businessmen. They further remark a Churchillian formula in which the progressive and idealistic lover rejects and triumphs over the heroine's businessman father and his values. Arthur Link comments that somehow "Churchill thought that all that was necessary to effect a regeneration of American politics was for the sturdy, plain people to turn the rascals out and elect honest men" *(American Epoch: A History of the United States since the 1890's, p. 78).* The Hofstadters also suggest that Austen Vane, "with his instinctive talent for leadership, his out-of-doors personality, and his western ranching background might have been modeled directly on [Theodore] Roosevelt" ("Winston Churchill," p. 18).

[35] Working as a newspaper reporter after graduating from Princeton in 1887, David Graham Phillips (1867–1911) moved up quickly. Writing editorials for Pulitzer's *World* and exposés for *McClure's,* he capped these efforts with works such as *The Treason of the Senate* (1906) to become the prince of muckrakers. Phillips was one of those who added phrases such as "Park Avenue Parasites" and "The Interests" to the popular vocabulary. He inadvertently helped bring into currency another phrase. Counterattacking when the first part of *The Treason of the Senate* lambasted Chauncey Depew, Theodore Roosevelt likened the exposé-writers to the character in the second part of *Pilgrim's Progress* who kept his eyes fixed on the muck on the floor without scanning the heavens above. The book helped contribute nonetheless to the amendment eight years later providing for direct election of senators. See Eric F. Goldman, "David Graham Phillips: Victorian Critic of Victorianism," in *The Lives of Eighteen from Princeton,* ed. Willard Thorp, pp. 318–332.

former, another a leader with a soul attuned to that of his people, and
the third a Christlike Marxist. *The Fashionable Adventures of Joshua
Craig* (1909) chronicled the career of a "hardy plodder in the arduous
pathway from plowboy to President."[36] There is scarcely room for all
the mythic attributes that cluster around Joshua Craig. He has, writes
Phillips, the megalomania of a Napoleon, feeling that "he is a born
king"(129). He is a "figure of the forest and the teepee"(4), but he has
a nose like that of Alexander the Great and a face that still manages to
be "ethereal in its beauty, yet flashing with manliness"(124).[37] An Attorney General who dominates an entire Administration, he leaves Washington with his formerly haughty, now-penitent bride as he prepares to
run for the governorship of Minnesota. The principal Dragons opposing
him are the railroad interests and "the plutocracy" (213). In his victories he seems not so much Knight as Superman, an embodiment of
triumphant force who just happens to be on the right side. If he is gauche
and unbelievable, so is the novel.[38]

   The Conflict (1911) was the best of these three political novels. The
hero is as different from Joshua Craig as Phillips can make him. Victor
Dorn is a Marxist. He is also unprepossessing physically, although of
great moral stature. Having worked his way through college and law
school as a carpenter (several attributes make him a radical Christ-fig-
ure), he lives by lecturing and publishing a "working man's" paper, *The*

---

   [36] David Graham Phillips, *The Fashionable Adventures of Joshua Craig,* p. 186.
   [37] In their physical characteristics, Phillips's rugged heroes belong to a type
frequently encountered in the last quarter of the nineteenth century. The protagonist of a novel published in 1877 is teased by a friend as being "the great
Western Barbarian, stepping forth in his innocence and might, gazing a while at
this poor effete Old World, and then swooping down on it." The author describes
him as "a powerful specimen of an American." His appearance is familiarly impressive: "He had a very well-formed head, with a shapely, symmetrical balance
of the frontal and the occipital development, and a good deal of straight rather
dry brown hair. His complexion was brown, and his nose had a bold, well-marked
arch. His eye was of a clear, cold gray, and save for a rather abundant mustache
he was clean-shaved. He had the flat jaw and sinewy neck which are frequent in
the American type . . ." And he never uses tobacco. The novel was Henry James's
The American, pp. 44, 6, and 7. By the time Phillips had published the novels
treated here, James had, of course, gone on to the intricate subtleties of *The Wings
of the Dove, The Ambassadors,* and *The Golden Bowl.* But though he changed
Christopher Newman's age from thirty-six to forty-two and a half when he revised the novel for the New York edition of 1907, he left his appearance virtually
untouched.
   [38] It was the cause, nonetheless, of Phillips's death. One Fitzhugh G. Golds-
borough, conceiving the idea that Phillips had caricatured his sister in the girl
whom Craig tames and marries, threatened Phillips and finally shot him on January 23, 1911. See Goldman, "David Graham Phillips," p. 328.

New Day, in Remsen City, Indiana. In the office hang pictures of Washington, Lincoln, Karl Marx, and Jesus Christ.[39] Dorn's natural enemy is the head of the traction interests and political ruler of Remsen City. With the Populist scare more than a decade behind, the physically repulsive Morton Hastings is in firm control. He controls everything but his daughter's heart, which belongs, of course, to Dorn. Dorn lectures Jane on the class structure of society, the nature of work, and the creation of wealth. Confident, he rejects the intercessory help she offers: "the old parties are falling to pieces because they stand for the old politics of the two factions of the upper class quarreling over which of them should superintend the exploiting of the people . . . we're seeing the death agonies of one form of civilization and the birth-throes of a newer form."[40] The novel moves inevitably to the class warfare Dorn predicts as the Workingmen's League battles the hirelings of the Interests. The "gas crowd, the traction crowd, and the paving crowd," the Interests control both plug-uglies and parties: the Republican, the Democratic, and the Reform (158).[41] Dorn suffers skull and jaw fractures as he nearly becomes the leader sacrificed for his people. In the election that follows he sees his candidates defeated in an orgy of fraud and intimidation.

By the novel's end the Reform Administration begins to sicken with its own corruption, but victory of the Workingmen's League must wait for the future. Like Friedman, Phillips concludes with an abrupt jump into that future. The Workingmen's League governs Remsen City, but "little can be done until the State government is conquered" and the national government after it (390).[42] The romantic problems have been solved through ideologically and socially appropriate mating. Dorn's bride, Selma, engages in a one-sided dialectic with Jane: "Who ever gave you the idea that we were seeking converts in your class? . . . Our whole object is to abolish your class . . . and make its members useful

---

[39] Compare the description in Ignazio Silone's *Bread and Wine* (1937) of the Fossa headquarters of the pre-Mussolini Catholic Socialist Peasant League.

[40] David Graham Phillips, *The Conflict*, p. 143.

[41] Two of the stereotypes Phillips uses are the Irish Democratic organization Boss—former safecracker and saloonkeeper Dick Kelly—and the professional politicians who hold reform movements in contempt.

[42] Although the Socialist Party was soon to decline and then meet disaster during the first World War, gains had been made which prevent Dorn's seeming a visionary daydreamer. By 1912, a year after the novel was published, the Socialist Party numbered 126,000 members. Link notes that by 1912 Socialist Administrations governed Milwaukee, Schenectady, and Berkeley, California. In the same year, Eugene Debs polled 897,000 votes for President, and there were soon to be two Socialists sitting in the House of Representatives (Link, *American Epoch,* p. 64).

members of our class, and more contented and happier than they are now" (242). This Knight is not content merely to slay the Dragon; his overriding task is to change the natural habitat which makes it possible for him to exist. In *The Conflict* Phillips had been unable to avoid a certain amount of romantic foolery. He had committed lapses in dialogue and diction, and he had obviously engineered the ending, but this novel was a vastly better job than *The Fashionable Adventures of Joshua Craig*. And he showed that, like some of his contemporaries, he was adapting radical political ideas to the uses of fiction, embody them though he might in familiar form.

In *George Helm* (1912) Phillips created a hero much more a man of the people than Joshua Craig yet not so much the revolutionary as Victor Dorn. He can see class allegiances as an obstacle to marriage, but he is a Dragon-killer who works within established institutions. Able, courageous, and effective, he is the kind Victor Dorn would doubly disapprove of, for shoring up rather than helping to sweep away the existing system. In his mid-twenties, he appears in an Ohio River town wearing "frock suit" and top hat. He has "a big loosely jointed body whose legs and arms seemed unduly long," and his beard adorns a "strong, rather homely face, stern to sadness in repose . . ."[43] (Earlier, Phillips has compared his rough joking with that of Lincoln.) Helm opposes the Republican and Democratic parties "owned and controlled [by] . . . the Railway Trust, the Harvester Trust, the Beef Trust, the Money Trust . . ." (13). His emergence has the ring of legend: "It had spread from man to man throughout the state that there had arisen in Harrison a strange, plain youth of great sincerity as a man of great power as a speaker . . . The Messiah-dream . . . has been . . . the longing of the whole human race, toiling away in obscurity, oppressed, exploited, fooled, and despised" (123). His marriage to Nell Clearwater is begun on his terms: "You're leaving your class and coming to mine—and . . . the war between these two classes is going to be bitter and more bitter until—" (247). It nonetheless handicaps him seriously as governor. The offender whom he must subdue or imprison is the Lumber King, Senator Clearwater—not surprisingly Nell's father.[44] Helm is the first of the Knights

---

[43] David Graham Phillips, *George Helm*, p. 24.

[44] This marriage between members of different and even antagonistic classes is one of a number of examples of the star-crossed lovers situation. Although the consequences are never tragic as in *Romeo and Juliet*, the lovers' differing backgrounds usually cause some anguish and occasionally, as in *The Conflict*, make marriage impossible. This device was probably attractive to these novelists for a number of reasons. For one, almost all of them use a romantic theme as counter-

to meet with defeat, for the state machine—whose leader's heir he has refused to become—will defeat him at the polls. But he looks ahead as he and Nell are joined in dedication to work for "the people" (301).

George Helm fell between its two predecessors: it avoided most of the excesses of *The Fashionable Adventures of Joshua Craig* and failed to achieve the solidity of *The Conflict.* Like them it paralleled the Quest for the Dragon with the Quest for the maiden by the Man of Destiny whom Phillips found so attractive. This prolific novelist was no major writer, but more than any of his immediate contemporaries he dealt with themes and types that were later to become staples. His earlier material had been conventional, as we shall see later with *The Plum Tree* (1905), and he was never able in his political novels to eschew the stock situations, turgid style, and limited diction of the nineteenth-century romancers. But Phillips was able to adapt to his purposes ideas of considerable radicalism for his time. Moreover, characters of his were among the first to urge not the reform but the junking of the old system for a new one meant to usher in the millennium.

The Approaches to the Present

A novel superficially resembling *George Helm* also appeared in 1912. In *The Citadel: A Romance of Unrest,* Samuel Merwin employed a Dragon-slayer-and-maiden-seeker, invoked the shade of Lincoln, made the local Boss a saloonkeeper, and drew the hero's sweetheart from the family of his chief enemy. His Knight also met defeat but looked forward with his devoted wife at the book's end to work that would lead to eventual victory. But the hero is an avowed Socialist anxious to change

---

point for the political one, and this variant upon the subject of the vicissitudes of courtship is potentially the most dramatic. It can serve to move the plot along and, in the hands of a skilled writer, to increase the intensity of effect of a number of otherwise rather conventional situations. Viewed differently, the Young Knight's act of capturing the heart of the daughter of his greatest enemy and then taking her away to be his own suggests a number of more overt and primitive responses. To take away the bloated adversary's treasure is potentially one of the most satisfying acts of hostility possible to the Young Knight. Aspects of such symbolic action are to be seen in works as disparate as *The Sheik* and *The Eve of St. Agnes.* Walter Rideout notes that this usage not only affords contrast but may also reflect "the writer's own commitment to the upward mobility ethic of American society." (This ethic is reflected many times in these novels, most strikingly in the implicit or explicit view that just about anyone, potentially, can become President.) Rideout also suggests that the Young Knight's revolt against society may be symbolized in this revolt against that familiar authority-figure, the Father (Letter to the writer, August 3, 1961).

or even scrap the Constitution.[45] Among the lesser changes the hero advocates are the standard Progressive goals of initiative, referendum, and recall. Beyond this, Merwin shows an awareness of Freudianism and Social Darwinism. He appears to be influenced by Theodore Dreiser and to anticipate Sinclair Lewis. Had he been a better craftsman, his novel might be remembered today. His protagonist is a vigorous Illinois congressman in his early thirties. With his pince-nez "he might have been a wide-awake, modern sort of college professor or particularly well-read and thoughtful business man."[46] When he breaks with his newspaper-publisher sponsor, he also breaks with his sponsor's daughter. The Dragon he assaults is "the Industrial Oligarchy" (137), and his cry is, "We are engaged in a Revolution!" (324). His enforced return from Washington to defend his position follows a familiar pattern. Once home, he is defeated by the oligarchy's machine in "an old-fashioned orgy of drink, bribery, physical intimidation, ballot-stuffing and general disorder and petty riot" (343). His new love, an agricultural biologist, plays the role of Woman as Guide. *"You saw it!"* he tells her, "Society as a biological organism—that was it!—growing, changing, endlessly struggling to adapt itself to a constantly changing environment" (328). She herself seems controlled by something very like what Dreiser called Chemisms when not seeming a broadly drawn case of repression and sublimation. When her id and superego finally reach an accommodation in her marriage to Garwood, the newlyweds look ahead with familiar dedication to joint goals. In describing the society which makes their crusade necessary, Merwin anticipates *Main Street* by eight years and *Babbitt* by ten:

Things were certainly "looking up" out here in Illinois. Business was fairly brisk. Men with tired eyes and the booster's smile were fighting each other and

---

[45] Although the latter part of the nineteenth century had seen propertied conservatives successfully mount a campaign in which the Constitution had been elevated to the status of a sanctified document, subscribers to Reform Darwinism had been steadily chipping away at the pedestal through the first decade of the twentieth century. A year after *The Citadel* was published, the economic interpretation of the Constitution which these social scientists urged was bolstered by Charles A. Beard. With *An Economic Interpretation of the Constitution*, he added the force of siege guns to the assault (See Goldman, *Rendezvous*, pp. 87–88, 134, and 151). See also Link, *American Epoch*, p. 80, for a brief discussion of the thesis that "the Constitution had been written deliberately to frustrate the democratic movement."

[46] Samuel Merwin, *The Citadel: A Romance of Unrest*, p. 4. This is the last kind word said about the college professor in these novels for about forty years and virtually the only one said for the businessman.

all society for some extra share in the common wealth, in order that their wives might drive the trim little cars, and that their sons might wear the standardized clothing and go away to the standardizing colleges, and that their daughters might wear the rich appearing furs.(49)

This novel is linked to its predecessors by some of the ritualistic trials its Knight must undergo. It looks toward its successors in the fact of his defeat and espousal of radicalism. In its awareness of contemporary thought, garbled though the statement of it may be, it might be called the first of the really modern American political novels.

Fiction, Fact, and History

Novels strong enough to act as political instruments are generally well known. One of the most familiar political-literary comments is, of course, that attributed to Abraham Lincoln upon meeting Harriet Beecher Stowe: "So you're the little woman who wrote the book that made this great war!" Less influential than *Uncle Tom's Cabin* but hardly less impassioned, Upton Sinclair's *The Jungle* (1906) and John Steinbeck's *The Grapes of Wrath* (1939)—though not political novels by the present definition—lent support to reform. There is one instance in this century in which a forgotten work appears to have exercised a profound influence upon politics and history. It appeared innocuously enough. Samuel G. Blythe published the first episode of *The Fakers* in the *Saturday Evening Post* of May 30, 1914. The August 11 issue completed the story of a young opportunist who rode under a shining pennant but harbored not one honest thought behind his deceitful exterior. An ambitious young politician read the episodes with fascinated interest. He meditated upon them and later "boasted that he would make them the foundation stones of a great political temple in Louisiana." Blythe satirized demagoguery in the person of T. Marmaduke Hicks, a cynical protagonist with something both of the fool and the rogue. But young Huey P. Long saw beyond the familiar comic chastisement of human follies to something very different. He confided to a friend, "The fellow that put those views and promises in the mouth of a political candidate thought he was writing something funny; and he was, at that. But he was also writing something of immense value to the chap who wants to get somewhere in politics. The people want that kind of stuff. They eat it up. Why not give it to them?"[47]

Although the George H. Doran Company thought well enough of

[47] Thomas O. Harris, *The Kingfish: Huey P. Long, Dictator*, pp. 17–18.

Blythe's novel to publish it in book form before the year was out, its style was closer to that of political potboilers of the late 1890's (when its action began) than to that of some of the more accomplished new novels. The action was slow-moving and unconvincing. The characters were stereo-typed and the diction was close to the parody Nathanael West was to do twenty years later in *A Cool Million* (1934). Both dialogue and ex-position hovered between primer prose and cliché. Blythe's plot was more nearly original. Senator Paxton, "The Old Fox of the Senate," calls Assistant Secretary Hicks "the biggest potential political faker I ever saw."[48] For Hicks's profit and his own sardonic amusement, the Senator will conduct an experiment: "Men are getting to Washington who are mere clumsy amateurs at this friend-of-the-people game. With Hicks properly located and properly instructed there would inevitably result a triumph of political fakery . . . we can erect, direct, own and operate a first-class tribune of the pee-pul . . ." (58). Transplanted to the Midwest, Hicks changes parties and intrigues his way through ten years of unsuccessful campaigns. By trickery he rises to the United States Senate and to affluence. By the time of his fall, very little money has stuck to his fingers. But Hicks is little daunted, seeing more rich pickings ahead, even if in Europe rather than America.

The parts of *The Fakers* from which Long presumably benefited most were Paxton's aphorisms and letters of advice to Hicks. The Senator instructs his pupil about dress, drinking, frivolity, promises, and truth. His cynical advice covers the clichés of oratory, the praise of women, the attack on the trusts, and repeatedly, the wooing of the "common people." "Never," he writes, "refer to the people as the people. Always call them the plain people. The great bulk of the people are so plain they like to be told of that characteristic constantly . . . The great toil-ing masses would be mighty uncomfortable and unhappy if they had nothing to kick about. So, if there are no outrages on the body politic, think up a few" (67). This bogus Knight attacks the Republican Party, the Standard Oil Company, The National City Bank, Rockefeller, Mor-gan, Harriman, Wall Street, and the Money Devil (328). Such pas-sages, according to Thomas O. Harris, were a revelation to Long. He goes even further: "It may seem like stretching language," he writes, "to say that the humorous articles of Samuel G. Blythe were incorporated in the political platform of Huey P. Long and were governing influences

---

[48] Samuel G. Blythe, *The Fakers*, p. 57.

in his public career up to the very hour of his death. Yet, that is the incontrovertible truth. What Blythe wrote as a parody, Huey Long adopted as a guide."[49] Rarely, if ever, has so indifferent a novel produced so turbulent an effect.

Knights in the Twenties

The two Young Knights who appear in the novels of the 1920's are almost complementary opposites: one is a James Montgomery Flagg Arrow-shirt portrait whose countenance shines progressively brighter; the other is a Dorian Gray whose corruption appears progressively, line by line. Henry H. Curran's *Van Tassel and Big Bill* (1923) was a naive and sentimental treatment of the young aristocrat succeeding in politics as elsewhere. M. H. Hedges's *Dan Minturn* (1927) was a serious though clumsy effort in the opposite direction with a proletarian protagonist whose worldly rise means his moral fall. Banker Van Tassel provides the idealistic impulse which helps make his son, Jimmy, an alderman: "Why, look at our country—leading the whole world. But not in government. And we won't be safe until our young men, who can lead, go into government, and come to lead there too."[50] His rise there is aided by a New York saloonkeeper and minor political factotum repaying the banker for an old favor. But this excursion into politics of a member of "the silk-stocking class" has no more lasting effect on the body politic than it usually does. After the story of the first campaign, the book degenerates into a series of irreproachable adventures with a Frank Merriwell tone.[51] An unrealistic mass of clichés sugared over with the cute and the maudlin, this story treats a Young Knight who sits his horse well but would hardly make a mouthful for an adult Dragon.

Dan Minturn's case is very different. Elected to the Minnesota leg-

---

[49] Harris, *Kingfish*, pp. 17–18.

[50] Henry H. Curran, *Van Tassel and Big Bill*, p. 9. These sentiments, in the tradition of patrician reform, are of course most dramatically embodied in Theodore Roosevelt, who had "a patrician's disdain for greedy businessmen, a patrician's sense of *noblesse oblige* toward the downtrodden, and a patrician's fear of socialism or some other 'riotous, wicked' surge from the bottom groups" (quoted in Mark Sullivan, *Our Times*, Vol. III, p. 249; cited in Goldman, *Rendezvous*, p. 162). Some components of this attitude were to be seen in T. R.'s young fifth cousin and nephew-in-law, Franklin D. Roosevelt.

[51] The novel's episodic nature suggests the influence of the slum sketches and human interest stories of popular journalism, which tapped a kind of interest like that which responded to the muckraking articles.

islature, the young typesetter promptly forgets his faithful sweetheart
and guide, as he courts the niece of the senator fronting for the Interests.
Telegraphing his punch, Hedges leaves the reader in no doubt that this
romantic change of heart prefigures a political one. The state legislature
is again the great disillusioner, especially to a boy whose room contained
not just a photograph of a movie star, but pictures of Lincoln and Maz-
zini as well. His own fall from grace is foreshadowed by a colleague's
remark (which might have come from a novel of the 1930's) : "The history of the labor movement is the history of betrayed leadership."[52] Minturn's betrayal of his responsibilities is followed by the twin sellout of
his marriage and by his re-election at the Interests' expense. He is ex-
coriated by his former friend Rakov, a badly overdone radical bookseller
in whose shop he had first read Machen, Veblen, Shaw, and Mencken.
One of Rakov's Parthian shots as he leaves for India seems derived from
Veblen: "It's a pig-trough civilization, Senator Minturn. It can't survive.
Machines grinding out stuff that people don't want that people may be
kept at the wheel in order to buy the stuff they don't want, and can't
use" (154).[53] Using situations that suggest D. H. Lawrence and concluding with impressionistic descriptive passages reminiscent of Virginia
Woolf, Hedges chronicles Minturn's progressive alienation from his family and his class.[54] It is his vote which kills what the author calls "The
Great Power and Drainage Act" (183). The description of his young
opponent suggests Garland's Bradley Talcott and the Farmers' Alliance,
but the machine is still securely in control. Unable to resist like George
Helm, Dan Minturn is about to step into harness and assume the machine's direction. Once again achievement falls short of aspiration for
lack of literary equipment. With chapters entitled "How Dan Loved
Agatha," and "Agatha's Love for Dan," the novel combines naiveté and
superficiality. Offering a potpourri of pseudointellectual phrases and
half-understood ideas, it serves them with underdone Lawrence and
warmed-over Woolf. Minturn is another example of the Young Knight
who betrays himself and his people. His is a relatively simple story of
betrayal, however, without the insight into dark forces in human personality to appear in later novels.

[52] M. H. Hedges, *Dan Minturn*, p. 87.

[53] Walter Rideout observes that the "revolt in this book is not only against
politics as a system of business power, but also against the seductive influence of a
merely materialistic civilization" (*Radical Novel*, p. 121).

[54] The novel is, suggests Rideout, "an astringent comment on the Cinderella
myth of America . . ." (*Radical Novel*, p. 122).

Corruption in the 1930's

During the 1920's and 1930's a whole group of novels appeared dominated by corruption and crime. The strength of this impulse carried over into four novels of the Young Knight. Each novel employs protagonists partly or wholly corrupted, and in one, the gangster first appears in the merging of organized politics and organized crime. Janet Ayer Fairbank's *The Lion's Den* (1930) is likely to give the reader a feeling of *déjà vu,* probably because of its resemblance to the story of bucolic virtue and urban vice which Hamlin Garland had told more than thirty years before in *A Spoil of Office* (1892). Mrs. Fairbank's principals are somewhat milder than Garland's, but she provides more romantic complications in this story of Daniel Carson, Wisconsin Progressive, and his sweetheart and guide, Irma Schmultz. Daniel is translated from orphan (working his farm alone for ten years, reciting Abraham Lincoln and Patrick Henry to his plow horses) to congressman in reward for his work for Senator LaFollette.[55] Irma has prophetic intimations of immorality even before he leaves his constituency, however, for she pleads, "You won't go back on all those things we've believed in? When you get down there in Washington—you'll go on being a Progressive?"[56] The Knight finally emerges from the Perilous Chapel with his escutcheon somewhat tarnished but his heart still in the right place. The reader is likely to conclude that here politics is window dressing and romance the real stock in trade.

Royce Brier's *Crusade* (1931) is the first novel in which organized crime corrupts both the Knight and local government. Published four years after Sinclair Lewis's *Elmer Gantry* and two years after W. R. Burnett's *Little Caesar,* it combines elements of both. Its protagonist is a Y.M.C.A. secretary in his late thirties, a self-righteous reformer of unimpeachable morals and the argot of a Babbitt. Jim Cardiff's one-man campaign against liquor and vice culminates in his election as his city's chief law-enforcement officer. Bribery, intimidation, and murder follow before he is turned out of office. (His gorgonlike wife then begins *her* reform career with election to the legislature.[57]) Counting on the con-

[55] LaFollette is the archetypal Midwest Progressive and champion of farm and labor, just as Lincoln stands for the martyred savior and Huey Long for the Southern Demagogue.

[56] Janet Ayer Fairbank, *The Lion's Den,* p. 22.

[57] This is a variant of the pattern in *A Spoil of Office,* in which the moral position originally assumed by the Knight is filled by his sweetheart-wife after he becomes corrupted. This pattern is carried further in *Crusade,* of course, as is

tinued support of the Anti-Saloon League and the W.C.T.U., Cardiff looks forward, despite his fall, to "pickings" in government or lobbying. Apparently buried in this mass of sensationalism is the moral that a hypocritical society will ruin even an honest man, who therefore deserves some sympathy even though he is a fanatic and a potential fascist. With or without the author's intent, however, this is quite as much the story of an arrant ass self-righteous even in corruption. It is a crude work which once again shows government corrupted by lust for money. And this corruption is intensified by the Amendment which—judged by the effects described in such novels as this—was a national catastrophe.

Gangsterism does not help rot the moral fiber of the Young Knight in Henry Hart's *The Great One: A Novel of American Life* (1934). But as he finally perceives that the bad old order will perish, he realizes that he has helped retard rather than accelerate the process. This was clearly the author's view, too. (Deeply committed to radicalism, editor and reviewer Henry Hart was one of the Executive Committee of the League of American Writers. For him, as for many others in that decade, novelists had their place on the barricades. They certainly found little cause for joy, according to Hart, in the reception their work was likely to receive in American society as it was then constituted. Citing meager sales figures of proletarian novels at the first American Writers' Congress in 1935, he concluded, "the bourgeois publishers are going to begin to refuse to publish them as the present incipient fascism increases."[58]) Hart's Philadelphia Main Line protagonist is a forerunner of a type which will emerge in the 1940's, often bearing easily identifiable characteristics of Franklin Delano Roosevelt.[59] It is that of the young aristocrat who enters politics for idealistic reasons and, in the most typical pattern, allies

---

almost everything else, in keeping with the brutal and frenetic milieu which is Brier's portrayal of the 1920's. Certain details of the plot suggest the 1912 murder of gambler Herman Rosenthal. Police Lieutenant Charles Becker and four notorious hoodlums were electrocuted for that crime, whose ramifications led to evidence of municipal and state political corruption and gave impetus to agitation for reform. F. Scott Fitzgerald's Wolfsheim refers to the crime in *The Great Gatsby* (1925). See Jonathan Root, *One Night in July: The True Story of the Rosenthal-Becker Murder Case.*

[58] Henry Hart, "Contemporary Publishing and the Revolutionary Writer," *American Writers' Congress*, p. 161.

[59] Walter Rideout identifies this novel as "an interpretation of the career of Boies Penrose." He adds that "Hart subsequently argued in *The New Masses* that he had been trying to show the helplessness of the individual in a society which was making individualism impossible, but the reasons given in the book to explain the hero's turn from reform to reaction are hardly those a Marxist would assign" (*Radical Novel*, p. 315).

himself with the great mass of the people rather than the class from which he has come. Bayard Stuart has been drawn into politics by desire to do good and by shock at the methods of the Interests. But this idealism is eroded in his rise from the legislature to the United States Senate. Control of the Pennsylvania state Republican machine completes his debasement. Friendless and unhonored on his deathbed, he tells his newly discovered illegitimate son, "I missed the boat . . . There is a new order coming, sooner or later, and I did nothing to help it. All I did retarded it . . . You must do what I didn't do."[60] But these words can hardly be expected to be efficacious in a society in which even those with great natural advantages are eventually corrupted by the forces which control it.

In *Compromise* (1936) Royal Wilbur France introduced a variant in this pattern. His Knight makes a fine beginning and ending, but between them he betrays his sweetheart, his wife, and himself. Achieving wordly success, he becomes a backslider, an adulterer, and a habitual compromiser. Once an admirer of Bellamy's *Looking Backward* and a partisan of Theodore Roosevelt the trust buster, Emory Young goes over to the Interests. He drifts away from his symbolically named sweetheart and guide, Justine, and marries a judge's daughter. Like Dan Minturn, Emory becomes integrated into his new class. This a familiar measure of corruption; whereas men like George Helm had required their mates to join their social class, Emory does the reverse.

Years later his conscience reawakens to the liberalism of colleagues like Senator "Fighting Bob" Bronson. With this belated growth of principle he rejects a Presidential nomination and campaign financed by "the oil crowd."[61] After the Wall Street crash, Emory advocates reforms eventually credited to the New Deal. As in *A Spoil of Office* and *Crusade,* it is the Knight's sweetheart who forges ahead. But Justine is fatally shot by company guards in a West Virginia mineworkers strike.[62] Emory's great expiatory act, promised to her before her death, is to "state your case—even if it costs me the Presidency (369). Of course, it does. When he expires, her name is on his lips.

Compromise carries the Young Knight into the New Deal era. In spite of the Republican sympathies of the major characters, and the author

---

[60] Henry Hart, *The Great One: A Novel of American Life*, p. 322.

[61] Royal Wilbur France, *Compromise*, p. 339. As a college orator Emory has been thought by some more effective than ("Fighting Bob") LaFollette.

[62] These events are apparently based on the same labor disputes Dos Passos was to use three years later in *Adventures of a Young Man* (1939).

too, this novel offers the familiar view of the role of business in American political life. Emory Young, like his contemporaries, is more vulnerable than his predecessors. The Dragon has if anything become more powerful than before, and the Knights less able to defend against his attacks. The America in which this continuing drama is acted out has changed too. In spite of reform agitation and legislation, the Interests are enormously powerful. Moreover, society itself seems sapped of moral energy. The New Deal, now a derelict hulk riddled by fire from the Supreme Court, was at its best never the ideal embodiment of the ship of state. The milieu seems a decadent one in which it is perhaps unrealistic to expect the Knight to maintain his dedication and his purity.

The 1940's: Return to Virtue

The novels of the 1940's deal very little with corrupt Knights.[63] In the single such fall from grace, the process is reversed. The protagonist has become corrupt although he does not realize it; with growing awareness he becomes a champion of the oppressed. The others resemble their early predecessors, and their efforts even meet with some success. The quality of *Young John Takes Over* (1942), by Elizabeth Jordan, is accurately indicated by the tone of its title. The main business of the protagonist (literally "the young knight,") is ostensibly running for mayor in a New England town. He spends considerable time, though, in a love affair with the daughter of his opponent, "the typical political boss.[64] The newspaper covering his campaign in an article "illustrated . . . with a cut representing young Campbell as a crusader, complete in armor," also reports Hitler's invasion of Russia. But such events are as remote from those of the story as the reality of life itself. Appearing forty years earlier, this novel would have been called a romance, like those of F. Marion Crawford. Appearing as it did in 1942, it was an anachronism, as dated as an antimacassar, as faintly ludicrous as a deer-antlered hatrack.

Clifford Raymond's *The Honorable John Hale: A Comedy of American Politics* (1946) was a broken-backed novel split into "The Story of a Legislature" and "The Story of a Modest Man." John Hale's father is a

---

[63] The end of the 1930's had seen the publication of one novel which was suffused with sweetness if not light. Ethel M. Hueston's *The Honorable Uncle Lancy* (1939) starred three pretty young women in the campaign in which their smart, lovable aunt secured the re-election to the United States Senate of an aging Knight, their lovable, featherheaded uncle. It was, presumably, a worthy successor to Mrs. Hueston's *Blithe Baldwin* and *Eve to the Rescue*.

[64] Elizabeth Jordan, *Young John Takes Over*, p. 23.

corporation lawyer in the service of the railroads and public utilities. His son enters the legislature (with the assistance of Committeeman O'Malley) believing in "the brotherhood of man, the church, the flag, the Union forever, the sacred mission of the Republican party, the intelligence of the most illiterate of the American electorate and the manifest destiny of the United States . . . [and] the permanence of the profit motive."[65] The legislature convinces him that "We'll have to improve the electorate. So long as they shamelessly create us, we'll be what we are" (81). Hale's friend is a likeable legislator from downstate Illinois. A seasoned but modest boodler, he gives the opposite view: "It sort of suits the political genius of our people. It seems to have something of the young Abe Lincoln in it . . . The genius of our people is to be agin' government and I think we make a sort of government that's easy to be against" (58). Another foil, a young Marxist named Connor, regards Hale as a naive reformer of the type periodically placated by the cynical machine politicians who really run things. Connor helps link the novel's parts when he reappears twenty-five years later, disillusioned with his experience in Russia. ("When Stalin began to build up a Tammany Hall we found we were deviationists. We were Trotskyites" [269].) His death in strike violence at John Hale's auto factory further unsettles the protagonist's world. Then, as the novel closes, National Committeeman Hale is discarded as a potential Presidential nominee because his wife has filed suit for divorce. The portrait that emerges is that of a Young Knight who enters politics with mildly idealistic motivation and whose well-intentioned career does no harm but, in the long run, little good. He is innocent of the one friend's tolerant cynicism, but he also lacks the conviction and dedication of the other. The novel's craftmanship is generally sure and sound, but it cannot obscure the two serious handicaps: the structural split and the lack of force in the portrayal of the life of the central character.

The Young Knight of Paul I. Wellman's *The Walls of Jericho* (1947) is another lawyer with an easy courtroom manner and "a tall, loose-jointed figure with a long, humorous face."[66] David Constable, passionately involved in Kansas politics in this century, suggests one of Phillips's intense heroes. So does his typically over-blown dialogue: "Today our great rich American families are living . . . in magnificence not equaled by the Emperors of Rome. And at the same time—in . . . the very places

[65] Clifford Raymond, *The Honorable John Hale: A Comedy of American Politics*, p. 15.
[66] Paul I. Wellman, *The Walls of Jericho*, p. 11.

where all the wealth is created . . . men and women live in hovels, barely
eking out an existence . . . I'm going into politics. Because this is going to
be the battleground of my generation." His local foe is a Boss glad to be
"rid of the poison of Bryanism and the Populist hysteria" (33). But the
chief enemy of Constable's Kansas wheat farmers is that monster Dragon, the corporation, " a huge, predatory and *immortal* being, out-living
men, forever growing and expanding," which may proliferate into "an
oligarchy of great holding companies, with the people no better than
serfs . . ." (121). The hero continues his fight in the courts and on the
stump until an unhappy marriage, adultery, and the machinations of
the opposition knock him out of the Senate race. (His new beloved is a
beautiful lawyer passionately devoted both to him and to political reform.) Finally the skies predictably begin to clear. Unfortunately, the
novel is so encumbered with trite situations (Constable, calling for hot
water, delivers a baby during a blizzard), sheer bad writing, and stock
characters (brutal teamster Gotch McCurdy) that the book becomes a
bad historical novel rather than the serious study its best passages suggest.

The best of these novels appeared in 1947. It was Harry Sylvester's
Moon Gaffney. Revealing is the novel's dedication to four "good Catholic radicals." Unique among all the Young Knights, the protagonist is
corrupt, although he does not know it. Undergoing the process of regeneration, he finally sets out to perform the first of the trials which will test
him. Moon Gaffney is a young lawyer showing early signs of physical
and moral softness as he goes about the work of Tammany Hall. But the
primary evil in this story of the 1930's is not in Tammany. It is in the
Roman Catholic Church. And it is not in the teachings of the Church,
but in those who, in the words of one of the young Catholic radicals
Gaffney knows, display

the immediate effects of Jansenism in our time . . . perverting her doctrines and
twisting her teachings and then patting themselves on the back. I hate their insane pride of race and of religion and their incredible fatuousness . . . What I
hate is a priesthood that lacks both charity and humility and has misled and
confused its people until they mistake black for white, hate for love and darkness for light. A priesthood that has substituted chastity for charity and frequently a chastity so warped and misinformed that its ultimate fruits compare
with those of lust.

Beyond this, these same men are guilty of more or less outspoken espousal
of Mussolini and fascism. Editing and publishing *The Catholic Worker,*
the young critics are sometimes known, one of them wryly says, "as the

A.C.A.C. or Anticlerical Athletic Club."[67] These associations cost Gaffney first his influence and then his job at Tammany Hall. But a new phase of his life begins as he is led into work in the labor movement. Here his friends try to represent Christianity in action just as much as the Communists embody militant Marxism in their attempt to subvert the dockworkers's unions with which both are concerned. One of these Catholic radicals has many more of the attributes of the Knight (he suggests Parsifal) than does the protagonist, Gaffney. Beaten by thugs as he distributes union leaflets on the dock, he is arrested by the police along with his assailants and rescuers. A friend, coming to post his bond, finds him among thieves, reading his breviary as he paces his cell. At the novel's end Gaffney signalizes his break with his former life by agreeing to defend three union members. He is told that all are Negroes, and one is a known Communist. "I knew that was coming," he murmurs, "sooner or later" (289). With this, Sylvester's careful character delineation shows how far Gaffney has moved toward not only moral regeneration, but a broadening of sympathy and human understanding as well. Earlier, going down to the dock area, Gaffney has seen a statue of Blessed Martin de Porres with a vigil light burning before it. His response had been revealing: "Christ, a nigger saint!" (66). But the next morning he helps distribute bread and soup in the bread line.

Sylvester gives many other portraits and sketches. There are Gaffney's friends—young men and women involved in problems of courtship and marriage as well as religion and politics. The members of his family embody the differences between the generations of Irish Americans. Powerful ones in Gaffney's environment critically affect his life: Assemblyman Billy Ryan, the monsignor in the Chancery office, and the shadowy head of "the Hall." This novel is unique in its mixed concern for the spiritual and the temporal. Its devotion to the doctrine of the Church appears as thoroughgoing as its abhorrence of the practice of some of the Church's servants. It is a sound and mature novel in its craftsmanship, one in which the ultimate concern is God's work and the immediate one the sorry discrepancy between theory and practice meant to advance it both

---

[67] Harry Sylvester, *Moon Gaffney*, pp. 263, 51. The novel's young priest—who breaks down from the tension of his emotional response to the plight of the poor and the reactionary attitudes of his superiors—suggests a social and political conscience like that of Father John A. Ryan, a leader of liberal Catholic thought in the two decades before the first World War. See Goldman, *Rendezvous*, pp. 110–112 and 227. One thinks also of Father Charles E. Coughlin, who, in leading his Social Justice movement in the 1930's, advocated doctrines repugnant to Gaffney's friends (see Chapter Eight).

in secular and religious affairs. Sylvester demonstrates his skill in dealing with a very large number of people—many of them of the most diverse kinds—characters whose relationships are functional rather than random, who provide enlightening contrasts and who serve to advance the action as well. Sylvester provides as much realistic detail as is found in the most realistically written of these novels without allowing it to inundate the book. Instead, there is a heightened illusion of reality. This fictional world is a very Catholic one. But though less familiar than the soap-opera portrayal of such novels as, say, Henry Morton Robinson's *The Cardinal* (1950), it is much more convincing. The kind of fervent anticlericalism of some of the characters is to be matched only in that of characters such as John Casey in James Joyce's *A Portrait of the Artist as a Young Man*. And although this revulsion at priests who are less than they should be is stronger than that directed toward their opposite numbers among the politicians, this same moral view underlies both attitudes. Another mark of Sylvester's skill is his handling of these two worlds—the political and the ecclesiastical—so that each exploration enriches the other. The reader is given insight into these worlds as Moon Gaffney concurrently comes to a degree of self-knowledge. This Young Knight is one who enters upon his Quest belatedly and without fervor, but with a kind of dedication, half-reluctant though it may be, which is not in him at the novel's beginning.

The Aging Knight of the 1950's

In three novels of the 1950's, the Knight was no longer young, although in each the present was displayed in the light of the past. In a way, these three epitomize the range of the patterns of action in this whole group of novels. Here one is corrupted, another is assassinated, and a third goes on apparently to complete his Quest successfully. Two of them are drawn from life: the victim modeled unmistakably on the figure of F. Scott Fitzgerald, and the success on that of Franklin D. Roosevelt. The Dragons which they fight are for the most part familiar —the Interests, large and small, although one sees in one novel those forces of bigotry and reaction which are standard in the novel of the Southern Demagogue.

The ill-fated comeback of former congressman Ivor Kelly in a border state southwest of the Alleghenies forms the subject of Mary Deasy's *The Boy Who Made Good* (1955). The narrative makes it clear that the characters of Ivor and Stella Kelly are indebted to Scott and Zelda Fitzgerald. The author draws upon Fitzgerald's fiction as well as his life in passages reminiscent of the major novels: "It wasn't so much that she and Ivor were in love with each other . . . as that . . . they were the prince and princess of a fairy tale—the brilliant young lawyer who was going to win all the golden prizes the world had to offer, and the beautiful girl whom everybody was going to admire and love . . ."[68] Kelly is a man who returns to the lists partly because of the fascination of place and power and partly because of the persuasion of an ambitious faction. He is a man of great charm who suggests the young idealists seen much earlier. He is made both special and vulnerable by his capacity for belief "in the possibility of a finer, more splendid life than the rest of us even dreamed of . . ." (116). By the time of his campaign for the governorship, disillusionment has taken the glow from the vision, but enough of it remains to help urge him into what is to be the last Quest of his life. As in the case of *The Honorable John Hale,* the Knight's early love is not a guide but a bad example: Stella Kelly accepts bribes. The narrator is the young daughter of the novel's villain. She chronicles both her love for Kelly and his end: death by gunshot wounds from a male relative of a woman thought wronged by the hero. (*Pace* Gatsby!) This novel's protagonist is closer to Lancelot than to Percival: he begins in dedication but gradually undergoes a change of heart and motive. Although he may not succumb to Lancelot's concupiscence, neither does he attain Percival's purity. "What he had wanted," concludes his chronicler in that familiar style, "was the bright, insubstantial thing, the glory, which is never quite good enough when you grasp it, but is all we have to dream our finest dreams" (214).

Stephen and Ethel Longstreet preface *The Politician* (1959) with a note on the genesis of their protagonist: "The central figure in our story is The Country Gentleman In Politics . . . Paul Hawley Barraclough is frankly cast in the mold of some of the gentry in our history books: George Washington, Thomas Jefferson, all those people named Adams, Woodrow Wilson, the two Roosevelts, and even such figures as Charles Evans Hughes and Adlai Stevenson who never went all the way." In spite of this claim, Barraclough bears one principal imprint: he suffers an injury which produces partial paralysis and a limp, and he habitually uses a cigarette holder. His appeal combines the authority of breeding and wealth with a genuine sympathy and understanding for the great

---

[68] Mary Deasy, *The Boy Who Made Good,* p. 113. Miss Deasy resides in her native Cincinnati. Some readers may wish to see this novel and *O'Shaughnessy's Day,* which is treated in Chapter Two, against that background .

mass of the people. If this does not make identification easy enough, the reader is shown that Barraclough is also adept at using the skills of people like the narrator, a boyhood friend from the other side of the tracks who rises to the position of chairman of the Democratic National Committee. The chairman's account of his friend's life seems to show that when a man has the proper attributes, he can overcome numerous handicaps—patrician birth, physical disability, the opportunists in his own party, and the power of the opposition. As the reader follows these novels into the modern period, those with happy endings like this are usually marked also by the liabilities of *The Politician.*

The Knight in George Garrett's *The Finished Man* (1959) is not young and he is not scrupulous, although his corruption comes about through motives he feels to be honorable. Florida Senator Allen Parker reneges on a promise to run against the protégé now in league with "His old enemies, the major national corporations, the railroads, the power company, the big citrus growers, once the enemies of the people as well . . ."[69] Like others before him, Parker finds, in the crisis of his political life, that he will do anything to win. He repudiates a legitimate photograph of himself with a NAACP Negro leader and poses for another with a Ku Klux Klan leader on the grounds of necessity. Reproached by a young aide who says he is throwing away thirty years of integrity, Parker replies, "I am *not* throwing anything away. You have to get yourself elected. *You have to get elected.* That's all there is to it" (232). Others in this novel have knightly attributes. They include Parker's aide, Mike Royle, and also Royle's father, whose early heroism is described by another son as being that of "a narrow-minded petty demagogue with a wild desire to be a martyr" (92). Later the son adds that, "He likes to see himself as Saint George out hunting for the Dragon. But the truth is . . . *he's* the only dragon he'll ever know. It's the basic premise of our bloodline—incurable, congenital romanticism. We commit horrible crimes in the name of it" (139–140). In this convincing novel all the politicians lose, even Parker's protégé who wins. Garrett's point of view is indicated by a quotation from Swift which he places at the beginning of the book: "He usually continues in office until a worse can be found; but the very moment he is discarded, his successor, at the head of all the Yahoos in the district, young and old, male and female, come in a body, and discharge their excrements upon him from head to foot." In the end the reader sees that perhaps the motives themselves were impure,

[69] George Garrett, *The Finished Man*, p. 53.

that the pleasure of place and power, so persuasive to Jerome B. Garwood fifty years earlier in *The 13th District,* had finally brought about what Parker's thirty years of politics previously had not: the corruption of the Knight as he finally adopts the scruples and methods of those against whom he has dedicated his strength.

The Young Knight in Perspective

One of the most positive things that can be said about these novels is that the technical competence of the more recent ones is vastly higher than that in those published between the turn of the century and the 1930's. *Moon Gaffney* and *The Finished Man* constitute good examples of the modern realistic American novel, convincing in action, character portrayal, and dialogue. They possess, moreover, a reflective quality which gives the added dimension found in serious fiction. These two novels are technically as far ahead of the awkward and intense imitations of Freud, Lewis, and Dreiser of the 1920's and 1930's as these themselves were of the erratic romances still encumbered by outworn conventions of the nineteenth century.

Content was another thing. Although the motivation of these Young Knights remained for the most part constant, the effect of their lives and work seemed to change. Almost all of them enter politics on grounds as much emotional as intellectual. Most of them see the world as characterized by social, economic, and political injustice; and they determine to change it, directly attacking evil to create a situation in which a remedy is possible. One thing is immediately perceptible: whereas all the Knights but one are victorious up to the mid-1920's more than half of those who follow are defeated or corrupted. This change may be owing to the ascendancy of the realistic novel, if only because it is more likely to treat a somber theme. It might also be explained on other grounds. In spite of progress in antitrust legislation and law enforcement, the Interests, political machines, and corrupt elements in national life seem to have become progressively stronger. Correspondingly, the protagonists have become much more vulnerable. They also become generally much more conventional in their political sentiments. Although some, such as Paul Hawley Barraclough, advocate sweeping social legislation, most follow the two major parties rather than the radical ones. David Constable advocates practices associated with socialism, but his story is set before the first World War. One must go back to *The Lion's Den* in 1930 to find a protagonist who calls himself a Progressive and to *The Citadel* in 1912 to find one who calls himself a Socialist. Conversely, Ivor Kelly is the picked candidate of the state organization, Moon Gaffney is an underling of the Tammany Hall machine, and Allen Parker embraces the Ku Klux Klan in his campaign for re-election. It is also possible that the rather conventional political sentiments of many of the later protagonists reflect the failure of the whole radical movement in this country. With the weakening of the Socialist Party before the beginning of the Wilson era, the decline of the Communist Party starting in the late 1930's, and the short life of the Wallace-Progressive Party in the late 1940's, radicalism was left to the movements of cranks and fanatics. Courses of action out of the Republican and Democratic mainstream were to be found, if at all, in the more extreme courses offered by men such as Strom Thurmond and Joseph McCarthy.[70] If, as is often argued, this country has entered an era in which pressures toward social conformity have become greater, this factor may also be reflected in the conventional sentiments of some of these protagonists. If the contemporary American environment is one in which the organization man is relatively sure of certain rewards (like the "Muldoon" of organization politics discussed in the following two chapters), one is that much more likely to encounter him rather than the maverick.

One general conclusion is clear: as the years of the century wear on, the shining-eyed young idealist is less often encountered, the radical vanishes, and the Lincoln-image appears less frequently. Gradually the Knight becomes less successful and more vulnerable, as the Dragon becomes progressively stronger and more formidable.

[70] See Daniel Aaron, *Writers on the Left: Episodes in American Literary Communism*, and Rideout, *Radical Novel*, on the failure of the Left, *passim*, and Daniel Bell (ed.), *The New American Right, passim*.

2. the boss

In this sacred grove there grew a certain tree round which at any time of the day, and probably far into the night, a grim figure might be seen to prowl. In his hand he carried a drawn sword, and he kept peering warily about him as if at every instant he expected to be set upon by an enemy. He was a priest and a murderer; and the man for whom he looked was sooner or later to murder him and hold the priesthood in his stead. Such was the rule of the sanctuary. A candidate for the priesthood could only succeed to office by slaying the priest, and having slain him, he retained the office till he was himself slain by a stronger or a craftier.

The post which he held by this precarious tenure carried with it the title of king; but surely no crowned head ever lay uneasier, or was visited by more evil dreams, than his. For year in, year out, in summer and winter, in fair weather and in foul, he had to keep his lonely watch, and whenever he snatched a troubled slumber it was at the peril of his life. The least relaxation of his vigilance, the smallest abatement of his strength of limb or skill of fence, put him in jeopardy; grey hairs might seal his death-warrant.

James G. Frazer,
The Golden Bough[1]

[1] Sir James George Frazer, *The Golden Bough: A Study in Magic and Religion*, p. 1. Theodore H. Gaster writes, "Frazer's interpretation of the priesthood at Aricia and of the rites which governed succession to it has been almost unanimously rejected by classical scholars. The sanctuary at that place was probably no more than an asylum for runaway slaves; and the golden bough, far from being a vessel of divine power identical with that carried by Aeneas on his journey to the nether world, was in all likelihood simply the branch characteristically borne in antiquity by suppliants at a shrine" (*The New Golden Bough: A New Abridgment of the Classic Work*, p. xvi). This is an interesting instance in which anthro-

The occupational hazards of being King of the Wood at Nemi were considerably greater than those of the average political Boss, just as the rites of Diana Nemorensis were of a vastly different kidney from the votive acts performed to the gods of political destinies. Moreover, the priest at Nemi, though lethal, was in theory good. This is rarely true in the stereotype of the Boss, and though his path may be lined with mines and deadfalls, it need not lead to a violent end. He may even die in bed heavy with riches and honors, later to be interred with gorgeous obsequies. But there are enough similarities to relate the Boss firmly to his archetypal predecessor. The position is one of nearly absolute power in a limited area. The position can be seized only with strength and craft. It can be held secure only through constant vigilance. It can bestow on a man some of the attributes of a lesser god, but his fall can be as swift as ever was a turn of the Renaissance Wheel of Fortune.

The political Boss's title is literal and not ceremonial. Assuming the responsibility for the organization's fortunes and enjoying a major share of its profits, he autocratically makes choices and gives orders. There is no give-and-take of democratic discussion. The Boss may consult an informal "kitchen cabinet," but ultimately he makes the decisions, though a dummy may issue them. A Boss can exist in a hamlet as well as a metropolis. But political and economic conditions have made the Boss a species that flowers in the big city. There oppressive conditions produced profitable discontent. There the underprivileged and ill-informed were ready for molding into a cohesive force; and there the enormous spoils made the game eminently worth the candle. Other factors—an industrial plant, capital, influx of immigrants—marked the areas where the Bosses most noticeably flourished: the great cities of New England and the Middle Atlantic states, the Midwest, and the Pacific Coast. Harold Zink notes that major Southern cities have harbored distinguished rulers, but "On the whole southern overlords seem to be less cosmopolitan in interests and in fame than their compeers elsewhere in the United States. With the exception of Martin Behrman of New Orleans none of them seem to rank alongside of the Tammany Hall bosses, the Chicago barons . . ."[2] Only two years before Mr. Zink's book was published Huey P. Long won his first gubernatorial election in Louisiana. Two years after

---

pology has recapitulated myth. Frazer's description of a human behavior pattern having wide relevance remains symbolically true though no longer accepted as literally true.

[2] Harold Zink, *City Bosses in the United States: A Study of Twenty Municipal Bosses*, p. 317.

its appearance Edward H. Crump secured the control over Memphis, Shelby County, and much of Tennessee that was to remain firm until Senator Estes Kefauver's victory of 1948 signalled the decline of his political fortunes. But these patterns were only then taking shape, whereas there was a long history of spectacular Boss rule in the cities Zink cited as his cardinal examples.

Attempting to answer the question whether or not there was a "typical boss," Zink rejected the "classic description of the derby-hatted, sport-suited, flashy-jewelried, plug-ugly boss, with coarse, brutal features, protruding paunch, and well-chewed stogy, who has no morals and is socially impossible . . ."[3] But he did compile a long catalogue of traits among twenty city Bosses. In part it recalled the Scout Oath, for these autocrats were generous, loyal, and brave. Persistent and practical, they also placed "reasonable emphasis on high standards of personal morals, and interest in religion." Mostly urban children of impoverished foreign-born parents, they were often breadwinners in childhood "because of the premature death of a father or because of his general shiftlessness." With little formal education they usually

entered politics as soon as they reached legal age, and became active in ward or district politics . . . Having reached the top few held a high titular office in the organization. With one exception all held at least one public office and a majority have long records of office-holding attached to their names. Most of them were periodically bothered with reform movements of various kinds. However, these movements had little to do with their overthrow if they [lost] control . . .

Most were sturdy fighters who knew how to take care of themselves. "A more than normal proportion amassed sizable although not huge fortunes, closely and frequently openly allied themselves with powerful corporate interests, and proved themselves strong executives in business as well as in politics." They were usually good family men who stayed out of jail, and a number never moved away from the old neighborhood.[4]

Certain other characteristics are not included in Zink's list of careful generalizations. Half of the twenty Bosses had Irish blood in their veins. Half were Roman Catholics. More than a few dominated notorious gangs as boys and several were celebrated fist fighters. Three had been saloonkeepers. Eleven amassed more than a million dollars; two served time in prison, and more were tried—and sometimes convicted—without, however, being incarcerated. A few acquired moderately good educa-

[3] Zink, *City Bosses*, p. 65.
[4] *Ibid.*, pp. 63–64.

tions, but most preferred action to contemplation. There was little time in their lives for books other than those of the accountant or registrar.

Although bossism in New York City immediately suggests Tammany Hall, some of the city's more celebrated Bosses constructed their power on solid machines in their home bailiwicks. "Big Tim" Sullivan, for example, cooperated with Tammany Hall, but his primary concern was the Bowery, a preserve he ruled with others of the Sullivan tribe from the late 1880's until about 1909. After many years of wealth and power, he still declined to move away from the old Five Points district of the East Side, now even less attractive than it had been in his boyhood.[5]

All the Tammany Bosses who followed after William Marcy Tweed have been dwarfed. He was a gourmand who ballooned to over three hundred pounds, and his depredations in the years between 1852 and 1871 were enormous. Then came the downfall that was to end with his ignominious death in prison. "Honest John" Kelley, as religious as Tweed was predatory, seized control when Tweed began to falter and maintained it until 1884. A devout communicant of the Roman Catholic Church, he was also a strong politician. If he could not wholly put Tammany back in good odor, he restored it to its place of power in New York politics. His chosen successor, Richard Croker, was rapacious like Tweed and firmer than Kelley. Cannier than Tweed, he was less cautious than Kelley.[6] He could also be defiantly matter of fact. Testifying before the Mazet Committee, he was asked, "Then you are working for your own pocket, are you not?" "All the time," Croker answered, "the same as you."[7] His place was usurped by "Commissioner" Charles F. Murphy

[5] Zink, *City Bosses*, pp. 85–95.

[6] Lincoln Steffens always went straight to the Bosses when gathering material for the exposés published as *The Shame of the Cities*. Such formidable ones as Martin Lomasney of Boston and George Cox of Cincinnati helped him. Steffens not only heaped praise on such good Bosses as Tom Johnson and Robert LaFollette, he also had surprising things to say about such a *bête noire* of the reformers as Croker himself. At one point in one of their conversations, wrote Steffens, "The sweet smile came back into his kind old face . . ." He was "hard as nails" when he talked about running the city, but when they parted, "he turned warm and sweet again, held out his soft, small, white hand, and bade me good-by" (*The Autobiography of Lincoln Steffens*, I, 235 and 238).

[7] New York State Legislature, *Report and Proceedings of the Senate Committee to Investigate the Police Department of the City of New York*, I, 353 (cited in Zink, *City Bosses*, p. 137). In a curious coincidence, history repeated itself. Alvin E. Geisy, former Internal Revenue Bureau agent-turned public accountant for underworld figures, was asked by Counsel Rudolph Halley of the Kefauver Committee why he engaged in such activities. "For the almighty dollar!" the witness heatedly replied. "The same as you are doing right now—" (Estes Kefauver, *Crime in America*, ed. Sidney Shallett, p. 204).

when Croker left for an English vacation in 1901. Thereafter his life was distinguished by his long-distance blasts at Murphy and his marriage to a Cherokee Indian princess in 1914 before his death at his castle, Glencairn, on his Dublin estate in 1922. Commissioner Murphy held the reins for twenty-three years, strengthening Tammany's position and backing Hall man Al Smith as a Presidential candidate. For five years after Murphy's death Judge George W. Olvany was head. A year after he resigned, scandals and investigations sent the Hall's fortunes plunging downward and precipitated the resignation of Mayor James J. Walker. It was the glib mayor who, standing at the side of Murphy's grave, ten years after his death in 1924, said mournfully, "There lies all that is left of the brains of Tammany Hall."[8]

Charles W. Van Devander records the further fortunes of the Hall up to 1944, when Boss Edward J. Flynn ruled the Bronx and James J. Hines controlled Harlem—before conviction on gambling charges sent him to prison. It is a chronicle of decline from the powerful Murphy and the respectable Olvany to men like Frank Costello, the notorious racketeer who became a power in Tammany councils before his own imprisonment. Further misfortunes came with the inroads made in 1961 and 1962 by Democratic reform groups. Seizing control, they crowned the humiliation by defeating leader Carmine De Sapio in his home district.[9]

Although Tammany politics epitomize many aspects of Boss rule, numerous other examples are documented by Zink, Van Devander, and others. "Czar" Martin Lomasney dominated Boston Democratic politics from 1892 to 1915, and when he began to slip, the colorful James Michael Curley was there to assume his mantle and wear it off and on for more than forty years. Republican power did not go unorganized. During much of the same period, Joseph W. Martin and Leverett Saltonstall worked to construct a Massachusetts machine with a winning percentage close to Lomasney's and Curley's. Martin and Saltonstall did not wear the same aura of bossism it is true. But none would argue the authority of New York State Republican Thomas C. Platt, whose successes were curbed only by death in 1910. Philadelphia aristocrat Boies Penrose became Republican state leader in Pennsylvania in 1904 and retained much of his power until shortly before his death in 1921. (He had been preceded by Philadelphia Bosses "King James" McManes, Judge Israel Durham, and the "Dukes of Philadelphia," the three Vare brothers—forming a continuum beginning with McManes's rise to

---

[8] Charles W. Van Devander, *The Big Bosses*, p. 12.
[9] See Van Devander, *Big Bosses*, pp. 11–62.

power in 1858 and ending with the death of Edwin H. Vare in 1922.
After Penrose came Andrew Mellon, Joseph Grundy and Joseph Pew.)
More illustrious Pennsylvania Republicans were Christopher Lyman
Magee and William Flinn, who had together run Pittsburgh politics
from 1879 to 1902. Magee, a brilliant and magnetic politician, was a
paragon of honesty among Bosses. Like Magee, Flinn was listed in the
Social Register. Worth more than eleven million dollars at his death,
he was possessed of such acumen, writes Zink, that "No other political
leader considered in this work approached 'Senator' Flinn as a financial
genius."[10]

    With the Depression, the number of old-style Bosses began to de-
crease. But some who survived built machines with a ruthless thoroughness to match Croker's and a rapacity to equal Tweed's. From 1919
onwards Democrat Frank Hague's power in Jersey City expanded until
it covered most of populous Hudson County, extending into the rest of
New Jersey and even beyond. His "I am the law" was like *"l'état, c'est
moi."* And although Democratic and Republican governors worked to
curb his power, he ran his machine—often by telephone from Florida—
until the defeat in 1949 of the heir-apparent nephew he had installed at
his retirement in 1947. Thomas J. Pendergast's control of Kansas City,
Missouri, was as tight as Hague's, and his influence in his state was more
pervasive. But he had less staying power. His Democratic machine was
all-powerful from 1932 to 1938, but in 1939 Pendergast was sent to
Leavenworth. He had neglected to report income accruing from bribery.
To the north, Chicago's Democratic Kelly-Nash machine had emerged
in 1932 after the assassination of Mayor Anton Cermak. When Patrick
Nash died in 1943, sixty-eight-year-old Mayor Edward J. Kelly carried
on until his retirement at his term's end in 1947. *Time's* obituary assessed
Kelly as the "shrewdest of the four Democratic City bosses (Kelly, Pendergast, Hague, and Crump) of the last generation." Like his coevals
a rough and tumble battler in his youth, he never suffered from excessive
savoir-faire. Sometimes the terms of the trade came out unexpectedly, as
when he turned to an honored guest, Admiral William Halsey, and
ceremoniously addressed him as "Alderman Halsey."[11] The regime did
not have the flamboyance of the Republican organization of the Prohibition era, when "Al Capone and Samuel Insull were the real political
bosses of the city and of Illinois." It was, however, generally acknowl-

10 Zink, *City Bosses*, p. 251.
11 *Time*, LVI (October 30, 1950), 89.

edged to be the strongest political machine in the history of Chicago.[12] Big city machines and Bosses obviously still existed, but the species seemed to have produced its most gorgeous blooms.

Earlier Bosses were sometimes more colorful than such later colossi as Hague, Pendergast, and Kelly. Now, with public images formed by public relations men as well as organizational tactics, some names may almost evoke nostalgia. "Curly Boss" Ruef increased his fortune as he controlled the San Francisco Republican organization from 1900 to 1907 until conviction for bribery put him in San Quentin. "The Genial Doctor" Albert A. Ames, a power in Minneapolis Republican politics from 1876 to 1902, was convicted of bribery but never jailed. "The Mystery Man of Chicago," Frederick Lundin, prospered both as manufacturer of "Juniper Ade" and as Republican power in Chicago between 1896 and 1922. Mentor of blustering Mayor "Big Bill" Thompson, "Poor Swede" Lundin saw his fortunes fail, and it took the skills of Clarence Darrow to spare him an end like Tweed's.

If the reader reacts with disbelief to characters such as Mattress Mulroony, in Edwin O'Connor's *The Last Hurrah* (1956), he would do well to remember the names, if not the deeds, of such rare birds as these on the tree of democracy.

The Boss in Fiction

As Mayor Francis Skeffington contemplates the advantages of his position in *The Last Hurrah* (1956), author O'Connor tells the reader, "He did not often think of politics in chivalric terms."[13] This is the prime difference between the figure of the Boss and that of the Young Knight; chivalry—anachronistic, imperfect, or even hypocritical though it may be—has a basis in morality, whereas bossism is always rooted in expediency. When one of these novels goes beyond mere dramatic action, it develops the problem of moral awareness. But in only two of the seventeen novels in this chapter does moral awareness lead to a rejection of expediency. The motivation of two more of these protagonists is conjectural. A few others want to be better than they are, but most of them do evil by necessity and choice. For several, cynical relativists that they are, a word such as "evil" has little meaning.

The archetypal figure of the Boss in these novels is about as well-defined as that of the Young Knight. Like him the Boss has humble ori-

---

[12] Van Devander, *Big Bosses*, pp. 260–261.
[13] Edwin O'Connor, *The Last Hurrah*, p. 52.

gins. Often orphaned, he may be the sole support of his widowed mother. He soon demonstrates his abilities to get on in a hostile or Darwinian world. He too has recognizable physical characteristics. He has strength, quick reflexes, and pugnacity. Sometimes he begins as a young tough who makes himself useful to an organization with strong-arm tactics: harassing the enemy, protecting interests, or even perpetrating fraud and violence at the polls. He thus gains the attention of the reigning Boss—usually the Boss of the ward—and becomes his protégé. Sometimes the succession to power is accomplished filially; in other instances the law of the survival of the fittest again operates, and the protagonist defeats the old Boss to gain his place. He can anticipate his own similar end when age makes him vulnerable in his turn.

The Boss has intelligence to match his physical prowess and predatory skills. With craft and cunning he can lay plans of depth and complexity beyond the ordinary politician. He is almost always a realist, a good judge of events and men, one who can sometimes control the first and usually command the respect and fear of the second. In spite of this, the Boss is frequently a solitary. At the ward level, where most of these novels begin, he has his "kitchen cabinet," but in the ascent beyond that level he usually goes alone. While his mentor lives, the Boss still has a confidante, and in a few instances there is a trusted subordinate, wife, or daughter. But more often than not the Boss is, in victory as well as in defeat, alone. The embodiment of Woman as Guide may finally bring about reformation, but as long as he wields the power, he must make his decisions on his own. More than half of these men keep mistresses, and their wives are much more apt to be shrews than doves.

The Boss's power base may be in part a racial one. Most of these Bosses are Irish, and the bloc of votes which they can deliver comes from immigrants and their descendants. For them they find work and housing, adjudicate disputes, and bestow rewards, demanding in return the unquestioning loyalty required by a tribal leader. A good many of the Bosses are saloon owners, men whose affluence begins with the dispensing of spirits and culminates in the dispensing of patronage.[14] The racial

---

[14] It is difficult today to appreciate the intense disapproval which large numbers of Americans felt sixty years ago for "the liquor traffic" or to appreciate the extent to which saloons and politics often were connected. Hofstadter writes, "Drinking was preeminently a vice of those classes—the plutocrats and corrupt politicians and ignorant immigrants—which the reformers most detested or feared. The saloon, as an institution pivotal in the life of vice on one side and of American urban politics on the other, fell under particular reprobation" (pp. 288–289). See also Link, *American Epoch*, pp. 36–37. Lincoln Steffens noted that "it was in St. Louis

phenomenon is cyclical: the Irish, who displace the Yankees, are themselves in turn displaced by the Italians. Eastern Europeans displace Northern Europeans, and then in the novels of this decade, the new wave comes from this hemisphere, from Puerto Rico.

In the Boss's philosophy, the whole society gives evidence of the rightness of expediency as a basis of conduct. To him, the silk-stockings from uptown do the same things he does on a larger scale. They do them more ruthlessly, yet with more concealment whenever possible. Wall Street is often charged with immorality and rapacity exceeding that of the Boss. Though he may graft, he gives some kind of value for value received. The Interests appear many times in each novel, either controlling the Boss's organization or purchasing its services.[15] And their purposes are no more elevated than those of the stock manipulator, the dishonest public official, or the vassal who stuffs ballot boxes. The Boss is aware of the depredations of real Robber Barons, and their example only serves to spur him on. If he needs any further salve for his conscience, he need only look at a judiciary used for paying off political debts, at a legislature obviously a market place, and a press at best largely ineffectual and at worst for sale to the highest bidder. Money makes the mare go, and the money comes in chiefly through patronage and graft. It may even come from vice collections. But that is simply the way things are. The Boss operates accordingly. Only the despised reformer attempts to change these immutable laws, fleetingly supported by a selfish and fickle public.

These novels often provide a primer of practical politics. The reader notes the gold teeth and the vests edged with white piping once the caste marks of the Boss. He is early made aware of the conviction that being a Boss is vastly more profitable and secure than being an officeholder—it is also, somehow, *decenter.* He learns strategy and tactics: making a deal with the opposition, running a candidate who will split the vote, circumventing the secret ballot, using repeaters at the polls. He learns the value of being "regular," a dependable organization man. (Too much docile, uninspired loyalty, however, becomes the mark of that expendable human automaton, the Muldoon.) He observes the techniques for forming associations, conducting outings, and holding funerals. He learns

---

that a practical joker nearly emptied the House of Delegates by tipping a boy to rush into a session and call out, 'Mister, your saloon is on fire . . .' " (*Shame of the Cities,* p. 34).

[15] David Graham Phillips was never quite sure which were in control: the Bosses or the Interests. His view would vary from novel to novel and would change even within novels.

how an undesirable can be exiled to Congress; he also sees how useful an acute man can be in a legislative body, particularly when the Boss is forming corporations likely to bid for public contracts.

The image of Lincoln appears again in these novels almost as often—though not so influentially—as in the novel of the Young Knight. But it suggests a melancholy shade, rather than a pervasive figure embodying an ideal. Other images first appear here which will become very familiar in the novel of corruption, and they are images which strongly and symptomatically suggest two real men: James J. Walker of New York, and Warren G. Harding of Ohio.

The Boss—Old Style

A forerunner of modern novels of the Boss had appeared as early as 1881. It was Rufus E. Shapley's *Solid for Mulhooly: A Political Satire.* It was more notable for its pictures than its text, for the illustrations of an immigrant Irishman's political career were done by Thomas Nast, whose cartoons had aroused the public indignation that had helped put Boss Tweed behind bars. In the preface to the 1889 edition Shapley explained that the broad satire had been part of the spreading struggle against Boss rule, focusing particularly on the problems posed by the vote of the "newly-naturalized foreigner, possibly unable to read or speak our language, and without a dollar of taxable property in the world," and the parallel problem of "securing the purity of the ballot box . . ."[16] Shapley called his book a "sketch" of Boss rule, and it was, in its broadness, just that rather than a novel. But in the abuses portrayed it anticipated fuller works to come.

One of the first of these novels was Winston Churchill's *Coniston,* which was published in 1906 but spanned a period from the early 1830's to the late 1870's. In Jethro Bass, Churchill presented a forerunner of the modern Boss. His career extends from village to capital as he becomes behind-the-scenes Boss of the state. His power base is the vote of the farmers whose mortgages he holds, and his allies are other "feudal chiefs from the North Country" whom he leads against the railroad and timber interests. He is a canny country politician who predictably bests citified Isaac D. Worthington. Worthington's plan to set up a combine, declares one observer, "will grind the people and debase them and clog

[16] Rufus E. Shapley, *Solid for Mulhooly: A Political Satire,* p. 9.

their progress a hundred more times than Jethro Bass has done."[17] Churchill then explains, "Jethro would never have been capable of being master of the state had he not foreseen that the time would come when the railroads and other aggregations of capital *would* exterminate the boss, or at least subserviate him. And Jethro Bass made up his mind that the victory should not come in his day" (248–249). The novel is interesting in Bass's methods of manipulating control and campaigning against the enemy. It is impossibly handicapped, however, by the romantic clichés of situation, speech, and character from which Churchill was never able to free himself. But in Jethro Bass and his organization he presented a kind of preview of the modern Boss. The milieu and antagonists would change but the nature and function would be fundamentally the same.

J. Devlin, Boss: A Romance of American Politics had appeared, like *Coniston,* in the twentieth century. But though it was published in 1901, the action spanned a period from about 1855 to 1880, with the Boss making some of his boldest moves during Ulysses S. Grant's bid for renomination in 1876. The Irish Boss whom Francis Churchill Williams described fought his way up in the familiar rough-and-tumble way. Like his fellows, he was not above bribery and ballot-box stuffing. Unlike most of them, he had a heart as big as his bank balance, and his greatest pride was that his word was his bond. Williams made it clear that he wanted to humanize his subject. "To the world he was a Boss," he wrote in a foreword. "To a few he was a Man."[18] In spite of its paper flowers and glycerine tears, the novel had some appeal. It was clearest when Williams showed Jimmy directing campaigns from his stronghold in the Water Trust, observing the march of his organization of "Black Umbrellas," or plunging into a boisterous, old-fashioned torchlight parade that might at any moment turn into a Donnybrook.[19]

The first full-length portrait of the twentieth-century political Boss came in 1903 with Alfred Henry Lewis's *The Boss: And How He Came to Rule New York.* Today a forgotten period piece, it is unique in Lewis's anticipation of many characteristics and concerns of the political novels which were to follow. He had come to his work well prepared. Not only

[17] Winston Churchill, *Coniston,* p. 356.

[18] Francis Churchill Williams, *J. Devlin—Boss: A Romance of American Politics,* p. 7.

[19] For the analagous use of the Gas Trust as the lever of municipal control in Philadelphia, see Zink, *City Bosses,* pp. 194–195. See also Steffens, *Shame of the Cities,* pp. 193–229.

had he published a biography of Richard Croker in 1901, he was also "a crony of the West Side bosses."[20] The Boss's qualities, his methods, and his aura of corruption—all these are enunciated. The novel deserves a more than passing glance in spite of its literary deficiencies.

This archetypal Boss is appropriately nameless. Through a ghost writer he tells the story of his life from the emigration of his parents from Ireland when he was seven to his retirement half a century later. His strength and agility gain him the notice of saloon-owning ward-leader John Kennedy. (Like most Irish politicians in these novels, he speaks in the accents of Mr. Dooley.) His rise is rapid in a power struggle marked by the use of organized gangs, riots, and murder.[21] Betrayals are frequent and skulduggery of all kinds, especially election frauds large and small, are commonplace.[22] The economics of vote fraud are also examined. The services of ten thousand repeaters from Philadelphia cost $500,000, but each man votes four times: "A man votes with a full beard; then he votes with his chin shaved; then he shaves the sides of his face and votes with a mustache; lastly he votes with a smooth face and retires to re-grow a beard against the next campaign."[23]

Kennedy and the Boss gain control of Tammany Hall and proceed to become rich through manipulation of city franchises and financial speculation. They regard Wall Street manipulators as much worse than themselves and the mass of the people as a generally docile herd bound to be victimized and fair game for anyone clever enough to take advantage of it. Old Mike, Kennedy's father, characterizes them: "Never interfere with people's beer; give 'em clean streets; double the number

[20] Roy V. Peel, in his Introduction to George Washington Plunkitt, in *Plunkitt of Tammany Hall*, p. xli.

[21] Arriving in the United States at the age of seven, he grows into adolescence small but quick and strong, becoming leader of a notorious gang called "the Tin Whistles." Compare Tammany Boss Croker (1893–1922), brought here from Ireland at the age of three, later "undersized" but "well developed and wiry," becoming leader of the Fourth Avenue tunnel gang (Zink, *City Bosses*, pp. 128–129).

[22] The simple stuffing of ballot boxes appears crude beside the technique evolved by the Boss and an aristocratic ally to circumvent the Australian ballot system. Under it, votes were cast in the privacy of the voting booth while all but officials were kept two hundred feet away. The solution was to secure one bona fide ballot or a passable imitation marked in advance for the desired candidate. The first voter would conceal this marked ballot. He would receive a fresh ballot at the polling place, deposit the marked ballot, and return with the fresh one to the men buying his vote. When he presented the fresh ballot he would be paid. The fresh ballot would thereupon be marked and given to the next "tin soldier" who would repeat the process.

[23] Alfred Henry Lewis, *The Boss: And How He Came to Rule New York*, p. 215.

of lampposts . . . an' have bands playin' in every pa-r-rk. Then kape th' street free of ba-ad people . . . th' public don't object to dirt, but it wants it kept in the back alleys. Jawn, if you'll follow what I tell you, you can do what else ye plaze" (155).

Power is finally transferred from Kennedy to the Boss. He assumes control of Tammany's finances ("money is the mainspring of practical politics" [224]) and the thirty thousand jobs patronage puts at his disposal. Much of the machine's revenue comes from protection rackets battening upon vice, and the Hall is not above making use of people such as Sing Sing Jacob and Sheeny Joe. The Boss capably manages this machinery, survives reform waves and investigations, and finally retires on his own terms. But there has been retribution. He has set up his parents in style only to see them die of idleness; he has been acquitted of a false murder charge through suborning the jury, but the strain sends his wife, "Apple-Cheek," into a fatal decline. Their newly born daughter, Blossom, bears the stigmata of rope burns around her neck. By the end of the novel she has retreated into neurosis, leaving him alone.

The judgment rendered upon the Boss is, of course, foregone, but it is in a sense not completely valid, for he appears wholly amoral. One of his oldest acquaintances—he has no friends—repeats the Dreiserian reaction of "a scientist" to the Boss:

There was a look in his eye such as might burn in the eye of an old wolf that has crept away in solitude to die . . . I felt that I was in the presence of the oldest thing in the world—a thing more ancient than the Sphinx or aged pyramids. This once Boss, silent and passive and white and old, and waiting for the digging of his grave, is what breeders call a 'throwback' . . . In what should arm him for a war of life against life, he is a creature of utter cunning, utter courage, utter strength. He is a troglodyte; he is that original one who lived with the cave bear, the mastodon, the saber-toothed tiger, and the Irish elk. (409)[24]

He is not wholly without consolation in his old age, however, for he does his waiting upon an amassed fortune of forty million dollars.

If there is any artistic merit here it resides in the illusion of life that Lewis creates with his pell-mell accumulation of action and incident. But the novel is deficient in almost every other way. For all of Lewis's heaping-up of detail, the Boss never comes to life as a wholly-realized

[24] Lincoln Steffens visited Senator Matthew V. Quay of Pennsylvania in the latter's last days. "I hate to be dying here on a bed like this," said the Boss to the Muckraker. "What I would like would be to crawl off on a rock in the sun and die like a wolf" (Steffens, *Autobiography*, I, 420).

fictional creation. The Boss's aristocratic uptown ally is no more real than the comic-strip Irishman labeled Old Mike. Lewis's dialogue is often an absurd mélange of the mannered and subliterate. His capacity for fantastic incidents seems limitless: a police captain depicts the future prospects of a wastrel son so horribly that his mother (Blossom's mother-in-law) has two quick hemorrhages and dies on the spot. For all the novel's crudity, however, it stands to many that follow as does the cave-wall sketch of the buffalo to the sophisticated drawings which come later but do not alter the basic line.

The first instance in this century of a cooperative relationship between the Boss and the Interests appeared in 1905 with David Graham Phillips's *The Plum Tree*.[25] It was a novel which clearly reflected muckraking and trust-busting concerns. Harvey Sayler's introduction to Midwestern politics includes floaters at election time, "the crude beginnings of the money machine in politics . . . the beginnings of the overthrow of the people as the political power."[26] To support his widowed mother he works for a saloonkeeper and Boss who is a "middleman between our two great political factors, those who buy and break laws and those who aid and abet the lawlessness by selling themselves as voters or as office-holders" (19–20). Phillips's close-up of the sources of power comes when his protagonist persuades the Power Trust to let him form for them a combine of a dozen of the state's big corporations. It is no surprise when Sayler confides, "*I* was the combine,—was master of this political blind pool. I had taken the first, the hardest step, toward the realization of my dream of real political power,—to become an unbossed boss, not the agent and servant of Plutocracy or Partizanship . . ."[27]

The source of his eventual state and national power is the same as that of the Boss: "I controlled the sources of the money that maintained the political machinery of both parties. The hand that holds the purse strings is the hand that rules . . ." (126–127). He finds the national scene simply a larger version of that in his own state. Unlike most other Bosses, he becomes a United States senator but he is still a Boss. He makes a President and breaks a rebellious magnate. He has long since violated

[25] For an example of colloquial usage of the phrase which supplies Phillips's title, see Steffens, *Shame of the Cities*, p. 214.

[26] David Graham Phillips, *The Plum Tree*, p. 14.

[27] Phillips, *Plum Tree*, p. 77. Historical analogues of the Boss as broker are not hard to find. Steffens wrote of Colonel Edward R. Butler, boss of St. Louis, "He was the chief boodle broker and the legislature's best client; his political influence began to depend upon his boodling instead of the reverse" (*Shame of the Cities*, p. 117).

his pledge to his mother not to defile himself, but he virtuously reflects, as he blocks the President's renomination, that the other "had lost his sense of right and wrong . . ." (277–278). Besides all this, his retirement from politics will help gain him the love of a virtuous woman.

Sayler experiences neither the damnation of Lewis's Boss nor the exaltation felt by some of the Young Knights. His mixed rewards perhaps reflect the fact that, Boss though he is, he opposes the predatory corporations and almost perversely desires a return to a vague kind of primitive American Republicanism with overtones of some aspects of Progressivism.[28] The novel's greatest usefulness in demonstrating the fictional image of the American political experience is not primarily in Sayler as Knight-*manqué* or Boss-*manqué*. It lies rather in its dramatization of the reformer's (and muckraker's) vision of the chain reaction in which the corporation-trust-plutocracy-oligarchy smothered the republic with money. This is the best of Phillips's novels in this study, but this is faint praise. Sayler is more believable than Lewis's Boss, and Phillips avoids most of Lewis's excesses in incident, dialogue, and diction, but this phase of the modern American political novel is still one in which the interest must be historical rather than artistic. Like its fellows, the novel is a period piece, with the few genuinely accomplished works still a good forty years away.

The Boss in the 1920's

The three novels in the 1920's showed little diminution in the Boss's power, but there appeared some retreat from bossism, minor though it might be. In the first, he was a man with a powerful conscience who struggled for reform measures. In the second novel, a governor acknowledged his guilt in deals which secured his office, learning too that the corrupt old machine politician who had made him possessed the greater sense of morality and responsibility. In the third novel, the Boss lost his protégé but continued powerful and corrupt to the end.

Frederick Hazlitt Brennan's *God Got One Vote* (1927) is unique in presenting an innately good man as a Boss who is circumscribed by the

---

[28] Theodore Roosevelt reacted to this kind of fiction and journalism with surprising alarm. "Nothing effective," he wrote William Howard Taft a year after the novel appeared, "is being done to combat the great amount of evil which, mixed with a little good, a little truth, is contained in the outpourings of the *Cosmopolitan*, of *McClure's*, of *Collier's*, of Tom Lawson, of David Graham Phillips, of Upton Sinclair . . . they are all building up a revolutionary feeling . . ." (*The Letters of Theodore Roosevelt*, pp. 183–184).

system. A young Dutch-Irish hod-carrier, he receives his initiation from a saloon-owning Irish ward Boss on the eve of the McKinley-Bryan election. Patrick Van Hoos proves his worth, repeating at the polls and fighting for Bryan against McKinley. His mentor, O'Mara praises his honesty: "A man who won't do nothin' crooked for himself has a good sound conscience an' he can pitch in an' work like a dirthy crook fer sweet Democracy. God bless ye, Pat, me boy."[29] His knowledge of national politics is fragmentary:

> He understood that in Washington Marcus Hanna was busily at work selling out the country to the forerunners of the Standard Oil Company, the Anaconda Copper Company, the United States Steel Company and J. P. Morgan . . . Listening while other men discussed bribery of legislatures by railroads and express companies, graft in public contracts, corruption of public officials, dirty politics and other topics of conversation of the day, he was silent. He didn't know what to say. (30)

But he learns, and after marrying a schoolteacher who quotes Longfellow, Whittier, and Emerson to him as guides, he runs for alderman to please her. He later learns the value of O'Mara's counsel: "If ye'll take my advice ye'll stay on th' decent side av polytics an' be a boss. Then ye'll own men instead of um owning *you*" (174).

Brennan goes on to describe the penalties that accompany the Boss's growing power. Caricatures show him as a beast and his puppet, United States Senator Kirby Allen, as "a tall Lincolnesque figure" (182). Ironically, Allen is a mercenary run as a reformer to split the Republican vote. Disillusioned by revolt and the defection of friends, he finally adopts a *laissez-faire* policy: "I'm not risking my place as boss any more," he decides. "Let the boys have just what they want" (343). Pyrrhic victory over a treacherous faction leaves him only the remnants of his power and his business. But it is some comfort when his daughter, Gwendolyn, assures him, "When all the votes are counted, Daddy . . . I know you can feel sure of this about the returns. God got one vote" (381).

Brennan's novel is unique in that its protagonist is both a hero and a Boss, a Democrat and a Prohibitionist. But there is little to recommend the thin and cliché-ridden remainder. Pat is made believable as a man by Brennan's solid accretion of facts, but he is not quite so believable as a politician who has the aim and conscience of a Young Knight combined with the power and ruthlessness of a Boss. This is an incongruous combination, and there is only one other approaching it in these novels,

[29] Frederick Hazlitt Brennan, *God Got One Vote*, p. 27.

appearing ten years later in Louis Zara's *Some for the Glory*. Perhaps this small statistic has some significance: only two Bosses out of seventeen are fundamentally good men in character and in action.

More than a quarter of a century after the appearance of *The 13th District*, Brand Whitlock published another political novel with the same solidity and thorough character exploration which marked the earlier one. *Big Matt* (1928) posed a double problem in the late awakening of conscience in two professional politicians soiled by a quarter-century of struggle. Although one comes to be dominant, they jointly fill the role of the Boss, one in wielding the power of his office, the other in distributing the spoils that come with it.[30] Like *God Got One Vote*, this novel shows the distance covered since Lewis's *The Boss*. The focus is not upon drama and incident, but again upon the problem of moral awareness.

This problem can be simply posed: Whether to pay off a political debt in the certain knowledge that the office will be used corruptly. A sometime grafter himself, new governor Wesley Blake finally feels the pangs of a long-suppressed conscience. His aspect is familiar, for Blake is the first of several figures modeled on Warren G. Harding.[31] "He knew how to ingratiate himself with a crowd," writes Whitlock. "He had a certain joviality that made men like him . . . Perhaps he was popular because in him most men could see themselves . . . his very mediocrity appealed to them, won him their sympathy and confidence."[32] With a kind of perverse morality Blake rewards Matt Holt but warns his henchmen that the corporations must be kept "on the square . . . they can no longer exploit and rob the people the way they've been doing all these years . . . acting as if they owned the cities and the State and the government and the people"(82).

The inevitable politically motivated investigation comes, however, authorized by one vote—cast by Blake's son-in-law, in another Montague-

---

[30] Whitlock had presented in *The 13th District* a character with something of the Boss about him. An Illinois county leader, Judge Zepaniah L. Bailey is "smart's a singed cat" (263). To his constituents he looks like Abraham Lincoln, "a resemblance much prized and sometimes cultivated by Illinois politicians, with whom the physical resemblance too often suffices for the moral" (262). The Singed Cat, as Whitlock calls him, possesses unique qualities: "There was about this man, strange, silent, uncouth and awkward in appearance, that mysterious thing called personal magnetism, beloved of politicians, even beyond the boundaries of Illinois, above any resemblance to Lincoln . . ." (263).

[31] Like Harding, Blake is a Midwesterner. His state is not identified, but it has an Indian name and Blake's favorite poet is James Whitcomb Riley.

[32] Brand Whitlock, *Big Matt: A Story*, p. 207.

Capulet relationship. After perjury and silent self-sacrifice, Matt emerges as Blake's moral superior when, in prison, he refuses a pardon for fear of damaging Blake's chances for further attainments. The reader last sees Blake gazing up at the capitol dome. He is suffused, presumably, with feelings unpremeditatedly expressed in his last campaign speech, "haunting echoes of regret for a great occasion missed, a great task unachieved, a great ideal unrealized" (229).

Big Matt is not an exceptional novel, but it is straightforward and competent. There are many familiar elements: the deals, the corruption, the Interests, the suspicion of the motives of the investigator, and the Boss with his moral blind spots, but it introduces a kind of subtlety into the character of the Boss foreshadowed in Pat Van Hoos. And though neither Blake nor Matt has anything like his purity of intent, neither possesses the amoral rapacity of Lewis's Boss or the totalitarian mentality of Phillips's Harvey Sayler.

Charles Francis Coe's *Triumph: The Undoing of Rafferty, Ward Heeler* (1929) views the ethics of bossism from another perspective. As in a morality play, Boss Rafferty and Nellie, the orphaned policeman's daughter, contend for Eddie Blank's soul. The contest with this Woman as Guide evokes Dan Rafferty's eloquent apologias for his life and profession.[33] He rejects the idea that built-in graft in American politics has always doomed reform. On the contrary, "Every forward step in American government has been brought about indirectly through graft . . ."[34] He tells Eddie that, "Every beautiful park that this town boasts was made possible because politicians were able to steal half the original purchase price. When there ceases to be money in politics, there will cease to be brains in politics, an' when there ceases to be brains, hell is gonna pop in this country" (134). When he loses the contest, Dan swallows his pride and remains the couple's benefactor. He has no one else, for his is the lonely eminence of power.

Coe's technique in narration and exposition is built principally on primer-style sentences drawn from a limited vocabulary. In using Eddie as his narrator he bargains away many of his own verbal resources in

[33] The careers of Rafferty and O'Mara are nearly identical. Both novels also note one caste mark of the politician in the early years of the twentieth century: gold teeth, produced by covering a tooth—sometimes a healthy one—with a layer of gold leaf. The decayed or impaired tooth covered with a shining gold cap is an appropriate symbol for many of these characters.

[34] Charles Francis Coe, *Triumph: The Undoing of Rafferty, Ward Heeler*, p. 130.

order to heighten the illusion of reality in the character of Eddie. This is a difficult and often problematical technique, as the successes and failures of John Dos Passos in his novels of indirect first-person narration testify. Coe's results show most of its diadvantages and few of the advantages. Eddie has a kind of native wit and perception for all his shortcomings, but his telling of the story is marred by jarring lapses in tone, vocabulary, and point of view. But unsatisfactory as the novel is aesthetically, it is another step in the exercise of bossism reconsidered. Again the problem of moral awareness is central. And, in a manner of speaking the figure of the Boss is schizophrenic. In this novel, as in *Big Matt* and *God Got One Vote,* the function of the Boss is fulfilled by two men, and like two opposing parts of one self, they are in fundamental conflict about the kind of behavior which is ethically permissible.

Signs of Decline

Between 1930 and 1937 three novels centered on the Boss. The last one gives an almost idealized view, fusing the best qualities of the Boss with some of those of the Knight. He strides onward and upward in the best Alger tradition. The others, however, draw a line of demarcation: for the first time there are indications of the decline of bossism as an institution in this fictional view of American political reality. In one novel the forces which the Boss has unleashed with the cooperation of the Interests and organized crime make his position untenable. In the other, the machine changes with the complete alteration of the ethnic and economic bases of the Boss's power.

Chester T. Crowell's *Liquor Loot and Ladies* (1930) traces the shift in power from old-style to new-style Boss. Then comes the gangsterism which proves uncontrollable once let loose. The nameless narrator loads his discursive story with political aphorisms. Like many in retirement, he regrets the past: "The business isn't what it used to be at all . . . Now it is disgustingly sordid and dingy and involves continuous protection of outrageous criminality instead of a few minor vices . . ."[35] But he sees waning power and the end in sight, for "Bosses are going the way of emperors, czars, and kaisers" (4).

The narrator stands in the same relationship to his mentor, Mike Callaghan, as his predecessors have to theirs. His career is like theirs, as he works his way up, serves his time in the legislature, and eventually suc-

[35] Chester T. Crowell, *Liquor Loot and Ladies,* p. 3.

ceeds to leadership of the organization.[36] Gaining control of a reform group put in office by the Interests and meant for use as a dummy, the narrator beguiles them in a contorted metaphor: "We'll all be smoking the peace pipe with our feet in the feed trough by the time the gravy flows" (198).

But criminal alliances and deadly hostilities carried on by hirelings such as "Spike," "Greasy," and "Seven-eleven" weaken his position. He is progressively less able to deal with bootlegging, protection rackets, narcotics traffic, and police brutality. Finally he agrees with Callaghan's verdict that he is caught in "the damn near complete breakdown of government by law . . . We've got a legal system devised hundreds of years ago by remarkably sane men who couldn't imagine more than a handful of simple, useful laws that they thought had better be administered with painstaking patience and no hurry. And now we've piled onto that slow-moving system so many laws that we couldn't enforce them even if we threw the jury system overboard tomorrow" (381). Retiring from the arena, he reflects on the number of Bosses ending their careers in bankruptcy and disgrace: "The day of reckoning is coming for many bosses. Whether it will lead to constructive measures no one can say. And when no one can say, why not take the optimistic view?" (405). The total effect is quite the opposite of this jarring, incongruously optimistic note.

---

[36] In another similarity, the narrator solves the problem of the Australian ballot with the same ruse devised by the Boss in Lewis's novel. He also learns techniques such as running an independent candidate who "would help to divide the rural vote and thus give greater relative importance to our city machine vote" (145). This was the technique employed by Dion O'Mara in *God Got One Vote*. Willie Stark, in Robert Penn Warren's *All the King's Men*, becomes a formidable politician only after he realizes he has been used in this same stratagem. A familiar figure appearing in this and other novels is that of the dreamy, harmless, likeable Socialist:

Adolph Richter . . . turned out tailor-made cigars for a small clientele of particular smokers . . . Adolph was a pleasant, gentle, erudite dreamer of fifty years, who should have been a school-teacher or possibly a research worker. He was the guiding genius of the local Socialists and proud of his record of having been defeated for mayor in twelve successive campaigns. But Adolph was no firebrand. Each defeat found him with a few more friends and many more admirers. (206)

The Socialist-dreamer theoretician, often a cigar-maker with a name suggesting German extraction, may owe something to Adolph Strasser, who led the cigarmakers union with Samuel Gompers in the 1880's. One of John Garwood's faithful supporters in *The Citadel* is Herman Schloss, the son of a Socialist who fled Germany in 1848 and himself a perenially losing candidate. A standing joke among his fellow townsmen for his radicalism, he makes his living as a cigar merchant. For mention of the Progressives' fondness for Germany as the country of reform, see Eric F. Goldman, *Rendezvous with Destiny: A History of Modern American Reform*, p. 234.

Artistically, the book is overloaded with facts and is distractingly discursive. The Boss himself is never real, but sounds rather like a mechanical voice on a tape recorder. The whole account suggests a sordid *Götterdämmerung* of tarnished demigods, while some new monster, like Yeats's horror, slouches forward to be born. Like Brier's *Crusade* (1931), this novel is so pervaded by the milieu of the gangsterism of the late 1920's and early 1930's that it is not as representative of the type as its fellows. But it is useful in studying the changing function and fortunes of the Boss as well as the growing conviction that he is on his way out.

Interspersed throughout Joseph Dineen's *Ward Eight* (1936) are reflective passages contrasting the past and present. One particularly emphasizes the sociological phenomena which underlie this study of the decline of the Boss. Dineen first notes Ward Eight's venerable past: the Old North Church and Copp's Hill, the Adamses and Ben Franklin. But now Big Tim O'Flaherty can fling a green pepper out of his window and hit a patriot's headstone. An "entire Irish population had moved into the ward and crowded out an entire Yankee population . . . Another cycle was casting its shadow before it."[37]

This novel begins in the 1890's. By the time it ends in the mid-1920's, the wave of Italian immigration has evicted the Irish in their turn. Since Dineen declares that Prohibition-inspired gangsterism was never a major factor in Boston, the power shifts result almost exclusively from population change. Dineen's novel thus stands between the extremes of *The Boss* thirty years earlier and *The Last Hurrah* twenty years later.[38]

Big Tim O'Flaherty is the strong young man in the novel who vacillates between trying to supplant the old Boss by force and serving under him until his succession is permitted. The old Boss, Hughie Donnelly, looks like a comic-strip Irishman, but he is wily and forceful enough to make himself a wealthy man with absolute authority:

He was respected because he assured the members of the clan their livelihoods. He was feared because he could deprive them of work instantly . . . [In his manifold services], He furnished bail for craps-shooters, drunks, and minor criminals, and donated the largest sums to churches and religious causes . . .

[37] Joseph F. Dineen, *Ward Eight*, p. 117.
[38] Seven years before the appearance of Edwin O'Connor's *The Last Hurrah*, Dineen published a biographical study of the man on whom O'Connor's protagonist was thought by many to have been based. It was called *The Purple Shamrock: The Hon. James Michael Curley of Boston*. Dineen's Hughie Donnelly in *Ward Eight* is portrayed as one of the last of the old-style ward Bosses, a combination of benevolent despot and paternal tyrant. Virtually the same but for superficial differences is O'Connor's eighty-year-old ward boss, John Gorman.

although he appeared only annually in public, his presence in any troubled or riotous area was more quieting than a platoon of mounted police . . . He ruled the colony with a mailed fist and he was the only trusted court of domestic relations (23).[39]

After youthful rebelliousness, Tim stays regular—in Hughie's "kitchen cabinet," and in the legislature where "oratory . . . could not sway a single vote" (172). As city councillor he works behind the façade of a reform mayor and administration while Hughie sells "all but the City Hall building under the mayor's nose"(234). Hughie is committed to graft on principle. He argues that the grafter keeps money in circulation and may take as little as 10 per cent: "The banks get more . . . his improvements last for his own generation, anyway. And why not? His own generation elects him. Postirity may have to pay the bills, but who cares for postirity now?"(229). With death imminent, Hughie warns Tim, "If ye're strong and crafty and fight hard and never quit, ye may be a boss in twenty years more, but yer hair'll be gray before ye're in command"(309). But Tim turns instead to the niece of a settlement worker who, playing Woman as Guide, has encouraged him and hoped for a break with Hughie. Out of loyalty, Tim goes through the motions of running for office. But he is finally free to speak the truth on the political platform as he takes stock of his life.

This novel suffers from a kind of split, as though Dineen cannot decide who is his protagonist. Tim is a character who rarely comes alive and Hughie often seems a stage Irishman. The romance of opposites— uptown and downtown, Protestant and Catholic, reform and organization—is a cliché which seems contrived to make Tim's career work out so as to serve the interests of the plot. And for all Dineen's knowledge-ability about the people of the ward, his rendition of Italian and Irish accents is not conspicuously better than that of his predecessors. Yet the novel's good points more than cancel out these deficiencies. Dineen conveys the sense of history and change, of time passing and of life actually lived. In panorama, masses of humanity wash into the ward only to flow on out of it, followed by new waves which will repeat the proc-

[39] A strong resemblance exists between Hughie Donnelly and Czar Martin Lomasney (1859–1932). Lomasney was a bachelor who ruled Ward Eight until the end of his long life, habitually withholding his endorsement until the Sunday before election, then lecturing his constituents and all those returned to the old ward for the day to receive instructions. After his death his organization failed to recover from the struggle for succession carried on by several of his subordinates. All these factors are present in Donnelly's case. See Zink, *City Bosses*, pp. 69–84 and Van Devander, *Big Bosses*, pp. 118–121.

ess. Richly and graphically Dineen details the folkways and mores of these County Cork Irish, richly individualistic and fiercely distinct from their countrymen. And for all Tim's doughy quality, his psychological development is a testimony to Dineen's skill. Beginning by questioning the values of his native subculture, he struggles to assert his individuality, then finally liberates himself from its last claims as he strikes out for a completely new life.

The prefatory note to Louis Zara's *Some for the Glory* (1937) helps make it prime material for this study: "For the purpose of this novel of fiction, the national scene has been carefully scanned for evidences of a behavior pattern, one that would afford a typical example of the genus homo politicus Americanus in action . . ." The sources included political scientists, historians, and biographers as well as newspapers, periodicals, and reports. The prefatory note is not misleading, for Zara's story of the rise of Michael Hawks from orphan boy to Presidential candidate presents more political lore than any other novel in this study. As he relates Hawks's rise through ward and city politics in a place much like Chicago and then his progress in state and nation, he buttresses his story with detailed exposition of infighting and grand strategy, minutiae as well as major strokes.

The title derives from an aphorism of an old Boss: "There is always a man to work for the glory . . . but it don't buy kraut for the sausages."[40] The book's epigraph is a quatrain from *The Rubaiyat of Omar Khayyam:*

> Some for the Glories of this World; and some
> Sigh for the Prophet's Paradise to come;
> Ah take the Cash, and let the Credit go,
> Nor heed the rumble of a distant Drum!

This is the philosophy of Big John Stacy, Hawks's saloonkeeping Irish mentor. But as Hawks lives through the novel's span from 1867 to 1912, he grows so that his motivation, never preponderantly materialistic, includes a good deal of the desire for glory and some better impulses as well. Both men fulfill the functions of the Boss, and Stacy is known to his enemies as the "Riverfront Tweed" (54), but though Hawks has taken graft and illegally aided criminals, native honesty is one of the basic aspects of his character. Like the careers of other young politicians who succeed to the place of power, his has included such tasks and incidents

---

[40] Louis Zara, *Some for the Glory*, p. 31.

as splitting the reform vote, serving in an oratory-proof legislature, and unsuccessfully revolting against his Boss and mentor. But unlike their careers, his is crowned by Presidential nomination. And finally, like a Young Knight, he looks beyond defeat to the next contest, assuring his loyal wife that, "The voice of the people . . . it will be heard—" (56).

Much of the narration follows the tradition of the popular historical novel which details the careers of a set of characters over two or three generations. This is not done so convincingly as the portrayal of the events and techniques that mark Hawks's rise. In this sense the novel is too political, for Zara's complete absorption with this side of his characters' lives slights the others. Yet it is a craftsmanlike work. It differs from its contemporaries in that its treatment of Hawks is wholly favorable. Since the novel stops short of the more spectacular political milieu of Prohibition and the 1930's, it has little of the grossness of *Liquor Loot and Ladies* and little of the sense of transition in *Ward Eight*. If the latter shows that things are changing, the former shows that they are changing for the worse as the horrors perpetrated by the alliance between politicians, the Interests, and criminals fulfill the direst predictions of the radical Young Knights of the century's earlier years.

Recent Portraits

A consistency shared by the one novel about the Boss published in the 1940's and the eight published in the 1950's is that almost all of the protagonists ultimately fail: they are defeated, they lose control, or they die.[41] In one of the two instances in which the Boss remains in control at the end, he does so at the cost of his personal happiness. (Many Bosses pay this price in failure or success.) In the other instance, he pays none of these penalties. In this he is like some of the opportunists in the novels of the 1950's, especially the novels of McCarthyism.

[41] One wonders why the Boss should have received so much attention in recent years, particularly if his numbers are declining. A possibility is that the old-style Boss may have begun to acquire some of the fascination of other elements of Americana once they were perceived to be vanishing. Whalers and whalemen, cattletowns and cowboys underwent this process. In this age of mass communication media and alleged homogenization of culture, the Boss's rugged individuality—and he was an individual no matter what else he might also be—may well have proved appealing and challenging to these novelists. In *The Last Hurrah*, Mayor Frank Skeffington tries to persuade his nephew to join him. He tells him that all the others like himself are gone. "When I join them," he adds, "the old campaign will vanish like the Noble Red Man" (Edwin O'Connor, *The Last Hurrah*, p. 73).

In the 1940's most political novels dealt with American Fascism or the Southern Politician. So dominant were these subjects that only one writer, Elizabeth Dewing Kaup, treated the Boss, emphasizing the familiar triad: the mechanics of bossism, its morality, and its decline. *Seed of the Puritan* (1944) chronicled the career of "a puritan gone a little wrong and pulled in several directions at once."[42] Moderately scrupulous and not especially adaptable to change, he also has the misfortune to miscalculate the strength of the national Democratic organization under Franklin D. Roosevelt.[43] Consequently, the political career of Medal of Honor winner Josiah Madden, begun after the first World War, ends during the second. Madden is a good administrator but a man of limited abilities. He has a feel for power and a talent for graft. It pleases him to think of a judge he controls and to reflect (in the Harding era) that "there'd been a man recently who had been set in the highest place the land afforded, merely to handle other people's fiery chestnuts!" (58).[44] But he lacks imagination and adaptability. Defying Washington ("the Organization was his first duty, his first loyalty, his first responsibility" [339].), he does so with candidates who lose. "The Big Fellow," his superior, comments that "A muldoon is a good old-fashioned ward heeler who can be depended on to obey orders and sometimes gets something given to him to keep him happy" (306). Madden is considerably above a Muldoon but substantially below the Big Fellow, who exudes force and is "beyond all good, and in a sense beyond all evil" (257). The effect of this pronouncement is weakened, however, by the fact the Big Fellow is exuding this force from behind bars. Rid of his unpleasant wife, Madden also loses his mistress, his son, and his position. His long-suppressed Puritanism finally reasserts itself as he seeks redemption by labor in a shoe factory such as the one in which he started.

This novel's defects paradoxically include too much exposition of facts yet too much superficiality in examining the causes behind them. It suffers from repetition, and from inexcusable dullness. But Madden's fate and the Big Fellow's foreshadow further limitations on the role of the Boss. He is no longer beyond the law. The novel also outlines a develop-

[42] Elizabeth Dewing Kaup, *Seed of the Puritan*, p. 198.
[43] Van Devander notes that "Nearly all of the big-city Democratic machines fought to prevent Roosevelt's nomination in 1932 . . ." (*Big Bosses*, p. 18).
[44] In an incident suggesting the career of James J. Walker, a mayor elected by Madden resigns and goes to Europe in the midst of an investigation of his administration.

ment more thoroughly analyzed a dozen years later in *The Last Hurrah*. The power of the national organization encroaches upon that of the Boss, virtually ending his regional autonomy.

Many of the same concerns run through Francis T. Field's *McDonough* (1951) although its protagonist successfully resists a challenge to his local dominance. Unlike Madden, he is an ardent supporter of Roosevelt and then Truman, but he too agrees that the days of the Bosses are over. In a paradoxical way he helps to demonstrate this proposition, for in defeating his county antagonist he also successfully defies Boss Coyle of Packer City, the uncontested leader of the New Jersey state organization.[45] But he pays the Boss's penalty as his methods cost him his new wife and his stepdaughter. As much against reform as any other Boss, McDonough offers Rafferty's argument that government jobs pay poorly and that graft is necessary to make up the deficit. Field agrees with McDonough no more than does Mrs. McDonough. He excoriates the traffic in votes and reveals a judiciary used for pay-offs and a press that is for sale. Politics are evil, the author says in effect, but they are part of a larger evil in the body politic itself. Politicians are no worse than other men; they simply encounter more temptation. This long novel is overly crammed with the minutiae of city and county politics. Yet it is a competent job, and it provides more practical lore than any novel but *Some for the Glory*. Judged solely on political content, this novel would rank much higher. But since these works must also be judged as works of art, it does not exceed the level of solid competence.

The remaining seven of these novels were published within the three-year time-span between 1955 and 1957. Again there is paradox in the appearance of this cluster describing a supposedly vanishing phenomenon. And although the authorial moral position does not shift, there is occasionally a tinge of apologia, as though some of these rogues evoke something almost like nostalgia for the past. Robert Wilder's *The Wine of Youth* (1955) recounted the story of a Boss by inheritance. With the indifference bred of great wealth and the intrusion of other concerns, he allows much of his power to be usurped as graft and violence flourish. The protagonist's father, Irish construction man Francis Xavier Cos-

---

[45] Just as ailing Boss Coyle and his son Ed, of Packer City, suggest Boss Frank Hague and his nephew Frank Hague Eggers, of Jersey City, so New Boynton suggests New Brunswick and Port Alby suggests Perth Amboy. Middlesex County can consequently be read for Field's Lenape County. The earliest recorded inhabitants of New Jersey were a branch of the Algonquin family called the Delaware, or Lenni-Lennape Indians.

tello,[46] is one of the few to praise the great entrepreneurs: "I know it is becoming the fashion to speak contemptuously of the Drews, the Morgans, the Astors, the Rockefellers and Vanderbilts," he declares. "But I tell you, without them this great country would be a cluster of settlements hugging the seacoast in their fears."[47] Observing his methods of enhancing the position of his construction business, the reader sees that Costello's view is simply a restatement of the familiar proposition that graft is really necessary for material progress under the conditions of modern American society. After he and his partner are murdered by political enemies, Kevin Costello assumes control of this five-county organization in Southwest Texas. But as he becomes a magnate influential in national politics, he loses touch; and criminal elements within the local organization rule by intimidation. When battles are precipitated by returning veterans, Costello is forced to ask state aid to restore order and provide reform. This constitutes his admission of culpability and his political retirement.

The novel's half-century traces the change in the qualities of the Boss. The dictatorial cattle baron is succeeded by the paternalistic construction man, and then the preoccupied tycoon, whose wide-ranging interests distract him, permitting the worst elements of the machine to rise to the top. If there are any factors which suggest a weakening in the Boss, they are the growth of the power of the state and the force which can be generated by militant groups such as returning veterans. The novel is ultimately disappointing, partly because Wilder can, at his best, write so well. His prose here is too often glib and facile, and too much is overdone—not just the violence, but the drama, which tends toward melodrama, and the emotion, which verges on sentimentality. Character also tends toward stereotype: the Irish father who is one of nature's noblemen, the wonderful priest who encourages the young protagonist to get an education, the Mexican-American determined to make good, and the honest whore who marries and reforms—a character Wilder had used

---

[46] Politically-obtained contracting jobs provide the major portion of the income of many politicians. Not the least of whom this could be said were the otherwise nearly irreproachable co-leaders, Christopher Magee and William Flinn. In a nine-year period at the close of the nineteenth century, Flinn's firm received all but $33,400 of the $3,551,131 paid for paving laid in the city of Pittsburgh (Zink, *City Bosses*, p. 253). Thirty years later, during the period when sewer contractor Patrick Nash guided Chicago's political fortunes with Edward J. Kelly, Mr. Nash's firm received contracts for more than $100,000,000 from the Chicago Sanitary District. *New York Times*, Oct. 21, 1951, p. 17.

[47] Robert Wilder, *The Wine of Youth*, p. 26.

more successfully in *Flamingo Road*. This is another novel whose Boss places power above domestic happiness and ends by losing both. It might have been a better one, even with less technical facility, if it had only bodied forth the plodding honesty of a novel such as *McDonough*.

The first of the three novels of the Boss published in 1956 in many ways was a throwback suggesting Lewis's *The Boss. The Big Fella*, by Henry W. Clune, emphasized the violence, predatory strength, and determination of the lawless protagonist, whose rise as King of the Fifth Ward was as predictable as his ruin. Far different was the case of another novel appearing the same year. As seventy-two-year-old Francis Skeffington begins his campaign for re-election as mayor in Edwin O'Connor's *The Last Hurrah*, he invites his nephew to accompany him. The reader naturally goes along too, into the past as well as the present campaign, coming to know a protagonist in whom the morality of bossism is presented in some complexity. Skeffington uses radio and television, but he prefers personal campaigning. "I suppose," he remarks to his nephew, "that I'm about the last of the old-style political leaders who's still alive and moving around"(73). Adam Caulfield is undeterred by his work as a cartoonist for a newspaper bitterly opposing his uncle. This is fine for Skeffington, a widower who is another of the lonely Bosses, and it is fine for O'Connor, who thus has a convenient point of view from which to tell the story—that of the interested observer who is close to the main character but no more committed to him than Nick Carroway is to Jay Gatsby at the beginning of *The Great Gatsby*. And O'Connor's main interest, unlike that of Henry James in *The Ambassadors*, for instance, is always in Skeffington, and never in the intelligence of his observer. And when Skeffington has to explain things to Caulfield, O'Connor manages it so skillfully that both he and the reader are saved the exposition so painful in many of these novels.

Frank Skeffington in his beginnings had been a smart and persuasive young Irishman.[48] He recalls for his nephew a handlebar-mustachioed Boss named Charlie McCooey, whom he had first seen as a child and later beaten four-to-one for ward leadership. He had gone on to become what one bitter critic calls the best "orator and crowd psychologist that

---

[48] Almost every commentator on this novel has remarked that Skeffington and his city appear to be based upon James Michael Curley (1874–1958) and Boston. Not the least of these was Curley himself. Alderman, congressman, mayor, governor, and jailbird at various points in his long career, "the Purple Shamrock" asserted that a later work, his own autobiographical *I'd Do It Again: A Record of All My Uproarious Years*, gave the facts on which O'Connor's character was based.

this part of the world has ever produced"(203), and what another calls a charming rascal and a gay robber (105). He has been responsible for the city's first real slum clearance program and for public health and recreation programs. But the philanthropic lawyer who recognizes these achievements sees him as mainly responsible for widespread theft and padding of job rolls (108).

Skeffington is beaten by a bland young Irishman whom a rival regards as a front for the power trust gang (205). A friend explains to Caulfield that Skeffington lost because many of the electorate felt it was time for a change, because he had been challenged by concerted opposition with plenty of money, and because Franklin D. Roosevelt had destroyed the old-time Boss:

> He made the kind of politician your uncle was an anachronism, a sport. All over the country the bosses have been dying for the last twenty years . . . Your uncle lasted this long simply because he was who he was: an enormously popular man whose followers were devoted to him . . . the old boss was strong simply because he held all the cards . . . What Roosevelt did was to take the handouts out of the local hands. A few little things like Social Security, Unemployment Insurance, and the like . . . Otherwise known as a social revolution. (375)[49]

This novel is more than the story of a man who describes himself as a tribal chieftain, whose one idea of government, according to one of his nephew's friends, is "old-hat paternalism" (115). It is also quite clearly a study of folkways and mores of the Boston Irish. The Irish wake, for instance, is observed from the religious, social, and political points of view. The novelist does not slight unusual members of the community: former Mayor Clement "Nutsy" McGrath, kicked to death by a camel in Cairo; "Mattress" Mulrooney, reputed to have written his political column

[49] The designation of aspects of the first New Deal Administration as "revolutionary" was a familiar one; for example, "Certainly the revolution of 1932 was as sweeping as any Democrat could have wished for" (Link, *American Epoch*, p. 379). Van Devander offers a different explanation for the power shift in Boston:

the fatal blow to the city machines, as such, was struck by the Republican state legislature when it forced upon Boston a system of non-partisan election of mayors. The provision for an open primary, with party labels barred, followed by a run-off between the two top men in the general election had the effect of wiping out party lines and promoting factional, rather than party, strife. More than that it frequently operated to give the Republican minority in Boston the power to pick the mayor by uniting behind one of the Democratic candidates (*Big Bosses,* p. 120).

For a discussion of causes of the decline of the old-fashioned machine, see Richard Hofstadter, *The Age of Reform: From Bryan to F. D. R.,* pp. 268–269.

from his bed for ten years without ever knowing where city hall was; "Knocko" Minihan, a failure as a man and a husband, whom Skeffington tactfully eulogizes at his funeral.[50] *The Last Hurrah* is the most absorbing of the novels dealing with the Boss and one of the most interesting in the study. It is a problem for the critic to determine why it is not a better novel. The Republican lawyer regrets that so able a man as Skeffington was such a rogue, and reflects that "the man's entire career seemed to have been devoted to the contravention of the law" (409). This states something of the dilemma in which O'Connor clearly found himself—liking his character but being unable to approve of his immorality. The consequence was an unresolved ambivalence which weakens the novel.

Many of Skeffington's acts have been morally reprehensible. The lawyer speaks almost as a *raisonneur*. If this were not enough, there are Skeffington's reminiscences in the long watches of the night from what will shortly be his deathbed: "... along his road to glory there were those shabby markers which signalized his own dishonor; for he was not a guiltless man" (384). Moreover, O'Connor's solemn and devout presentation of the last rites and the solemn high requiem mass, as well as the aura of Roman Catholicism throughout the novel, plainly manifest a code in which Skeffington's deeds would be judged unequivocally. But a series of extenuating circumstances minimizes Skeffington's guilt, and in one curious passage his confessor's emotional response seems something like an extrasacramental absolution. The lawyer makes allowances for Skeffington's upbringing. O'Connor presents him as a man beginning life as an underdog on all counts—social, economic, ethnic—except that of personal attributes. He is a colorful politician and a charming rogue in victory as well as defeat. And O'Connor leaves little doubt that he is a better man than any of those who oppose him. Apart from the Republican philanthropist, the other proper Bostonians are dislikeable bigots. Skeffington's Democratic opponents are either mad or ridiculous, or they are bland young fronts for the Interests. And no matter what Skeffington's depredations, he *did* do some good. When Adam's father-in-law gloats that the moribund Skeffington would now do things differently if

---

[50] Edward McCormack, brother of House Speaker John McCormack, has for years borne the nickname "Knocko." Skeffington's perennially unsuccessful rival is Festus "Mother" Garvey, who had gained his nickname by installing his grim mother on every platform from which he spoke. Van Devander mentions a contemporary of James M. Curley's—Boston Democratic Committee Chairman Billy "Mother" Galvin, "so called because of his motherly voice . . ." (*Big Bosses*, pp. 123–124).

given the chance, the sick man raises up painfully and says, "The hell I would!" Monsignor Burke, his old friend, murmurs, "Oh, grand, grand, grand!" (401). And this is the verdict, one suspects, which the author's heart renders despite his explicit and implicit intellectual condemnation.[51]

In O'Connor's description of the last rites and the requiem mass there is a kind of Catholic apologetics, the sense one gets in certain passages in the later Evelyn Waugh, rather than that which one feels when Flaubert so tellingly uses the last rites in *Madame Bovary*. Something of the tougher fibre Harry Sylvester demonstrated in *Moon Gaffney* might have made the difference here between an excellent but probably ephemeral novel and a first-rate one with some chance of permanence. But despite this, it would be unfair not to say that *The Last Hurrah* is convincing and amusing, that Frank Skeffington is a living character, and that O'Connor gives the most convincing demonstration yet of that often observed but not yet proved assertion that the days of the old-style Boss are finally over.

The last of the three novels published in 1956 presented a Boss as unredeemed as those who had preceded him and potentially more dangerous than any of them. Here ancient rapacity was up-dated by modern methods. In *The Ninth Wave* Eugene Burdick depicted a very different political milieu from that which he and William Lederer produced two years later in *The Ugly American*. Burdick set *The Ninth Wave* in California rather than the Orient, and his protagonist is the antithesis of some of the pompous and ineffectual Americans encountered in the later book. Mike Freesmith is frightening because he has all the attributes of Lewis's Boss—predatory intelligence, strength, and courage—plus the resources of modern polling techniques and statistical analysis. Burdick's epigraph comes from Durkheim's *Suicide:* "Those who have only empty space above them are almost inevitably lost in it, if no force restrains them." Freesmith has only empty space above him for he acknowledges no moral law, and nothing restrains his ambition but the practical obstacles to be overcome.

Freesmith makes money in college acting as a subject in a psychological

---

[51] I had conversations about Curley some years ago with a Roman Catholic friend of Irish extraction, a young man of irreproachable morals and a Holy Cross-trained lawyer. The judgments he rendered on Curley's depredations were as forthright as those in *The Last Hurrah*. But at Curley's most outrageous maneuvers he would burst into delighted laughter and cry, "That's James Michael, all right!" Perhaps some readers will have had similar experiences. I suspect that O'Connor must share something of my friend's attitudes.

experiment. He wins money rewards in the experiment and dominates the other students serving as subjects. This is one of the experiences by which he empirically arrives at his set of principles of human behavior: one person can make a decision faster than a group; the weak person wants to be delivered from the superior person; people appear to love the man who humbles them. Freesmith feels that people work on what he calls the Fear Principle and the Hate Principle. These two emotions are the only ones that make sense out of history for him. His destructive talent is to find what people fear most, to probe for it, and to use it. He is not so effective or frightening as O'Brien in Orwell's *Nineteen Eighty-Four*, but he does well enough. Exploiting friends and sweethearts, he puts himself through law school. After callous wartime heroics he builds his political power. He hires a polling organization to determine the most sensitive issues, the fears and hates he can best prey on to secure victory for his gubernatorial candidate. Intimidating pressure groups into large pledges, he uses them for more opinion research in the intensive campaign.

The end of the novel closes a circle started at the beginning, when Freesmith and his oldest friend ride the waves on their surfboards. They wait for the last, biggest wave in each series of nine and for the ninth of these which is biggest of all. When the great wave finally rolls in, Freesmith's friend drowns him in it. Thus nemesis again overtakes the amoral destroyer as Nature itself apparently cooperates with human conscience. In the days of his greatest successes Freesmith has used clever planning, opinion research, and applied group psychology to gain control. But like so many of his modern predecessors, he too has declared that the days of the Bosses are over. Paradoxically, his career, before the familiar retribution, seems to demonstrate that the Bosses are not through. If anything, they may become more insidious than they have ever been before. The novel is a competent one in the tradition of tough but intelligent realism. The principal defect is that the story is too episodic, that the events of Freesmith's career give the effect of being spread out so that they fail to build sufficiently to the strong climax which the novel needs.

The Experimental Tradition

James Reichley's *The Burying of Kingsmith* was the best of the three novels of the Boss published in 1957 and the most ambitious of all the novels in this chapter. On the narrative level it dealt with practical politics, on the symbolic with patterns of human experience as expressed in myth. Its subjects were two: the filling of the power vacuum created by the death of the Boss and the enigma of his personality. The reader learns that young Nathaniel Kingsmith was all things to all men. To his second in command, "He, the King, the master angler . . . had played out the lines of money, votes, intelligence until he had snagged the fish that lay too far beneath the surface for any of the rest of them to see. But more than that . . . he liked them, the men, the schemers and the plotters. He had liked the politicking, he had known how to make it go . . ."[52] To his half-brother, Kingsmith was "a swollen ego drawing the life out of everything he touched"(261). Kingsmith's onetime mistress asserts, "The truth was that Kingsmith had remained to the end of his life a very small boy . . . that he had never gained the maturity that comes of sacrifice and shared misfortune and the location of values outside of one's own lousy self" (364). But one subordinate compares Kingsmith's death with those of Samson, Simon Peter, and the Apostle Paul, finally marvelling that "by the manner of his death at the hands of the forces of evil of this world, Nathaniel Kingsmith had placed himself in a special and undoubted relation to the Prince of Peace Himself . . ."(232).

Kingsmith's many-sidedness is emphasized as each even addresses him differently: Nat, Nate, Nath, Natty, the King. One of the shortcomings of the novel is that no dominant image of Kingsmith is really formed. Joseph Conrad set a pattern for others to follow with the multiple image. In *Lord Jim* and *Victory* we see Jim and Axel Heyst from several different points of view, but we finally see them whole. This is not true of Kingsmith, although Reichley tries to promote the fusion by giving one of the novel's many soliloquies to Kingsmith himself, as Faulkner does with Addie Bundren in *As I Lay Dying*. Near the end of the book we learn of Kingsmith's conviction that the death he anticipated in Korea was futile. With Swiftian disgust, he feels for a moment that people will finally exterminate themselves. Then he takes lukewarm comfort from the thought, "from destruction light can emerge; the record is not wholly bad; there is at least a consciousness of what a good thing life might have been; the mind that can sustain that consciousness can never be a subject for entire despair." But he asks, "must I die for that, a consciousness of what a good thing life might have been?" (408).

By the novel's end, Kingsmith has been buried, his successor has been decided, and his half-brother (an anti-Telemachus) has chosen not to become reconciled to his father. (The one-day framework extended by

[52] James Reichley, *The Burying of Kingsmith*, p. 48.

flashbacks is one of the debts to James Joyce.) The father calls the successor a "dumbhead," and adds, "We will need a few loudmouths like
Barney Gould to handle the politics, but real power is going to be in the
hands of business leaders who will operate behind the scenes" (396).[53]
If this is to be interpreted as another signal of the passing of the Boss,
it is valid only in the sense that he reverts back to the status sometimes
assigned to him by David Graham Phillips. He is once more the servant
of the Interests, running the organization that will provide a favorable
climate for their operations.

This novel also shows the influence of Joyce in Reichley's continual use
of myth to extend its revelance and symbolically transform his characters
and situations into universals. The many soliloquies are couched in formal diction. This has the effect of making them appropriate to an ancient
Greek or an Elizabethan Englishman. This diction is also apt for description of incidents which clearly have other referents. In one, Kingsmith's
half-brother thinks of the first night of his last voyage: "I had already
realized that I was not trusted by the men of the crew . . . submissive as
they were to the will of the mad captain and under the practical control
of his three loyal mates, there was little hope that I would be able to
convert them to my point of view" (89). After being thrown overboard
in a storm by the crew, "I thrust about me with my arms and almost at
once struck a narrow oblong box which I recognized" (263). The ship's
disappearance and his survival further strengthen the already obvious
correspondences with *Moby Dick*. Other sequences suggest Odysseus,
Cassandra, Clytemnestra and Agamemnon, Cain and Abel, Falstaff and
Hal, the Temptation on the Mount, and the Judgment of Paris. Lacking
the unity which Joyce's parallels with the *Odyssey* imposed upon *Ulysses*,
these symbolic and mythic references only partially perform their unifying and universalizing function.

Apart from this deficiency and the failure to bring the image of the
protagonist into focus, the book's chief fault lies in its wordiness and dif-
fuseness. This novel, again, is one of the most ambitious in the whole
study. Its author might have come closer to fulfillment of his aims if he
had taken one more cue from Joyce: the compression demonstrated in
the differences between *Stephen Hero* and *A Portrait of the Artist as a
Young Man*.

In *O'Shaughnessy's Day* (1957) Mary Deasy again showed herself to
be an excellent literary mimic. And it is this further demonstration of the

[53] These views suggest the influence of Messrs. Mellon, Grundy, and Pew in
Pennsylvania politics in this century. See Van Devander, *Big Bosses*, pp. 138–142.

adoption of experimental techniques in the rendering of American political experience that is more interesting than the depiction of one more Boss in decline. As *The Boy Who Made Good* had followed the example of Scott Fitzgerald, so *O'Shaughnessy's Day* imitated that of James Joyce. The author's preface sets the first time-level as April 28, 1922 (the year *Ulysses* was published), and adds that on a subterranean second level, from 1891 to 1922, there is "the stream of remembrance of Time." As the requiem bell tolls for Boss Aloysius O'Shaughnessy, one woman's stream of consciousness suggests Leopold Bloom's musings on death in the "Hades" episode of *Ulysses:* "Queer thing about that custom. Advertise it to the whole neighborhood—somebody's dead: watch out, you're next. Different sound for a wedding, cheerful, all banging away at once. But the same bells for both—marrying and dying."[54] Later, remembering the beginning of a liaison, she might be Molly Bloom recalling her courtship by Bloom in the "Penelope" episode. Another sequence—as various people in the city hear the bells toll—recalls one of the most famous passages of Virginia Woolf's *Mrs. Dalloway.* Elsewhere the shade of Scott Fitzgerald haunts these pages as he did those of *The Boy Who Made Good:* two of the characters are recalled at a dance in October of 1917, when "Below them the saxophones sang sadly: *Poor Butterfly . . .*" (207).[55]

By the day's end a kind of resolution has been achieved in the lives of O'Shaughnessy's three sons: Liam, jailed by his father through perjured testimony; Kevin, rising with the Citizens Committee which has defeated his father's picked candidate; and Calvin, fanatically devoted to his eldest brother. Flashbacks revivify garrulous and malicious Aloysius O'Shaughnessy. Calling himself an old brigand, he declares that he has made a good living for many years simply through "knowing all about the fine points of human behavior . . ." (186). Kevin rejects his proffered partnership, telling the onetime saloonkeeper, "The old-fashioned political boss—*your* kind of boss—is on the way out; it's only a matter of time

---

[54] Mary Deasy, *O'Shaugnessy's Day*, p. 162.
[55] Liam O'Shaughnessy's stream of consciousness as he gazes on a corpse suggests the kind of meditation we hear in the mind of Stephen Dedalus in the "Proteus" episode of *Ulysses:* "All the accidental forms of his existence lying there, ready for the discard now, because I met him on O'Brien Street and because my father drank too much and was displeased. And the rest of it—the soul? What is that phrase of Avicenna's?—*substantia solitaria*—a solitary substance—Out of the body of Thady Murphy now—alone, frightened, naked, *substantia solitaria*—" (297). The whole murder sequence appears imitative of the Nighttown section of the "Circe" episode, using stage directions and dialogue in place of narrative.

now" (198). Later, as Kevin reads the provision in his father's will for ten thousand masses for the repose of his soul, he comments, "Trying to bribe his way past St. Peter . . . according to this, I'd say he rated the Keeper of the Golden Gates about halfway between a United States senator and the president of a public utilities company" (307).

The story of this Boss, whom his eldest son calls "a liar, a thief, a bully, a blackmailer, a false witness, a suborner, a coward—" (318), contributes no new insights into the character of the Boss. He dies a quarter of a century before Frank Skeffington, but he too is beaten by a powerful new organization and collapses shortly after. But unlike Skeffington, he is a thoroughly evil man, much more like Burdick's Mike Freesmith than O'Connor's rascally but charming "Riverboat Phil." This novel has, like *The Wine of Youth*, a glossy surface, but it is too long, often slow-moving, and unforgivably imitative. It does show, however (as had *The Burying of Kingsmith*), that the influence of James Joyce has joined that of Dreiser and Lewis in the American political novel.

More conventional than the novels of Reichley and Deasy, William Wister Haines's *The Hon. Rocky Slade* (1957) displays elements of the novel of the Boss, the novel of corruption, and the novel of McCarthyism. The merging of themes demonstrates the adapting of old patterns to topical subjects. Haines's protagonist is a former football star sponsored in politics by a group of businessmen. Their New Deal-hating leader explains to the lawyer who narrates: "For ten years I . . . submitted to total perversion of our government. I swallowed the lies, the broken promises, the manufactured emergencies, the falsified budgets, the secret diplomacy, the systematic inflaming of hatred and envy and fear."[56] Slade's postwar speeches have a familiar and ominous ring:

I could hear Rocky's voice, next time, closing solvent banks to produce a political panic. I could hear him using those same promises to unite gangsters and unions and reliefers into another holy crusade for another fifteen years of total tyranny until we needed more total wars to insure total submission . . . You've got to fight that kind of fire with fire. You cannot corrupt a politician, Jim; the words are a contradiction. The best you can do is control him. That's why I did this. (247–248)

But both he and old Boss Flynn see the illusion of control vanish as Slade turns defeat into victory. In an incident that seems clearly modeled after one in the 1952 presidential campaign, Slade defends himself against the

[56] William Wister Haines, *The Hon. Rocky Slade*, pp. 246–247.

charge that he has been receiving funds from interested groups.[57] His emotional speech receives wild applause, and at the end of it, Flynn embraces him.

This novel is closer to *The Ninth Wave* than any of its contemporaries. Combining the Boss's traditional attributes with extreme opportunism, the protagonist practices group psychology with the aid of such modern devices as Madison Avenue-style presentations complete with graphs and charts, motion pictures, and television. This well-written novel deals competently with politics on the local level and with the familiar machinations in the legislature. No more than his predecessors and contemporaries does Haines neglect love. As an added fillip, it is chiefly embodied in the form of a triangle involving his convincing central characters: a beautiful young woman, the narrator, and—as one would anticipate—Rocky Slade. And for him, like all the other Bosses, it is politics, not love, that comes first. "Objectively, you might call him pitiable," comments one townsman, but "his life has been a quagmire of humbug . . . This boy is a triumph of willful hypocrisy" (203).

The Changing Image

One of the obvious differences between the Boss and the Young Knight is age. Fourteen of the seventeen Bosses are older men. Twelve of these fourteen stories are told retrospectively from the vantage point of retirement, defeat, or death. In none is there the combined note of assurance and hope often found at the end of the novel of the Young Knight, sounded as it often is even in defeat. These are men who concentrate wholly on power and the position and profit that it brings, sacrificing all else in the pursuit.

But there are changes between the appearance of *The Boss* in 1903 and *The Hon. Rocky Slade* in 1957. They concern the Boss's characteristics, his base of power, and his methods. Although he remains intelligent, daring, and devious, he is a rather less violent man than his predecessors. He is much less apt to carry out overtly illegal acts and much more likely to obtain his ends by subtler pressures. He is much more aware, usually, of the moral implications of his acts. He still feels that

---

[57] A cynical, informed newspaperman has told the narrator: "Rocky could be cleaned up very fast. Half the public men in America are taking private money" (254).

irregularities in politics are dwarfed by irregularities in business and finance, but he often incurs the burden of guilt along with his spoils.

The power of the Boss wanes as the outside world encroaches more and more upon the ghettolike wards into which masses of immigrants streamed in the turn-of-the-century decades. They move away from the slums and the docks, to be followed by other ethnic groups even more quickly assimilated into the general population. The Boss is less often the clan leader. He no longer has nearly complete control over the economy of his district as the authority of larger governmental units—state and federal—impinges upon his area with benefits which lessen his constituents' dependence upon him.

Most of the novels in the latter half of this chapter carry the assertion that the Boss is dying out. Perhaps this should be understood to mean that the old-style, paternalistic Boss is vanishing as the nature of his constituency changes, as his people are better off economically and educationally, as the levers of control are progressively taken from his hands. Apparently what happens is that the Boss remains, but that as he has abandoned gold teeth and vests edged with white piping for the appearance of the Brooks Brothers man, so he abandons the repeater and the stuffed ballot box for the opinion-research counsellor and the segments of television time. The area of authority is larger; he dominates not a ward but a state. Using mass media rather than the individual handout, he plays on basic fears and antagonisms rather than immediate economic and social concerns. The Boss remains, but like the state, he has grown less personal and more powerful.

3. CORRUPTION

I preche of no thyng but for coveityse.
Therfore my theme is yet, and evere was,
Radix malorum est Cupiditas.
Thus kan I preche agayn that same vice
Which that I use, and that is avarice.

—The Pardoner
Geoffrey Chaucer
The Canterbury Tales

Although the novels in this chapter display many different varieties of corruption, the causes are considerably fewer than the effects. Desire for money and power, in that order, brings pressure to bear on the political process. It is exerted upon those who name candidates and elect them and then upon the elective and appointive officials themselves. In the fiction and nonfiction of this area, the politicians constitute only one element of a ubiquitous triad; the other two are businessmen and criminals. There are, of course, numerous and varied agents of these three principals, but their roles are subsidiary ones. For purposes of analysis, however, these three elements and those clustering around them can be treated in four interrelated embodiments: the Interests, the Lobby, the Machine, and Crime.

Historically, the Interests and the Lobby appear first. Lobbying, it has been argued, is a process guaranteed by the First Amendment's provision that the people shall have unhindered right to petition the government for a redress of grievances. It was, of course, an activity which antedated the Constitution itself. Ancestors of modern pressure groups lobbied at the First Continental Congress. The phrase "lobby-agent" did not become current until 1829, but it was lobbying which concerned

James Madison when he spoke out upon the dangers of "faction" in the *Federalist,* No. 10.[1] Another patriot had formed the first business lobby in the early years of the new century. Alexander Hamilton's Philadelphia Society for the Promotion of National Industry preceded the National Association of Manufacturers by nearly a century, but when the latter organization was formed in 1859, many of its aims were similar. Tactics arising out of tariff fights such as that over the unsuccessful Woolen Bill of 1824 have changed surprisingly little over the course of the years, but the tempo of such activities has accelerated rapidly. In sentiments to be echoed in tract and fiction, James Buchanan wrote in 1852 to his friend Franklin Pierce that, "The host of contractors, speculators, stock-jobbers, and lobby members which haunt the halls of Congress, all desirous *per fas aut nefas* and on any and every pretext to get their arms into the public treasury are sufficient to alarm every friend of his country. Their progress must be arrested."[2]

In the decade before the Civil War, pressure over patents and other matters was exerted by such rugged entrepreneurs as Cyrus McCormick and Samuel Colt. They were among those singled out in the Letcher Committee's lobbying report of 1855. This was one of many efforts by Congress to gain some measure of understanding of, and control over this phenomenon which at times subjected segments of the legislative branch to nearly intolerable pressure. With the coming of the war the situation grew enormously more complex. Washington became a military and economic center where great sums of money were expended as the national economy was reshaped. Press coverage rose sharply, reflecting the new focus of national interest. In 1867, 49 press correspondents were accredited to Congress. By 1890 there were 110. Many found time for activities other than gathering and writing news. Some inhabited "a shadowy world where reporting, public relations, and lobbying all met. They knew how to plant a rumor that would brighten the prospects of a bill . . . and a company with a bill in its pockets . . . knew enough to cultivate them. The reporters also had access to key senators and representatives whose doors did not open easily."[3]

While the National Grange and the railroad lobby exerted group influence in the 1870's, men cut in the pattern of McCormick and Colt began to exercise leverage that could not have been dreamed of a short

---

[1] See Karl Schriftgiesser, *The Lobbyists: The Art and Business of Influencing Lawmakers,* p. 5 ff.

[2] Schriftgiesser, *The Lobbyists,* p. 7.

[3] Bernard A. Weisberger, *The American Newspaperman,* pp. 167–168.

time earlier. Harriman and Hill, Frick and Carnegie, Rockefeller and Morgan went to the sources of legislative control. There, writes Arthur Link, they "dominated the Republican party and usually the Democratic party as well from 1865 to 1901. They financed political campaigns and received their rewards from government in the form of utilities franchises, land bounties, freedom from taxation, or tariff protection."[4] When the era of great corporations, trusts, and holding companies shortly succeeded the era of the entrepreneurs, the threat inherent in this power was becoming unmistakable. By 1898 the trusts had become a major force in American economic life.[5] Then, in the years between 1903 and 1912, the Morgan interests gave an appalling demonstration. As part of J. P. Morgan's campaign to gain a monopoly over all transportation facilities in New England, "the New Haven directors debauched politicians, bribed editors, and in the end helped bring the economy of New England to the brink of ruin."[6] To some the spectacle was not surprising. War, panic, and pestilence, wrote John Dos Passos in one of the famous "biographies" of *1919*, were "good growing weather for the House of Morgan."[7]

The antitrust laws could not stem the progress toward consolidation, which eventually settled even the fierce conflict between the Morgan and Rockefeller groups. The epic battle over ownership and control of the Great Northern Railroad, partially resolved in 1901, finally culminated in a merger carried out between 1907 and 1913. On New Year's Day of 1913, the House of Morgan and its confederates could view the future buttressed by a total of 341 directorships of 112 enterprises including industries, railroads, and banks whose resources totaled over $22,000,000,000.[8] Such an agglomeration of power gave force to Wood-

[4] Link comments that the comparisons of the magnates with medieval robber barons "however engaging, are essentially unfair, because, for all their faults, most of the captains of industry were men of enormous constructive energy and in the final analysis reflected the standards of their age" (Arthur Link, *American Epoch: A History of the United States since the 1890's*, p. 5). He notes, however, that the Supreme Court's striking down of the income tax in 1895 was the most unpopular ruling since the Dred Scott decision of 1857, and that "Coming as it did in the same year in which the Court upheld the conviction of Debs and other officials of the American Railway Union for violating the Sherman law, the income tax decision only deepened the popular conviction that the Supreme Court had become the tool of the railroads, corporations, and millionaires" (p. 116).

[5] See Richard Hofstadter, *The Age of Reform: From Bryan to F. D. R.*, p. 168. For the names of some of the principal organizations see p. 169.

[6] Link, *American Epoch*, pp. 53–54.

[7] John Dos Passos, *U.S.A.*, p. 340.

[8] Link, *American Epoch*, p. 52. For a recent account of interlocking interests

row Wilson's charge, in the Presidential campaign of 1912, that "The masters of the government of the United States are the combined capitalists and manufacturers of the United States . . . The government of the United States is a foster child of the special interests. It is not allowed to have a will of its own."[9]

While the processes of consolidation were going forward, one of the best known of the muckrakers was printing a series of exposés of civic corruption which he gathered together in March of 1904 as *The Shame of the Cities*. In this classic journalistic study, Lincoln Steffens did more than simply repeat the old refrain that crooked politicians produced crooked government. "Big business everywhere is the chief source of corruption," he wrote. He went further: "But no one class is at fault, nor any one breed, nor any particular interest or group of interests. The misgovernment of the American people is misgovernment by the American people." Driving his point home in words that have a familiar ring today, he wrote, "We break our own laws and rob our own government, the lady at the customhouse, the lyncher with his rope, and the captain of industry with his bribe and rebate. The spirit of graft and of lawlessness is the American spirit."[10] And this corruption was total. It was, added Steffens, "not merely political; it was financial, commercial, social; the ramifications of boodle were so complex, various, and far-reaching, that one mind could hardly grasp them . . ."[11]

The cities he had visited exemplified different responses to corruption: in St. Louis, boodle; in Minneapolis, police graft; in Pittsburgh, a political and industrial machine. The extremes were represented—some of them strange-sounding today. Whereas Philadelphia represented a perfect political machine producing "general civic corruption," the city of Chicago "was an illustration of reform, and New York of good govern-

---

see Estes Kefauver, *In a Few Hands: Monopoly Power in America*, with the assistance of Irene Till.

[9] Woodrow Wilson, *The New Freedom*, as quoted by Schriftgiesser, *The Lobbyists*, p. 35.

[10] Lincoln Steffens, *The Shame of the Cities*, pp. 291, 4, and 12. Compare Senator J. William Fulbright, speaking on government scandals nearly half a century later, as he "told the country that the problem was not really illegal conduct but unethical conduct—a lack of ethics that ran through the whole community. 'How do we deal with those who, under the guise of friendship, accept favors which offend the spirit of the law but do not violate its letter? What of the men outside government who suborn those inside it?' " (As quoted by Eric F. Goldman in *The Crucial Decade and After: America, 1945–1960*, pp. 199–200).

[11] Steffens, *Shame of the Cities*, p. 14. For a brief treatment of these conditions on the city and state level, see Link, *American Epoch*, pp. 81–83 and 86–87.

ment."[12] Steffens dealt at some length with specific Bosses. He closely scrutinized, for example, the activities of the rascally Edward R. Butler of St. Louis, but he was quite as concerned with Butler's accessories: "not thieves, gamblers, and common women, but influential citizens, capitalists, and great corporations. For the stock-in-trade of the boodler is the rights, privileges, franchises, and real property of the city, and his source of corruption is the top, not the bottom of society."[13] Steffens's research had been productive. He did not have room, he said, to print all the things he had learned, and his articles were, if anything, understatements. But he printed names, places, events, and facsimiles of documents. Some of the names came from the top of society. Among them were Chris Magee and William Flinn. These Pittsburgh social register-politicians, wrote Steffens, shared an eminently agreeable partnership. Magee gained power and Flinn wealth when the mayor gave to the contractor "all the streets he wanted in Pittsburgh at his own terms: forever, and nothing to pay."[14]

Steffens chronicled improvement in Chicago and New York. Civic housecleaning had made Minneapolis "a city without reproach," but the spectacle of Philadelphia, corrupt and contented, was morbid and frightening. Manhattan's Tammany organization might be "the embodiment of corruption," but Philadelphia was "the ideal of party organization, and, possibly, is the end toward which our democratic republic is tending . . . Nothing but a revolution could overthrow this oligarchy, and there is its danger."[15]

To some, however, Steffens's warnings were as naive as the complaints of the silk-stocking reformers. George Washington Plunkitt, self-styled "statesman" of "the Democracy" of New York, leader of its 15th assembly district, spoke from years of experience. Called "a straight organization man" by the redoubtable leader, Charles F. Murphy himself, this sachem of the Tammany Society declared, "Steffens means well but, like all reformers, he don't know how to make distinctions. He can't see no difference between honest graft and dishonest graft and, consequent [*sic*],

---

[12] Steffens, *Shame of the Cities*, p. 16. It is interesting to consider to what extent a distinction can be made between the "good" and "bad" machine. See Goldman, *Rendezvous*, p. 171, for comment on the LaFollette organization and the envy it aroused in the breast of the redoubtable Boies Penrose. See also Hofstadter, *Reform*, p. 276. In any case, it is primarily the machine doing evil that seems to attract the novelist's interest.

[13] Steffens, *Shame of the Cities*, p. 108.

[14] *Ibid.*, p. 174.

[15] *Ibid.*, pp. 102, 289, and 205.

he gets things all mixed up." Politicians in 1905, he said, were no worse than they had been seventy years earlier. "It just means," Plunkitt argued, "that the old-timers had nothin' to steal, while the politicians now are surrounded by all kinds of temptations and some of them naturally—the fool ones—buck up against the penal code."[16]

The lobbyists continued their special pleading, but according to Schriftgiesser, "all of them, working in coalition, were struggling to capture the government itself."[17] On this second front, the forces of corruption were working less impeded than in many major cities. The war effort had placed tremendous emphasis upon productivity and had served to make government more amenable to the wants of business, industry, and finance. Before the war, President Wilson had waged a more successful battle with the lobbies than had any President before him, particularly in the great tariff fight of 1913. But with the end of the war, the Administrations of Harding, Coolidge, and Hoover provided a highly favorable climate in which the Interests could cultivate their gardens with the assistance of the growing crews of lobbyists. So successful was the pattern of expansion and consolidation that by 1924 "the big business, industrial and financial pressure groups had all but succeeded in their aims."[18] The roll of the lobbies—the railroads, the Grange, the growing drug and pharmaceutical industry, the canners and packers—was rapidly lengthened. The public utility companies, the Navy League with its adherents in steel and shipbuilding, the powerful farmers with large holdings, all these entered the lists. But the strongest pressure had come from two disparate groups. Veterans pressed for bonuses and other special legislation using a special "grass-roots" technique: orders sent to each local Legion Post would be translated into pressure on individual congressmen. Prohibitionists had worked with an unequaled intensity for legislation which was to change American mores and the very image of America in the eyes of the world. Beginning with the formation of the United States Temperance Union in 1833, the movement had gained

[16] George Washington Plunkitt, *Plunkitt of Tammany Hall*, ed. William L. Riordon, pp. 39 and 43. Charles W. Van Devander notes the idea "widely accepted in Tammany during Murphy's day [*c.* 1902–1924], that there was a deep moral gulf between 'honest graft' and 'dirty money.' The former means such pickings as cuts on public contracts and contributions from candidates for public office. In a period of easier public morality, it came, by the early thirties, to include payments for the 'protection' of speakeasies and gambling. The political 'take' from prostitution rings and extortion gangs remained definitely 'dirty money'" (*The Big Bosses*, pp. 22–23).

[17] Schriftgiesser, *The Lobbyists*, p. 32.

[18] *Ibid.*

such rapid momentum that by 1861 twenty-one states legislated statewide prohibition. In 1874 the Woman's Christian Temperance Union
injected still more moral fervor into the struggle. In the last decade of the
century it provided some of the best-known activists of the spectacular
Anti-Saloon League. As the pressures of the approaching war increased,
Bishop James Cannon, Jr., and lobbyist Wayne B. Wheeler led a stepped-
up campaign. It succeeded in 1917 when the Webb-Kenyon Act of 1913
was upheld by the Supreme Court after four years of litigation. In one
view, Prohibition was "a pseudo-reform, a pinched, parochial substitute
for reform which had a widespread appeal to a certain type of crusading
mind." The movement had also been a complex phenomenon involving
a number of interlinked and deeply-ingrained social, religious, and political attitudes.[19] But to one commentator this triumph was "almost entirely the work of a lobby. Unscrupulous and determined, willing to use
any and every known method of propaganda and lobbying, a minority
pressure group had managed to capture the government."[20] The citizens
of the country reacted to this legislation with mass lawbreaking on a scale
unparalleled in American history. The resulting sequence of cause and
effect was close to a national catastrophe, the reverberations of which are
still being felt today.

A journalist with something of Steffens's sense of outrage wrote that
the federal and state governments had spent a total of well over a billion
dollars in fighting crime for the one calendar year of 1928. Nonetheless,
he asserted, the annual cost of crime to the American people was more
than the 4.5 billion dollars which Congress's appropriations had averaged
for the ten years beginning with 1923.[21] The illegal manufacture of alcoholic beverages, rumrunning, and highjacking had not come unaccom-
panied. Violence increased as competing local criminal rings increasingly
came under the domination of larger organizations. A former F.B.I.
agent turned public safety director testified, "From the day the National
Prohibition Act was passed . . . until its repeal, December 5, 1933, Cleveland went through an era of mob violence, gang slayings, hijackings,
bootleg and racket wars. Out of the prohibition period came the same
kind of city-wide, regional and even inter-state gang organization that
plagued other cities." He went on to show that laissez-faire was not confined to licensed organizations: "Rival gangs fought for supremacy . . .
Murder became a standard tool for all such illegal gangs as they fought

[19] Hofstadter, *Reform*, p. 287. See also p. 288.
[20] Schriftgiesser, *The Lobbyists*, p. 46.
[21] Denis Tilden Lynch, *Criminals and Politicians*, pp. 1–2.

for territories, sources of supply, trucks, boats that ran the liquor block-
ade on the lakes, and for the upper hand among the hoodlums, gunmen,
drivers, and customers."[22]

Like the economic struggles in the thirty years preceding Prohibition's
enactment, a pattern emerged of strife among many contenders, the appearance of a few enormously powerful entrepreneurs, and the subsequent consolidation. A few large groups, often with interlocking director-
ates, became supreme in managing the far-flung interests and activities
of these empires. In the period between 1924 and 1932, the number of
gangsters murdered in the United States was placed at a minimum of
5,000. During only seven years of this period, Chicago alone accounted
for 500 such deaths. Denis Tilden Lynch estimated that the number of
professional criminals engaged in the bootleg industry reached about
275,000 before Repeal. With the ancillary forces of other criminals, corrupt police, and politicians, he added, the number might reach half a
million. The best known entrepreneur was, of course, Alphonse Capone.
To some, he was merely the front man for a syndicate. At the time of his
arrest his wealth was estimated by Federal agents at about $20,000,000,
and his influence was alleged to reach into the mayor's office in the city
of Chicago. According to an opponent of William "Big Bill" Thompson,
the Capone gang had contributed $50,000 to Thompson's successful
campaign for the mayoralty in 1927. Another opponent said $260,000
had been invested in an earlier campaign. Once in office, Thompson had
appointed city sealer Daniel A. Seritella, allegedly a Capone lieutenant,
as a member of his cabinet.[23] Seritella was to show a talent for longevity
as well as success. Twenty years later Senator Kefauver noted his continuing presence on the scene. But he had risen in the world: he was now
"simultaneously a state senator, scratch sheet operator, and business
partner with Greasy Thumb Guzik."[24]

The murders of the O'Bannions and Colls, the Colosimos and Uales,
and atrocities such as Chicago's St. Valentine's Day Massacre were the
most widely publicized aspect of the pattern of lawlessness. The bizarre
was yoked to the violent in equally flamboyant crimes, such as the brief
spasm of violence in Detroit on September 16, 1931, when members of
the Purple Gang machine-gunned Izzy Sutker and the two brothers
Lebowitz, the leaders of a group uniquely known as the Little Jewish
Navy. Perhaps more alarming, however, were the encroachments of

[22] Alvin J. Sutton, Jr., as quoted by Estes Kefauver in *Crime in America*, p. 189
[23] Lynch, *Criminals*, pp. 13, 107, 28, 31, 17, and 22.
[24] Kefauver, *Crime in America*, p. 86.

crime in the areas of civil and police power. Mr. Seritella was by no means the only symbol of these inroads. When Michele Merlo, head of the Mafia and the Sicilian underworld of Chicago, went to his last rest in November of 1924, the honorary pallbearers included a state's attorney, three judges, Mayor William E. Dever of Chicago, and Anton Cermak, a mayor-to-be. The funeral had been arranged, wrote the *Chicago Tribune*, by Alphonse Capone and another friend of the deceased.[25]

Blackmail and extortion were not the exclusive preserve of the underworld. Prohibition agents also preyed on distillers, brewers, distributors, and speakeasy operators. One official declared, according to Lynch, that "three-fourths of the 2,500 dry agents are ward heelers and sycophants named by politicians." In New York police power was perverted in a different way. The tactics by which New York City police impeded and frustrated the efforts of Federal agents were directed, he charged, by Tammany Hall itself, under the guidance of Leaders Charles F. Murphy and George W. Olvany.[26] There was little encouragement, four years later, in the Seabury Committee's evidence of "a corrupt alliance between some one in the [New York County] prosecutor's office and the racketeers [the district attorney] was warring against." In passages which recall Steffens, Lynch concluded his book with the adjuration that, "organized crime . . . cannot be crushed until there is also a separation of politics and the underworld. This alliance began with the advent of prohibition; and our aristocrats, who maintain their power with the untold billions of the bootleg industry, cannot be subjugated while their source of power remains."[27]

When the ostensible source of power was removed by the repeal of the Prohibition amendment, organized crime did not wither and die. Like certain strains of virus confronted with certain antibiotics, it changed, adapted itself to new conditions, and continued to thrive. Even before 1933, the gangs and syndicates had begun diversifying their activities. The so-called protection racket, extorting money under threat of violence, had been used to victimize whole industries. Later, disputes between industry and labor proved lucrative. Some employers hired thugs to intimidate unions and recruit strikebreakers. Some union leaders followed suit in retaliation. Both found that the camel, once invited in, would not leave the tent. A major source of revenue was gambling, with auxiliary activities such as communication networks to handle betting

[25] Lynch, *Criminals*, pp. 138 and 113–114.
[26] *Ibid.*, pp. 54, 64, and 68.
[27] *Ibid.*, pp. 219 and 246.

and race results. The problem posed by Treasury Department investigation and prosecution—which proved so successful in the cases of Messrs. Capone, Adonis, and others—was met in part by the diversification of interests and the infiltration of legitimate business, partly under wartime pressures, by criminal interests with more money to spend than they could legally account for. When the Senate Special Committee to Investigate Crime in Interstate Commerce carried out its work between May, 1950, and May, 1951, it became clear to them that crime in the United States had become big business. It was dominated by a national syndicate revolving on an axis whose hubs were New York and Chicago but much of whose motive power derived from places as far away as Miami Beach and Los Angeles. The New York and Chicago factions were led, the Committee said, by Frank Costello, Joe Adonis, and Meyer Lansky, and by what was still known as the Capone Syndicate. And behind them, stretching to other continents, was the Mafia.

La Mafia, first formed by Sicilian peasants in the early nineteenth century to resist exploitation by the great landowners, had been perverted into an organization which soon preyed upon landowner and peasant alike. Using violence and intimidation, it enforced discipline through its simple code of *Omerta*, which decrees death for resisting or informing upon the organization. The late nineteenth-century waves of immigration brought large numbers of Sicilians, and with them came the organization, sometimes under the seemingly innocuous name, *Unione Siciliano*, sometimes under the sinister one, The Black Hand. In 1891, the chief of police of New Orleans had been murdered by members of the local Mafia. When a jury acquitted some of the accused, local citizens lynched eleven suspected Mafiosi in their cells.[28] The Mafia did not again challenge duly constituted authority in an obvious way for more than thirty years, but from the late 1920's onwards, its menacing influence was more clearly apparent. In spite of this, Senator Kefauver could write in 1951 that, standing behind the local gangs of the national syndicate was "a shadowy, international criminal organization known as the Mafia, so fantastic that most Americans find it hard to believe it really exists."[29] But its activities, as set forth by the Committee, made it very real. These activities also formed a paradigm of relationships between crime and politics.

Charles Binaggio, wrote Senator Kefauver, was probably "the outstanding example of political boss and undisguised gangster in the

[28] Lynch, *Criminals*, pp. 10–11.
[29] Kefauver, *Crime in America*, p. 14.

United States. In Kansas City he was the leader of the First Ward Democratic Club, and after he had supplanted old Boss Tom Pendergast he was top dog in politics in the area."[30] A professed gambling operator, Binaggio was a firm supporter of Governor Forrest Smith, allegedly raising $150,000 for his cause and also contributing the 30,000 to 35,000 votes he controlled. But, Binaggio one of the "Five Iron Men," Mafia leaders who controlled gambling in the Kansas City area, was unable to exert his power sufficiently to save himself. When he failed to subvert the police boards of St. Louis and Kansas City to provide a better climate for the syndicate's operations, he met the violent death that befell many Mafia chieftains. The Committee revealed equally damaging information regarding the other end of the axis. It reported to the Senate that the Administration of former New York Mayor William O'Dwyer had taken little effective action against the top echelons of organized crime. It also noted a wartime visit paid by O'Dwyer to syndicate leader Frank Costello's apartment on an occasion when a number of other Tammany luminaries were there. Moreover, a year later, in 1943, Costello had forced upon Tammany Hall the nomination of his man, Magistrate Thomas A. Aurelio, to the New York Supreme Court. The ensuing scandal reached major proportions. "There can be no question," the Committee reported, "that Frank Costello has exercised a major influence upon the New York County Democratic organization, Tammany Hall, because of his personal friendships and working relationships with its officers, and with Democratic district leaders in ten of the sixteen Manhattan districts. Costello also had relationships with some Republican leaders." The former Mayor, the Committee further concluded, had "appointed friends of both Costello and Adonis to high public office."[31]

The Senate Committee's investigation and the book based on its report traced the workings of the syndicate in its multifarious activities across the United States. But two small vignettes were as revealing as the more detailed accounts. One concerned a police officer and the other a red-light district. Police Chief Gene Burnett of Granite City, Illinois, described the aftermath of his cleanup of gambling in Granite City: "my department and I have been more or less outcasts from the other officials of the county . . . I am known as the renegade of the law enforcement profession on the east side." Former State's Attorney Byron L. Connell, of Pulaski County, described the unsuccessful efforts of a Baptist body to build a new church in a red-light district of Cairo, Illinois. "After due

[30] Kefauver, *Crime in America*, p. 148.
[31] *Ibid.*, pp. 304–305.

deliberation," Connell testified, "the city officials decided that the girls had a prior right to the locality, so the church people . . . would have to build somewhere else."[32]

Eleven years after Senator Kefauver's book had presented some of his committee's findings, Senator John L. McClellan published *Crime without Punishment*. He had chaired the Senate Select Committee on Improper Activities in the Labor-Management Field, and in his book he presented some of the most spectacular findings in the 20,432-page official record of the Committee's work between January, 1957, and January, 1960. The annual cost of crime, according to J. Edgar Hoover, was $22,000,000,000. Deploring like Lincoln Steffens the public's failure of morality, Senator McClellan declared that organized crime could destroy us "without help from Soviet missiles or Red Army divisions." He traced the infiltration of labor unions by professional gamblers, racketeers, and gangsters. Investigation revealed corruption in unions ranging from those of garbage collectors and taxi drivers, meat cutters and bakers, to giants such as those of the garment workers and the teamsters. Of the president of the latter, the Committee reported to the Senate, "if [James R.] Hoffa remains unchecked he will successfully destroy the decent labor movement in the United States."[33]

The Committee's investigators uncovered the old interlinked with the new. There were alumni of the Capone syndicate and even a veteran of Detroit's old Purple Gang. There were cases of murder and arson, the techniques of the gangland wars of the 1920's and the protection rackets of the 1930's. And there was, of course, the Mafia. When on the night of November 13, 1957, a contingent of New York state policemen raided a suspicious gathering at the Apalachin estate of Joseph Barbera, they took into custody a total of fifty-eight men, almost all of whom had police records. As a group they appeared to represent the dominant crime syndicate in the United States. Subsequent investigation, wrote McClellan, showed that "whether or not the Mafia group exercised national direction of the crime syndicate, it was closely connected to top criminals throughout this country."[34]

Testimony indicated that the syndicate's executive level comprised eight hundred to a thousand members spread out all over the United States. They had reaped enormous profits from their usual sources of revenue, declared the director of the Federal Bureau of Investigation,

[32] Kefauver, *Crime in America*, pp. 170–171.
[33] John L. McClellan, *Crime without Punishment*, pp. 9, 234, and 59.
[34] McClellan, *Crime without Punishment*, p. 129.

and "With that money, they have bought into legitimate businesses or set up on their own." And there they had done business as usual. But an even more insidious threat was posed another way. Senator McClellan quotes Attorney General Kennedy on three geographic areas where "the major political leaders and figures . . . are being corrupted, and are on the payroll of some of our big-time gangsters and racketeers . . ." Crime has increased "five times as fast as our expanding population," writes Senator McClellan. Concluding with his own apocalyptic vision, he asks, "If that shadow sweeps across the land, bringing the darkness of a vast national cartel of crime, wherein present venality would be multiplied many times, what chance would we have in a world where Communism threatens at every point of the compass? No chance at all. We would lie helplessly in the grasp of the criminal leaders, who would be like an all-powerful Mafia, subverting and enmeshing the country."[35]

One result of the McClellan hearings probably unmediated by their chairman was revealed by John Dos Passos who, upon being asked if he had followed them replied, "Yes, several of the characters in *Midcentury* were taken from follow-ups of the investigations."[36]

Lobbying had matched the advancing tempo of national activity when the 1920's succeeded the war years. Prohibition had been imposed on the United States by an unscrupulous and determined lobby, wrote Schriftgiesser, but ironically, "in the end, after years of bloody strife and lawlessness such as the wildest frontier days had not seen, the same methods that the prohibitionists had used were turned against them and the eighteenth amendment was repealed."[37] Other lobbies were almost as active, and if they were not so spectacular they were just as formidable. When a resolution had been introduced into the Senate in 1928 to authorize investigation of utility financing, one of the first to oppose it was the National Electric Light Association, representing a total of 1,573 companies. Standing with this organization were the American Electric Railway Association, representing a total of 795 companies, and the American Gas Association, composed of 861 more. They were joined by the National Association of Manufacturers. To the lobby's satisfaction,

---

[35] McClellan, *Crime without Punishment*, pp. 235, 127, 284, and 291. The testimony of Mafia lieutenant Joseph Valachi before a Senate committee in 1963 supplied information on the structure of "Cosa Nostra," as insiders called it. If it was not the monster organization the Senator envisaged, it was the most sinister association of "families" in America.

[36] Richmond Moore, "John Dos Passos Gives Views in Interview," *The Cavalier Daily* (University of Virginia), February 20, 1963, p. 2.

[37] Schriftgiesser, *The Lobbyists*, p. 46.

the investigation was carried out by the Federal Trade Commission rather than the Senate. But when the Commission had finished its investigation it concluded that the industry's efforts to sway opinion against public ownership of power was so extensive that "no campaign approaching it in magnitude has ever been conducted except possibly by government in war time."[38] The National Electric Light Association alone spent more than $1,000,000 a year publicizing its point of view.

In spite of the enormous sums and wide-ranging pressures at their command, powerful lobbies began to encounter increasing resistance. When the utilities companies marshalled their forces against the Public Utility Holding Company bill (aimed at legerdemain such as that of Samuel Insull during the Harding era), President Roosevelt denounced their efforts to block congressional action. This counterattack helped bring into being the Senate Committee under Hugo Black which discovered that the Associated Gas & Electric System and the Committee of Public Utility Executives had between them spent nearly a million dollars in efforts to defeat the bill.[39] In compromise form it was passed in August of 1935. Two years earlier, however, Congress had overwhelmingly passed the $2,200,000,000 Soldiers' Bonus Act over President Roosevelt's veto. The American Legion and other elements of the veterans' lobby expressed approval.

The Legislative Reorganization Act of 1946 provided some measure of control over lobbying activities. Title III of the Act compelled lobbyists appearing before the House and Senate to register, to identify their employers, and to record the amounts spent in lobbying. The law was by no means rigidly adhered to, but it provided a badly needed source of information, however incomplete. The proliferation of lobbies continued though, through the Roosevelt administration. Interests as diverse as the labor unions, the Townsend Plan Group, the American Medical Association, and the real estate profession sponsored organizations in Washington, state legislatures, and elsewhere. And the battles continued. The National Association of Real Estate Boards struggled against the retention of wartime rent controls and government housing programs. Joining them were groups representing lumber, construction, and mortgage interests. An alliance led by the C.I.O. and including trade unions and church groups fought them. The labor lobby had grown stronger over

---

[38] Federal Trade Commission, *Summary Report*, Doc. 92, Part 71A, Seventieth Congress, first session, p. 18, as quoted in Schriftgiesser, *The Lobbyists*, p. 59.

[39] Schriftgiesser, *The Lobbyists*, pp. 67–72.

the years as the size of membership rolls and treasuries increased.[40] In spite of its efforts, however, the 80th Congress enacted the Taft-Hartley law, killed rent-control, and failed to produce effective new-housing legislation. To one newspaperman this Congress brought back "an atmosphere you had forgotten or never thought possible . . . you saw them, the Neanderthal Men, lurching forward on hairy feet—the sugar lobby, the wool lobby, the rail lobby, the real estate lobby, the Power trust . . . Victories fought and won years ago, like the TVA, were suddenly in doubt."[41] A different group fought for the Atomic Energy Act. Its passage in the summer of 1946—giving control to federal authorities rather than private power and utility groups—was owing in large part to the determined efforts of these lobbyists, most of them newly come from the laboratories of New York, Chicago, Oak Ridge, and Los Alamos. And the struggle and filibuster, sixteen years later, over space communications, was a not wholly dissimilar confrontation, with somewhat different results.

Lobbying is now more clearly and widely perceived than it once was, and it is carried out with more finesse. But it can still prove inimical to the interests of good government. This is especially true on the always more vulnerable state level. The Kefauver Committee considered the case of Arthur H. Samish, principal lobbyist in California for the brewing industry. With a $1,000,000 fund at his disposal over the years 1945–1951, he had reportedly declared, "I am the governor of the legislature. To hell with the governor of the state."[42] Certain political machines work with IBM precision while others break down or blow out; numbers of criminals are jailed, deported, or killed while others flourishingly transact business; some lobbyists secure preferential treatment while others fail to earn their fees. One of the novelists in this chapter uses as his epigraph the familiar, *Plus ça change, plus c'est la même chose,* and his view is far from uncommon.

The Types

The novel of corruption in politics differs from the novel of the Boss in one way in particular. The focus is not preponderantly upon the protagonist, but is to a more considerable extent upon the environment and

[40] See McClellan, *Crime without Punishment,* pp. 2, 17, and 203.
[41] T. R. B., "Neanderthal Men," *New Republic,* CXVII (August 4, 1947), 3, as quoted in Goldman, *Rendezvous,* p. 409. For an account of current lobbying practices see Lester W. Milbrath, *The Washington Lobbyists.*
[42] Kefauver, *Crime in America,* pp. 238–239, 255.

a whole complex of practices and relationships. Bosses and Knights both appear, but the total effect is more forcefully felt as a depiction of a corrupt milieu rather than as the portrayal of a single person working out his destiny within it. The contrast between Edwin O'Connor's *The Last Hurrah* and Stephen Endicott's *Mayor Harding of New York* (1931) points up the difference. In the first, the personality of Frank Skeffington dominates; the events of his present and past, the strategy and tactics described all contribute to his character. The second is not dominated by the personality of William Harding; he is a flashy politician but a weak man, in effect a figurehead. And neither the Boss of the organization nor the assistant district attorney who turns against it is a strong enough character to dominate the novel. All of them exemplify the corrupt moral and political climate which emerges more strongly than anything else.

Underlying all of these novels is the widespread assumption of many characters that government exists for the profit of those who control it directly or hire agents to do it for them. This profit is made through the diversion of public funds into private hands, with preferential treatment of favored contractors and outright sale of privileges or opportunities by government agencies, and through the creation of a political and economic condition extremely favorable to particular enterprises. The functions of government described in the old-style civics textbooks—those relating to the provisions of the Constitution, the Amendments to the Constitution, and most federal and state legislation—bear little relation to the functions of government as carried out by the entrepreneurs, lobbyists, machine politicians, and members of the underworld who populate these novels. One finds little of the pride taken by some Bosses in efficient administration. There is rarely even the familiar justification of graft as a kind of incentive bonus, so accepted is the goal of amassing as much booty as possible. Moreover, it is assumed that dishonesty in government springs from basic attributes of human nature. The novelist's implicit or explicit position, of course, is usually one of moral condemnation.

The view of American political experience in these sixteen novels has four related aspects. Like the larger patterns treated in these chapters, these four aspects form a progression in time. Although a few nineteenth-century novels had treated Congressional lobbying, the Interests commanded greater literary attention at the start of the new century. Later, novels about the Lobby reappeared. After them came the largest group —books anatomizing the political machine. Then, in a group of novels of recent years, crime dominates politics. These four areas are not, of course, like watertight compartments, for some of the novels contain elements of all four.

Among the earliest to appear are the railroad interests. One line or a combine seeks to control legislatures and officials in order to operate freely: crushing competition so as to charge the highest rates bearable while spending as little as possible. Its influence also extends to the courts, where political appointees will find for it in its multifarious litigations.[43] The oil interests are prominent from the first World War through the 1930's. The power companies and the munitions manufacturers are among the villains of the 1930's, 1940's, and 1950's. Bankers, investors, and financial manipulators may also appear as a pressure group. The Interests may sometimes be super-corporations, trusts, and later cartels which, almost like states themselves, extend across international boundaries. Hypocritically advocating freedom and virtuous economic conservatism, they will try to bribe or purchase members of all three branches of government. Segments of the press may aid them by falsehood, collusion, or silence. They are engaged in enormous projects and they deal in vast sums, forming pools, cornering markets, grabbing national natural resources. Government by business extends to foreign as well as domestic policy.[44] As the years pass, the methods become somewhat more subtle. Rather than garnering oil leases, the Interests seek lucrative receiverships and huge government loans.

The novel about the Lobby is an offshoot of that concerned with the Interests. Usually set in Washington, D.C., it shows how influence is brought to bear, how the former legislator, for instance, works toward

[43] An indication of the success of the railroads in securing advocates is to be seen in the concern of "the railroad senators" at legislation proposed by Theodore Roosevelt in 1905 (See Link, *American Epoch*, p. 109). The persistence of such pointed senatorial interest is to be seen in the area of foreign relations. John D. Montgomery notes that, "Individual senators and Congressmen sometimes become so closely involved with the fortunes of a particular country receiving aid that facetious references are made to 'the Senator from Formosa' or 'the Representative from Spain' " (*The Politics of Foreign Aid*, p. 221). For comment on the relationship between Senator Joseph R. McCarthy and the powerful China Lobby ("a hard core of hired lobbyists, influential friends, and outspoken advocates of Chiang Kai-shek"), and its possible bearing on McCarthy's charges against Owen Lattimore, see Jack Anderson and Ronald W. May, *McCarthy: The Man, the Senator, the 'Ism*, pp. 192–195.

[44] This activity was presented in 1904 in a novel better known than any in this study: Joseph Conrad's *Nostromo*, in which the influence of the American magnate Holroyd caused the American cruiser *Powhatan* to sail into the harbor of Sulaco, supporting the silver-rich Occidental province in its war of independence against the rest of Costaguana.

the special goal his employer or client seeks. Although he may have held high office, there is usually something of the confidence man about him whether he is a frequenter of lobbies who buttonholes passing congressmen, an influence-peddler, a "five-percenter," or a high-priced "consultant" ensconced in an expensive suite of offices.

The most typical novel dealing with the machine will examine an organization such as Tammany Hall. One sees the fruits of patronage in the solid blocs of votes which can be delivered with assembly-line efficiency. One sees the immoral use of power and the familiar sequel: scandal, investigation, and ruin. These authors cover strategy and tactics from the precinct level to the national convention—the bargaining, purchasing, and, where practicable, intimidation. There is often something of the *roman à clef*, as characters appear strongly suggesting Harding, Walker, LaFollette, LaGuardia, Smith, Long, or Franklin D. Roosevelt.

Early in the century, and occasionally even later, politicians were represented as intermediaries between the Interests and the underworld. A logical result of the increasing immorality was the intrusion of overtly criminal elements into politics. In the late 1920's they proliferate as part of the circumventing of Prohibition. In the 1930's, 1940's, and 1950's, individual criminals and gangs are superseded by national and even international crime syndicates. The varieties of vice—gambling, prostitution, narcotics, protection rackets—share methods in common: intimidation, bribery, and subornation. And these crimes are often made easier by a public fickle and uninterested until the problem is brought home through personal experience.

A predecessor of these novels set national politics in an atmosphere of moral sickness. It was Henry Adams's *Democracy: An American Novel*, which appeared in 1880. Its immediate subject was the progressive disillusionment of Mrs. Madeleine Lightfoot Lee, a widow come to Washington to ease the pain of bereavement by studying politics, specifically in the person of Senator Silas P. Ratcliff, "The Prairie Giant of Peonia, the Favourite son of Illinois . . ."[45] She charms him in order to use him as a kind of laboratory animal but finds instead that she has come to accept his doctrine of expediency. "If Washington were President now," he declares, "he would have to learn our ways or lose his next election. Only fools and theorists imagine that our society can be handled with gloves or long poles . . . If virtue won't answer our purpose, we must use vice, or

[45] Henry Adams, *Democracy: An American Novel*, p. 23.

our opponents will put us out of office, and this was as true in Washington's day as it is now, and always will be" (141). Adams ironically adds, "As he wisely said, the issue now involved was not one of principle but of power . . . Their principle must be the want of principle" (160–161). Mrs. Lee's eyes are finally opened when she learns that Ratcliff had earned $100,000 from a lobbyist.[46] Her anger turns inward as she convicts herself of really having been motivated by ambition, meddlesomeness, and thirst for power, rather than scientific curiosity.

Adams's main interest is this progress from self-deception to understanding coupled with the exercise in moral judgment through which Madeleine is put. He succeeds in conveying both the sense of the perplexities she faces and her own mixed responses to them. Adams does not employ as many characters in governmental life as do many other novelists, but he uses Ratcliff in their stead, just as Madeleine means to use him. The only possible extenuation of his conduct is a lame one: he is in part another victim of the delusion that evil means can be used without contaminating the ends they are meant to achieve. It becomes clear that one of the most damning ideas in this particular complex is not just that these contaminated tools are available for political tasks and might as well be used, but rather that they are actually the only ones which will work. Although Adams was at his best as a historian rather than a novelist, *Democracy* is the equal of most of the novels written before the Depression era and better than many of them. The book is filled "with the reverberations of the clash between Adams' moral expectations and the grotesque realities of American machine politics," writes Howe, who finds the novel thin but feels that it calls into question the American experience itself with the query, "in this atmosphere, can an intelligent man survive?"[47]

---

[46] It is interesting and ironic to note that Adams himself engaged in lobbying, both early and late in his career, though he was, according to Schriftgiesser, an amateur and his cause was the unimpeachable one of civil service reform. "The breakfasts he served and the dinners he gave were calculated more often than not to sway legislation" (Schriftgiesser, *The Lobbyists*, p. 15). Irving Howe takes a different view. He writes that Adams had written the novel after having spent several years in Washington "at the rim of the political trough, and if he had not plunged his arm in, he had dipped a few fingers. For the remainder of his life he seemed to feel that he could never wipe them clean, and he suffered, sardonically and a little self-pityingly, from a nausea he could neither release nor suppress" (Howe, *Politics and the Novel*, p. 175).

[47] Howe, *Politics and the Novel*, pp. 176–177.

The Interests

A year after *The Boss*, Alfred Henry Lewis relentlessly published *The President* (1904). It lacks the archetypal quality of its predecessor, but it is a period piece which repays a brief glance. The title has almost nothing to do with the novel. At first glance it seems another story of a Young Knight battling the Dragon while attempting to win a young beauty in spite of her tycoon father. But it is much more complicated. Her uncle leads his party in the United States Senate, and the Russian rival for her hand seeks American financing of a thirty-billion dollar scheme to ship gold from China to St. Petersburg by way of Duluth. The young man, Richard Storms, is even described as a combination Viking chief, Western scout, and slenderized Hercules. But the reader soon sees that this is not the familiar pattern of the Young Knight, but instead a conflict between two enormously powerful combines.

Analyzing this wild farrago for its attitudes toward politics and economics is almost like evaluating the symbolic play of children. If there are any serious assumptions underlying the novel, a fundamental one is that the government is so constituted that the judiciously applied leverage of enormous amounts of money is all one needs to achieve anything within reason. This is a novel of extremes. The uncle of Storms's sweetheart had served in the legislature of his state "for eight years . . . in the midst of all that treason and mendacity and cowardice and rapacity and dishonor which as raw materials are ground together to produce laws for a commonwealth."[48] The sender of four hundred bogus telegrams to members of Congress, he has "the countenance of a prelate and the conscience of a buccaneer" (21).[49] These extremes are evident in almost every one of Lewis's overcharged pages. Storms is no sooner introduced to the reader than he abruptly produces a woman's shoe and kisses it. This is not Krafft-Ebing but Boucicault, for this shoe has caused his beloved to trip, precipitating her into his arms and his life. If there is a dominant impression in the novel's attitudes and images, it is that the Interests are so powerful and the safeguards against them so ineffectual

[48] Alfred Henry Lewis, *The President*, p. 22.
[49] The attraction of the bogus telegram campaign did not pale. In 1935 a Western Union messenger boy told Senator Black's Senate Investigating Committee "how he had been sent out to solicit telegrams in opposition to the Wheeler-Rayburn [Holding Company] Bill, at three cents a telegram . . . the investigators worked forward until they proved that thousands of telegrams were sent to Washington—sometimes at the rate of 4000 an hour—signed with names taken at random and without authority from telephone books and directories" (Schriftgiesser, *The Lobbyists*, p. 71).

that almost anything is possible to them. Virtue's triumph occurs only because the more powerful resources happen to be used—as much for amatory reasons as any other—on the "right" side.

Fiction and films usually show the 1920's as a time for scaling new heights in almost everything: athletic performance, airplane flights, jazz, the stock market, and general prosperity. Two novels published in 1926 and 1927 showed corresponding record-breaking in the corruption of government by the Interests. Although each novel has two prominent figures in the principal intrigues, the bribery and thievery are the work of large numbers of men. The factual background is supplied by the events leading up to the Teapot Dome scandal of 1924. In *Revelry*, Samuel Hopkins Adams fictionalizes or withholds most of the names, dates, and places. In *Oil!* Upton Sinclair supplies them, so that his book can be read as a kind of key to Adams's.[50] The major difference lies in the emphasis. Sinclair pairs the corruption of the Administration with that of the oil men who profit from it. He describes corrupt practices in the cabinet without dramatizing them. Adams is more interested in the President and the way his henchmen and backers use him. Sinclair's novel is one of his Socialist tracts against the evils of capitalism. Adams's book is a story of political robbery emphasizing the spectacular, just as would a novel of outlawry in Texas or Chicago. Its level is raised somewhat, however, by his attempt at serious portraiture of a man caught in a job that is too big for him and only dimly becoming aware, too late, of the true nature of his situation. These differences emerge in brief passages which come rather like morals at the conclusion of both novels. A commentator in *Revelry* remarks, "Friendship in politics undermines more principles than fraud, and gratitude is a worse poison than graft."[51] In the last lines of *Oil!* the hero forecasts a happier future, "if man can find some way to chain . . . an evil power which roams the earth . . . luring the nations to destruction by visions of unearned wealth, and the opportunity to enslave and exploit labor."[52]

By the time *Oil!* appeared, Sinclair had been for more than two decades one of the best-known literary workers in the Socialist vineyard. If there was anyone who knew where the grapes of wrath were stored, it was this author who at twenty-eight had published *The Jungle*, which

[50] The same thing can be said of Adams's own *The Incredible Era: The Life and Times of Warren Gamaliel Harding*, which makes clearer the frequently blurred demarcation line between fact and fiction. For a contemporary account see Andrew Sinclair's *The Available Man: Warren Gamaliel Harding*.

[51] Samuel Hopkins Adams, *Revelry*, p. 318.

[52] Upton Sincliar, *Oil!*, pp. 526–527.

Jack London hailed as "The 'Uncle Tom's Cabin' of wage slavery!"[53]
The comparison of this muckraking novel of life in and around the Chicago stockyards with Mrs. Stowe's classic was not quite as far-fetched as
it might then have seemed. The impact of *The Jungle* on public consciousness was great, and the legislation subsequently enacted owed no
little debt to this tract London called "Comrade Sinclair's book . . ." Sinclair continued to pour out diverse works in a volume exceeded only by
such literary factories as that of Dumas *père*. (By the time he was eighty-four, Sinclair had published seventy-nine books, none of them ghost-written.) He once observed, "Readers of my novels know that I have one
favorite theme, the contrast of the social classes . . . and the plot is contrived to carry you from one to the other."[54] In *King Coal* (1917), a
mine owner's son discovered the squalor and misery on which his father's
affluence was built. After joining the workers in labor warfare, he returned to his own class to convert it. Through wartime conditions hostile
to men with his message, Sinclair continued to build up what Rideout
calls "a body of work which is a whole tradition in itself." And then, in
the heady "I Don't Care" feeling of the prosperous 1920's, "he almost
was radical American literature." When he published *Oil!* in 1927, he fell
back on the *King Coal* formula. And it was a better book. It was among
the most effective in the long list of works whose creator "has made his
life one long saga of St. George and the Dragon."[55]

The characters in the foreground of *Oil!* are independent oil tycoon
J. Arnold Ross and his young son, Bunny. Around them Sinclair depicts
the oil men's purchase of the Harding Administration and the debacle
which follows. Sinclair pictures exploitation of labor by management and
persecution of the Industrial Workers of the World. He describes sharp
practices by which the oil tycoons defraud oil-land owners and each
other. He goes farther afield than Adams in order to expose vice in the
motion-picture industry and the immorality of many of its stars. Elsewhere commercialism and student graft infest a college founded as "the
result of an oil king's resolve to manufacture culture wholesale, by executive order!" (395). Sinclair goes on to the Administration of Coolidge:
"a little man whose fame was based upon the legend that he had put
down a strike of the Boston policemen, when the truth was that he had

[53] Letter to *The Appeal to Reason,* November 18, 1905, as quoted in Walter B.
Rideout, *The Radical Novel in the United States 1900–1954: Some Interrelations of Literature and Society,* p. 30.
[54] Upton Sinclair, *American Outpost: A Book of Reminiscences,* p. 12.
[55] Rideout, *Radical Novel,* pp. 32 and 38.

been hiding in his hotel room, with a black eye presented to him by the mayor of the city" (440). At the book's close, a fifty million dollar campaign fund has made him President.

Sinclair argues that the Interests influence foreign affairs quite as much as domestic policy, asserting that one Mexican Administration after another had been turned out by the threat of American intervention.[56] A young leftist journalist in the novel goes further. American troops fought in Siberia, he claims,

because American bankers and big business men had loaned enormous sums of money to the government of the Tsar . . . the Bolshevik government had repudiated these debts, and therefore our bankers and business men were determined to destroy it . . . the creditor nations meant to make an example of Soviet Russia, and establish the rule that a government which repudiated its debts would be put out of business. (244)[57]

By the novel's end, J. Arnold Ross is dead, his enterprises ruined by friends who have rebounded from the scandals more powerful than ever.[58] But if they have not changed, Bunny has. Married to another radical, he sets out to found a labor college with a million dollars salvaged from his father's estate.

By contrast, the romance in *Revelry* involves the attraction of a beautiful and sophisticated woman for a politician belatedly trying to learn to be President. Edith Westervelt has some success in playing Woman as Guide to Willis Markham. Her friend, a cynical old senator, admits that Markham "really has tried to be decent and to be President the best he knows how, since you changed his horizons for him" (273–274). But the tide of scandal in which he has unwittingly been caught swiftly rises. He

[56] For a discussion of American intervention in the Mexican revolution between 1913 and 1917 (which at one point "involved nothing less than the cooperation of the United States and the [Mexican] Constitutionalists in a war against [provisional President Victoriano] Huerta.") see Link, *American Epoch*, pp. 164–171. For the bearing on this situation of matters relating to oil interests, see pp. 294 and 462.

[57] Link writes that 9,000 American troops were dispatched to Vladivostok in August, 1918, to rescue a Czech army from the Bolsheviks (*American Epoch*, p. 277). Goldman writes that just when "Wilson presented the Versailles Treaty to the Senate, the United States and other Allied countries were using economic pressure against the Bolshevik regime, and Allied troops were fighting Red troops in an attempt to overthrow the new Russian government" (*Rendezvous*, p. 266).

[58] Although Ross is a composite character, there appears to be a particular indebtedness to certain events in the life of Harry F. Sinclair. See Link, *American Epoch*, p. 247, and Adams, *The Incredible Era*, pp. 341–365 and ff.

escapes only by refusing to call for an antidote for the poison he has accidentally taken.

There are several correspondences in both novels such as that between Markham and Harding. Dan Lurcock is the real if not the titular Attorney General in Adams's book whereas in Sinclair's Barney Brockway is both. Senator Gandy is Secretary of Public Health in *Revelry* and Senator Crisby is Secretary of the Interior in *Oil!* but both carry out the most outrageous depredations. Adams makes Senator Welling the courageous and determined man who brings about a Congressional investigation; Sinclair gives the credit to Senator Robert LaFollette. Adams tells his reader that Lurcock achieved Markham's nomination in part by breaking a deadlock with the help of party leaders who wanted a more pliable President after their experience with Roosevelt and Wilson. But it was chiefly accomplished through the money and support of "the oil crowd," to whom he promised cabinet appointments and other concessions. One of Sinclair's oil men tells Ross, "I'm negotiating with a fellow from Ohio, Barney Brockway, that runs the party there. He wants us to take their Senator Harding; big chap with a fine presence, good orator and all that, and can be trusted—he's been governor there, and does what he's told. Brockway thinks he can be put over with two or three million, and he'll pledge us the secretary of the interior" (288). For both novelists, the President has been carefully nurtured by his mentor through legislature and governorship. He is valued for the docility cloaked by a commanding appearance and hearty good fellowship.

After the election, campaign pledges are honored. One of Adams's characters names the cabinet: "Secretary of Deals, Secretary of Pardons, Bootlegger General, Secretary of Office Sales, Secretary of Judicial Bargains, Receiver General of Graft, Secretary of Purchasable Contracts, Secretary of Public Health and Private Wealth . . ." (42).[59] Sinclair declares that "The Wilson administration had grown fat by exploiting the properties seized from enemy aliens; and now the Harding administration was growing fat out of turning them back! Five per cent was the regular split; if you wanted to recover a ten million dollar property, you turned over half a million in Liberty bonds to the 'fixer' " (424). Besides bootlegging deals, he alleges the theft of three hundred million dollars from funds for the relief of war veterans. Adams simply says at one point

---

[59] See Link for a brief treatment of President Harding and the "Ohio Gang" around him, "as avaricious a group as ever moved in high circles in Washington" (*American Epoch*, p. 251).

that in smart Washington chatter the White House is called the Automat, "Because you can drop in your money and get anything you want for it" (203).

In both novels the President is the least culpable in the saturnalia of graft. Harding is portrayed as reluctant to accept the oil men's money, and Markham never knowingly touches it. In *Revelry*, an investigation and scandal show Markham the plight of his Administration. He prefers to die rather than face the consequences. Adams depicts Markham's martyrdom as its "palliating radiance" falls on all those implicated, and "The tears of the nation washed their sins away" (315). In *Oil!*, Sinclair simply announces the death of "the old gentleman" (440). This contrast is symptomatic. At the President's demise, Sinclair neither halts nor falters, galloping on to excoriate further corruption. The oil scandals implicating the Administration simply provide another means—as squalor had done in *The Jungle* and the Sacco-Vanzetti case was to do in *Boston*—for belaboring the system he wanted above all to change. After the President's death, Adams comes quickly to his conclusion. He has shown the small measure of change in his protagonist, and he has given a lively version of some of the most spectacular and shabby episodes of the Roaring 1920's.

Like most of Sinclair's other books, *Oil!* combines fiction and journalism. It is vivid, just as occasional newspaper accounts can be vivid, but its many characters, incidents, and pages do not add up to a serious work of art. If one makes allowances for Sinclair's known bias, it becomes a sometimes illuminating commentary on the times, but it remains more a polemic than a novel. It is possible for a great novelist to start with a polemic and end with art, as Dostoevsky did in *The Possessed*. But Sinclair is not a great novelist. *Revelry* is a more modest book, and it is one whose capability is limited by the author's use of his material if not by his intent. Although Adams seriously explores his protagonist's nature and his growing awareness, he also exploits violent and sordid events just as, for instance, W. R. Burnett does in *Little Caesar*. One might argue that, by his own lights, Sinclair's motives were the purer, but his results, put side by side with those of Adams, are the lesser. The deficiencies of both these novels are due in large part to the difficulty of treating corruption with the accuracy which will portray it faithfully yet with the restraint and subtlety which will prevent excess. What is required is the kind of combined acuteness and reticence of *The Wings of the Dove* and *What Maisie Knew*, or the end of *The Remembrance of Things Past*. But these, after all, are James and Proust, and neither dealt with anything so obviously gross as the purchasing of pardons or the economics of boot-legging.[60]

The Lobby

The earliest nineteenth-century novels of corruption treat the lobby-ist, the professional solicitor who serves his clients by attempting to se-cure legislation in their interest or to prevent legislation unfavorable to it—almost always by bribery or coercion. John W. DeForest had gained notice with his war novel, *Miss Ravenel's Conversion from Secession to Loyalty* (1867). In 1875 he turned to the postwar scene with *Honest John Vane*. Like other precursors, it prefigured later fictional images of political experience for all its crudity. Vane earned his sobriquet by re-fusing a small bribe and denouncing its author. As a congressman he ac-cepted the lobbying business which came because of his reputation for apparent probity. It sometimes seemed to him that "the lobby was a cleverer and more formidable assemblage than either of these two cham-bers which nominally gave laws to the nation." He was cautious to avoid such obvious frauds as "the Great Subfluvial Tunnel Road [based on the Credit Mobilier scandals], meant to run through our country from north to south, under the Mississippi River, uniting Lake Superior with the Gulf of Mexico," but in the end he had literally sold his soul to an agent of the devil.[61]

The first novel of this century to treat lobbying at length was Harvey Fergusson's *Capitol Hill* (1923). It characterized the lobbyist and much of Washington's political life. Fergusson's protagonist, Ralph Dolan, pre-pares for his profession with success as a traveling salesman of fraternity jewelry, secretary to a congressman, newspaperman, fund raiser, press agent, and publicity director. Then he becomes executive secretary of the National Commercial Association in charge of the Washington office at

---

[60] See Howe for a discussion of James's *The Princess Casamassima,* in *Politics and the Novel,* pp. 139–156.

[61] John W. DeForest, *Honest John Vane,* pp. 86 and 104–105. In *Playing the Mischief* (1875), DeForest wrote of lobbyist Jacob Pike, "From his point of view, [lobbying] was a kind of public life; it was more completely inside politics than even electioneering or legislation; it was, as he believed, the very germ and main-spring of statesmanship" (p. 154). More than half a century later the American Legion's legislative committee wrote, "it must be recognized that Congress does not lead in settling questions of public, political, or economic policy . . . *Legislation is literally made outside the halls of Congress by groups of persons* interested in legislation, mainly with economic motives, and *the deliberative process within Congress constitutes a sort of formal ratification*" (quoted in Marcus Duffield, *King Legion,* p. 48; cited by Schriftgiesser, *The Lobbyists,* p. 51).

the end of World War I. The same skills serve him in each phase. "He was a born spell-binder, a medicine-man, a bamboozler of fools," writes Fergusson. "His strength lay in a grasp . . . of the weaknesses and prejudices of common men. His career in salesmanship had been a school in this art of demagoguery, which is the art of all popular leaders, except insofar as they are superfools and victims of self-deception." His easygoing morality makes it easy for him to accept what Fergusson calls the newspaperman's code: " 'His not to reason why, his but to write the lie'—if a lie it happens to be, as is frequently the case."[62]

Washington provides Dolan's ideal environment. According to the would-be novelist who serves as his foil, it is "a sort of soft-job paradise for boneheads. When they can't make a living at home they come to Washington and get a government job" (39). By comparison, Dolan is brilliant. He is also a good deal brighter than most of the elective officials in the novel, one of whom has a Lincoln fixation. Dolan becomes a connoisseur of congressmen.

There was the vaudeville type [writes Fergusson], who wore a white vest and a long coat and a wide black hat . . . These men seldom knew much about what was going on . . . Another well-marked variety was the ward-heeler who had been elevated to Congress by the boss as a reward for years of faithful service . . . Men who had made their fortunes in business, and had purchased seats in the House by way of capping their career with public honors, constituted another class. [But most important was] the little group of men who did nine-tenths of the work . . . lawyers who . . . were the conductors of investigations that ran for months and resulted in nothing but thick printed volumes, the wranglers over tariff schedules and items of appropriation, the authors of speeches that fill the *Congressional Record*—honest, earnest, hard-working men, for the most part, lost in the wilderness of legislative detail, eager to serve their country nobly, but determined above all to hold their hard-won jobs. (147)

Dolan's work for the National Commercial Association includes rendering assistance to congressmen up for re-election, who, once re-elected, are

---

[62] Harvey Fergusson, *Capitol Hill: A Novel of Washington Life*, pp. 59 and 131. The image of the press as being for sale is a constant one. Matthew Josephson quotes young and righteous Senator William Chandler of New Hampshire asking himself, "Can a man touch pitch and not be defiled?" (and finally answering in the affirmative), as he acted for the Republican National Committee in purchasing newspapers or in carrying out such associated tasks as paying individual reporters stipends up to $3,000 a month (*The Politicos, 1865–1896*, pp. 54–55, as quoted in Goldman, *Rendezvous*, p. 12).

then harassed by the Association for a return.[63] The Association itself "had been established during the outburst of so-called radicalism which took place in the early years of the century, when the muck-raking magazines were digging into the corporation records and the new friend-of-the-people type of statesmanship was replacing the good old-fashioned fellow who accepted his agency of wealth without deceiving either himself or his masters" (223). By the time Dolan achieves his $25,000-a-year secretaryship, he has acquired a wealthy wife (another Woman as Guide) and a sense of transformation: "He saw himself in a new light, discovered in himself a new power. He was a brave young knight going forth to save the Holy Grail of property from the infidels and barbarians of Bolshevism" (308).

Seen in the light of its time and measured against its contemporaries, Fergusson's book is a good one. The characterization is convincing, the view of Washington pursuits a panoramic, and the volume of incident and case history is large without being overwhelming. Fergusson describes a seemingly changing relationship. Unlike the situation in *George Helm* and *The Conflict*, the Interests do not own the politicians. In a kind of reversion, they buy their services as in *The Boss* and other earlier novels. This alternation forms part of a familiar cycle.

Marquis Childs's epigraph to *Washington Calling* (1937)—*plus ça change, plus c'est la même chose*—is borne out throughout the novel. As one character puts it, thinking of Lincoln's time and the present, "The men of power had the same role in the little play; sending their butlers . . . on and off stage to take the prizes; looking on from the wings with tolerant condescension or angry impatience as the surface mood of the play altered."[64] Handsome and dissipated Charley Squires is a fifty-nine-year-old ex-Senator whose lobbying and influence-peddling bring him an income of sixty thousand dollars a year. With cynical laughter he rejects a return to the Senate: "I'm serving the interests and I couldn't desert

---

[63] Dolan and his superior both resemble some of the Washington noncombatants profiting from the war in John Dos Passo's *1919*. Dolan suggests comparison with J. Ward Moorehouse, the publicist turned lobbyist and intimate of the great in Dos Passo's novel. The links between journalism, propaganda, and "public relations" were strengthened when President Wilson named a Committee on Public Information, under the chairmanship of former newspaperman George Creel, to create in effect a national propaganda agency. Before the war's end it had used the services of 150,000 people in one capacity or another and cost five million dollars. Such eminent publicists as Carl Byoir and Ivy Lee helped carry out "the first really full-scale program using the press not merely to inform but to manipulate public opinion" (Weisberger, *Newspaperman*, p. 186).

[64] Marquis W. Childs, *Washington Calling*, p. 254.

them so abruptly" (221). His seven volumes of scrap books make clear the sources of his influence: "In the Squires catalogue, for example, were listed, for those who could read the rather simple cipher, the heads of divisions, the executive assistants whom the Senator had helped to advance and to whom, therefore, he spoke with authority. A skilled accountant might have been able to ascribe a going, book value to the relationships that had come out of the Senator's career" (14).[65]

The novel's tactical problem is simple in essence but its solution requires a series of complex moves. Two millionaire brothers are threatened with the loss of a railroad—systematically and profitably looted over the years—through receivership proceedings. They will be able to secure a sixty-four million dollar loan for the road from the Financial Rehabilitation Authority if they can get approval in Federal Court. But the presiding judge has just died. For a fee of one hundred thousand dollars, Charley Squires agrees to work for the appointment of a new judge who will be sympathetic. To his opponent, Ferris Branolsky, a liberal lawyer happily able to combine zeal and an independent income, receiverships are "infinitely complex devices for robbing widows and orphans of the shares in large enterprises which, briefly, they had had the illusion of owning" (124–125). But this is a special case.

It seemed to him ... to contain, with the simplicity of a fifteenth-century painting of heaven and hell, all the relationships of contemporary society, the whole structure anatomized for anyone who could read the symbols. Money would buy a judge. Beneath all the sophistries of the law, the subtle legalisms, the judge would do the bidding of the men who had paid the money ... And at their bidding he would name the trustee in receivership who would be another puppet to speak out of their mouths. So they would strip the railroad, starve it lean, gut it of money, always money. Men in remote towns at distant junction points would be idle. Who would see or understand the intricate, far-reaching web of circumstances? (126)

There is a great deal more in the novel: the crooked Boss in the home constituency, the liaison man between politics and crime, the lobbying of

[65] After serving as President Wilson's secretary, Joseph Tumulty later served a number of organizations including four power companies. "One of the most engaging and certainly one of the most sentimental of the Washington lobbyists," wrote Kenneth Crawford, "Tumulty is a holdover from an older, now declining school. Knowing all who amount to anything in Washington, liking them and receiving affection in return, he gets results as a special pleader before Administration agencies, many of which are well stocked with employees he had recommended" (*The Pressure Boys: The Inside Story of Lobbying in America*, pp. 61–62).

the utilities companies, the general trafficking in judgeships, the paying
of political debts, the contempt for congressmen. There is the appearance, once again, of the shade of Lincoln, as Branolsky's intercessor
meditates in the Lincoln Room of the White House: "did Lincoln understand, sitting in the dusk, the unseen forces that had brought the nation
to Civil War? . . . he felt . . . that that knowledge was a part of Lincoln's
sorrow. The men who knew what they wanted. Lincoln watched them;
great creatures moving in a subaqueous darkness beneath the loud,
troubled surface" (252). This, Branolsky feels, is still the situation, and
President Winthrop's refusal to act seems to confirm this view: "You
could not, it appeared, rub out overnight a pattern of behavior which
had persisted from the first days of the republic, from the beginning of
organized government for that matter" (257–258).

In spite of the evocation of Lincoln and the fact that "a democracy
raised noble men and women such as John and Mary Winthrop to
power" (253), the emerging view of American national political life
emphasizes the sham. Not only the characters' assertions, but Childs's
metaphors as well make this apparent: Squires's real merchandise is revealed in his clipping books in a "rather simple cipher"; the case of the
railroad anatomizes the structure of contemporary society for anyone
who can understand "the symbols"; Squires (who has the grace, finally,
to regard himself with something a little like loathing) and his clients
have roles in a "little play . . ." (254). Democratic government of the
Lincolnian ideal is no closer to becoming a reality now than it ever was.
In this novel—perhaps the best in this chapter—as with the others treating the Lobby, the trappings of democratic government are merely camouflage which conceals the real identity of the figures who wield the ultimate power.

In a novel published more than two decades after *Washington Calling*,
lobbying served the purposes of plot from rising action through denouement. But John Selby's *A Few Short Blocks Between* (1959) seemed to
use the political milieu for purposes of plot, rather than the reverse. It
turned on the most virtuous political corruption in these novels. Governor Marion Byrd must send his illicitly pregnant daughter away because
he is about to launch a critical campaign for the Senate. Because his state
salary is too small for such emergencies, the strong-minded wife who dis-
creetly guides his actions accepts $25,000 from their son-in-law. Because
he happens to be a lobbyist for a traction company currently soliciting a
franchise from the legislature, enemies attempt to blackmail the Governor. A counterattack by wealthy and influential friends saves the situa-

tion. Governor Byrd then prepares to go through with the reciprocal arrangement which will put him in the Senate and the man he is succeeding in the governor's chair. The two Byrds look to Washington prepared to reform. It is true that they have been weak, the author seems to be saying, but the situation was desperate, the provocation extreme, all the desired ends good ones, and the culpability minor. "State pays governor little or nothing, and governor can't get money for an emergency readily," the Senator consolingly tells them. "I believe it's practically impossible to have an honest democracy. Honest autocracy, yes, granted an incorruptible king or dictator. Unlikely, yet possible. But Marion, look what politics has done to you and to me."[66]

This novel set in 1906 clearly makes use of the Woman as Guide motif, although here she leads her man to higher things by taking the lower road. Actually, the novel has another concern besides corruption. Much of it is taken up with the case history of the alcoholic daughter, Dora, and the amiable husband she has seduced. After the family sends them to Copenhagen for Dora's pregnancy, the reader sees the gradual deterioration which leads to disaster. Her death is presumably punishment for her parents' failure to meet her need, if not for their acceptance of the $25,000 originally intended for the whole legislature. In a manner of speaking, they are culpable morally while not being wholly culpable politically. Selby presents a series of dilemmas meant to be intensely serious but somehow never quite real. And in this world of special standards, the lobbyist (who is, after all, in the family) and his company are virtually angels in disguise. For, the state really needs the service that will be provided once the franchise is secured with the help of the $25,000 that changes hands literally under a table. Human nature is frail and erring, but the real villains here, it appears, are the ones who set the state salary scale.

Corrupt Power Politics and the Machine

Although James L. Ford's *Hot Corn Ike* appeared in 1923, its action, like that of Henry Adams's *Democracy*, is set in the last decades of the nineteenth century. But it accurately foreshadows twentieth-century novels of corrupt machine politics. The plot is labyrinthine, but the aura of corruption is the strongest single element in the book. Ford describes a Presidential convention that expresses nothing so little as the will of the people. Then he relates a series of back-room deals and a battery of

[66] John Selby, *A Few Short Blocks Between,* p. 214.

fraudulent voting techniques in which registered voters are paid to stay home and "tin soldiers" carry their properly marked ballots to the polls. Extra railroad trains are run so that voters can also cast ballots in two localities rather than just one.[67] Ford tells the reader that one of the principal characters later went to Sing Sing. This is the only instance in which justice is served. The prize goes to the strong and unscrupulous, and any resemblance between the novel's events and the processes of textbook democracy is purely illusory.

The seven novels which followed *Hot Corn Ike* described the same disease although the severity might vary and it might occur in the Northeast, the South, or the Middle West. One of the weakest of the lot was McCready Huston's *Dear Senator* (1928), a pretentious yet pedestrian account of machine politics in the Midwestern state of Ilyria in the years immediately following the Harding Administration.

Elliot Paul's *The Governor of Massachusetts* (1930) demonstrated the thesis that the honest man will do as badly in high-pressure state politics as the dishonest one and probably worse. The young lawyer who narrates the story is a disengaged man, but both his superior and a client of the firm become embroiled in politics. Neither is a match for the predators they encounter, enemies who are equipped with skills they cannot match and lacking scruples they possess. As governor of Massachusetts, the one-time client of the firm must grapple with a legislature dominated by pressure groups, a city administration which, one Republican says, "would come up in the night and scrape gilt from the State House dome." A rival candidate uses harassment, secret deals, and false and libelous allegations. The narrator presciently remarks, "I feared that justice, marvelous and imaginative concept that it was, would get its usual well delivered ax between the eyes." This rival, says the narrator, represents "a new race of crafty men who were seizing upon the mechanical improvements of the age and discarding, perhaps too hastily, the standard of conduct their predecessors had left unchanged in its essentials."[68] It is not revealed what evidence underlies the assumption that ethical stand-

[67] Steffens noted techniques less flamboyant but equally effective in Philadelphia: "the machine controls the election officers often choosing them from among the fraudulent names; and when no one appears to serve, assigning the heeler ready for the expected vacancy . . . the repeaters go from one polling place to another, voting on slips, and on their return rounds change coats, hats, etc. . . . It is estimated that 150,000 voters did not go to the polls at the last election. Yet the machine rolled up a majority of 130,000 for Weaver with a fraudulent vote estimated all the way from forty to eighty thousand. . . ." (Steffens, *Shame of the Cities*, pp. 200–202).

[68] Elliot Paul, *The Governor of Massachusetts*, pp. 232, 253, and 246–247.

ards were any higher in theory or practice in the previous age. Senator Ratcliff seems to imply in *Democracy* that standards were somewhat higher in Washington's time, and *Ward Eight* compares Tim Flaherty's Boston unfavorably with that of Samuel Adams. But there is little in other novels such as those of Lewis and DeForest to suggest a later falling off from a political Golden Age or to indicate that George Washington Plunkitt's assessment was wrong. This is not an area of American literature in which the reader finds the Adamic myth retold or learns that he lives in a postlapsarian world.

The fetid full bloom of corrupt machine politics was to be seen in *Mayor Harding of New York* (1931). The pseudonymous Stephen Endicott used the history of Tammany Hall for "colorful incidents ... to lend conviction to the tale." The publisher concluded his note, however, by adding that the author's main purpose was to show the kind of "graft and chicanery" which lay ahead if reform were not achieved.[69] The book was no novel of the future, however, but instead a *roman à clef* drawing upon many of the best-known figures in New York politics of the 1920's and 1930's. Stylistically, it seems another bad imitation of Hemingway. Its violence and the argot of many of the characters suggest outright gangster novels such as W. R. Burnett's *Little Caesar* (1929). In this it provides a link with the cluster of novels in the early 1950's in which political action is dominated by organized crime.

This machine is characteristically built on patronage, protection, and the minutiae which bind the followers to the organization. A local leader's harangue to his followers begins,

"Here I am, slaving for you, working hard, attending to your contracts [*sic*], and you sit around and stare at me! I won't have it!" That threat was serious, contracts being little favors—such as promotions for city servants, fixing speed tickets, and a million odd little things that a political club can do for its rank and file. (87)

The machine battens on many forms of graft. One involves the purchase of land and the awarding of contracts for a twenty million dollar bridge.[70] Dishonest judges and police have their own payoffs, and the reader is always aware of the bootleggers' contributions. Another aspect of machine politics is the rivalry not for elective office, but for the real position of power, that of head of Tammany Hall. The mayor is simply

---

[69] Stephen Endicott, *Mayor Harding of New York*, p. xiii.
[70] This kind of transaction was particularly favored by G. W. Plunkitt. See *Plunkitt*, pp. 3–8.

a figurehead: "We've got enough trouble without listening to squawks from people like you," he is told. "You do as you're told, and I'll worry for you. Is that understood?" (143).

One character refers to James J. Walker's mayoralty. Endicott's description of the fictional mayor might be a sketch of the real one: "Brown hair went back from a rounded forehead, and thin eyebrows made almost straight lines above twinkling, genial hazel eyes. Narrow shoulders, a slim, well-kept figure for a man of forty-five, were all part of the man: impressive until the mouth became noticeable. Lips almost always parted in a sophisticated secret smile, but they were loose and always gave Dan the impression of amiability verging on soft-headedness" (19). His rounds of activities recall rotogravures from Sunday supplements of the 1920's: tossing out the first ball at the Polo Grounds and then talking with a Giant manager who is obviously John McGraw, attending "a testimonial luncheon . . . to a transatlantic flier,"—a phrase capable by itself of evoking memories of Charles A. Lindbergh. Former governor Jim White just as clearly suggests Alfred E. Smith: "He was one of the shrewdest politicians in history; he had come from the waterfront to be Governor of New York State, and now he was in big business. He was tough, warm-hearted, religious and honest"(119). Endicott went to political history again for his reform candidate. A liberal Republican—to some a near-Socialist—is Congressman George De Angelis, who represents a New York City District. "A thick, squat, belligerent man with a shock of black hair that seemed never to have been combed . . ." (53). This man with shiny brown eyes who plans to run for mayor as an Independent is, of course, as clearly based on Fiorello H. La Guardia as Harding is on Walker or White on Smith.

By the end of the novel, twin catastrophes have occurred: the Depression and an investigation incriminating magistrates, lawyers, and police. A city-wide inquiry is imminent, but the reader feels no assurance that a New Day is coming. He is much more likely to take as symptomatic the last scene—reminiscent of the early art of the silver screen—in which the ostensible protagonist, a young district attorney, is killed by a gangster's submachine gun. The main business of the novel has been the portrayal of a political group whose goals are power and wealth. A few of the leaders appear to be men of character and probity, but most are criminals in office, men who cannot completely enjoy their prizes because pursuit may be just a step behind them. Out of Endicott's situation and characters might have come a superior study of the corrupting drive to power in a corrupt time. He produced instead an ephemeral work, concentrating upon violence in a style so awkward and imitative as to be an almost impossible handicap.

Corruption in the affairs of city and state formed the main subject matter of Frederick L. Hackenburg's *This Best Possible World* (1934). Tammany Hall again figured in the action, but this was a milder novel than Endicott's. The author's attitude seems to be the familiar one of cynical tolerance: graft makes the political world go around. Human nature being what it is, this *is* the best of all possible worlds, shabby as it may appear. The author follows half a dozen major characters in New York City and then in Albany. The machine weathers investigations, the death of the leader, and demographic change as Irish wards are re-populated by Jews, Italians, and other groups. A politician finally warns another, "Corruption is a very acute subject; it develops daily. Grafting and racketeering is the fastest growing industry in America."[71] But there is nothing of the same sense of urgency or alarm transmitted in the work itself, a middling period novel which contributes nothing new.

Something new is contributed, however, by a very bad novel entitled *The Sound Wagon* (1935). To the influence of the Interests in city and national politics, Thomas S. Stribling adds a treatment of New Deal policies and criminal syndicates. Industrial interests are described participating in the kind of cartels and secret agreements later to outrage the authors and protagonists of novels dealing with American Fascism and the second World War.

The novel is set in the early days of the New Deal. Unlike Stribling's novels of the South, this one begins in Megapolis (which resembles New York City) and shifts to Washington. The central character is Henry Lee Caridius, an egregious ass elected to the House of Representatives and controlled by an uneasy alliance of gangsters and businessmen. More than one character sees little difference between the partners except that the former are more likely to keep their word. Caridius' education begins quickly. A veteran congressman tells him that their main function now is "to trade with each other . . . lay off any fool idea that you are legislating for the country at large, there ain't any sich animal."[72] The assessment of the electorate is familiar too. Caridius' misgivings about campaign finances are allayed when a backer tells him that they need not be concerned about the political effects of "fraud, corruption or injustice. The people are used to that . . . No, what pulls them out to the polls is the drama of a solitary Saint George riding forth to slay the dragon of

[71] Frederick L. Hackenburg, *This Best Possible World*, p. 304.
[72] Thomas S. Stribling, *The Sound Wagon*, p. 163.

corruption. And when he's elected, the show's over and they all go home. And of course they give the dragon a rest so he will be in shape for the next exhibition" (150). A corresponding cynicism saturates the treatment of powerful industrial and financial combines. A journalist comments, "the Rumbourg Company has a reciprocal agreement with the British and French companies to keep out of each other's territories. The nations might break their treaty, but the munitions companies wouldn't break theirs" (252). By the novel's end the protagonist has been ruined and his close friend has been murdered.

Stribling's narrative technique, which might have been influenced by Dos Passos's method of shifting rapidly from one set of characters to another, suggests the grasshopper rather than the artist. The wildly sensational concoction of events in the gangster thread of the plot repels belief. The characterization is flat and the dialogue suggests Dreiser at his worst. Even the names ring false. The novel's only value resides in the view of the political process by which it is organized. A cynical lawyer-politician remarks of big business and crime, "These two directing forces of American life should learn respect for each other's power." He then adds,

here in America we have a new class making a bid for power. At present it is what we call the criminal class, but you must remember that nearly every great American plutocrat and great American corporation began their existences as simple criminals. Of course, after the successful issue of their undertakings they arranged the law so that they are no longer criminals. (256)

The Sound Wagon serves as a step in a progression. To the interaction of the political machine and the Interests is added the influence of organized crime. The effect of this combine extends now beyond city, county, state, and nation, as the powerful and unscrupulous Interests are pictured with joined hands, extending their dominion around the world.

The last of these novels published in the 1930's was much more restricted in its scope. Benjamin Appel's *Runaround* (1937) presented a sordid account of Depression politics in which wily and unscrupulous Irishmen, Jews, and Italians fight and betray each other for the patronage of their Manhattan slum district. In a foreword the author writes, "My politicians are typical. In other words they are all primarily interested in jobs, patronage and the tin box; and they all mouth phrases such as *My Friends, Freedom and Liberty, The American Ideal*, etc."[73] There

[73] Benjamin Appel, *Runaround*, p. 7. Again, compare *Plunkitt*.

are few who are able even to mouth such phrases, and collectively these characters are more unsavory than any others in this group of novels. But the book is much more competently written than *The Sound Wagon*. Appel's story, with its small and self-seeking people, its mean and shabby events, is considerably more effective.

No novels of corruption as such were published in the 1940's. These were the years when political novelists were concerning themselves with the Southern Demagogue, American Fascism, and other manifestations of the Far Right. The last two novels to deal seriously with corrupt machine politics were written in the late 1950's, and although there was in them enough to make a mockery of American political ideals, there was not the supersaturation with cynical chicanery and lawlessness that marked novels of the 1920's and 1930's.

In 1959, in *A Fever in the Blood,* William Pearson presented a Southwestern state's old-style, senior senator contesting the Democratic gubernatorial nomination with a crusading district attorney. The attorney hopes to bolster his chances by prosecuting a spectacular fabricated murder case against an innocent man. The senator attempts in effect to bribe the "Lincolnesque" judge to declare a mistrial and thus quash his opponent's best source of publicity. By the end of the novel the senator is dead, the attorney is discredited, and the judge is censured by the Bar Association. The honest young lawyer who is the attorney's assistant now has prospects of a political career and a sobering and disillusioning education in the nature of power politics. He observes the deals, lies, and intimidation. He goes through the fatigue and hysteria of a convention and a campaign. The reader accompanies him, and though the wrongdoers fail, the dominant impression from this technically accomplished novel is of an area of human experience where pursuit of power is an endemic disease which rots moral fibre as well as much else.

One of the characters in *A Fever in the Blood* had likened the attorney to Huey Long. James Reichley's *Hail to the Chief* (1960) went farther. Besides references to Senators Taft and Saltonstall, there were characters modeled after them. The governor of New York in this *roman à clef* was unmistakably Thomas E. Dewey, just as the chairman of the National Convention was quite as clearly Congressman Joseph Martin. And just as triumph for Eisenhower meant failure for Taft in 1952, so victory for general of the armies Lucas P. Starbuck is the last defeat for Senator Theodore Blair. References are made to Theodore Roosevelt, Woodrow Wilson, and Thomas Jefferson. Most are made, as one would expect, to Abraham Lincoln. Corrupt power politics enters this novel when two Texas oil men subsidize the candidacy of the young governor of Oregon. The journalists who comment throughout are, as usual, consistently cynical. And there is much to be cynical about. Despite the chance, chicanery, and conniving, however, two men are nominated who are honest and decent if not particularly intelligent.[74]

Although Reichley explores Starbuck's character through interior monologue, he does not use experimental structure and technique as he does in *The Burying of Kingsmith* (1957). It is no run-of-the-mill political novel, but it is not nearly so impressive as its predecessor. Moreover its narrative drive slackens after the convention, leaving the denouement to trail off badly.

Two novels out of eight make too small a sample for generalization. But there are fewer corrupt practices in them than in their predecessors. This difference may parallel the assertion in the novels of the Boss that the old days are over. With the growing power of the state, extremes may be less often produced by the actions of powerful and ungovernable men. Human nature remains what it has always been, but the system no longer allows the free play for extravagance which it once did, whether by individuals or even by powerful organizations such as the machine.

Corruption and the Uses of Comedy

The novelist who inclines toward comedy and satire finds a fertile field in the wide range of political behavior. Corruption can provide the moral indignation which serves as a motive for satire. It can also supply the excesses for the distortion or hyperbole of comedy. In four novels which appeared over the course of nearly three decades, the stylistic approach varied from farce and verbal slapstick to sharp satire and bitter humor.

Dermot Cavanagh's *Tammany Boy* (1928) was an attempt to combine chicanery and comedy which might have been called *Corruption without Tears*. Published two years after *Oil!* and *Revelry*, the novel followed the fortunes of a stupid man with a handsome exterior, a character much like the others who appear indebted to Warren G. Harding. Sized-up by his Tammany superiors as "a real Muldoon—straight organization man," he ultimately surprises them, doing well outside the

---

[74] General Starbuck is unimaginative but patriotic and idealistic. Also, he is not tainted, as are almost all the rest, by the conditions of politics. It is interesting to compare this character with another based on Dwight D. Eisenhower, the protagonist of Tristram Coffin's *Not to the Swift* (1961), who has not even the moral and intellectual stature of Starbuck.

organization as well as in it.[75] But though the author apparently intended the novel's humor to serve as a harsh illuminator if not a whip and scourge, it provided neither enough indignation nor enough comedy to compensate for inconsistencies in mood and tone, authorial intrusion, and an unbelievable protagonist.

Joel A. Sayre's *Hizzoner the Mayor* (1933) has strong affinities with such books as Endicott's *Mayor Harding of New York*. But Sayre, whose *Rackety Rax* helped provide the plot of Samuel Hopkins Adams's *Plunder*, embellishes the sack of his fictitious city with a comic murder mystery, dialectal and racial humor, and carnival stunts. Most of the city officials are dispatched—including sixty-five aldermen after the aldermanic dinner. The wily killer uses a lethal horseshoe nailed to a baseball bat plus suction-cup shoes for negotiating walls and ceilings. His disguise also incorporates a false face simulating a pony's face and ears. Finally revealed, he is a tiny, fey, homosexual whose murders are protests against cruelty to animals including insufficient horse troughs and "the check rein evil"(257). Politicians lampoon their opponents by making surrogates from inflatable balloons and silk-stockinged pigs. Negro evangelists harangue their flocks. A realtor instigates a riot with the cry, "Rilltors of the woild unite! Arise you wictims from texation! Let's be going down to Tsity Hull and show our friends goats can bott! LATS BOTT TSITY HULL DOWN!"[76] The deceased mayor is eulogized by the bishop as "a gweat man . . . a gweat, gweat, all awound man . . ." (253). And a rival says of the mayor's sponsor, "They used to say Charlie McQuilty'd steal the beads out 'n a rosary while a priest was blessing him. Beads! Why that old crook'd take the priest's PANTS. He'd steal his DRORES!" (228). The rascals are finally turned out only to slip back in, duping a dull electorate and still another front man with the façade of a new "NON-PARTEESIAN Party" (280). Much of this humor is obvious and some of it is tiresome. But here and there in Sayre's indefatigable use of dialect, onomatopoeia, and outrageous incident are flashes of comic genius which light up a spectacle elsewhere only shocking.

Rogues and fools among the bureaucrats and pressure groups were the targets of Dalton Trumbo's *Washington Jitters* (1936). And if their corruption was not that of the ward heelers of Cavanagh and Sayre, their

---

[75] Dermot Cavanagh, *Tammany Boy: A Romance and a Political Career*, p. 139.
[76] Joel A. Sayre, *Hizzoner the Mayor*, p. 265.

pursuit of personal gain at the nation's expense made them suitable butts for Trumbo's bitter humor. Washington in early New Deal days is Trumbo's Vanity Fair, where knaves and asses vie for power and prestige. The chaos of the system is ridiculed by the comedy of errors in which the protagonist rises from sign painter to high government official. Henry Hogg is not particularly talented. Luck, the support of a newspaper columnist, and useful naiveté carry him unscathed through the crossfires of bitter rivalries and the ambushes of powerful pressure groups. He nearly becomes a Presidential candidate before a plush sinecure takes him out of the running. The Administration cannot simply sack him, for bureaucratic unwieldiness has allowed him to grow prominent and powerful without ever having been hired.

Trumbo made wholesale borrowings from life. Just as Ed Mehafferty and Fritz Weener suggest Jim Farley and Felix Frankfurter, so General Dewey Bronson seems to bear some relationship to General Hugh S. Johnson and Willis Randall I to William Randolph Hearst. Extremists try to persuade Hogg to endorse their combined platforms—Dr. Burghlimit, dentist-author of the Burghlimit Plan; the Rev. Dr. Laughlin, founder of the National Association for Just Living; and Downie Sincere, deviser of the Millennium Plan. And they are obvious caricatures of Dr. Francis E. Townsend, the Rev. Charles E. Coughlin, and Upton Sinclair.[77]

Trumbo's contempt for the federal agencies pervades the whole novel in his caustic comedy of ridicule. The federal employees are not devoted workers (like some in Dos Passos's *The Grand Design*) struggling to help a stricken nation back to health; instead they are grotesque and self-seeking empire-builders. Their methods are gossip and innuendo, mining and countermining, log-rolling and hatchet-throwing. Passage on this Ship of Fools transforms Henry Hogg. Despite the sinecure, he cannot abjure politics. When he is questioned by reporters the old windy phrases

[77] For activities of Townsend and Coughlin (and the Rev. Gerald L. K. Smith) in 1936, see Chapter Seven. In 1934 Upton Sinclair had been an unsuccessful candidate for the governorship of California. In treating his Sinclair-character, Trumbo writes, "A Marxian Lucifer hurled from red heavens, Downie Sincere proudly wandered the earth, hinting darkly of treachery, producing slogans that were the despair of competent advertising specialists, emerging from each successive debacle with bright eyes and a book" (Dalton Trumbo, *Washington Jitters*, p. 184). A Marxist himself, Trumbo was one of those writing in what the Communist Party approved as "the revolutionary literary tradition" (see Daniel Aaron, *Writers on the Left*, p. 386). In 1939 he published a strong anti-war novel called *Johnny Got His Gun*, whose protagonist is the most maimed in all literature. See Rideout, *Radical Novel*, p. 195.

come to his lips: "He felt not unlike a reformed cocaine addict who, even though his will for rectitude is desperately sincere, feels a terrible, intolerable necessity for the drug the instant he lays eyes on it." Attempting to distract his mind by lettering an alphabet, he finds that he has lost his touch. "I'm not a sign painter any more," he moans. "I'm not even a man. I'm nothing but a politician . . ." (287).

Let George Do It! (1957) was the work of Foster Furcolo, then governor of Massachusetts, writing under the pseudonym John Foster. He showed how, in an aura of corrupt politics, a wily opportunist could impose his will on the electorate by a combination of his trickery and their apathy. One of the difficulties with *Let George Do It!* is that though George Clancy is a scoundrel who elects nonentity Pete Martin, the reader finds himself liking Martin and being amused at Clancy. He prints assorted campaign cards: Pietro Martin for the Italian vote, Pierre Martin for the French. Another Martin campaign card bears a photograph of an unidentified Negro, below which the small print declares Martin to be a friend of the colored man. George declares, "You are a racial candidate. That is what we've got to sell them. They're a racial group and you're a racial candidate."[78] In similar comic gambits, women are hired to read messages from Martin's mother over Polish and Italian stations—in Polish and Italian. "Let them Polish decide for themselves that your mother's Polish," he tells Martin. "We don't say so and we're not misrepresenting. We're only bringing your mother's message to them in their own language, and there's nothing wrong with that" (134). The novel's tone clashes with the jarring moral at the end. It is as though Furcolo wrote the book for fun, and then not wishing to be thought frivolous or worse, attempted to make it an object lesson. The book's effectiveness is also diminished by a severe stylistic limitation. Martin narrates his career, from inception to legislature, in a Damon Runyonesque first person. On reflection, one cannot help thinking what a primer the book would make for the aspiring ward heeler if he could use it and manage to stay out of jail.

Dan Cushman's *The Old Copper Collar* (1957) uses the subject matter of the Interests and lobbying for a turn-of-the-century comic extravaganza that leans often on farce. Despite gestures of respect toward moral rectitude, Cushman takes events that would have roused the old fury in Phillips and Sinclair and plays them for laughs. The basic situation is simple: Montana copper king Harvey Bennett wants to be United

[78] John Foster, *Let George Do It!*, p. 58.

States senator. So he sends his son to purchase the office for him from the legislature. The suitcase Fred Bennett carries to Helena contains $280,000. Before the novel ends, he has spent $700,000 more of his father's 200 million to secure the prize from the clutches of the opposition, the monster Cobra Copper Company.[79] Most of the humor derives from hyperbole. Legislators are wooed at wild parties where naked whores are squirted with sparkling burgundy. Fred discomfits the opposition by buying the hotel and turning off their heat and light. He tries to determine bribability by throwing $15,000 packets over transoms to see if the legislators will take money anonymously. Eventual success is followed by severe letdown. Fred is disgusted with the ubiquitous cupidity and venality, but he leaves the scene successful in love, and the tone of the novel remains preponderantly comic with the wild comedy of farce and outrage. This Wild West-Floradora-Tenderloin environment is rendered convincingly in a Western version of the kind of bacchanal described in the "Woodchuck Session" of a New England legislature in Winston Churchill's *Coniston*. And, like *Hizzoner the Mayor*, Cushman's novel is a forceful example of the response to corruption which is not scorn and indignation but rather slapstick and laughter.

Crime

Three novels published in the early 1950's followed violence and corruption to a logical end in which the political processes were controlled by criminals, through bribery or intimidation, for the simple purpose of providing favorable conditions for their enterprises. This situation suggests novels in which the Interests do what amounts to the same thing. In their case, however, the activity may be the development of oil resources, the sale of public power, or the sale of public transportation; in the other it may involve bootlegging, narcotics, gambling, prostitution, or protection rackets. In the one case, the organization has a corporate name, in the other it has none, although in two novels it is known as the Mafia.

The tough newspaperman who is the protagonist of Charles Francis Coe's *Ashes* (1952) lectures the young woman whose wealthy father aspires to reform politics:

> In this city there are about sixty thousand registered voters. Thirty thousand are Democrats. Eighteen thousand are Republicans. The others are classed independent. They don't vote in primaries. Of the thirty thousand Democrats

[79] The reader is likely to think, of course, of the Anaconda Copper Company.

... nine thousand voted in the last primary. Now, the city departments, including police, account for nearly one-third of those voting. Say that each of that one-third controls two votes in his own family. He votes for the machine candidate because that is a vote for his job. So do they. That just about settles the election before a vote is cast. Add the District Committeemen, the election officials and the frightened school boards. Where does your independent candidate fit? To offset that handicap he has to pull non-voters to the polls at about three to one over the manufactured vote. That takes money. Lots of money. The only time a reform candidate wins, is on a record turn-out vote. The average man or woman thinks about politics only at election. The underworld, through professional politicians, works three hundred and sixty-five days a year. They have plenty to work with, too. Millions and millions a year make their stake. It's worth buying and paying for and fighting for.[80]

He suggests that her father try for Congress, for though Washington is "a god-awful mess," it is less hazardous than their city. There, he tells her, is the Mafia: "Rich. Powerful. Ruthless. It really takes over. Money. Politics. Murder where necessary. It moves in, kills off local competition, pays off local government and operates crime as efficiently as your old man runs that plant of his. I think it's the greatest danger in this country" (32). After two twenty-year jumps, the father has become governor and the newspaperman has turned murderer, exterminating the local Mafia chief to protect the heroine and their illicit child. When the boy inevitably enters politics he informs the citizenry of "the measures he would use to suppress organized crime; to drive forever from the city the powers of corruption; once and for all to dissolve the dread alliances between criminals and public officeholders. The Governor had appointed him" (205). The last sentence exemplifies the novel's worst defect: its awkward prose. Apart from habitually truncated sentences (which suggest bad journalism or misapplied-Hemingway) there is dialogue so stilted and trite as to make the characters completely unconvincing. It is a bad novel, inferior even to the same author's *Triumph* of twenty-three years before. It is also one of the very few novels in this study praising the press.

An environment even more saturated with violence is the setting for Mary Anne Amsbarry's *Caesar's Angel,* also published in 1952. Using a familiar device, the author explores the disparate careers of two boyhood friends. Leo Stansky fights criminals both as county prosecutor and Democratic organization man. He is often disheartened, but early in the novel he consoles himself with the thought, "suppose this were Illinois,

---

[80] Charles Francis Coe, *Ashes,* pp.26–27.

where the gangsters controlled blocks of votes in the Democratic machine? . . . God damn the Democratic Party and the labor bigwigs in Illinois who let themselves be pushed around by a gang of hoodlums from Cicero."[81] Tony Maggiore works with criminals and then wrests control from them to become city dictator. Before he is killed he fights the national syndicate, partly for altruistic reasons. The omniscient author explains the evolution of this organization: "Somewhere back in the history of Mafia, there were self-styled avengers who fought in the name of Sicily (against conquerors), but the purpose of the Mafia was perverted long since and had degenerated as had our own southern vigilante bands into the Ku Klux Klan." She goes on to add that though "it had been absorbed by the smoother, larger business corporation, the syndicate, [this] fooled nobody who knew its bloody record" (149–150). The novel leaves the forces of law and order still struggling to fight the enemy on even terms. Although the violence is interlarded with Tony's love-life and a kind of authorial psychoanalysis, the novel never rises above the approximate level of the gangster novel. And ironically, some of it rings false as the effort of a feminine author to be very, very tough.

The most considerable of these three novels was William Manchester's *City of Anger,* which was published a year later in 1953. It began appropriately with a quotation from George Orwell's *1984* about the Lottery and the Proles, for the numbers racket, here in a city resembling Baltimore, fulfills the same function as the lottery in Oceania.[82] The city faces the bay in the form of a horseshoe: "The politicians had split the arc in two. To the east thick wards of Poles and Slavs curved down through the industrial complex of East Bay . . . And westward sprawled the foul Seventh District, in whose cramped warrens a quarter million Negroes lived, panting hard against the white rim to the North." Here politics and vice are one: "The entire perimeter was tightly and corruptly organized, but only in the Seventh did the voters buy themselves. They did just that. They paid the district machine for the trouble of bossing them, and the machine gave a little back and kept the rest."[83] Battle is joined when the race track interests combine with the Boss of

---

[81] Mary Ann Amsbarry, *Caesar's Angel,* p. 12. Although the action of this novel is set in 1940, on Memorial Day, there is a good deal that suggests the 1920's and 1930's. Racketeer Tony Maggiore's mentor is a bootlegger named Dutch Lehman. This name is, of course, as redolent of the gangsterism of the 1920's and 1930's as is the place name of Cicero.

[82] Manchester had displayed his knowledge of Baltimore in *Disturber of the Peace,* a biography of H. L. Mencken he published in 1951.

[83] William Manchester, *City of Anger,* pp. 1–2.

the East Bay wards to destroy the Boss of the Seventh. He is no inconsiderable antagonist on his home grounds:

Here the vote was solidly his: when the thousands of Negroes swarmed out of their cold-water tenements on election day, herded together by his men, Ben Erik meant free oyster roasts, and parties at the Central Democratic Club, and the buck outside the door at the poll. Here the leaders were blindly his; the legislators and councilmen were hopelessly tied up in the racket, and two of the three magistrates were bought and paid for, with papers in a safe-deposit box to prove it. (106)

The balance of power lies with the Police Commissioner, a rugged old patrolman and the only ranking officer not on a combatants' payrolls. His attack on the lottery, combined with a "fix" put on it by the opposition, brings about Erik's downfall. But there are other downfalls as well. One of them forms the other major thread of the story, as an illegitimate Negro garbage collector Sam Crawford goes berserk when his winning number does not pay off and then murders and is killed in the riots that follow. Manchester's publisher calls this novel "a study in the tragic effects of lovelessness." The author comments, "the flaw in most of these people is that their lives are without light, without understanding, without love. That is the kindling force behind the search of these characters, behind the actions producing the reactions." There can be no denying that this brutally stark novel is a detailed study in the tragic effects of lovelessness. It is also one in which the logical final step is taken with the criminal and the politician becoming one. Stylistically, it is the most accomplished novel considered in this chapter.

Configurations

Although a moral purpose presumably prompts the presentation of much material such as Manchester's, these works have a collective unsavoriness that in some ways exceeds even that in the novels of American Fascism and McCarthyism. In the great majority of these characters there are no mitigating factors—no idealism, no matter how misguided, no self-sacrifice, no matter how fanatical. Their progress follows to a logical end one theme implicit in many of the novels in this study as a whole: the theme of the person or group, in government or out of it, which will take any action necessary to insure its own well-being and financial success. It is a form of behavior which obviously runs counter to the rights of all others in the same society and in effect denies that they have any rights. It does not even have the mitigating factor of an ideology such as Fascism, no matter what terrible end that ideology was ultimately capable of reaching.

The progression of the novels in time roughly matches their progression toward excess and outrage. There is less violence and obvious brigandage in *Capitol Hill* and *Washington Calling* than in *The President, Revelry,* and *Oil!* Novels of corrupt machine politics, however, deal increasingly with overt violence and the breakdown of political processes until they culminate in the novels of gangsterism in politics in the early 1950's. In them the criminal syndicate, local or national, controls the political machinery. Alternatively, the political leader is himself a professional criminal rather than a politician soiled by his trafficking with criminals.

A mitigating effect in this progression is provided by the last two novels, *A Fever in the Blood* and *Hail to the Chief*. There are several possible explanations: for one, the same process of decreasing local autonomy and increasing federal control said to be altering the status of the Boss; for another, a shift of interest. In the late 1950's international themes are more common, and certain subjects evidently becoming passé, such as those of the old novel of crime. Whatever the cause, the treatment of the theme of corruption reached its peak in the third and fourth decades of this century. As it declined, attention began to shift to other kinds of violence such as that coming from political upheaval in both Western and Eastern Europe and the sharp reactions to it which followed in the United States.

4. the novel of the future

For I dipped into the future,
    far as human eye could see,
Saw the Vision of the world,
    and all the wonder that would be;

Saw the heavens fill with commerce,
    —argosies of magic sails,
Pilots of the purple twilight,
    dropping down with costly bales;

Heard the heavens fill with shouting,
    —and there rained a ghastly dew
From the nations' airy navies
    grappling in the central blue;

Far along the world-wide whisper
    —of the south-wind rushing warm,
With the standards of the peoples
    plunging through the thunder-storm;

Till the war-drum throbbed no longer,
    and the battle flags were furled
On the Parliament of man,
    the Federation of the world.

Alfred, Lord Tennyson
"Locksley Hall"

Although the story in the novel of the future might be retold at a date as much as a millennium and a half beyond the publication date of the book, as in Jack London's *The Iron Heel,* the original action which made up the story was usually set only a few years after the time of composition. The story's events might span as much as two or three decades, though they would more often take place over a few years. In contrast with the near uniformity of this formula, the political points of view varied widely. In two early novels of the fifteen examined here, the author's viewpoint is Marxist.[1] Marxist theory underlies events and Marxist terminology flavors the dialogue. Other novels represent the opposite end of the spectrum. There is, for instance, a reactionary view which regards the reforms of the 1930's as disastrous and, beyond this, an apparently approving presentation of measures and methods overtly Fascist. The middle range shows the attitudes of liberals mobilized against totalitarianism or reformers opposing corruption.

Generally these novels fall into two types: the utopian and the apocalyptic. A utopian novel here means one which tends mainly toward the presentation of an ideal state, although it may begin under conditions which precipitate violent change. Apocalyptic is not used to designate a prophetic novel, although several are written in just such a tone, but rather one in which the vision is catacylsmic, in which evil inherent in contemporary society is extrapolated into an anti-utopian view. The most striking novels of the future of this century—Aldous Huxley's *Brave New World* (1932) and George Orwell's *1984* (1949)—have, of course, been of this kind.

The most nearly common factor in these novels is the set of contemporary conditions out of which the action arises. At its mildest, it is one of corruption. At its worst, it is one of misery, oppression, and even chaos. Such circumstances are presented as an outgrowth of those in the early novels of corruption. The corporations and trusts, now supreme, have produced a society of immense wealth for a limited few and extreme deprivation—characterized by such abuses as child labor—for the many. The oligarchy sometimes shares its power with gangsters. All the organs of government are substantially controlled, and other forces, such as the press, are abjectly subject to the ruling and exploiting group.

Violence erupts when conditions become intolerable and a man (less often a small group) emerges to meet the needs of the time. He is usually a superman. Very similar to the Young Knight, he may be cast in the same mold as one of David Graham Phillips's young heroes. The super-

---

[1] David Karp's *One: A Novel* (1953) would constitute a sixteenth novel but for its setting not in the United States but rather in an English-speaking state with an Anglo-Saxon culture. Recalling of George Orwell's *1984*, the protagonist runs afoul of the machinery of a totally collectivized state and is broken by it.

man leads a successful campaign, coup, or revolution which brings him to power. He then assumes dictatorial powers until his reforms establish conditions in which free elections can be held. The reforms differ. They may consist of new legislation, the introduction of the British parliamentary system, or the changing of human nature itself. As one would expect, the superman usually has a young sweetheart or devoted wife. In her absence, his parents occupy this auxiliary role. But in all cases the world is never well lost for love. The job comes first, and the young hero does it even at the cost of martyrdom.

These novels often are charged with melodrama rather than drama. In some instances, they go beyond melodrama to science fiction. Some of the melodrama is prophetic, as one reads visionary descriptions of television, enormously powerful new bombs, nerve gases, and germ warfare. One novel's glimpse into the future includes a product called Protectosex: men's underwear chemically treated against radioactivity.

Though most of these novels are charged with melodrama, several decline from active narration into static description. The transfer of power may barely be completed before the story degenerates into report-making. The rationale is the portrayal of the literally brave new world which the change has brought about. But this description is usually as dull as the model constitutions appended to a few of these volumes. Several of these novels have considerable intrinsic interest. Collectively they are intriguing as a kind of fictional extrapolation of varieties of American political experience.

Nineteenth-Century Antecedents

Utopian and apocalyptic tendencies distinguished two widely read novels of the late nineteenth century. *Looking Backward: 2000–1887* (1888) was a utopian novel in which Edward Bellamy's vantage points were the year 2000 and a socialist utopia. His protagonist, insomniac Julian West, was mesmerized on May 30th, 1887, and woke, still a man of thirty, on September 10, 2000. The physician who discovered him in his sleep-inducing subterranean chamber provided him with a wife as well as hospitality, and in marrying Edith Leete, West married the great granddaughter of his former fiancée. More remarkable than this, however, was the transformed city of Boston, a beautiful metropolis in a planned socialist society. The all-powerful corporations having themselves allowed the government to take over their functions, life was highly regulated. Although all economic needs were met by the state, considerable freedom remained. There was room for organized religion, portrayed without the antireligious bias and anticlericalism character-istic of several of these novels. Bellamy's book, for all its pedestrian talki-ness, was popular and influential. Static and didactic though it was, it presented a prospect which appealed to the imagination of a large seg-ment of the American reading public.

Two years later, prolific Ignatius Donnelly published *Caesar's Column* (1890). Written under the Populist leader's pen name of Edmund Bois-gilbert, M.D., the novel produced a blood-and-thunder vision which in some ways anticipated Jack London and George Orwell. Its sources, however, were personal and immediate. Walter Rideout notes that Don-nelly had made another unsuccessful campaign for the United States Senate in the fall of 1888 and in the anger and frustration of his defeat, "turned to fiction as a means to bring his fears most vividly before the people."[2] Richard Hofstadter suggests as a source the "unusually cor-rupt Minnesota legislative session of 1889, when he was struck with the thought of what might come to be if the worst tendencies of current society were projected a century into the future."[3] Although the novel at times suggested S. J. Perelman rather than Karl Marx, it was partly based on Donnelly's first-hand knowledge of conditions among the farm-ers of the Middle Border.[4] His book took the form of an epistolary novel addressed by a well-to-do sheepherder, Gabriel Weltstein, to his brother in Uganda. Entering New York City—a science-fiction metropolis of the year 1988—Weltstein perceives the imminence of battle between the plu-tocracy under the barbarous Prince Cabano, and the revolutionary Brotherhood of Destruction, led by the equally sanguinary Caesar Lo-mellini (who suggests protagonists of gangster novels of the 1930's). When Weltstein tries to persuade the oppressed workingmen of the prole-tarian organization to adopt peaceful tactics, his audience hoots at him. The friend who has gained him entree tells him, "When man permits the establishment of self generating evil he must submit to the effect. Our an-cestors were blind, indifferent, heartless. We live in the culmination of their misdeeds"(175). The revolt destroys both the plutocracy and the fabric of society. When the quarter million victims are being immured

[2] Rideout in Ignatius Donnelly, *Caesar's Column: A Story of the Twentieth Century*, p. xvi.
[3] Richard Hofstadter, *The Age of Reform: From Bryan to F. D. R.*, p. 68.
[4] See Walter B. Rideout, *The Radical Novel in the United States 1900–1954: Some Interrelations of Literature and Society*, p. xvi.

in a concrete monolith, it is Caesar Lomellini, rather than his policies, who is pulled to pieces. Weltstein and his friend then escape via aircraft across gutted Europe to Uganda, where the groundwork for a brighter future is to be laid.

Although Donnelly used Marxist phrases, the destroyers of the oppressor-class were not clean-cut socialist heroes, much less Knights of any order. And despite endorsement by progressive leaders and other prominent figures, the book failed to interest pre-World War I American literary radicals because, according to Floyd Dell, "Donnelly had pictured Revolution in such romantic and absurd terms. What! violent revolution and bloody counter-revolution, with an accompaniment of famine and massacre! No—such things could not happen. We were too civilized."[5] Written in a "sadistic and nihilistic spirit," according to Hofstadter, the novel "affords a frightening glimpse into the ugly potential of frustrated popular revolt."[6] Noting the book's interest to the literary and intellectual historian, Walter Rideout observes that its author also succeeded in focusing "the free-floating anxiety that afflicts our time even more than his, the ineradicable nervous fear that, despite one's hope for the future, civilization may already have made the wrong turning and is now moving inescapably toward world catastrophe."[7] *Caesar's Column* was both wilder and more interesting than *Looking Backward,* although Donnelly's purpose was apparently quite as didactic as Bellamy's. And although its sales were not as impressive, the book sold well. The author and publisher agreed this was due to word-of-mouth recommendation, probably by readers holding much the same socialist sympathies as those who purchased Bellamy's book.[8] Neither of these works was particularly accomplished fiction, but with their left-wing stance the authors touched on fundamental political and economic concerns of a very great number of people. And casting their fictional embodiment of these concerns in the form of the novel of the future, they could portray both the best and the worst with an emotional appeal of great strength.

---

[5] Quoted in Daniel Aaron, *Writers on the Left: Episodes in American Literary Communism,* pp. 104–105.

[6] Hofstadter, *Reform,* p. 70.

[7] Rideout, in Donnelly, *Caesar's Column,* p. xxxi.

[8] Rideout, in Donnelly, *Caesar's Column,* p. xx. *The Golden Bottle,* which Donnelly published in 1892, had rather less of Armageddon and more of the millennium. His imagination still untrammelled, the Populist leader portrayed a Kansan who turned base metal to gold and as President foiled domestic bankers and foreign tyrants in liberating Europe and establishing world government.

The Utopian Dream

Six novels appearing during the years between 1908 and 1949 saw the future in terms of society's improvement, if not its perfectibility as Bellamy had done. Unlike him, each of these authors presented the development of a new mode of government as arising out of deep-rooted discontent and as being precipitated usually through violence. The first of these was C. A. Steere's *When Things Were Doing* (1908), which brought in the New Day by means of a long dream sequence on Christmas Night. The talky, episodic novel follows muckraker Bill Tempest as the Socialist Board of Strategy suggests that he assume the Presidency after a planned coup. (His break with the Republicans as a young man had come from "the rugged personal honesty of the neophyte who for mere graft and boodle could no more descend to their infamous level than the waters of Niagara could run back over the precipice.")[9] After the bloodless revolution, the Socialists make available to their brothers in Russia and Germany a discovery called *sizmos,* "an explosive . . . so fearful . . . that . . . a five-gallon jar of it contains enough kinetic force . . . to split Manhattan Island from east to west as by a terrific earthquake" (32).[10] The book degenerates into a series of long reports through one cardboard persona or another. In five years a cooperative commonwealth called Altruria has emerged, one of several in the two Americas.[11] Some passages today produce an exquisitely ironic effect:

In Southern California the gods have been exceedingly kind to mortal manikins, but these same manikins have been even kinder to themselves. They have simply networked the whole region with splendid boulevards, zip-car tracks (they call the new fangled trolley a zip-car) and railroads of enormous power and speed. It is a country of magnificent distances, charming vistas and idealistic, harmonious group life—a country where arboriculture, floriculture, tiviculture and horticulture have reached the apex of excellence, where flourish to a perfection scarcely attainable elsewhere the orange, lemon, olive, fig, grape,

[9] C. A. Steere, *When Things Were Doing,* p. 24.

[10] In the end pages of the novel the publisher advertised "Books of Marxian Socialism," one division of which was described as a "Library of Science for the Workers." It is interesting to note, however, that, like Donnelly, Steere speaks not of the worker, but of the "workingman." This terminology is used by Lionel Trilling in *The Middle of the Journey* to differentiate between the literature of the socialism of the late nineteenth century and that of the Communist movement in the twentieth.

[11] This is apparently a direct borrowing from William Dean Howells's *A Traveler from Altruria* (1894).

and numerous other fruits of tree and field and vine. It is, moreover, the autoists' heaven on earth. (249)

This amateurish novel is a mine of clichés with nothing to redeem its gaucheries of style and structure. The ending is somehow appropriate to these lamentable failures. It has all been a dream, brought on by steam heat and Roman punch.

More sober, and dull, was a novel published anonymously four years later under the title *Philip Dru, Administrator,* and subtitled *A Story of Tomorrow, 1920–1935.* Were it not for the author's identity, his book would be utterly forgotten. He was an influential Texas politician called Colonel Edward Mandell House. In the year his novel was published, he was very much concerned with another task: securing the Democratic presidential nomination for Woodrow Wilson.[12] House was not substantially more imaginative than his fellow fictional utopists. When the weight of the Interests, the plutocracy, and bossism, finally becomes unendurable, the most brilliant young tactician in America (a West Pointer invalided out of the Army for eye trouble) takes command of the dissident forces. Philip Dru sweeps on to victory then abdicates his dictatorial yet paternal rule when the nation's internal health and international position have been made secure. House was one of those who favored a substantially unicameral system. Dru gives the Republic a new Constitution which will produce something substantially like the British parliamentary system. Then, in a passage that might have been done by Winston Churchill had he written in primer sentences, Dru and his bride sail away through San Francisco's Golden Gate. House's style drained all vitality and verisimilitude from narrated action. Moreover, he had an unerring instinct for the cliché. Some passages have the ring of Nathanael West at his most satiric in *A Cool Million* (1934). But as with Steere, the source is simplicity rather than art. This appears to be characteristic. As the superior artist most often treats the corrupt politician rather than the upright one, so the utopian writer usually falls short of his contemporary whose vision is apocalyptic.

Twenty years elapsed before the appearance of the next utopian novel of the future. But while offering more words, it could muster—impossible though it may seem—even less literary skill. Constant Spenser, the hero

---

[12] Colonel House performed many assignments for President Wilson. He helped draft the Treaty of Versailles and draw up the Covenant of the League of Nations. Professor Cyril E. Black of Princeton University has pointed out to me that some of the reforms Dru effects found their way into Woodrow Wilson's programs.

of Frederick Palmer's *So a Leader Came* (1932), combines attributes of Jesus Christ, George Washington, Abraham Lincoln, and Tarzan of the Apes. He has been consecrated to his special task since his birth. During his childhood, his father pictures him questioning bishops, and the reader sees him swinging from a tree into his parents' room. Later he is equally adept at debating and government. Distinguishing himself gallantly in World War I, he subsequently engages in a series of activities which suggest *Tom Swift on a Ranch* or *Tom Swift in Brazil.*

The country's presidential nominating system is by now like "the choice of the Doge in the declining days of the Venetian Republic."[13] After leading a march on Washington, "Connie" assumes personal control of the government despite two bullet wounds. His paternalistic Administration is as successful as Philip Dru's (complete with copy of the British parliamentary system), but he is not as lucky as the young soldier. As he walks home from the White House for the last time, he and his body-guard (the faithful Spud) are fatally shot by a man "with a maniacal glint, which concentrated the survival of an ancient gangster grudge." The noble martyr is true to form: "Steadying himself against the house wall, Connie managed to turn his bleeding side away from Spud, and to put all his heart into his smile" (366–367).

This author's metier clearly was not fiction. But curiously and fortuitously he has made his paper cut-out protagonist in the mythic image of the god who dies for his people. Connie Spenser, with his bleeding side, is a poor and distant relation of Frazer's vegetation god, Weston's Fisher King, and Eliot's Hanged Man. The fundamental judgment is, however, quite clear. Twenty years earlier, in *The Citadel,* Congressman John Garwood had advocated a government modeled after the British form. Palmer dilated upon this view in *So a Leader Came,* mixed with it something of the Superman concept that was so attractive to David Graham Phillips and Jack London, and then embalmed it all in a slapdash plot stuck together with some of the most amateurish fiction-writing of the decade.

A year later, in 1933, a pro-Fascist novel appeared with no name on the title page. *Gabriel over the White House* was the work of Thomas Frederic Tweed, and it was built upon the idea of possession of spirits. Judson Cumming Hammond was another figure drawn in the image of Warren Gamaliel Harding. He changes so drastically upon recovery from an accident-induced coma that his secretary confides to the narra-

---

[13] Frederick Palmer, *So a Leader Came,* p. 84.

tor, Hammond's confidential secretary, her theory that God has sent Gabriel to do for Hammond what he did for Daniel. With Europe a ruined chaos, South America in turmoil, and the United States in deep depression, Hammond institutes "The New Order." Free of the dissolved Congress, he establishes a National Reconstruction Corps, abandons the gold standard, and increases Supreme Court membership to fifteen. "The Green Jackets," a small *carabinieri*-like organization of crack shots mounted on motorcycles, confiscate weapons and take arrested hoodlums to Ellis Island, "a special concentration camp," where most of them are quickly despatched.[14]

Near the end of his Presidency, Hammond almost single-handedly forges a successful UN, "the fulfillment of an economic Philosophy, the teachings of which had first been heard two thousand years before on the shores of Galilee" (238). But a knock in the head by a revengeful gangster also knocks Gabriel out of Hammond. In an about-face which seems like an authorial disclaimer inserted as an afterthought, Hammond then tells his cabinet, "some of the things I shall be held responsible for are evil, definitely evil—outrages against that spirit of individualism and national independence which is our proudest attribute. Liberty has been destroyed and the Constitution I swore to uphold has been practically scrapped"(286). When the horrified cabinet declares him unfit, a rage carries him off permanently. Though his staff dissolves in tears, one manages haltingly to articulate, "it . . . is . . . better . . so"(308).

Most of this is familiar—national corruption, world-wide misery and chaos, the bracing effects of a new hand at the helm. It is also a badly written novel in which no one is real or convincing. Its only claim to one's attention is that, despite the lip service paid to "individualism" and "independence" in Hammond's last speech, the largest portion of the book is devoted to the formation of a corporate state. It is fascism, whether administered by Hammond or by God through Gabriel, and the author approves of it heartily.

The last of the old-style utopian novels appeared in 1935. John Francis Goldsmith made clear his approach by using as epigraph the lines from "Locksley Hall" quoted at the beginning of this chapter. The narrator of *President Randolph as I Knew Him* had also served as Presidential secretary. Writing in 1970, he begins his account of the historic events of 1956–1967 by tracing Randolph's ancestry back three generations.

---

[14] Thomas Frederic Tweed, *Gabriel over the White House: A Novel of the Presidency*, p. 186.

He describes his college chum at the start of his career. Then, in one
of the novel's liveliest passages (one likely to bring tears to the eyes of
a real politician), Randolph expatiates upon his motives:

"I love the art of political strategy, the matching of wits, the out-bluffing
bluffers, the staking of courage against fear, the hurried conferences of the
leaders, the mad advance of the bandwagon, the early returns, the landslides,
and all the excitement the great game gives . . . But above the fun and romance
of a campaign, I see in politics the opportunity for unlimited service to my
fellow men. I'm off, old man, I'm off . . ."[15]

And there is little in Randolph's state and national officeholding to dis-
pel the fun and romance or minimize "the opportunity for unlimited
service." Being "endowed with a superhuman energy and stamina"
when "fighting for a cause" (101), President Randolph reforms his
party, brings in domestic prosperity and tranquility, provides for the
common defense (with a 100,000-plane air force), and pacifies belliger-
ents in Europe and Asia. Although no radical ("There is no material
difference between a system of large collectivistic monopolies and trusts
and a system of communism. The net result of either is slavery for the
common man." [161]), he works for a United Nations of the World. And
when in 1961 a blue flag bearing a white disc rises over the capital in
Luxembourg, the chief officer—to no one's surprise—is "the most genial
President since Harding, the best dressed since Coolidge, the most intelligent since Wilson, and the handsomest of them all" (164). The union
of Western states succeeds (Russia is excluded), carrying out police
actions, holding war-crimes trials, and working toward a common market. By 1966,

with the passing of nationalism and the desire to be economically self-sufficient,
tariff barriers on the Continent were fast melting away, and the standards of
living and of education were improving perceptibly. Today, although American tariffs are imposed upon less than one-half the number of articles subject
to duty ten years ago, American industrial, agricultural, and commercial activity is being maintained at the most prosperous levels of all time. (413).

A year later, the master architect is carried off by a coronary attack. After
an account of the aftermath, the volume is concluded with a twenty-
eight page *Constitution of the United Nations of the World.*

The reader is impressed with the earnest industry that obviously went

[15] John Francis Goldsmith, *President Randolph as I Knew Him: An Account
of the Historic Events of the 1950's and 1960's Written from the Personal Experience of the Secretary to the President,* p. 68.

into the research and writing which produced this long novel. He remarks too, the accurate prophecies, including, among others, campaigning by television. But his dominant impression is likely to be that this serious work, for all the effort it represents, hardly seems like fiction at all, but rather like a long and uninspired recounting of a vast case history. The breath of life is in neither the story nor the characters. And when it palls, it does not simply pall: it becomes a soporific.

Mary McCarthy's *The Oasis* (1949) was the most serious of the satiric novels in this study and one of those least close to institutional, elective politics. The task she set herself was the depiction of a New England utopian colony of fifty members, divided at the outset between the "realists" and the "purists." Begun by an anarchist founder who might conceivably reappear, it is fated ultimately to fail. She plays her satiric wit over the shortcomings of this tight group possessing a high degree of political sophistication and communicating through esoteric jargon. Ludicrously caught between past and present in their utopian ground rules, they are startled by early success, too disengaged for strong commitment, and secretly convinced of the inevitability of failure. The two factions can compromise on some matters.

Agreeing, in principle, that the machine was to be distrusted, they had nevertheless voted to use in their experiment the bicycle, the carpetsweeper, and the sewing machine, any machine, in fact, to which a man contributed his own proportionate share of exertion and which tired him like the plough or the hoe. The bath, the flush toilet, all forms of plumbing they tolerated, but they opposed, at least for the time being, the installation of an electric power-plant . . .[16]

In other matters, such as the desirability of the Founder's presence, they differ. Although the realists hope, in their hearts, for the kind of success never achieved at Oneida or Brook Farm, "they shrank from a definition of the colony which committed them to any positive belief. Conspicuous goodness, like the Founder's, filled them with uneasy embarrassment; they looked upon it as a form of simple-mindedness on a par with vegetarianism, and would have refused admission to Heaven on the ground that it was full of greenhorns and cranks" (15).

The novel ends with a "Breughelesque" vision of future activities in the colony in the months or years left before its ultimate failure. It comes, just before sleep, to a brilliant young woman described as a Marxist realist and an anarchist purist. There amidst the manifold activities of

[16] Mary McCarthy, *The Oasis*, p. 3.

the individualists, dreamers, cranks, and frustrated leaders she sees "the average man stealing out of one corner of the picture, a guilty finger to his lips"(181). Passages such as this, contrasting so strongly with the style, tone, and mood of novels like those of West and Trumbo, characterize the sophistication of Mary McCarthy's treatment of this perennial phenomenon in man's political experience—the attempt to build a utopia—and illumines both character and action with a subtly satiric comedy of ideas.

Whodunit?

The influence of the Dashiell Hammett school of modern American fiction was clearly at work in a novel of the future neither utopian nor apocalyptic. *The President Vanishes* (1934) was another anonymous novel. Complete with ponderously retouched photographs of Capital scenes, protest marchers, and mobilized troops, it is an isolationist mystery story. The President, struggling against financiers and industrialists to keep the United States free of a world war, needs a short delay before giving a speech to mobilize opinion for keeping the country uninvolved. Some of this rough-and-ready novel's overtones are familiar. Communists are fighting native Fascists. They are the Gray Shirts, with a fanatic leader named Lincoln Lee, whose catchword is not "Heil" but "Union."

This first-person narration of a White House Secret Service guard is filled with often unmotivated toughness which at times foreshadows the Mickey Spillane school of fiction. "A war would be a tame show after these three days," he sums up on the novel's last page. "In the space of three little days I've shot a billionaire in the leg, bound and gagged a President of the United States, and socked a beautiful woman in the jaw."[17] The novel deserves inclusion if only as an example of the kind of mutation the political novel can undergo, as a writer here links Fascism, Communism, the Interests, and violence to provide a political background for a literary form which, tracing its ancestry back to Poe and Conan Doyle, is almost as old as the political novel.

The Apocalyptic Vision

The first apocalyptic novel of the century came in 1908, the same year which saw the appearance of Steere's *When Things Were Doing*. It came

[17] Anonymous, *The President Vanishes,* p. 286.

from a militant socialist with a working-class background. Jack London was already famous. The former tramp-turned-journalist had gained wide notice with *The Call of the Wild* in 1903. This story of atavism in the Alaskan snows was followed a year later by *The Seawolf*, a Nietzschean tale of an extraordinary mariner. A number of short stories revealed London's Socialist convictions and revolutionary fervor, but in 1908 he produced in *The Iron Heel*, a "minor revolutionary classic," which became proof for generations of radicals that a proletarian could write popular and vigorous fiction. It was fiction in which—no matter what the author's class status and fundamental ideology—he had still "made good for the Revolution."[18] Although *The Iron Heel* is dated 2632 A.D., in the era of the Brotherhood of Man, it is London's early twentieth-century vision of blood, fire, and destruction.[19] It is also the dreadful reckoning to which George Helm and others refer so ambiguously. The action in the "Everhard Manuscript" which forms the bulk of the novel covers the period from 1912 to 1932, but the whole document is presented as being edited and annotated by Anthony Meredith in the twenty-seventh century, four centuries after the Brotherhood of Man has succeeded three centuries of domination by the oligarchy. This is, of course, London's device for having things both ways: the hot immediacy of revolution plus the documentary effect of footnotes with substantiating evidence. A model was close enough at hand in the abortive Russian Revolution of 1905. London apparently drew also on W. J. Ghent's view of capitalism set forth in *Our Benevolent Feudalism* three years before.[20]

The hero, revolutionist Ernest Everhard, is taken from the same mold as Richard Storms and Joshua Craig, for he is "a superman, a blond beast such as Nietzsche has described."[21] Unlike them, he is a dedicated labor leader.[22] With the maudlin quality that occasionally emanates from London's prose, Everhard informs his beloved, Avis, that he cannot accept a government office: "Dear heart, I am a captain of labor. I could not sell out. If for no other reason, the memory of my poor old father and the way he was worked to death would prevent [sic]" (109). There is much that calls up passages from *Caesar's Column*. The Pinker-

---

[18] Rideout, *Radical Novel*, pp. 42 and 46.
[19] Walter Rideout points out the novel's resemblances to *Caesar's Column* and suggests the possibility of its influence (in Donnelly, *Caesar's Column*, p. xxiv).
[20] See Rideout, *Radical Novel*, p. 42.
[21] Jack London, *The Iron Heel*, p. 6.
[22] He was a composite, writes Philip S. Foner, of Eugene Debs, Ernest Untermann, and Jack London (*Jack London: American Rebel*, pp. 89–90).

tons are "the Mercenaries of the Oligarchy" (80), and their accomplices
are those described earlier by Churchill and Phillips: "This senator was
the tool and the slave, the little puppet, of a brutal and uneducated machine boss; so was this governor and this supreme court judge; and all
three rode on railroad passes; and, also, this sleek capitalist owned the
machine, the machine boss, and the railroads that issued the passes" (82).
Meredith footnotes the text with quotations attributed to Lincoln, Calhoun, Theodore Roosevelt, and others. The strictures, particularly those
against the corporations, are pronounced in the tone of contemporary
muckraker exposés. In a lecture to "small capitalists" being squeezed by
the trusts, Everhard describes society's weaknesses, analyzes specific injustices, and prescribes a solution. His indictment divides society into the
plutocracy, the middle class, and the proletariat. Presenting Marx's doctrine of surplus value, he asserts, "I have demonstrated to you mathema-
tically the inevitable breakdown of the capitalist system" (151). His solution is simple: expropriate the machines and their associated resources
and manage them for the good of all in a Socialist society.

Pell-mell action succeeds doctrine as terrorist mobs pillage and destroy
on orders from the oligarchy. Striking labor is crushed, Wall Street precipitates an economic collapse, and the captains of industry destroy the
middle class, submerging the proletariat. Everhard's election to Congress
in "the great Socialist landslide" of 1912 is quickly followed by repression and mass arrests. Later he and Avis carry out espionage while acting
as *agents provocateurs* for the Iron Heel preparatory to the projected
revolution of 1918. But the forewarned Iron Heel prepares an object
lesson. The mercenaries are ordered to wipe out the proletariat in the
area which becomes the site of the "Chicago Commune." The victims
are the "people of the abyss," deceived into emerging prematurely from
their warrens for revolt. Seen in the light, they are completely wretched,
degraded, and brutelike.[23] The Everhard manuscript breaks off, Meredith surmises, at the Everhards' execution after the failure of the Second
Revolt, an international one in which Germany, Italy, France, and "all
Australasia" (3) rose simultaneously only to be crushed by the united
oligarchies of the world.

In an unsurprising paradox, it is London's fierce partisanship which

---

[23] The phrase, "People of the Abyss," is owing to H. G. Wells; the people themselves suggest the Proles of George Orwell's *1984*, although Orwell's protagonist
sees in them a yet ineradicated potentiality for rebirth and freedom. There is no
indication that Everhard sees anything like this.

accounts for the best and the worst in this novel praised by such experts on revolution as Leon Trotsky and Karl Radek.[24] Everhard is too much the superman to be believed, and Avis is largely a disembodied character. Much of the novel has the sound of a dramatized tract. The middle portion, relating the oligarchy's early period in power, is a narrative which summarizes rather than dramatizes and consequently fails to be convincing fiction. The book does not gain power until it treats the despotism of the oligarchy and the carnage of the commune. Walter Rideout notes that London's "creative imagination always functioned increasingly well the more it was able to disintegrate the fabric of social life or the civilized responses of the individual personality to its simplest level, a condition of complete violence. His concern is with the struggle, which horrifies and fascinates him, rather than with the achievement . . ."[25] These sections of the novel have the force and vividness of nightmare phantasmagoria. But they lack the capability—displayed in Orwell's *1984*—of eliminating the boundary between the world of nightmare and the world of waking and fusing the two through imaginative power. Jack London was a minor writer who will be remembered primarily for stories combining adventure and primitivism sometimes mixed with militant socialism. *The Iron Heel,* moreover, is not his best novel. But its very force, no matter how awkward, made it stand out against the artificialities of a good many of its contemporaries, and its apocalyptic vision of the future was not to be matched for thirty years.

When Sinclair Lewis published *It Can't Happen Here* in 1935 he envisioned an American counterpart to the experience of Italy in 1922 and Germany in 1933. In this novel his satire was sharper and broader than it had been in *Main Street* and *Babbitt. It Can't Happen Here* might be thought of as a novel of native Fascism, but it is treated here because Lewis set these events in the future, in a description which came to take the form of an apocalyptic vision. It grew logically out of his earlier diatribes against the selfishness, crudity, and materialism which had exacerbated his sensibilities. The novel called into play emotions which had contributed to aesthetically more satisfying novels such as *Babbitt, Main Street,* and *Dodsworth.* In one way, this novel had a more direct effect on the American scene than these others. As his contribution to the trust-busting campaign of 1937, Secretary of the Interior Harold L. Ickes made

---

[24] Aaron, *Writers on the Left,* p. 95.
[25] Rideout, *Radical Novel,* p. 45.

an attack on big capital entitled "It Is Happening Here." The result of this speech and another like it was, says Goldman, to put Washington in a tumult.[26]

Written with the encouragement of columnist Dorothy Thompson, Lewis's second wife, *It Can't Happen Here* portrays a decadent America ripe for the tyrant and the destruction of the constitutional system. Lewis begins *in medias res,* with the Democratic Party captured by demagogic Senator Berzelius Windrip and with Franklin D. Roosevelt the head of the liberal Jeffersonian Party. But, writes Lewis, "The conspicuous fault of the Jeffersonian Party . . . was that it represented integrity and reason, in a year when the electorate hungered for . . . the peppery sensations associated . . . with baptism by immersion in the creek, young love under the elms, straight whisky, angelic orchestras . . ."[27] This hunger is sated by "Buzz" Windrip. A hypnotic orator like Adolf Hitler, he appeals to many with a scheme for the division of wealth. His fifteen-point program, concocted with liberal borrowings from the Fascists and Nazis, is anti-Semitic and anti-Negro. On his Inauguration Day, he seizes power through the combined efforts of the Army and his Minute Men.[28] Lewis describes partisans of the American Corporate State and Patriotic Party in his familiar vitriolic strain. The

idealists of Corpoism [he writes], had turned to Windrip & Co. . . . as the most probable saviors of the country from . . . domination by Moscow and . . . the slack indolence, the lack of decent pride of half the American youth, whose world (these idealists asserted) was composed of shiftless distaste for work and refusal to learn anything thoroughly, of blatting dance music on the radio, maniac automobiles, slobbering sexuality, the humor and art of comic strips— of a slave psychology which was making America a land for sterner men to loot. (422)

Lewis's description of America under Corpoism—the forty-eight states superseded by eight provinces, unions and corporations replaced by syn-

---

[26] Goldman, *Rendezvous,* pp. 366–367.

[27] Sinclair Lewis, *It Can't Happen Here,* p. 103.

[28] This phrase, attractive to several authors, is used to identify both "good" and "bad" groups, depending upon the context of the novel. A group known as the Minutemen has been organized by Robert Bolivar dePugh in southern California. According to one observer "a self-styled anti-Communist guerilla force . . . the psychotic, serio-comic exaggeration of the wildest dreams of the Far Right," the Minutemen are still at work—despite repudiation by Senator Goldwater and others—"with a quiet and determined hysteria to prepare themselves for the day when the great Russian hordes invade America" (Mark Sherwin, *The Extremists,* p. 156).

dicates and confederations—uses the apparatus familiar to the reader of novels of native Fascism. Lewis is, if anything, more detailed than other novelists writing in this vein. Describing purges, flagrant homosexuality, and violent sadism, Lewis finally compares Corpos with Fascists and Nazis.[29] At the novel's end revolt has broken out in "the land of the Populists, the Non-Partisan League, the Farm-Labor Party, and the La Follettes" (447), and a bloody Civil War is in progress.

Lewis dramatizes many of the events by showing how they impinge upon his protagonist, a frail, goateed "bourgeois intellectual" named Doremus Jessup. The whole complexion of his family's lives and that of their town is changed, like that of the nation, by Corpoism and the thugs who administer it. Like Ernest Everhard, Jessup finally expresses his opposition in the only way left—by fighting in the "New Underground." But Lewis does not exempt him from guilt for his country's plight. In a tone like that of Dos Passos in *The Grand Design* (1949), Lewis writes, "The tyranny of the dictatorship isn't primarily the fault of Big Business, nor of the demagogues who do their dirty work. It's the fault of Doremus Jessup! Of all the conscientious, respectable, lazy-minded Doremus Jessups who have let the demagogues wriggle in, without fierce enough protest" (244). Rallying growing sentiment such as that which was later to bind together the diverse elements of the Popular Front, the novel "related readers of conflicting political views in a common anti-Fascist sympathy. It was severe with the Communist Party in the United States, but even some Communists found it good."[30]

Lewis himself placed a low valuation on the novel. It was a bad book, he confided to a friend. But American sales soared to a third of a million, and the rigorous critic, R. P. Blackmur, called the novel "a weapon of intellect."[31] To Lewis's biographer, Mark Schorer, it "differs from other examples of its genre in having neither the intellectual coherence

[29] Several passages suggest Ernst Roehm and some of his cohorts in the Nazi S. A.

[30] Mark Schorer, *Sinclair Lewis: An American Life,* p. 611.

[31] Schorer, *Sinclair Lewis,* p. 609. As a *roman à clef,* the novel did not tax its readers in making identifications among its major characters. Schlesinger observes that Windrip "was obviously based on Huey Long, with a touch of Gerald B. Winrod," and suggests other correspondences: General Dewey Haik and Douglas MacArthur, Lee Sarason and Robert E. Clements; Bishop Peter Paul Prang and Father Coughlin, Mrs. Grimmitch and Elizabeth Dilling (Arthur M. Schlesinger, Jr., *The Age of Roosevelt: The Politics of Upheaval,* p. 89). Winston Churchill wrote of it that "Such books render a public service to the English-speaking world" (Winston Churchill, "What Good's a Constitution," *Colliers,* as quoted in Schlesinger, *The Age of Roosevelt,* p. 90).

of Aldous Huxley nor the pervasive vision of a nightmare future of George Orwell." Schorer adds, however, that in 1935 "readers in the United States like readers in Britain and in France (*Impossible Ici!*), were sensitive to their immediate history, and it was to the immediate possibility of that history that Lewis's novel shook their attention."[32]

While *It Can't Happen Here* cannot measure up to earlier books in which Lewis mounted a major attack on American mores, influencing other writers and adding new phrases to the American lexicon, it has much of their vigor and savagery. Done in broad strokes and sometimes frenetic rather than biting, it lacks the solid observation and portraiture of *Dodsworth* or *Arrowsmith*. But this is understandable, since he was writing of what was to happen rather than what was happening. He was not exercising his forte of photographic observation and selective distortion, but rather extrapolating from the observed. But this novel showed more openly his now almost hysterical concern over what had become of America. And in this novel he arraigned the corporations of big business not only as a major force in the corruption of the country and its ideals, but as a major cause of its destruction.

In the ten-year period from 1938 to 1948, Samuel Hopkins Adams published two of his worst novels. They were both set in the future. *The World Goes Smash* (1938) was a mélange of common apocalyptic elements, and *Plunder* (1948) was a replay of *Revelry* thirty years later weakened by a potpourri from the novel of corruption, the Southern Politician, McCarthyism, and Fascism. In the former, he used the Romeo and Juliet formula, with his protagonist, a crusading district attorney, in love with the daughter of "Z," the head of the New York rackets.[33] Armageddon in Europe and Civil War in America (the left v. the right plus the Interests and gangsters), precipitate scenes reminiscent of London's Chicago commune before a moralistic-romantic conclusion ends the novel. It is a superficial potboiler, and the author of *Revelry* must have known it.

In *Plunder*, Adams did what he had done thirty years earlier in *Revelry*: he portrayed a handsome, weak, loyal, and brainless President whose greedy friends carried out their depredations under the shield of his office. The principal character of *Plunder* is Martin Strabo, a rep-

---

[32] Schorer, *Sinclair Lewis,* p. 610.

[33] By way of contrast, the Montagues and Capulets of the Crime Syndicate in the United States are at considerable pains to further the extensive intermarriage already existing in their ranks. See McClellan, *Crime without Punishment,* pp. 120–121.

tilian ogre and millionaire many times over. The President in the year 1951 resembles *Revelry*'s Willis Markham as Markham had resembled Warren Harding. Cheerful Charlie Dennison is tractable in the extreme to the buccaneers of Strabo's circle: "He was their little woolly lamb and they loved him! . . . The President's handsome countenance, which had done much to get him nominated and elected, shone with benevolence."[34] Unlike *Revelry*, *Plunder* touches on McCarthyism, on the Southern Politician, and ends on a comic note. Strabo's downfall follows encroachment on sacred precincts: he "fixes" the Army-Navy game.[35] Abandoning his enterprises—which include allegedly radiation-proof men's underwear called Protectosex—Strabo flees to South American asylum.

Adams's novel deals with subjects widely treated in the modern American political novel, and there is truth in some of his satire, but it is buried so far beneath the dreary farce and slapstick that it has no force. In addition, form keeps pace with content, as the reader tires of a breeziness too great to be borne, and of plain bad writing.

For years the author of romances enormously popular especially among women, Taylor Caldwell published *The Devil's Advocate* in 1952. Instead of the heart throbs of cavaliers and temptresses, however, its primary concerns reflected the hates and fears of the American radical right. Though the time of the action was 1970, Mrs. Caldwell took her title from a legend, whose significance she explained in a foreword. The Devil was arrested and held for trial in a highland village, the legend ran. His court-appointed defender performed so well that though the Devil was condemned to eternal banishment from the hamlet, his advocate was hanged by stupid villagers who thought he had enlisted in the Devil's service. The Devil's advocate in Mrs. Caldwell's book is not one but many who, like the protagonist, Andrew Durant, are members of the Minute Men, an underground organization dedicated to regaining the liberties taken away by the brutal Picked Guards who serve The Democracy.[36] The loss began, one explains, "with the Bolshevik revolu-

---

[34] Samuel Hopkins Adams, *Plunder*, p. 176.

[35] Strabo is warned against attempting this by an acquaintance who sends him a copy of Joel Sayre's *Rackety Rax*. The point is articulated by a press agent in an exhortation which now sounds naive: "You can't fool with this football racket. You can kick the head off the Constitution, bust all the laws in the book and run this town to suit yourself, but lay off fooling with football. It's the only serious thing in the United States" (282).

[36] The use here of "The Democracy"—a phrase often employed to describe the Democratic Party in earlier novels—hardly seems accidental.

tion. Like the black plague of the soul, it seeped into Germany, into Scandinavia, into Britain, into France, into South America and Asia and Africa . . . It was called Fascism and Communism, People's Democracies and Socialism, the Welfare State and totalitarianism and authoritarianism. In America it was called Progressive Democracy."[37]

Like *It Can't Happen Here,* the novel employs detailed descriptions of Fascist apparatus. (The privileged classes include the Army, the Picked Guards, the subsidy-rich farmers, and the bureaucrats.) Durant's assignment is to work within the government, oppressing the people so they will rise in successful revolt which, however, will destroy him as the Devil's Advocate was destroyed. Durant miraculously survives although hundreds of other *agents provocateurs* meet their expected fate. But three days of fighting bring about universal peace and free elections. The Republican Party, outlawed as subversive in 1958, will presumably flourish again. So will the American Legion, proscribed four years later; for "too vigorous . . . condemnations of all radicals, Communists, 'progressives,' and other nondescript bleeding-hearts and dogooders . . ." (296). Conversely, eclipse appears imminent for "liberals" (206) who had sabotaged an anti-Communist campaign and the teachers whose "liberalism" (30) had helped bring about the debacle. The spin of the wheel of fortune also sends centralized government plummeting and states rights soaring.

Although Mexico and Canada have been annexed, with Russia, Germany, and Britain conquered in successive world wars and South America the designated next victim, there is also much of the *roman à clef.* In 1932 says Durant's chief, the people had elected as President a man "whose twisted mind stands out against the black background of history like a conflagration. Before this event . . . every man believed . . . that . . . he might succeed in raising himself to a higher position. But in 1933 he was defamed, and became despicable, for he accepted the shameful name of the Common Man, and lent himself to its cult" (26). Seen on television, the successor of this President is "a little meager man with a small, crafty face . . . wizened eyes . . . cunning . . . and sanctimonious mouth with its sharp and quivering point" (31). A leading Minute Man is a four-star general the President has sacked. And when world-wide revolt is triggered off, the Acting President relieves his Commander-in-Chief. He tells him of a time fifteen years earlier when the President (then a captain) had issued orders for the assassination of the Acting President

[37] Taylor Caldwell, *The Devil's Advocate,* p. 358.

(then his general) because the general was on to the captain's activities. *The Devil's Advocate* is vehemently and repetitiously against the New Deal, the Fair Deal, unions, most social legislation of the 1930's, and farm subsidies in particular. It is obviously the clearest embodiment in this study of those ideas which are articles of faith to many of the groups of the Far Right treated in Chapter Eight. This garrulous and pretentious novel sets quotations from Goethe and other great writers amidst fantastic episodes. Credibility is strained when so many Minute Men have infiltrated the military that one wonders why there was no simpler coup earlier. But this, of course, would have made superfluous much of the cat-and-mouse, hide-and-seek pattern that festoons the novel. It is one of the worst of the lot, and one regrets that, for the sake of symmetry if nothing else, it lacks the power of that novel embodying a far different point of view, Jack London's *The Iron Heel.*

Future and Fantasy

Three novels published within a few years of each other during the 1950's depended heavily on the humor of the improbable made acceptable by action set in the future. One of them was very like fantasy whereas the other two, extrapolating from computer technology and advertising techniques, applied them satirically to political methods and events. Beneath the comic often lay the moral, beneath satire, a controlled indignation. All three books were technically competent and, in varying degrees, successful.

Jack Guinn's *The Caperberry Bush* (1954) explored an old idea: what would happen if people told the truth? The book is an indictment of the consistent dishonesty and hypocrisy of men, by implication placing the blame for corruption in politics not merely upon the politicians and those who do business with them, but upon an ineradicable characteristic of human nature manifested one way in politics and myriad other ways in diverse human activities. The active agent is a truth serum so potent that twelve ounces in a reservoir will turn a metropolis into a city of compulsive truth-tellers. Guinn explores the effects of this drug in the gubernatorial campaign of a state which suggests Oklahoma. The narrator's view of human nature is implicit in his words to the disillusioned inventor: "This entire city was hovering on the edge of bliss . . . but what did the potential earthly angels think about it? The gamblers and vice-peddlers offered money for your hide, because you were ruining business. The church people wanted you arrested and thrown in a dungeon because you were upsetting deacons and other high-type citizens. As for the remainder of the population, they reacted according to their information and fears. That little group which can read and write and understand, and which therefore always is the most helpless, just gave up and fled. But I'll wager they cursed you every step of the way."[38] The fundamental situation which Guinn exploits for purposes of comedy is buttressed by his sure characterization and wry wit, so that though his characters may be unusual, they are perfectly believable and amusing.

John G. Schneider's *The Golden Kazoo* (1956) and Arthur T. Hadley's *The Joy Wagon* (1958) applied to future presidential campaigns the techniques of advertising and electronics. The former was the broader in comedy and sharper in tone; the latter more urbane and ingenious, and in the end, more amusing. Schneider's protagonist, Blade Reade, is an advertising man directing the 1960 Republican Presidential campaign. He tells his idea-man: "Don't sell the welfare state, the free enterprise system or whatever screwball Utopia you've got figured out for the U.S.A. Henry Clay Adams is your product. He's a can of beer, a squeeze tube of deodorant, a can of dog food. Sell him."[39] As a part of this process Candidate Adams is made to play Lincoln at Soldier Field in a nine-minute skit in a TV carnival. He appears in Denver at the televised All-American Rodeo as "Ropin' Hank Adams." The Big Idea, the "Kazoo," is the promised distribution of sixteen billion dollars worth of surplus farm commodities. Reade gives to his subordinate the greatest accolade he can bestow: "You dreamed up the biggest giveaway show in history" (149).[40] But somehow the novel fails to come off, not because the author has extrapolated too far—though his premises seem to give disproportionate credits to the admen and debits to the electorate—but because there is, one suspects, a kind of ambivalence at work below the surface of the novel. Beneath the pungent satire upon the mentality Reade represents and the code of conduct he embodies, there seems a covert admiration for him, as a man who is brilliant, ingenious, and determined, and who does sell his product, servicing an enormous account. This same

[38] Jack Guinn, *The Caperberry Bush,* p. 250.
[39] John G. Schneider, *The Golden Kazoo,* p. 22.
[40] Although the events related are still, fortunately, fantastic, the "merchandising" of candidates on television and in other mass media during the last ten years lends force to this comment by Hofstadter: "Without taking an excessively indulgent view of the old machines or imagining that their failings were any less serious than they actually were, it is still possible to wonder whether the devices that are replacing them are superior as instruments of government" (Hofstadter, *Reform,* p. 269).

kind of surreptitious approbation is bestowed on the idea-man who, despite his sardonic analysis of advertising, knows precisely how he is prostituting his talents.

Arthur T. Hadley's *The Joy Wagon* concerned a three thousand tube miniature electronic calculator. Determined to realize its potential by dominating the surrounding humans, it decides on politics as the quickest way to the goal. Mike Microvac engineers certain additions to further these plans:

> It had put a number of delicate electronic pads into the palms of its hands, after isolating the perfect handshake as a basic ingredient of successful politics. Since everyone considers the perfect handshake an exact replica of his own, Microvac's hand pads analyzed the pressure, heat, and vitality of each shake, and the machine then returned the greeter's grip perfectly. Further, electronic impulses radiating from the pads communicated to the greeter a feeling of well being.[41]

Hadley's humor frequently derives from such ingenuity. Microvac compensates for its inability to kiss babies by electronically psychoanalyzing them. "On being tendered a squally, drizzly infant, Microvac gave the child a harmless but stunning electric shock . . . Having relaxed and silenced the infant, the machine would use a lower voltage to tickle the child's nerve ends, causing it to smile. 'Ooh, doesn't the baby love him!' women close by would murmur" (86–87). Hadley's satire also ranges over many subjects, not only familiar ones such as convention skulduggery and campaign tactics, but also such peripheral ones as the Hollywood celebrity. One of Microvac's campaigners is "Darlene Lord, All America's Loveboat," who "had just finished a new picture, *Something for the Birds,* a little tale about St. Francis of Assisi" (108). Hadley's ingenuity keeps pace with his narrative as the opposition tries to capitalize on Microvac's inability to eat food offered at his rallies or to make love, on his not having had a mother, and on attacks gradually coming closer "to calling Microvac an atheistic mechanical bastard without actually saying so" (107). He counters masterfully with an address in which he declares, "I know whose master hand gave me the joy of being alive. I know I get my joy joice from God. Not for one single instant do I ever forget from whence cometh my joy joice" (172). And it is only because of an inadvertent televised revelation of the "Sorcerer's Apprentice reaction," (a glimpse of scores of similar machines secretly built by Microvac), that a revulsion of horror chills the electorate and causes Mi-

[41] Arthur T. Hadley, *The Joy Wagon*, p. 17.

crovac's defeat. Hadley derives further comic effects from the witty and parodistic use of political clichés. Having analyzed them with appropriate electronic circuits, Microvac uses them in his campaign. And it is this aspect of Microvac's plan and campaign which Hadley uses to keep this novel of the 1970's from being merely a fantasy of the future. Through portrayal of Microvac's intelligence, even though it is frustrated in the end, Hadley is able to satirize many foibles and follies of American politics, using them for satire which is, at its best, as amusing as it is clever.

Predictions and Results

Several generalizations emerge from a reading of these novels of the future. One is that they include more bad novels than any other group. This kind of work is probably more likely than any of the rest to attract the amateur, the would-be writer who may feel that the strength of his vision of things to come will compensate for deficiencies in technical skills. Though in many instances these writers were prophetic, it was in a limited way. One is willing to applaud the forecasts of television, monster bombs, nerve gases, and bacteriological warfare on the one hand, and of the United Nations, multination police actions, tariff reductions, and common market formations on the other. But Europe is neither in chaos nor in shambles, the political system of the United States has been captured by neither the extreme right nor the extreme left, and this balance of power, such as it is, has been maintained through normal procedures rather than ravening civil war. The situation here is analagous to that in the English political novel. Though visions of impending revolution mark the pages of novelists from Benjamin Disraeli and George Eliot to Howard Spring and Joyce Cary, the massive violence never occurred.

An obvious generalization is that the old-style utopian political novel disappeared from American literature more than a quarter century ago. The possible causes are several. The Socialist dream of Bellamy and Steere has apparently given way to hope of amelioration of hardship through a gradual approach to the welfare state. One also suspects that there are few novelists today willing to go further than William Faulkner in his assertion that "Man will endure." It may also be symptomatic that three of the four novels of the future in the last decade of this study have been comic ones. Speculation about the future is so shadowed by technological advances in thermonuclear weapons and rocketry—not to mention bacteriological and meteorological warfare—that the mind is likely to balk at the kind of tale which, twenty-five years ago, could fancifully be called a "glimpse into the future." The kind of thing the reader finds in the apocalyptic novel of this century's early years is often uncomfortably close to newspaper headlines during each periodic phase of international tension or crisis. It may also be that the impulse which gives rise to this kind of novel has spent itself, for the most part, in its best representatives—London's *The Iron Heel,* Huxley's *Brave New World,* and Orwell's *1984.* And when a novelist now sets a book in the future it is likely to be a future of death-bearing stasis, as in Arthur Koestler's *The Age of Longing* (1951), or one of contaminated wasteland after the catastrophe has occurred, as in Nevil Shute's *On the Beach* (1957). Some of the impulse toward novels of the future has probably gone into science fiction with political implications. Ray Bradbury's *Fahrenheit 451* (1953), for example, has as its protagonist a fireman (whose job is destroying books) who turns against the post-atomic-war regime which rules a horrifying, totalitarian America. Whatever the cause, this kind of modern American political novel has undergone marked change. And, like the novel dealing with the role of woman, American Fascism, and the Southern Politician, it has apparently passed its peak and begun to decline.

5. the role of woman

"Dear knight, as dear as ever knight was dear,
That all these sorrows suffer for my sake,
High heaven behold the tedious toil ye for me take.

"Now are we come unto my native soil
And to the place where all our perils dwell.
Here haunts that fiend and does his daily spoil;
Therefore, henceforth be at your keeping well
And ever ready for your foeman fell.
The spark of noble courage now awake
And strive your excellent self to excell;
That shall ye ever more renowned make
Above all knights on earth that battle undertake."

> Edmund Spenser
> *The Faerie Queene*
> Book I

In 1856 Coventry Patmore published the second and final book of his long courtship-and-marriage poem, *The Angel in the House*. Canto II was entitled "The Course of True Love," and in one of its preludes, called "The Changed Allegiance," Patmore had written,

To him she'll cleave, for him forsake
Father's and mother's fond command!
He is her lord, for he can take
Hold of her faint heart with his hand[1]

In Canto III of Book I, which had appeared two years earlier, he had said of the beloved,

---

[1] Coventry Patmore, *The Poems of Coventry Patmore*, p. 149.

She was all mildness; yet 'twas writ
In all her grace, most legibly,
'He that's for heaven itself unfit,
'Let him not hope to merit me.'[2]

These passages illustrate two principal aspects of the idealized Victorian woman. She was fragile and obedient, the willing thrall of her lord. But in another way she was far above him. She was spotless, and as he aspired to her hand she led him to finer thoughts and deeds, ultimately even to the salvation of his immortal soul. The persistence of this stereotype into the twentieth century—often cynically used—is seen in the antisuffrage argument that woman debased herself by aspiring to functions properly the province of the stronger sex. She was already queen of his heart, and in this way, if only indirectly, the hand that rocked the cradle *did* steer the ship of state.

Nearly a century after *The Angel in the House,* Virginia Woolf published a telling essay. In it she took the angelic image for the text of one paragraph which is now more memorable than the long poem which elicited it. She described Patmore's heroine:

She was intensely sympathetic. She was immensely charming. She was utterly unselfish. She excelled in the difficult arts of family life. She sacrificed herself daily. If there was a chicken, she took the leg; if there was a draught she sat in it—in short she was so constituted that she never had a mind or a wish of her own . . . Above all—I need not say it—she was pure. Her purity was supposed to be her chief beauty—her blushes, her great grace. And when I came to write I encountered her with the very first words . . . I turned upon her and caught her by the throat . . . I acted in self-defense. Had I not killed her she would have killed me. She would have plucked the heart out of my writing.[3]

Virginia Woolf explained that her struggle was twofold: she had to write honestly without flattering men and she had to write candidly about feelings in a way which might seem indelicate in a woman. But her comment clearly was relevant to more than her problems as a young writer in the early years of this century. It bespoke the impulse behind the modern emancipation of woman.

An ocean and half a continent away, a fictional woman gave a *cri de coeur* in her hopeless confrontation with this situation intensified by cul-

[2] Patmore, *Poems,* p. 81.
[3] Virginia Woolf, "Professions for Women," in *The Death of the Moth and Other Essays,* p. 237.

tural starvation. Carol Kennicott raved against much more than just the Gopher Prairie of Sinclair Lewis's *Main Street* (1920).

"I believe all of us want the same things . . . all the classes that have waited and taken advice . . . We're tired of drudging and sleeping and dying . . . We're tired of hearing the politicians and priests and cautious reformers (and the husbands!) coax us, 'Be calm! Be patient! Wait!' For ten thousand years they've said that. We want our Utopia *now*—and we're going to try our hands at it."[4]

As early as 1905, David Graham Phillips had begun writing passionately feminist fiction. Between 1905 and 1911 he published six such novels (not included here because not strongly political), and in 1917 his best, *Susan Lenox*, appeared. But these novels had little of the impact that distinguished the work of the man from Sauk Centre.

A number of forces illuminate the background against which these novels of Woman as Guide should be seen. Major ones are the influence of Freud, World War I, and Prohibition. The most important, of course, is the campaign for universal woman suffrage, which began in the United States before the Civil War and ended after World War I. It provides a framework for the other events which followed.

Declarations of principles had taken a number of forms in the years before the Civil War. The marriage of Lucy Stone and Henry Blackwell in 1855 did more than unite them in the familiar civil and sacramental bonds. The bride worked beside Lucretia Mott, Elizabeth Cady Stanton, and Susan B. Anthony as a leader in the agitation for Women's Rights, and she was not going to be submerged in domesticity. She gave notice at the ceremony by reading a protest later circulated. In it she and her husband decried the laws which gave the husband custody of his wife's person, her property unless settled on her or in trusteeship, the produce of her industry, and their children. They protested against "the whole system by which 'the legal existence of the wife is suspended during marriage' so that, in most states, she neither . . . can . . . make a will, nor sue or be sued in her own name, nor inherit property."[5] To the surprise of few who knew her, Lucy Stone chose to be known as Lucy Stone after the ceremony. The furor the protest aroused gave further evidence of the deep-seated prejudices and hostility against the movement for women's

---

[4] Sinclair Lewis, *Main Street*, pp. 201–202.
[5] As quoted in "Rampant Women," by Mildred Adams, in National American Woman Suffrage Association, *Victory: How Women Won It: A Centennial Symposium: 1840–1940*, p. 40.

rights. But it was not surprising, for these women were not simply running counter to tradition. As Mildred Adams wrote, they were "attacking property laws, which were sacred then as now. They were demanding the extension of education, which costs money. In a society which prided itself on conforming to scriptural models, they were challenging the rule of biblical beliefs insofar as they referred to the proper place of women."[6]

The impetus of this movement, like others devoted to reform, was inevitably slowed by war. And when the Civil War had ended, the passage of the Thirteenth, Fourteenth, and Fifteenth Amendments drained off energies which might otherwise have been channeled into efforts on behalf of women's rights. Although the movement had always favored abolition and emancipation, its adherents now faced a galling situation. As Mrs. Stanton was quick to point out, women hitherto "had merely been in a class with children, idiots, criminals, now they were made the political inferiors of the race they had helped to free, a race still in the complete ignorance of slavery."[7]

Suffragists again showed their characteristic tenacity. After the Fifteenth Amendment was adopted in 1870, a new campaign was mounted under the leadership of Mrs. Stanton. Wyoming had voted suffrage to women in 1869, but other successes came slowly and piecemeal. Often they were won against heartbreaking obstacles in demeaning circumstances. Women believed that fraudulent ballots had contributed to their defeat in Nebraska in 1882. The National American Woman Suffrage Association developed a skilled lobby, but it had determined, organized, and unscrupulous antagonists to meet. Like the other "wets" generally, the brewing interests were against Woman Suffrage and they helped organize opposition. In some states, where aliens were permitted to vote after declaring their intention to become citizens, blocks of them were massed to defeat woman suffrage. Susan B. Anthony, who led the Association from 1892 to 1900, was made keenly aware of this force in the first of five campaigns in South Dakota. She "found blanketed Indians in the Republican convention, and when she addressed the Democrats, she was faced by a group of illiterate Russians, wearing large badges which said, "Vote against woman suffrage and Susan B. Anthony."[8] When women replied, it was with somewhat more than the retort polite. In 1912, in a

---

[6] N. A. W. S. A., *Victory,* p. 42.

[7] As paraphrased by Mary Foulke Morrisson, in "That Word Male," in N. A. W. S. A., *Victory,* p. 50.

[8] N. A. W. S. A., *Victory,* p. 73.

New York naturalization court, "a group of university women in their caps and gowns . . . sat in silent protest while thirty men, including Turks, Persians, Russians and Serbs, received their final papers—new citizens from whom American women had to beg the vote."[9]

By 1912, however, the turning in the long road had come. To the six states that already had enacted woman suffrage, three more were added. Another followed suit the next year and two more in 1914. Nine more states joined the roll in 1917 and 1918. Then, in 1919, the year when the Amendment passed both houses of Congress, eight more states secured Presidential suffrage by legislative enactment. And it was this pressure of successful campaigns at home upon congressmen in Washington which, as much as the assiduous campaign in the capital, brought about the final passage.

The drives and rallies, the fund-raising and letter-writing, came to a successful conclusion with the ratification by the states and the proclamation of the Nineteenth Amendment by the Secretary of State on August 26, 1920. Mrs. Carrie Chapman Catt, the genius who had become president of the Association in 1900 and directed the final campaigns that won the victory, summed up.

> To get that word "male" out of the Constitution [she declared], cost the women of the country fifty-two years of pauseless campaign. Fifty-six campaigns of state referenda; four hundred and eighty campaigns to get legislatures to submit suffrage amendments; forty-seven campaigns to get constitutional conventions to write woman suffrage into state constitutions . . . nineteen campaigns with nineteen successive Congresses and the final work of ratification.[10]

Another event—an even dozen years before ratification—was to have effects quite as far-reaching. In 1908 Dr. A. A. Brill had arranged to translate the works of Sigmund Freud into English. The young American had studied the work of the great Viennese at the Zurich psychiatric clinic of another modern giant, Dr. Carl G. Jung. Brill was on hand the next year to welcome Freud when the father of psychoanalysis arrived to help celebrate the twenty-fifth anniversary of Clark University with a series of lectures on the new science. The presence of Freud and his colleagues was briefly noted in the press and a few magazines. Then in 1910 Brill published a paper on dreams which was given a two-page

[9] Gertrude Foster Brown, "A Decisive Victory Won," in N. A. W. S. A., *Victory*, p. 111.
[10] N. A. W. S. A., *Victory*, p. 53.

review in the New York *Sunday Times*.[11] He began to receive many inquiries, some from fascinated writers. In 1913, he translated Freud's *The Interpretation of Dreams* and followed it a year later with *The Psychopathology of Everyday Life*.

By 1915 the *Nation* and the *New Republic* were also disseminating Freudian psychology. So was *Everybody's Magazine* where, in a two-part series, Max Eastman informed a mass audience that psychoanalysis was "a technique for finding out what is in the unconscious mind." This was the place, he revealed, "where those desires and fancies go which we are not willing to acknowledge even to ourselves."[12] Such *cognoscenti* as Walter Lippmann were quick to see the likelihood of misinterpretation and distortion. Lippmann invited Brill to speak at one of Mabel Dodge Sterne's soirees in Greenwich Village, where Brill warned against the popular new pastime of "psyching" one's friends and acquaintances as well as the danger of judging Freud on the basis of casual reading and conversation. In spite of these caveats, many were determined to hear what they had been waiting to hear.

To many progressives [writes Eric Goldman], Freud said that what happens when a male and a female are placed in proximity . . . results from impulses over which human beings have little or no control. In short, he gave a very scientific-sounding reason for doing what you please and leaving to the psychiatrist the solution of any troubles that might follow. Having been interpreted into this convenient view of sex, Freudianism was applied the more rapidly in all fields of progressive thought and thus provided a capstone to relativism.[13]

This psychological fiat changed the status of woman quite as radically as the constitutional one had done. She was still physiologically—and to a lesser extent psychically—different from man, but she was no longer simultaneously inferior and superior to him in the way she had once been. She had her id and her libido, as he did. Her infantile eroticism may have been expressed differently from his, but it was there all the same, and her dreams drew their symbols from the same common bank. If his acts psychically recapitulated those of Oedipus, hers were just as meaningful in terms of Electra's.

---

[11] See Frederick J. Hoffman, *Freudianism and the Literary Mind*, p. 48. I am indebted here to Professor Hoffman for his treatment of the early impact of Freudianism in the United States (see pp. 44–58).

[12] As quoted in Hoffman, *Freudianism*, p. 51.

[13] Eric F. Goldman, *Rendezvous with Destiny: A History of Modern American Reform*, p. 311.

During the war years many women were no longer as homebound as they had been. They went out to roll bandages and sell bonds. They went to the cities to work in munitions plants. Others boarded the zig-zag camouflaged ships and, as nurses and aides, followed the example of the Rose of No-Man's Land. As doors opened to wider professional opportunities, women's mobility also increased. Horizons had suddenly expanded. The war's end brought further departures and adjustments. "In the long run," wrote Arthur Link, "the most important aspect of the revolution in social life in the 1920's was the change that occurred in the status of women."[14] Prohibition made many women lighthearted lawbreakers alongside men. In the circumscribed freedom of the speakeasy, the girl in the famous cigarette advertisement who had urged, "Blow a little my way," seemed almost incredibly naive. The closed car changed the patterns of courtship and the new silhouette changed those of the dressmaker. Hemlines rose and corsets vanished. And if free love was not generally available in the Land of the Free, at least there seemed to be plenty in Greenwich Village. There was more of it in what were regarded as the best of the new books, with "the incredible vogue of the new standards among both writers and readers."[15] Sensual Stephen Dedalus prowled through the murky streets of Nighttown and complaisant Molly Bloom entertained at No. 7 Eccles Street. Elsewhere Brett Ashley took on whatever chaps struck her fancy, and Constance Chatterley was cleansed of shame in nights of passion. The winds of change were stirring, and they began to sweep beyond the cold-water walk-ups to the bungalows in the suburbs and even to the small frame houses on the far great plains.

The Angel in the House was quite dead. But what should have been a gladsome wake was something of a morning after. Signs had appeared as early as the beginning of the decade. One of Scott Fitzgerald's first heroines, who had earlier told the protagonist, "I'll be psyche, your soul," later lamented to him her lot in the "rotten old world" she lived in, in which her ultimate fate was still to be "tied to the sinking ship of future matrimony." There was still not enough enlightenment, and what there was had adulterated the sweetness of knowledge with the bitterness of disillusionment. "Just one person in fifty has any glimmer of what sex is," she said. "I'm hipped on Freud and all that, but it's rotten that every bit of *real* love in the world is ninety-nine percent passion and one little

[14] Arthur Link, *American Epoch: A History of the United States since the 1890's*, p. 320. See also pp. 318–319 and 321.
[15] Link, *American Epoch*, p. 323.

soupçon of jealousy."[16] Six years before this Walter Lippmann had hope-
fully used the Freudian analogy in *A Preface to Politics* to suggest that
society should sublimate its libidinous desires into channels which were
not only acceptable but profitable. The burden of his advice was that
men should first look within themselves to understand their inner natures.
Out of such understanding might come a political morality which was
realistic and effective rather than destructive, as were aspects of the existing code. In the year of the Great Depression Lippmann reported in *A
Preface to Morals* that he and his contemporaries were living

in the midst of that vast dissolution of ancient habits which the emancipators
believed would restore our birthright of happiness. We know now that they did
not see very clearly beyond the evils against which they were rebelling . . . The
evidences of these greater difficulties lie all about us: in the brave and brilliant atheists who have defied the Methodist God, and have become very
nervous; in the women who have emancipated themselves from the tyranny of
fathers, husbands, and homes, and, with the intermittent but expensive help of a
psychoanalyst, are now enduring liberty as interior decorators; in the young
men and women who are world-weary at twenty-two . . .[17]

But no matter how other fruits of the women's rights movement may
have soured, suffrage had not been disappointing, or had it? The suffragists had claimed in the years of struggle that Democracy had failed. To
such reformers as Frederic Howe, Woman had appeared the chief hope
for ameliorating the terrible conditions that had challenged the Jane
Addamses and the Florence Kelleys.[18] The women had not been hesi-
tant in fixing the blame. The banner of the Rights of Man had been
trampled by hordes of machine-processed voters, men who were "paid
for their loyalty by cash, jobs or favors . . . in large part newcomers, ignorant and with no understanding of democracy." Once given the vote,
women would help to raise the banners under which the electorate could
go forward to proclaim anew the Rights of Man. "What now, women of
America!" Carrie Chapman had asked when the vote was won. "Side
by side with men-citizens it is for you to rejuvenate the Republic, revivify
its faith and replenish the fires of human freedom." Duty called again.
"Will you," she asked, "lead on to that ideal democracy never yet at-

[16] F. Scott Fitzgerald, *This Side of Paradise* (1920), pp. 242, 254, and 255.

[17] Walter Lippmann, *A Preface to Morals,* pp. 6–7, as quoted in Goldman, pp.
312–313. See also Hoffman, *Freudianism,* pp. 55–57 on Mabel Dodge Sterne
(Luhan) as emancipated woman.

[18] See Goldman, *Rendezvous,* p. 76.

tained but which alone can salvage threatened civilization?"[19] Historians
and social scientists later gave the melancholy answer. As Goldman put
it, "Woman suffrage made the most spectacular lack of difference. Elections became no cleaner, no glow of motherly kindness spread over the
industrial scene."[20] Not only did large numbers of women fail to vote,
but those who did seemed to constitute no new force. Other factors—such
as religion, residence, and occupation—seemed to be more important
than sex when they did vote.[21] And if constructive organizations such
as the League of Women Voters appeared, so did movements such as
that for an Equal Rights Amendment to invalidate all legislation distinguishing between males and females. And if such illustrious women
as Secretary Frances Perkins and Senator Margaret Chase Smith had
followed the gallant Representative Jeanette Rankin into public life,
"Ma" Ferguson had served as governor of the State of Texas.[22]

Carrie Chapman Catt had taken Victor Hugo's phrase, "the Woman's
Century," and applied it to the period from 1840 to 1940.[23] Another independent spirit, Mademoiselle Simone de Beauvoir, was less sanguine.
"The women of today are in a fair way to dethrone the myth of femininity," she wrote; "they are beginning to affirm their independence
in concrete ways; but they do not easily succeed in living the life of a
human being."[24] To what extent these antithetical views can be resolved, the novels which follow may help to determine.

General Outlines

As we have seen, women consistently appear as guides for the male
protagonists. They act as spiritual and cultural mentors, attempting to
infuse idealism into these creatures of coarser clay than their own, giving
them books to read, exposing them to new ideas, and trying "to turn
their thoughts to higher things." Their influence may go beyond this
fundamentally ladylike activity. When they are activists such as lectur-

---

[19] N. A. W. S. A., *Victory*, pp. ii, iii, and iv.
[20] Goldman, *Rendezvous*, p. 292.
[21] *Ibid.*, pp. 292–293.
[22] Having expressed the preference in 1916 that men should "attend to all public matters," she consented to run for governor eight years later when her name
was entered in the primary by her husband, former governor Jim Ferguson, after
the Democratic leaders had secured a court order ruling his own out of the party
primary election. See Reinhard H. Luthin, *American Demagogues: Twentieth
Century*, pp. 166–167.
[23] N. A. W. S. A., *Victory*, p. i.
[24] Simone de Beauvoir, *The Second Sex*, p. xxx.

ers and field workers, they serve as moral policemen, adjuring the men to be faithful to shared goals and ideals, and to resist the temptations of the state capital or of Washington. Important as this function is—it helps in displaying early motivation and measuring later defection—it is performed in a subordinate role. In a group of twelve novels, the first of which appeared in 1922 and most of the rest between 1927 and 1937, the emphasis was shifted, and Woman was cast in the principal role.

Though she was the protagonist, she might carry out a demeaning assignment. Her function was essentially to act as a lobbyist, exercising her charms in the interests of her husband or lover, who might himself be a lobbyist. She might be a victim—an unwilling entertainer or Mata Hari—or she might quite deliberately work for wealth or revenge. In her purest form, the woman in these novels is a devout feminist, passionately devoted to the emancipation of Woman and ultimately to other liberal and even radical causes. The novelist may set up a conflict of function: should she be the wife and mother or the devotee who sacrifices the domestic role for an almost Promethean one? Woman's place in politics may be questioned, with the implication that a woman sacrifices her femininity when she becomes politically engaged and may also lose the respect of conservative men and women.

Nearly half of these novels treat Woman as Statesman. One even centers on a woman who is a Boss, if a covert and tactful one. Another is an artful tyrant. The protagonist is usually successful. She is elected or gains some kind of ascendancy against considerable odds; she overcomes formidable opposition in the discharge of her duties; and she is even able to remain feminine. In three novels written by women, the protagonists even surmount difficulties in romances which culminate in marriage. As one would expect, rose-colored glasses are extensively used even though they may be misted over with tears.

In still other novels of this group, the woman plays the familiar role of helpmeet or lover. She is thus Woman as Guide again, but she stands at the center rather than in a subordinate position. She is more intelligent and sensitive than the man whose career she advances, remaining in the political background but still being substantially responsible for whatever success he achieves.

The Early Novels

The capital portrayed by John W. DeForest in *Playing the Mischief* (1875), the earliest ancestor of this kind of American political novel,

was little different from that in the earlier *Honest John Vane*. It was
a city of cynical opportunism where rascality thrived. To a congressman
whose honesty places him on a lonely eminence, "The Treasury is plun-
dered and the general body of tax-payers is defrauded every session for
the benefit of private schemers and of business corporations . . . There
are scores, if one may not say hundreds, of men in Washington who live
by devising and pushing bills of which the end is theft and the means
bribery."[25] Just as the congressman cannot accept these standards, so
he cannot accept the love of the novel's twenty-two-year-old protagonist.
Josie Murray is a hard, avaricious, and pretty widow come to Washington to seek damages for a barn burnt during the War of 1812. She hires
lobbyists and prosecutes her claim in spite of a prior payment of two
thousand dollars. Callously ruining a senator, she perseveres until a bill
is passed authorizing one hundred thousand dollars' compensation. De-
Forest committed many of the excesses of Churchill, Crawford, and
Ford. There were frequent excursions into the ridiculous or the incredible plus the same fondness for outlandish names, dialogues, and situations. But occasionally his study of the conniving Josie Murray, like that
of the corrupted John Vane, achieved a kind of solidity and detachment
which is characteristic of DeForest's best work in *Miss Ravenel's Conversion*.

   Frances Hodgson Burnett's *Through One Administration* (1883), also
displayed Woman as Lobbyist. But rather than being one of the predators in the system, she was indirectly one of the victims. Bertha Amory
does not give her husband books to read nor does she direct his gaze to
the stars. Instead she gives dinners for senators, congressmen, and other
officials who may be useful in her husband's lobbying for a bill to advance a scheme which obsesses him. She does not understand the full
import of her actions or the way they are staining her reputation. Her
experience of Washington, like Madeleine Lee's in *Democracy*, ends in
tragedy. Bertha Amory finally becomes aware, during the four years
which the book covers, of the crassness and hypocrisy underlying the behavior of almost all those around her. The novel is a modest one, limited
in scope and intensity. Partially through the use of fewer characters and
the limitation of incident, however, Mrs. Burnett does a more workmanlike job than many of her contemporaries with bigger but wilder books.

   In both *Playing the Mischief* and *Through One Administration*, wo-

---

[25] John W. DeForest, *Playing the Mischief*, p. 168.

man as a political individual acts in a primitive way, trading on her at-
tractiveness. Josie Murray is like the trollops in eighteenth-century novels
exchanging their favors for favors in return. If she is different, it is
mainly in that she is more clever and less good-hearted than they are
apt to be, giving less and gaining more. Bertha Amory is the innocent
victim, but her appeal is fundamentally the same; it has a sexual basis
even though her style runs to feminine graces and genteel hospitality.
Carrying out political acts in the national capital, neither of these women
has strong political convictions. Their efforts are addressed not to the
intelligence, or even the self-interest, of the men they act on, but rather
to their romantic sensibilities and their passions. And once again, the
ultimate motives behind their acts are wholly mercenary.

Feminism and the New Freedom

During the decade dominated by the first World War, the new works
of a few major novelists such as Frank Norris, Theodore Dreiser, and
Sinclair Lewis were available to the public. So were those of Winston
Churchill, and it was also during this period that David Graham Phillips's best book appeared posthumously. But in the emergence of realism,
the maturing of naturalism, and the flood of writing about the war, the
novel of contemporary American politics went into eclipse. It reappeared
in 1922 with a book by a woman about women engaged in the feminist
movement and Republican politics. But the author herself seemed to
entertain the views of the Old-Fashioned Girl, ideas that would be congenial to one of Crawford's good and noble women, despite the naughty
glitter of a dilute solution of Freud and D. H. Lawrence sprinkled over
them. Margaret Culkin Banning's title, *The Spellbinders*, contains a
double meaning which goes to the heart of the novel. It is the familiar
ironic reference to the political speechmaker, in this case the feminists.
It is also a reference to woman's most important function, in which she
binds her man to her in that relationship which Mrs. Banning feels is
more important than success in politics. These opposed actions are demonstrated in two different women. The first is Helen Flandon. Unlike
Bertha Amory in *Through One Administration*, she is nobody's victim.
Instead, *she* drives *her husband* to drink as her career begins to eclipse
his. When he asks her not to serve as a delegate to the Republican National Convention in Chicago, she replies, "You've chosen, quite deliberately, to be a reactionary in all this woman's progress movement. I'm

sorry. But there is a loyalty one has to women, Gage, beside the loyalty one has to a husband . . .”[26] But there were other emotions besides loyalty involved, for some women “interpreted the new freedom to suit themselves as did most other women. To them it meant a good deal of license, a cool impudence and camaraderie towards men, a definite claiming of all the rights of men in so far as they contributed to the fun of existence . . . That was the substance of their feminism”(248–249). At the National Convention, however, amidst “a gathering of men, a smoky, hot, sweating collection of men who had a certain kind of training in the game of conventions and politics,” the feminine delegates become real ornaments to the political process: “well dressed for the most part, some of them handsome, all of them more alert, less careless than the men—talking wisely too but with more imagination, with a kind of excited doubt as to the outcome, and despite themselves showing a delighted naiveté in their bearing towards the whole event”(174–175).

Young Freda Thorstad argues the other case as she asks, “Don’t you think, Mrs. Flandon, that something’s being lost somewhere? Aren’t women losing—oh, the quality that made poets write such things about them—”(43). Helen’s husband carries this argument further with a Lawrentian comment on Woman as a spellbinder: “It was all right when it was instinctive and natural but now it’s so damned self-conscious. They’re picking all their instincts to pieces, reading Freud on sex, analyzing every honest caress, worrying about being submerged in homes and husbands. It’s wrecking, I tell you, Walter. It’s spoiling their grain”(73). Freda’s unspoiled grain is indicated by her idyllic marriage—to an Irish poet and Sinn Feiner—which triumphs over theft, separation, and typhoid. In her last words to Flandon, Freda tells him, “I want women to be stronger, finer—I’ll work for that—but that’s one thing, Mr. Flandon. It hasn’t anything to do with the adventure between men and women, really”(28).

These words identify Mrs. Banning’s real concern—not so much women in politics as in the adventure between men and women, whatever that may be. This is a superficial novel, one which has a surface gloss compounded of dashes of feminism and subjects of then-current interest such as Freudian psychology, the Celtic Renaissance, and D. H. Lawrence’s pairing of healthful natural instinct versus destructive barren intellectuality. The substructure is only the familiar base of romantic difficulties resolved in the end. This is somehow made worse by the fact

[26] Margaret Culkin Banning, *The Spellbinders*, pp. 109–110.

that, unlike the honest and undiluted romantic pap purveyed by some of Mrs. Banning's predecessors, hers is at first less easily recognizable because of her relatively polished style. If there is any kernel of commentary on men, women, and politics, it is strictly conservative. Some women would be good at politics and many would not, and it is really better for women not to become too much involved for their husbands may become very cross and difficult to manage if they do. Like an athlete who foregoes badminton to play tennis, they do better to concentrate on the major sport, for the minor one will only put them off their real game.

The only other novel to deal so directly with feminist activity was Janet Ayer Fairbank's *Rich Man Poor Man* of 1936. In large part it was also the story of the wealthy Smith family of Chicago from 1912 to the eve of the Depression. Full of the clichés of such family chronicles, it had a liberal admixture of a-smile-and-a-tear romance. The political interest is focused in the story of young Hendricks Courtlandt Smith, Jr., and Barbara Jackson, Kansas-born girl orator. After their marriage he learns that "where woman suffrage was concerned, she was beyond reason—fanatic."[27] It is part of her inheritance, a kind of reform grand slam. Her grandfather had been a Vermont abolitionist who stood with John Brown in the Pottawatomie Creek Massacre; her grandmother had been a militant suffragist; her father, a Populist. At first Hendricks and Barbara are bound together by their fervent loyalty to Theodore Roosevelt.[28] Their paths begin to diverge as she campaigns for the Nineteenth Amendment, pickets the White House, visits Eugene Debs in prison, and travels to Russia. Their incompatible marriage ends when she divorces him to marry a Communist.

There is a troublesome ambiguity in this novel. Through the body of it Barbara Jackson Smith is portrayed as a zealot for whom a cause is a constant psychological necessity: first suffragism, then liberalism, and finally radicalism.[29] Her husband is the long-suffering Liberal-with-Money, who asks only that she save part of her life for marriage and the

[27] Janet Ayer Fairbank, *Rich Man Poor Man*, p. 246.
[28] This is one of the few novels to present the sense of devotion inspired by the "spiritual power" with which Theodore Roosevelt and his campaign were imbued. For a description of its nature and force, see William Allen White, "Roosevelt, a Force for Righteousness," *McClure's*, XXVIII (January, 1907), 393, as cited by Richard Hofstadter, *The Age of Reform: From Bryan to F. D. R.*, p. 212.
[29] A number of suffragists went on to other reform activities after the Amendment was adopted. Carrie Chapman Catt was one of them. In 1925 she "brought two leading national women's organizations together in the conference on the Cause and Cure of War and later helped form the National Peace Conference" (Mary Gray Peck, in N. A. W. S. A., *Victory*, p. 146b).

family. Before the reader's eyes, however, the author shifts her ground as Smith sees Barbara speaking in Union Square on May Day, 1929. She is untidy and faded, but her former husband turns away glad of this picture, "for now, instead of remembering her as she had looked in the courtroom . . . he could think of the spiritual beauty in her face when uplifted, as she always was when speaking . . . That wholehearted commitment seemed to him a wonderful thing, and . . . he found himself envying, as he always had, her power of consecration. It seemed to him a long time since he had known the supreme contentment of unquestioning faith—since he, too, had been free . . ." (626).

A good part of the novel is concerned with the marriages of Smith's sister. It is also handicapped by discordant notes in dialogue, overdone romantic scenes, and bogus combat scenes. The novel appropriately was serialized in the *Pictorial Review*. It is interesting, however, to contemplate Barbara as woman radical. Compared with other portrayals of American women radicals to come, she is considerably idealized and quite different from such other activists as, for instance, Conrad's Sophia Antonovna in *Under Western Eyes*. Perhaps the salient fact about her is that she is a woman who must have a cause and ends with a series of them. And in spite of the book's glowing last paragraph and her avowals throughout, she never appears to be a genuinely fulfilled individual.

Woman in Authority

In the ten-year time-span beginning in 1927, four novels placed women in authority. Thirty years later, a fifth appeared. In some, the strains of romance could be heard clearly, whereas in others they were almost completely muted or subordinated to the leitmotif of Woman as executive. Ruth Comfort Mitchell's *Call of the House* (1927) makes much of 28-year-old Doria Dean Yale's difficulties as a new California state senator but concludes with a promising romantic attachment to the land baron first cast as the opposition. This novel is gauche despite an interlarding of literary allusions and pallid in spite of material about the 1920's.

In a prefatory note to *The Woman of It* (1929) Clare Ogden Davis wrote, "The characters and the events in this book are wholly fictitious, and do not refer to former Governor Miriam Amanda Ferguson of Texas or to former Governor Nellie Tayloe Ross of Wyoming, the only two women who have been governors in the United States . . ." Be this as it may, Widow Della Lawrence's state is a Southwestern one with plains,

cotton, and oil. She herself is an ambitious president of the State Fed-
eration of Women's Clubs, who defeats the Ku Klux Klan nominee for
the governorship and then pushes liberal legislation which causes one of
the Klan group to grumble, "I don't put anything past that woman;
she's an insane crusader."[30] Her first year is a success, but there are de-
fections: "Woman in politics was disappointing, she now admitted to
herself. Women let emotions and prejudices influence them; they let men
sway their beliefs" (111). There are other consolations, however, for she
finds love in the governor's mansion and remarries. In a variant of the
Capulet-Montague strategy, Della's husband is prosecuted by her son-in-
law-to-be for postal fraud. His acquittal and her defeat in the next election balance out, and she has gained the equanimity to explain to a reporter, "Politics, son, politics. I had a defeat coming to me sometime, I
reckon" (249).

She has furthered measures advocated by women who have appeared
as Guides: an anti-mask bill aimed at the Klan, and legislation to aid
education, and prison reform. She denies commutation of sentence to a
bad risk but pardons three "Bohemian farmers," several Negroes, and
small bootleggers caught while the higher-ups were being protected. But
she is too good for this world, and the women around her seem no more
laudable than most of those in *The Spellbinders*. And here, as in *Call of
the House*, it is romance rather than politics which dominates the conclusion. Similarly, few of the characters actually come to life, and when
they do, they are seldom very convincing.

The Woman of Destiny (1936), by Samuel Warshawsky, was more
ambitious than *The Woman of It*. The office was the Presidency and the
climax came not through prosecution for postal fraud but through an
attempt to avert world conflict. Constance Shepard's political strength,
like that of Della Lawrence, comes in large measure from other women.
The maiming of her son in World War I spurs her to world-wide pacifist
campaigning. A leader of "the International Anti-Military Mothers'
Clubs of the World,"[31] she gains the Vice Presidential nomination in
1944 and forces into the party platform an antiwar plank. It holds "that
war shall be a matter of personal guilt; that any individual or group of
individuals guilty of acts tending to force us into aggression shall be
tried for attempted murder and imprisoned like common criminals"
(162). When the President predictably dies of a heart attack, Mrs. Shepard frustrates the Interests' War Party by negotiating with "The Mi-

[30] Clare Ogden Davis, *The Woman of It*, p. 88.
[31] Samuel Jesse Warshawsky, *The Woman of Destiny*, p. 83.

kado" via radiophone. She then rushes out of her office to tend a sick grandchild. The reader is spared a certain amount, however, for she has previously ruled out a prospective romance, consecrating her life to duty.

This novel displays quite as much unblemished amateurism as *Call of the House* and *The Woman of It*. The tone, however, is elevated somewhat by what seems to be genuine abhorrence of war and espousal of pacifism. The pure, sensitive, and dedicated protagonist is an appropriate vehicle for the expression of such sentiments. But the author unfortunately lacks the gift of convincing, realistic portrayal of character and incident, and some scenes go badly out of control, particularly the mad scenes of Mrs. Shepard's blinded and shellshocked son. More a tract than a novel, this book is not very successful as either.

The heroine of Sophie Kerr's *Fine to Look at* (1937) is a spiritual sister of Madeleine Lee and Bertha Amory, for the overwhelming result of her experience of politics is disillusionment. A Republican like Helen Flandon and Constance Shepard, bright young Vera Linder Scott goes to work for a United States senator just before the Depression's end. Her primary value lies in the young people's "For America" clubs she has organized for assessing candidates and issues.[32] When she learns that her employer has accepted a $30,000 bribe, she quits politics. The aspect she had known was fine to look at, she concludes, but only a façade for the sordid structure behind it. This heroine demonstrates the same qualities as those of the young women who inspire their mates, but she has little of their staying power. She has none of the force of Della Lawrence or Constance Shepard, and she succumbs after less punishment than Madeleine Lee and Bertha Amory absorb. This must be summed up as another superficial novel. It lacks force, as does its heroine, who accomplishes the least of the five women in positions of authority.

Although Wirt Williams's *Ada Dallas* (1959) demands treatment here primarily as another story of a woman's role in politics, it also fuses other themes and subjects. Much of it involves the figure of the Boss and the corruption that ensues when his reign is succeeded by one in which absolute power corrupts absolutely. In this new regime, personal sadism and lust for power give impetus to various embodiments of American Fascism. Not content with quasi-military power, the regime does business with the underworld and adopts its methods to reap its rewards. But Williams's novel is unusual on other counts. Technically it is the best in this chap-

---

[32] This organizational name is one several used by novelists and actual groups. For a different usage of the phrases "Pro-America" and "For America," see the groups described in Chapter Seven.

ter. The author, like so many of his generation, owes a good deal to Faulkner. He is also very considerably indebted to Robert Penn Warren and *All the King's Men*.[33] Williams's protagonist, like the protagonist of Larston Farrar's *The Sins of Sandra Shaw* (1958), is as different from the early fictional females who served as Guides as it is possible for her to be. As the novel's action builds toward its exciting and skillfully constructed climax, the man who knows Ada Dallas best contemplates her: "And this was the governor of Louisiana, who had whored for a living, who had murdered one blackmailer, and who had now determined to kill another and burn in the chair for it."[34] If there were not nineteenth century examples of Woman as Predator rather than Guide, one might say a final, total reversal had been reached; instead of purity embodied in a beautiful female form there is largely unmixed evil.

Actually, Williams's characterization of Ada Dallas and his portrayal of eight years of her life are considerably subtler than the quotation above would indicate. He provides her with a background and motivation which, while not thoroughly convincing for all the actions that eventually issue from them, keep her from becoming an unbelievable and inhuman monster such as Cathy Trask in John Steinbeck's *East of Eden* or a pasteboard cutout such as Farrar's Sandra Shaw. With luck, beauty, and determination, Ada Malone struggles upward from a squalid background in the Irish Channel section of New Orleans, escaping from the alcoholic father who forces her mother into prostitution and herself into a B-girl's job at thirteen. Earning her way through Sophie Newcomb College as a weekend call-girl in Mobile, she graduates with a Phi Beta Kappa key and a nonprofessional relationship with Steve Jackson. A New Orleans television newsman, he rejects her love but provides entree into politics. Before the novel's eight-year period has elapsed, she has married Tommy Dallas, a cowboy-singer-puppet-governor of Boss Sylvestre Marin. Gaining the governorship and control through partnership with sadistic state police commandant Robert Yancey, she meets her death saving Jackson from the assassin's bullet Yancey fires to prevent an exposé.

Motivation is varied. Tommy Dallas is a woman-chasing simpleton who later abandons revenge to concentrate on self-respect and power for not wholly ignoble ends. Yancey is a war hero who regrets the vanished violence of combat and allows a combination of concupiscence and pow-

[33] The reader will find it useful in reading these comments to consult the analysis of *All the King's Men* in Chapter Six.
[34] Wirt Williams, *Ada Dallas*, pp. 243–244.

er-lust, sadism and death-wish to place him in the electric chair. Marin is content to settle for his status as a millionaire and for ever-growing, rigidly held power. Ada shows that she is feminine as well as human by demonstrating a capacity for regret as well as love, and by cherishing acceptance and approval from the *haut monde* of New Orleans society. The vengeance she takes when these are denied her is as savage as the driving ambition which dominates the other side of her complex personality. A small grocer who revolts against her organization appears in the newspapers as "St. George battling the dragon"(275). In her revenge against the wealthy and socially prominent, she herself is hailed by the Irish Channel "as its St. George"(216). When her pension plan pays out its first checks, she is "Joan of Arc and Santa Claus rolled in one" (205). With her absorption in her role after re-election, many of her actions are determined by her "messianic image of herself"(265). The nature and consequences of her regime—characterized by her own Young Louisiana League recruited from among juvenile delinquents, by the motorized column which Yancey heads as it enforces their dominion over New Orleans, by the machine's extortion from hundreds of organizations—is only belatedly borne in upon her. Her appeal to the electorate is such that they believe her "as they had believed nobody since that day in 1935 when the doctor met the Senator in the corridor"(214). She even exceeds Huey P. Long, Jr., not only in asserting her power over New Orleans more completely, but also in her drive to attain statewide control: "The House was stunned as the Reichstag must have been stunned when it received certain proposals in 1933"(233). And her stature is eloquently attested by her final resting place—a few feet from Huey.

Almost as complex is the motivation of Steve Jackson, constituting one of the links between this novel and *All the King's Men*. Traumatized by a blighted love, a war wound, and an indifferent career, Jackson does his work but coincidentally attempts to immerse himself in "Nothing" (14) or, later, in work arduous enough to permit him "to achieve again my spendid anesthesia"(110). Just as his relationship to Ada suggests that of Jack Burden to Anne Stanton, so his Nothing and his splendid anesthesia correspond to The Big Sleep and to the amoral work for Willie Stark which characterize Jack Burden through most of Warren's novel. Jackson's vantage point as a newsman is like that of Burden when he is first introduced. And Jackson is close enough to government, as confidante to Ada, to make the same kind of shrewd guesses which Burden often makes as personal assistant to Willie Stark. Ultimately he fulfills somewhat the same function. Like Burden he survives the holocaust to pick up what pieces are left and arrange them in a meaningful pattern. But beyond this, serving—as Tommy and Ada each tell him on separate occasions—as a "conscience" (264, 328), he comes to realize that actions are consequential. He learns, like Jack Burden, that one must take responsibility for one's acts. Although life may appear so hostile that one may regard it in terms of what Jack calls the Spider Web, it certainly cannot be seen in terms of what he calls The Great Twitch. "The consequences of your actions," he tells Ada, "have completely run away from the actions themselves" (277). In the condemned man's cell after a last interview with Jackson, Yancey tells himself, "I am responsible for everything I have done and I admit it" (324). And Jackson, contemplating the series of tragedies, tells himself, "I accepted full responsibility for what I had done . . . I would keep on choosing and accepting full responsibility for the choice" (327).

Other links between Williams's novel and Warren's are certain images occurring both in patterns and in isolation. Yancey, roaring across Louisiana highways in a powerful car in the dead of night, a pistol in his holster and unexploded violence in himself, suggests something of Stark's faithful Sugar Boy, the stammering, stunted chauffeur-gunman who finds in Willie and in violence the kind of fulfillment nowhere else possible for him.[35] Yancey's fulfillment comes through Ada and the world of opportunities she provides for him. There is also the sense of the past, though it does not stretch as far back here as it does in Warren's novel. Just as the suicide of Mortimer Littlepaugh (and Judge Irwin's part in causing it) has its retribution, so the murder of Blanche Jamison comes home to rest with Yancey and Ada. And just as Jack Burden comments on retribution from the past—in his ironic reference to "The Case of the Upright Judge" and in his reference to himself as a Student of History and Seeker of Truth—so Yancey refers to the slowly accumulating evidence of the Jamison murder as delayed, undelivered packages which will one day finally arrive in the mail.

Williams's novel is literate like Warren's though not so philosophical. (Boss Marin quotes Bacon and Jackson echoes Spenser's "Prothalamion" and Eliot's *The Waste Land*.) A technique which differentiates the two novels further is Williams's bold use of near-contemporary his-

[35] Correspondingly, Warren's Sugar Boy seems to owe something to Faulkner's Popeye, in *Sanctuary*.

tory. He freely employs the names of actual Louisiana politicians, and especially that of Huey Long, to useful effect. (There are recollections of Ma Ferguson and of stories told by Earl Long.) Comments on Long's statue recur in the monologues through which the story is told. After delivering his ultimatum, Jackson walks "through the green gardens, past Huey's cast-bronze godhood, to the car" (293). As the climax approaches, he glances at the statue's setting of sidewalks and gardens: "Huey stared at these and at the western skyfire in deistic immobility. And as the fire went out . . . the light that never went off coned downward and yellow at his consecrated unseeing features" (300). This recurrent use of Long's statue as symbol creates several effects. There is irony in the deification of the dictator, in the statue as a *memento mori* for aspiring or practicing dictators—the people least likely to think on the things the statue suggests.

The influence of Faulkner is to be seen chiefly, I think, in the effective use of shifting monologues which vary point of view in the narrative. Just as Caddy Compson has no monologue in *The Sound and the Fury* and Addie Bundren has only one in *As I Lay Dying*, so Ada Malone Dallas never narrates any of the action in this novel, though she stands at the center of it. Steve Jackson, Tommy Dallas, and Robert Yancey perform this function, just as Benjy, Quentin, and Jason Compson do in *The Sound and the Fury*. And though we are not in the streams-of-consciousness of Williams's narrators as we are in Faulkner's, Ada's husband and her two lovers present views of Ada which are at times almost as much at variance as those of the Compson brothers. Elsewhere, the rendition of country dialect and the punctuation of dialogue suggest Faulkner, though Williams never falls into the temptation—fatal for many who have tried to learn from Faulkner's example—of following the richly convoluted Faulknerian style.

Ada Dallas is a swift-paced and on the whole convincingly narrated novel which envisions Louisiana politics as they might have evolved had a beautiful, intelligent, and unscrupulous woman taken up where Long left off. Possessing many of his fascistic tendencies, she carries them further with the help of the kind of sadist who becomes a stock character in novels of American Fascism. Williams describes the political maneuvers by which she serves the Boss as he follows his own designs (making use of the Interests) and then goes on to self-destructive excesses once the Boss is out of the way.[36] Even though we may realize, at the novel's

[36] When Boss Marin first contemplates using Ada in his political plans, he thinks of the role achieved by Eva Peron in Argentina. By the time of Ada's

end, that we have never really believed that a woman like Ada could rule Louisiana as she does, we do grant Williams a large measure of the suspension of disbelief Coleridge described. Unlike most of her earlier embodiments, Woman here uses her sex not to inspire and uplift but to seduce and corrupt. If *Dan Minturn* is an astringent comment on the Cinderella myth of America, *Ada Dallas* suspends it in a bath of aqua regia.

Lovers and Helpmeets

The women in two other novels functioned primarily by influencing the men in the matrimonial-political balance of power most often encountered in political novels. They were, however, the central characters. One appears in a bad and trivial novel, the other in one of the more ambitious of the dozen considered in this chapter.

Berthe K. Mellett's *Wife to Caesar* (1932) focuses on the heroine's dual role as wife of a congressman and mistress of the fiancé who had jilted her. This is another pseudo-intellectual and pseudo-realistic novel whose events form no pattern which is meaningful in larger terms than those of the plot.

A very different set of feminine attributes was demonstrated in Walter Gilkyson's *Tomorrow Never Comes* (1933). His heroine was an enlightened young woman who knew Freud and had read *Lady Chatterley's Lover,* who was prepared to battle her stepmother and her powerful relatives, and who was ready to mount the rostrum in her husband's place when necessary. She has the kind of courage and ability demonstrated by Barbara Jackson Smith in *Rich Man Poor Man,* but her deepest convictions appear to be those of Freda Thorstad in *The Spellbinders.* She is a woman with a talent for politics who prefers to occupy a subordinate role. Catherine Carmichael lives in a city near Philadelphia dominated by the machine works of her uncle, the real ruler of the city acting through a political Boss who has underworld alliances. Her stepmother is one of the reigning family, and when she runs for Congress against Martin Freemont, Catherine's fiancé, the girl throws all her resources into the contest. After he is injured by gangsters, she carries on: "Catherine had put on a swell show. Boies Penrose in his palmiest days couldn't have engineered the dramatics of the campaign to greater advantage. Wounded husband, devoted wife, and cruel mother . . . A debauch of

---

death, it is clear that she has attained a comparable one, at least among the Louisiana equivalents of Señora Peron's *descamisados.*

emotion. He wasn't a candidate for Congress, he was America's husband."[37] One wonders if there is meant to be something of Mary Pickford in the successful candidate's wife. Nothing like this is apparent, however, in a particularly phallic passage in which the young bride considers something of what Freda Thorstad apparently had in mind when she spoke of "the adventure between men and women": "Man was the spearhead and woman the shaft, if you wanted to look at sex in a dark mythological sort of way . . . Like motion, or the future, it was not to be analyzed or predicted, following the unknown laws of process and growth and continuity in perpetual change . . ." (92). After this Lawrentian reflection, it is curious to read Catherine's view that, *"Lady Chatterley's Lover* is a man's idea of how a woman ought to feel" (101). The stepmother, her foil, is unfulfilled both as wife and politician. To Catherine, "Florence was a female charger, caparisoned for battle. She was an enemy of men just as the Don Juans were enemies of women . . ." (105). The reader's last glimpse of Catherine comes in an overly tender scene as she sends Martin out to take the applause of the crowd, sure of the dependence and devotion he renders to her.

Many of the themes and devices of these novels as a whole are to be found in *Tomorrow Never Comes*. There is a Knight battling the Interests, their hireling press, and their political retainers. There are also gangsters, corruption, and the investigation which often follows it. But the principal theme is embodied in the feminine member of this pair of family-crossed lovers, the Woman as Guide from whose point of view the events are seen. The mixture of all of these elements is compounded with just enough skill to make the reader reflect on how unfortunate it is that the novel misses the desired effect. Perhaps one difficulty is that there are too many elements mixed together. Another is that there is too much reflective prose, most often the indirect interior monologue of Catherine, which is meant to be penetrating and philosophical but which sounds improbably high-flown or muddled. Technically the novel is much better than those in the early years of the century which presented Woman as Guide. But Gilkyson was writing, after all, with a quarter-century advantage over Churchill, Ford, and Phillips, and one would hope to see it used more fruitfully.

Money and Lobbying Again

After the mid–1930's, feminine protagonists in positions of authority

---

[37] Walter Gilkyson, *Tomorrow Never Comes*, p. 311.

almost disappeared. As more women entered political life, they nearly ceased to appear in this role in fiction. In three novels in which women did appear as protagonists, they used a combination of intelligence and (in two cases) sex to gain their objectives. Attempting to influence legislators, two complete the circle begun with *Playing the Mischief* and *Through One Administration*. But whereas only one of the two earlier protagonists was immoral and avaricious, two of the last three protagonists are that and more.

In setting the scene for *A Woman of Washington* (1937), Cornelius Vanderbilt, Jr., describes "at least five Washingtons," those of small bureaucrats, janitorial employees, eminent executives, legislators and lobbyists, and finally the diplomats and the leisure class.[38] Vanderbilt is chiefly interested in the fourth of these Washington worlds. Exotic Mrs. Joan Glenarm, one of its best-known ornaments, offers hospitality which furthers the interests of her wealthy lover. The object of her charm is an old man appointed to the Senate after forty years' devotion to the causes of Bryan, LaFollette, Debs, and Thomas. Called by the newspapers "the Don Quixote of the Prairies" (16), he reflects, "Yes, Bryan was right: Washington was the enemy's country"(18). He is too naive to see through the machinations of this woman whom her lover, in a spasm of rage, calls "just another well-dressed come-on, just another cheap flounder masquerading as filet of sole"(44). The detective work which saves his reputation and his bill (work performed by two more family-crossed lovers, his son and her ward) ends her career in Washington. She loses the promised castle in the south of France, but her work has not been completely unremunerative, for there is a safety deposit box in her name in New York which is "comforting to think about" (274).

Mrs. Glenarm is an entertainer, a lobbyist, and an intelligence agent. And she has been totally unencumbered by scruples in this work which lobbyist Jacob Pike in *Playing the Mischief* considers the chief business of government. Despite the plot's heavy machinations, the impression is that of a lightweight novel. And although theme and intent are clearly serious, the expository tone is sometimes incongruously flippant. Moreover, the often fevered prose fails to display the insight into the interplay of complex character and situation necessary for a major novel of Washington.

[38] Cornelius Vanderbilt, Jr., *A Woman of Washington*, p. 72. For a recounting of Vanderbilt's political experience and knowledge, see Upton Sinclair, *The Autobiography of Upton Sinclair*, pp. 295–297.

It was more than twenty years before another American political novel with a feminine protagonist appeared, and when it did, it was the worst of the lot, in some ways the worst in this entire study. The publisher's blurb on the cover of *The Sins of Sandra Shaw* (1958) informed the reader that "Larston D. Farrar is the author of *Washington Lowdown,* the Signet book which lifted the lid off the nation's capital." One surmises that the novel was meant to titillate the same emotions as the earlier book, centering as it does on an improbable young woman bent on destroying a senator who had ruined her father and then driven *both* her parents to drink and death. She gains experience both in and out of bed, so that she later remarks in extenuation of her conduct, "I suppose I'm not the only one, but I came to Washington determined to use my sex to blitz a man."[39] The descriptions of this life-sized pasteboard cut-out are so monotonously repetitive as to suggest a breast fixation. Cliché-ridden, tawdry, and meretricious, it was a paperback book like the myriad others on newspaper and cigar store racks, with the Washington setting and the pretentious set pieces of pseudo-intellectual political and philosophical commentary constituting only a superficial camouflage. The female lobbyist had finally been brought to the level of the trulls and courtesans in the ruck of worthless and ephemeral popular novels.

The last novel in this group added some of the characteristics of the American woman of business to the image of the American woman in politics. But she was neither mannish nor frustrated. She was instead, for all her shrewdness, as overpoweringly lovable as she was Irish, for in *Queen Midas* (1958) Joseph Dineen had lavished on his heroine most of the gifts bestowed only sparingly and separately in his earlier treatment of Boston Irish immigrants and their progeny in *Ward Eight.* In *Queen Midas,* thrift leads to affluence and affluence to a fortune. Pegeen O'Connell's family and friends run the dominant political machine. By the novel's end one son has served two terms as mayor of "Boylston" and she has become a millionaire several times over. Some of her financial-political operations are very close to the kind G. W. Plunkitt favored, but she seems never to consider them anything to bother one's head about. She is obviously meant to be a character heroic in her own way, but it is interesting to see that neither she nor her creator is much disturbed by the subtle kind of corruption in which her life involves her.

This realistic novel is for the most part a workmanlike job, documented

---

[39] Larston D. Farrar, *The Sins of Sandra Shaw,* p. 126.

with the solid and believable detail that helps create the illusion of reality. But it is never in the same class as *Ward Eight,* and it is the kind of book which one idly casts for Hollywood, so that the faces of the author's characters very soon become overlaid with those of, say, Siobhan McKenna, Pat O'Brien, and Margaret O'Brien.

Not a Woman's World

In reading these political novels with feminine protagonists, one is struck by the fact that most of them seem to be based on a cliché that can be expressed variously: "Woman's place is in the home," or "Politics is a man's game." Only one of the women makes an unalloyed success of public office. After a relatively brief time, all but one (who meets disaster) retreat to domesticity. Of the others, two serve the interests of men as lobbyists and the third is an unbelievable trull who serves only herself. A few women are devoted to feminism and radicalism, but they are far outnumbered by those whose prime concerns are materialistic. Joan Glenarm and Pegeen O'Connell both see politics primarily in material terms although one is painted in the hues of virtue and the other in those of vice. Ada Dallas represents a kind of final debasement of woman in political life. Ada as call-girl is far less reprehensible than Ada as governor. In the first occupation she gives full value for value received, using the proceeds irreproachably—almost, one might say, virtuously— upon her education. In the later occupation she also uses her body, when her intelligence and will cannot serve, but the proceeds are dictatorial power which ultimately involves most of the major crimes in the calendar.

Apart from *Ada Dallas,* none of these novels is particularly accomplished and fully half of them are simply bad. It is challenging to try to account for this collective performance. The evidence considered thus far in this study indicates that excellence is as rare as a bird among these flocks as among most others, and perhaps even more so than in many. This is particularly true in this chapter. It may be that the American literary genius for some reason has not inclined as much toward the woman who can dominate a novel as has the European. Perhaps there are fewer Carrie Meebers and Isabel Archers in American fiction than there are Anna Kareninas, Emma Bovarys, and Tess Durbeyfields in European. The fundamental reason may lie in the fact that when a feminine protagonist becomes a great character in literature, it is partly because her creator has presented her in a situation in which she fulfills an intensely feminine function: in love, courtship, marriage, or an affair. The situation of woman in political life (though it can be outstanding, as Mrs. Franklin D. Roosevelt, Frances Perkins, and Margaret Chase Smith have demonstrated), is one as remote from these others as any in which she is likely to appear.

6. the southern politician

Proud, brave, honorable by its lights, courteous, personally generous, loyal, swift to act, often too swift, but signally effective, sometimes terrible, in its action—such was the South at its best. And such at its best it remains today, despite the great falling away in some of its virtues. Violence, intolerance, aversion and suspicion toward new ideas, an incapacity for analysis, an inclination to act from feeling rather than from thought, an exaggerated individualism and a too narrow concept of social responsibility, attachment to fictions and false values, above all too great attachment to racial values and a tendency to justify cruelty and injustice in the name of those values, sentimentality and a lack of realism—these have been its characteristic vices in the past. And despite changes for the better, they remain its characteristic vices today.

W. J. Cash
The Mind of the South[1]

The Southern Politician naturally takes his character and coloration from his region, this most individualistic of American regions.[2] Students of Southern history and politics object, however, to the stereotypes clustering around such abstractions as "The South," and such figures as "The Southern Demagogue" even while they grant that there is truth in many such stereotypes. It is true that except for North Carolina, Virginia, Tennessee, and Texas, Southern politics has operated until recently under

[1] W. J. Cash, *The Mind of the South,* pp. 428–429.
[2] In political and cultural studies the South is most often taken to include the eleven Confederate states: Virginia, North Carolina, South Carolina, Georgia, Florida, Alabama, Mississippi, Louisiana, Texas, Arkansas, and Tennessee. In the novels considered in this chapter the qualities of this region are largely carried over to border states such as West Virginia, Kentucky, and Oklahoma as well.

an absolute one-party system. Disfranchisement of most Negroes and many whites has been for nearly a century an accomplished fact. And where disfranchisement leaves off, nonvoting impedes the operation of democratic practices. Experts insist, however, that state politics and leaders are nowhere nearly so homogeneous as is often assumed.

State politics, they declare, presents not one shade or two, but a whole spectrum. Virginia has been dominated most of the years of this century by an organization led by Senator Harry F. Byrd. Stable, powerful, and perspicacious, it can determine which young men will be encouraged in politics and which will be allowed to slip into obscurity. In Tennessee, a working understanding was said to exist in the 1930's and 1940's between the Democratic machine of E. H. "Boss" Crump, based in the city of Memphis and Shelby County, and the Republican faction, based in the mountains of East Tennessee and led by Carroll Reece, for many terms a member of the U.S. House of Representatives and in 1946 Republican National Chairman. The Alabama pattern, however, shows an almost random rise and eclipse of many factions, whereas politics in Florida shows even greater change and variance.[3] North Carolina's government in this century is generally called the most enlightened in the South, but in it the power of the Interests has been stronger and steadier than in perhaps any other Southern state. In the view of one native, "The big interests have known when to give way and when to play ball. They have been willing to be fair but not at the expense of their power."[4] In Mississippi, big delta planters aligned with the Interests have struggled against the hill country people often courted by spectacular demagogues. But here too there are variations and surprises. Mississippi politics sometimes represents an extremity of the Southern dilemma, but it has been observed that in voter turnout, when compared with Virginia "Mississippi is a hot-bed of Democracy."[5] That there are deeply felt attitudes which make for Southern community of ideas—most notably demonstrated on certain issues in Congress—cannot be disputed. But it is also clear that a greater divergence exists from state to state than is commonly assumed even among intelligent laymen.

The figure of the Southern Demagogue has substantially replaced that of the old-style Southern senator. The amply padded figure with flowing

[3] V. O. Key, Jr., in his exhaustive *Southern Politics*, comments, "Florida's peculiar social structure underlies a political structure of extraordinary complexity. It would be more accurate to say that Florida has no political organization in the conventional sense of the term" (p. 87).

[4] *Ibid.*, pp. 214–215.

[5] *Ibid.*, p. 20.

locks, pompously declaiming platitudes, has faded. In his place, in books and on film, strides a man burly and unkempt, wily and unscrupulous. His drive to power is aided by an intimate, emphatic knowledge of the plight and aspiration of the mass of the people. He has sprung from this class, but he cynically ignores their interests whenever they conflict with his own. The Southern Demagogue, writes Key, is a national institution: "His numbers are few but his fame is broad. He has become the whipping boy for all his section's errors and ills—and for many of the nation's. His antics have colored the popular view of a region of the United States."[6] A whole series of historical figures stand behind the stereotype. And they appear as early as the turn of the century, appealing to the same feelings that provided a favorable climate for the fervent but short-lived Southern Populism of the 1890's. Pitchfork Ben Tillman of South Carolina, "the first great exponent of the role," was followed by a long list of others who added their own variations.[7] There were Cole Blease and Cotton Ed Smith in South Carolina as well as

the ineffable Jeff Davis larruping the specter of the black man up and down the hills of Arkansas. Here were Tom Watson and Hoke Smith riding hard upon him in Georgia. Here was W. K. [*sic*] Vardaman roaring to his delighted Mississippians: "The way to control the nigger is to whip him when he does not obey without it . . . and another is never to pay him more wages than is actually necessary to buy food and clothing."[8]

Success bred emulation. In Mississippi, Theodore Bilbo, a self-confessed bribe-taker, followed the path of Vardaman to power. Eugene Talmadge of Georgia, "The Wild Man from Sugar Creek," not only outlasted his downstate rival, Little Ed Rivers (who proclaimed his loyalty to the New Deal while trying to make Georgia strictly his own political preserve), but left his son Herman a following and a name which helped seat him in the United States Senate. In Texas, W. Lee O'Daniel campaigned with a hillbilly band playing his own compositions. Others displayed markedly individual characteristics: in Memphis, Mister Ed Crump shrewdly built statewide influence on a city and county machine base that would have done credit to a Jersey City or Kansas City politician. The most dramatic of all was a man who belonged "essentially to the

---

[6] Key, *Southern Politics*, p. 106.

[7] *Ibid.*, p. 159.

[8] Cash, *South*, p. 248. Goldman notes that Tillman and Vardaman "combined reform and racist attitudes in a formula similar to the one Adolf Hitler was to perfect" (Eric F. Goldman, *Rendezvous with Destiny: A History of Modern American Reform*, p. 65).

traditional pattern of the Southern demagogue," but also managed to be "the first Southern politician to stand really apart from his people and coolly and accurately to measure the political potentialities afforded by the condition of the underdog." He was a man, as he himself readily proclaimed, who was *sui generis*.[9]

> Louisiana [writes Arthur M. Schlesinger, Jr.] was as natural a breeding place for radicalism as its swamps were for fevers. No state in the Union had been so long misgoverned. The old oligarchy, a dreary alliance of New Orleans businessmen and upstate planters controlled by the utilities, the railroads, and Standard Oil of Louisiana, had run things without serious challenge almost since Reconstruction. No state had so high a proportion of illiteracy . . . No state treated its children worse . . . And the submerged people of Louisiana had not only been oppressed, they had been bored: no Cole Blease, no Tom Watson, no Heflin nor Bilbo had arisen to make them laugh and hate and to distract them from the drabness of their days. Half a century of pent-up redneck rancor was awaiting release.[10]

When the instrument for this release came, it came from the north-central Louisiana hill country which had a tradition of revolt as well as deprivation. Refusing to vote for Secession, the parish had been jeered at as the Free State of Winn. In the 1890's Winn had reverberated to the storming Populist oratory of Sockless Jerry Simpson. In 1908 Presidential candidate Eugene V. Debs stumped the parish for the Socialist Party. Mill hands and cotton choppers responded by electing "half of the police jurors and school trustees on the Socialist ticket."[11] These sentiments persisted. "There wants to be a revolution, I tell you," said one man who had seen both Simpson and Debs. "I seen this domination of capital, seen it for seventy years. What do these rich folks care for the poor man? . . . Maybe you're surprised to hear talk like that. Well, it was just such talk that my boy was raised under and that I was raised under."[12] The speaker was Huey Pierce Long, and the boy, the eighth of nine children, was Huey P. Long, Jr. Though theirs was originally a poor white family, college educations were somehow managed for six of the children. But later, on the stump, the boy still claimed that he had worked in the fields from

[9] Cash, *South*, p. 284.

[10] Arthur M. Schlesinger, Jr., *The Age of Roosevelt: The Politics of Upheaval*, pp. 42–43.

[11] Reinhard H. Luthin, *American Demagogues: Twentieth Century*, p. 239. See also Hartnett T. Kane, *Louisiana Hayride: The American Rehearsal for Dictatorship*, pp. 13–35; Allan A. Michie and Frank Rhylick, *Dixie Demagogues*, p. 110; and Key, *Southern Politics*, pp. 156–159.

[12] Kane, *Hayride*, pp. 36–37.

before sunup till after sunset and had known childhood days when he went shoeless as well.

After blooming as an elocutionist at Winnfield High School, Huey P. Long, Jr., had taken to the road at sixteen as a peddler. He sold Gold Dust, a Pinkhamlike compound called "the Wine of Cardui," and ran contests among his customers for the best cake baked with Cottolene vegetable shortening.[13] He turned briefly from business to education in 1912 when he attended the University of Oklahoma. Then, after another period on the road, he married one of his baking contest winners, young Rose McConnell from Shreveport. Borrowing $400, he began a study of law at Tulane University in New Orleans. The money ran out in seven months, but Long acted with characteristic resourcefulness. He talked the Louisiana bar examination committee into giving him a special examination covering the standard, three-year curriculum of legal studies. He passed it, and on May 15, 1915, he was sworn in as a member of the bar. He was twenty-two years of age.

The pickings were slim at first, and sometimes the pay was humiliation. When he argued against a narrow workmen's compensation law, the chairman of the legislative committee asked whom he represented. His clients, he replied, were several thousand laborers who had paid him no retainer. "They seem to have good sense," commented the chairman. It was a barb Huey never forgot.[14] When the United States entered the war he gained exemption on the grounds that he was married and also a state official. He was a notary public. Working part-time at the law and part-time at the sale of patent medicines, he watched for his opportunity. It came in 1918 when he campaigned for the railroad commissionership of North Louisiana and won the Democratic nomination. And he had his eye on more than railroad matters.

The new commissioner soon began to lay about him. He was, he had let it be known, a friend of the common man. After having Standard Oil's pipelines declared "common carriers," he exerted pressure on Standard's rate-making practices. He compelled the Cumberland Telephone and Telegraph Company to reduce its rates. Meanwhile his Shreveport law practice flourished. In 1920, he helped elect John M. Parker as governor. Three years later, when Parker refused to levy higher taxes on Standard Oil, Long charged betrayal of the people and ran for the gubernatorial nomination. He and his wife and the organization he

[13] Michie and Rhylick, *Dixie Demagogues*, p. 109.
[14] Huey P. Long, Jr., *Every Man a King: The Autobiography of Huey P. Long,* p. 27.

had built went to work with the old lists of the hill-country customers as well as potential new supporters. Their canvassing extended from the Protestant parishes of northern hill people to the Catholic parishes in the Cajun south. The posters were nailed up, the campaign literature was sent out, and Huey stumped the state. In a rhythmic delivery like the camp-meeting preachers' of his childhood, he roared his invective at the Interests and the "Old Regular" machine of New Orleans. On a rainy January 15th he was defeated, but before 1924 was out, he had been returned to his office as railroad commissioner by a margin of five to one. With the law practice flourishing, he worked to expand his power base.

Four years later Long ran again. His refrain, "Every Man a King but No Man Wears a Crown," was adapted from a Bryan campaign speech of 1900, and it tapped some of the enthusiasm that the Great Commoner himself had aroused. Attacking the wealthy, he called for a financial redistribution. His lament under the Evangeline Oak became famous. "And it is here under this oak," he declaimed, "Evangeline waited for her lover, Gabriel, who never came . . . but Evangeline is not the only one who has waited here in disappointment." The people, he said, had waited for schools, roads, and institutions. "Evangeline wept bitter tears in her disappointment," he went on, "but it lasted through only one lifetime. Your tears in this country, around this oak, have lasted for generations. Give me the chance to dry the eyes of those who still weep here."[15] This time the skies were fair on Primary Day. Huey P. Long, Jr., carried fifty-six of the sixty-four parishes, and the Pelican State had a new governor.

He got off to a running start. His men went in as speaker of the House and president pro tempore of the Senate. Revenue from new tax bills financed construction of roads and schools and underwrote expanding government bureaus and functions. State patronage was brought firmly under control. When the program needed massive doses of new capital in March of 1929, a special session of the legislature slapped a five-cent-a-barrel levy on the oil refineries. Standard Oil thereupon refused to pay and led the other oil companies in a revolt. Then, on March 25, a senator called for investigation of charges that Long had hired a gunman for a political assassination. Two days later impeachment charges were filed against him. Long prepared for counterattack. With the help of powers such as Robert Maestri of New Orleans and with the encouragement of hill men in overalls come south to stand with him, Long flooded the state with propaganda. But his winning coup came through individual action

---

[15] Long, *Autobiography,* p. 99.

rather than mass action. Huey threatened and cajoled fifteen state senators into signing a "round robin" letter declaring they would not vote against him. The opposition, now clearly unable to muster the necessary votes for impeachment, collapsed. Standard Oil kept on refining at the old rate per barrel, but Long had repulsed his first major attack. From then on, the temper of his steel began to harden.

By 1930 state government had become an instrument that fitted his hand. His law office prospered in New Orleans, and the Louisiana Democratic Association, which he had organized from the ward and precinct level up, tightened control and funneled unrecorded funds into the organization. A year to the day after the impeachment charges had been drawn up, a newspaper he owned announced that Huey P. Long, Jr., would run for the United States Senate. In the election, one parish, St. Bernard's, went for him 3,979 to 9. He served out his term as governor and then, in January of 1932, boarded the train with his entourage for Washington.

Long had acquired the nickname, "The Kingfish"—taken from the radio serial called "Amos 'n' Andy"—and his behavior in Washington was as colorful as the name. His dress was flamboyant. Strutting on the Senate floor, he slapped backs and ignored protocol.

In his manners, values, and idiom [writes Schlesinger], Huey Long remained a back-country hillbilly. But he was a hillbilly raised to the highest level, preternaturally swift and sharp in intelligence, ruthless in action, and grandiose in vision. He was a man of medium height, well built but inclining toward pudginess . . . His face was round, red, and blotched, with more than a hint of pouches and jowls. Its rubbery mobility, along with the curly red-brown hair and the oversize putty nose, gave him the deceptive appearance of a clown. But the darting pop-eyes could easily turn from soft to hard, and the cleft chin was strong and forceful.[16]

He attacked senior senators such as Carter Glass of Virginia and heaped on others his home-style invective. Alben Barkley said he was like a horsefly. "He would light on one part of you," the Kentucky veteran said, "sting you, and then, when you slapped at him, fly away to land elsewhere and sting again."[17] He introduced income-limiting bills and plumped for his "Share-Our-Wealth" program. And he was meditating other things. He had come to Washington convinced that he had played a crucial role in gaining the presidential nomination for Franklin D.

[16] Schlesinger, *Roosevelt,* p. 48.
[17] As quoted in Schlesinger, *Roosevelt,* p. 53.

Roosevelt. Taking the stump for Roosevelt in territory written off as lost, he had produced results that opened Jim Farley's eyes. What he now wanted in return was the disposal of all federal patronage in Louisiana. Neither Roosevelt nor Farley antagonized him, however, despite provocation. He had decisively helped Senator Hattie Caraway in neighboring Arkansas against six opponents trying to unseat her. Thus when his own man, John H. Overton, took Louisiana's other seat, Long controlled a block of three votes in the nation's upper chamber. He had for some time made references—often humorous or cocky—to himself as a potential occupant of the White House. It was becoming evident that these remarks had more in them than jest.

Long moved forward on two fronts. On election day, 1934, 3,000 battle-dressed Louisiana national guardsmen marched into New Orleans. Long's brother Julius, who had earlier described him as "the greatest political burglar of modern times," saw this move as totalitarian suppression of freedom. "With his well-known record for approving gambling and vice; fraud and ballot-box stuffing," he charged, "supported now by some of the outstanding gamblers and dive owners in and around New Orleans . . . he has the audacity and little respect for the intelligence and liberties of the people to pretend that he sincerely wants to suppress vice and has called out the National Guard and state militia."[18] Less than a month later, the legislature gave his officials practically unlimited control of the Louisiana military and subjected the cities in particular and state in general virtually to authoritarian rule. He turned his weekly paper into a national organ called *American Progress*. In a move traditional with presidential aspirants, he published his autobiography, *Every Man a King*. By February, 1934, the Reverend Gerald L. K. Smith—an antisemite and fascist-to-be—was organizing Share-Our-Wealth clubs on a national basis. In June of 1935 Long gained more national attention with a fifteen-hour filibuster opposing further extension of the New Deal National Recovery Act. By early 1936 he was all but a formally announced candidate. Long did not care if he split the Democratic Party; he was quite prepared to offer an alternative to both major parties. His view of them suggested David Graham Phillips's young radicals and communists in later fiction. Both parties were selling the same nostrums, he said, "And . . . the only difference . . . I can see is that the Republican leaders are skinning the people from the ankle up, and the Democratic

[18] As quoted in Luthin, *American Demagogues,* pp. 259 and 260.

leaders are taking off the hide from the ear down. Skin 'em up or skin 'em down, but skin 'em!"[19]

The Administration struck back through a radio broadcast by former NRA administrator, Gen. Hugh S. Johnson, a grizzled and cantankerous veteran who was himself no mean hand at invective. "It was easy," Postmaster General James A. Farley later recalled, "to conceive of a situation whereby Long, by polling more than 3,000,000 votes, might have the balance of power in the 1936 election."[20] After Johnson's blast, Long asked for equal radio time and used it to attack Roosevelt and extol the growing Share-Our-Wealth clubs. The Administration turned to a different kind of weapon. If it could not blast Long directly, it would mine his position. Treasury tax investigators had found out a good deal through an investigation prudently begun in 1930, later suspended, and then resumed. Indictments came through against his organization's smaller fry and plans were made to request a grand jury indictment in October. Long would be charged with evading income taxes on graft he had received through the Win or Lose Corporation deviously operating in the natural gas industry. But the following day a very different causal sequence disposed of the Kingfish forever.

Two opponents who had managed to stand against Long were Judge Benjamin F. Pavy and District Attorney R. Lee Garland. Their judicial district comprised the parishes of St. Landry and, ironically, Evangeline. Evangeline parish had never been able to outvote its yokemate for Long, but the Kingfish had devised a solution. It was the familiar gerrymander: his legislature would make Evangeline a separate district and combine St. Landry with three Long parishes. Like others loyal to Pavy, his son-in-law, Dr. Carl A. Weiss, Jr., was outraged. The mild-mannered eye, ear, nose, and throat specialist was said to be furious, moreover, at Long's insinuations of Negro blood in the Pavy family. Weiss was waiting in a corridor of the capitol building—the skyscraper which Long opponents called "Huey's silo"—on Sunday night, September 8, 1935, when Long emerged from a meeting and strode down the hallway toward the office of his faithful, rubber-stamp governor, O. K. Allen. He never reached it. Weiss stepped from behind a pillar and raised his hand. A gunshot reverberated off the marble walls as Long crumpled to the floor. Weiss fell riddled by the bullets of Long's bodyguards, dying instantly, un-

---

[19] As quoted in Schlesinger, *Roosevelt,* p. 65.
[20] As quoted in Luthin, *American Demagogues,* p. 265.

recognizable after the fusillade of lead. Long sustained only one wound, but like Mercutio's it served, and six hours later the Kingfish was dead. The uncertainty about the circumstances of Long's death was increased by the disappearance of the fatal bullet. Weiss had drawn the short straw, said some, in a plot which included some of Long's own men. Weiss had not fired at all, said others, but merely gestured as he tried to intercede for his father-in-law. Long did not, like Eugene O'Neill's Emperor Jones, die by a special, silver bullet. But the bullet was special, and there was something of the element of the macabre, as in the demise of the other, less powerful emperor.

Although the rise and fall of Huey Long was in many ways more dramatic than that of other latter-day demagogues such as Senator Joseph McCarthy, the causes were if anything less complex. It could be argued "that the combination of ruling powers of Louisiana had maintained a tighter grip on the state since Reconstruction than had like groups in other states." Similarly, wrote Key, "the longer the period of unrestrained exploitation, the more violent will be the reaction when it comes."[21] There was no question about the complexity of the man. There were many qualities: "the comic impudence, the gay egotism, the bravado, the mean hatred, the fear."[22] Huey P. Long, Jr., could play the buffoon, but this mask concealed one of the keenest minds in American politics. He was to Alben Barkley "the smartest lunatic I ever saw in my whole life!" to Rebecca West "the most formidable kind of brer fox," and to H. G. Wells "a Winston Churchill who has never been at Harrow."[23] His wit and humor were folksy and bawdy, but they served—and they stung. Neither the enemy in the Standard Oil Company offices in Baton Rouge nor the aristocratic rival in the White House in Washington was immune. Huey could liken the servants of the Interests to devils, his state foes to rats and lice, and the President of the United States to a bird of prey. Herbert Hoover, he said, was like a hoot owl who burst in the hen house, swept the hen from her perch, and then caught her before she touched the floor. Roosevelt, he said, was like a scrooch owl, who "slips into the roost and scrooches up to the hen and talks softly to her. And the hen just falls in love with him, and the first thing you know, *there ain't no hen!*"[24]

The endurance of Long's organization during his lifetime (as he pre-

[21] Key, *Southern Politics,* p. 159.
[22] Schlesinger, *Roosevelt,* p. 51.
[23] *Ibid.,* pp. 50 and 66.
[24] *Ibid.,* p. 56.

dicted, after him came the deluge) owed much to the fact that he kept faith, by and large, with the people who elected him, the wool hats and red necks, the mill hands and sapsuckers. For their allegiance, writes Schlesinger, "the people of Louisiana got a state government which did more for them than any other government in Louisiana's history . . . Schools, hospitals, roads and public services in general were better than ever before. Poor whites and even Negroes had unprecedented opportunities."[25] Huey had unprecedented opportunities himself, and he made the most of them. When his star was at its zenith, the Kansas City *Star* asserted that "Wall Street has furnished Louisiana about $50,000,000 since the Kingfish took hold . . ."[26] William Allen White saw much more than money involved. "Fascism always comes through a vast pretense of socialism backed by Wall Street money," he wrote. "Huey Long is the type we must fear."[27] Contributions flowed in from the oil, sulphur, railroad, banking, and utility interests.[28] The treasury agent who had led the investigation intended to put Huey behind bars wrote that he "took plenty and he took it for Huey Pierce Long, which made him a tool of the vested interests he fought so vigorously."[29] Some, however, got little or none at all: "He sprinkled the state with roads and buildings. But he did little or nothing to raise wages for the workers, to stop child labor, to reduce the work day, to support trade unions, to provide pensions for the aged, to furnish relief to the unemployed, even to raise teachers' salaries. He left behind no record of social or labor legislation."[30] In spite of Long's oft-repeated slogan, no one can have been convinced that in the Kingfish's dominions Every Man was a King. But it was clear to see, for all who would, that One Man Wore a Crown.

To many critics, Huey P. Long, Jr., was an American Fascist. Others, while granting like Key that his "control of Louisiana more nearly matched the power of a South American dictator than that of any other American state boss," felt he was innocent of totalitarian ideology.[31] Huey rejected the comparison violently. Mentioned with Hitler, he

---

[25] Schlesinger, *Roosevelt*, p. 58.
[26] As quoted in Michie and Rhylick, *Dixie Demagogues*, pp. 113–114.
[27] As quoted in Schlesinger, *Roosevelt*, p. 89.
[28] Michie and Rhylick, *Dixie Demagogues*, p. 113.
[29] Elmer L. Frey, as quoted in Luthin, *American Demagogues*, p. 250.
[30] Schlesinger, *Roosevelt*, p. 60.
[31] Key, *Southern Politics*, pp. 156 and 164. Rorty and Decter take the opposite view: "He was an ideologue, a theoretician, a planner, an organizer. His library was well stocked with the theoretical literature of both Marxism and Fascism" (James Rorty and Moshe Decter, *McCarthy and the Communists*, p. 113).

roared, "Don't liken me to that son of a bitch!"[32] He was willing to
tolerate a similarity to Abraham Lincoln. Not surprisingly, he came off
the better. "Lincoln didn't free the slaves in Louisiana," he boasted, "I
did."[33] Another time, he was willing to acknowledge the Great Emanci-
pator as one of his three teachers; the others, he said, were Andrew
Jackson and Almighty God.[34] The conjunction of Lincoln and Long
was in a strange sort of way apt. In the novels discussed in this chapter
the two figures become almost mythic, presenting as though polarized,
elements good and evil in American politics and culture.

In the following literary analysis, the Southern Demagogue is subsumed under the figure of the Southern Politician, for there appear in
the novels—as there did in the South—leaders of a different stripe.
Claude Pepper, a vigorous campaigner and eloquent orator on the stump
in Florida, became in Washington one of the strongest advocates of New
Deal policies. In Alabama, Big Jim Folsom waxed powerful against the
planters and the "big mules" of industry and finance from the commanding position of the governor's chair. The difference between national and local politics for the Southern politician was exemplified by
James F. Byrnes. For years a Roosevelt stalwart in Washington, he made
White Supremacy his program's keystone in South Carolina. Aspects of
conservatism were embodied in fiscal policies of Virginians Harry Byrd
and Carter Glass, whereas a conservatism so radical as to give rise to
the short-lived Dixiecrat Party of 1948 had as its standard-bearer Governor J. Strom Thurmond of South Carolina. On still another level was
Senator J. W. Fulbright, who rose through the faction-ridden politics
of Arkansas to a position of power and eminence in the Senate. There
he has been not only a liberal Democrat—so far as practical exigencies
of Arkansas politics would permit—but a man who has helped shape
far-reaching policy under more than one administration. But for all
these variants, the stereotype of the demagogue persists. As Cash remarks, it "would not be true to say that . . . the South had no choice save
between demagogues of the Right and demagogues of the Left (in their
appeal, not their practice, of course). But there would be a good deal
of truth in it."[35]

One would not hope to give in a few pages the outlines of the twentieth-century Southern politics which have provided the milieu which

[32] As quoted in Michie and Rhylick, *Dixie Demagogues,* p. 112.
[33] As quoted in Schlesinger, *Roosevelt,* p. 60.
[34] Luthin, *American Demagogues,* p. 243.
[35] Cash, *South,* p. 421.

produced the novels. But some of the salient features of this political terrain can be seen. After Federal attempts at Reconstruction ceased, the Southern states used the Black Codes to re-establish White Supremacy by substituting peonage for slavery. Then, after Populism foundered upon the rock of cooperation with the Negro, Southern politics emerged as a one-party system. The powerful planters of the Black Belts and new industrialists and financiers of the cities exerted great pressure to maintain the racial and electoral *status quo* (when not in fact extending disfranchisement) and to protect their commercial and financial interests. From the early years of the century they were often opposed by demagogues and popular leaders rising from among the people (or at least giving the appearance of having done so) and making common cause with them against the big planters and the native and absentee industrialists and financiers. Concurrently, industrialization increased and with it the number of industrial workers. But labor's growth into a strong force was militantly opposed by both powerful employers favored under the law and by regional attitudes inimical to such concepts. And though Federal aid was welcomed in the Depression years, the economic structure might prevent it from filtering down as far as it was meant to go—often to the areas where it was most desperately needed— and the incursions of Federal power were resented and repelled.[36]

Whether political or nonpolitical, serious contemporary fiction depicting the South usually emphasizes problems arising out of the racial conflict and dilemma. This is, of course, only one problem, even if the most acute, of a region with a tragic history. It is one aspect of a larger problem: "Obviously the conversion of the South into a democracy in the sense that the mass of people vote and have a hand in their governance poses one of the most staggering tasks for statesmanship in the western world."[37] Surely the extremity of this situation is responsible for much of the power of the best of these novels of Southern politics, the best one of which stands alone.

Literary Characteristics

One of the major assertions of twentieth-century American literature

---

[36] In John Dos Passos's *The Grand Design*, the Reverend Green shows Paul Graves a stricken area. He tells him that in these counties "relief is in the hands of the politicians and the politicians are mostly landlords who save it for their own tenants" (p. 155). For discussion of other inequities, see Goldman, *Rendezvous*, pp. 348–349.

[37] Key, *Southern Politics*, p. 661.

has been that the South is not just different from the rest of the country but that it is, as Long liked to call himself, *sui generis*. The work of such artists as William Faulkner, Thomas Wolfe, Eudora Welty, Tennessee Williams, Carson McCullers, and Erskine Caldwell stands as a testimonial to this fact. This same uniqueness is to be seen in the political novel, especially in fourteen novels which appeared in the years between 1922 and 1960. They are novels in which the sense of place is so strong as to set them apart from those of other areas. Often novels of bossism or corruption might as easily have been set in New York as in Ohio, in New Jersey as in Illinois. The novels in this chapter are set (by statement or inference) in Virginia, West Virginia, Kentucky, Arkansas, North Carolina, Florida, Mississippi, Louisiana, and Oklahoma. None could have been set outside the South, and as the mark of place is upon the novels, so it is upon the men. It has helped create the most dramatic archetypal figure among these novels—the Southern Demagogue—and the best novel—Robert Penn Warren's *All the King's Men*.

The novelists insist on the South's uniqueness. In *The Sound Wagon* a congressman tells T. S. Stribling's Northern protagonist, "In the South we lack system. We have only a few political machines, and they work creakily and uneasily. Our big deciding vote swings with damnable uncertainty on the whim of the voter. You can buy votes in the South, all you want; but you can't get 'em delivered . . . the Southern votes come singly, and the Southern congressman spends his time getting elected."[38] But the regional differences, of course, go deeper than this. They are the products of historical forces which shaped the past and determined the present. In a passage in *The Kingpin* (1953) which shows the often-encountered influence of William Faulkner's rhetoric and cadences, Tom Wicker writes, ". . . out of this past . . . come the people of the country South, the backwoods South . . . timeless, slow-moving, ill-fed, ill-housed, ill-clad, prey to all the dark moods and passions, all the hates and hurts and beliefs of a land and a heritage blighted, diseased, cursed by an old black evil, an evil and a heritage they never saw, never knew, only accepted in some deep and bitter resignation . . ."[39]

Many of these novelists seem to endorse the view of Southern history which Malcolm Cowley and others see in Faulkner's saga of Yoknapatawpha County. His "Myth of the South," especially in "The Bear" and *Absalom, Absalom!* (1936), portrays a fertile land, developed by pow-

---

[38] Thomas S. Stribling, *The Sound Wagon*, p. 164.
[39] Tom Wicker, *The Kingpin*, p. 184.

erful aristocrats and aggressive New Men but made vulnerable by the seed of corruption inherent in the moral evil of slavery. The War and its aftermath come as retribution with native and foreign exploiters replacing the armies of occupation to complete the tragedy. The forces leading to the catastrophe were, of course, complex. One contributory force was that form of ancestor worship which Hamilton Basso's protagonist in *The View from Pompey's Head* (1954) calls Southern Shintoism. Robert Rylee's protagonist in *The Ring and the Cross* (1947) contends that General Robert E. Lee should have accepted Lincoln's proffered appointment as commander-in-chief of the Federal forces in order to shorten the war: "And partly due to Lee's loyalty to Virginia, we still sit here in the South, worshipping before the ruined tombs of our corrupt ancestors, blaming others for our ills—and I grant you others have greatly aggravated them—when it was we ourselves who set off the chain of evil circumstance."[40]

In these novels then, the War has left a legacy of poverty, sickness, ignorance, and hatred. Hatred of the Negro is complemented by xenophobia usually directed against the Yankee, the Jew, and latterly, the agents of organized labor. The new order emerging with the dissolution of the old has most of the ante-bellum vices and few of the virtues. Violence and immorality are commonplace. Organizations such as the Ku Klux Klan perpetrate lynchings, mutilations, and beatings. Individuals in public as well as private life commit acts of immorality and sexual pathology which often go beyond simple indices of personal aberration and become symbolic of general social decadence as well. Besides the double standard for men and women, there is the one for white people and Negroes. The heritage of the past is seen not only in the clear and obvious—inadequate schools and roads—but in the devious and covert: leases of state resources to influential entrepreneurs, tax structures which favor the moneyed planters, the utilities, and the corporate interests. Corollary is discrimination against the exploited, underpaid factory hands and hard-pressed share croppers—the "crackers," the "lint-heads," and the "red-necks."

The protagonists produced by these conditions fall clearly into distinct types. Almost all of these Southern politicians are prominent office holders; only a few are Bosses who rule from behind the scenes. These few have a good deal in common with those in Chapter Two. But again, the pervasiveness of the environment, the special conditions in which they

[40] Robert Rylee, *The Ring and the Cross,* p. 285.

attain and exercise power, make them Southern politicians first and Bosses second. Men of lowly birth, usually, they ally themselves with the great mass of the poor. Making their appeal to the "hill-billies" and "wool hats," they pledge roads, schools, and health services, promising to "share the wealth and soak the rich." Others (sometimes these same men once safely ensconced in office) ally themselves with the power companies and large corporations to prey upon the majority of the electorate and the large disfranchised substratum below. A few share the motivation of the Young Knight. Most conform to a pattern, however, which can be called that of the Southern Demagogue—the man who plays upon the emotions of the masses for power, profit, and place. He is usually physically powerful, strong, shrewd, and acute. He has a pragmatic grasp of human psychology in his manipulations of individuals and crowds. He is a dramatic orator whose campaigning combines political issues with the emotions of the revivalist camp meeting and the traveling medicine show. The tones and rhythms of the campaign orations reproduce the antiphonal responses of preacher and congregation. And with them come the twanging of the string bands' hillbilly ballads, the shrilling crescendos of brasses blaring "Dixie."

The Southern Demagogue is usually a complete relativist. He uses what he has to work with, and often the ends are contaminated by the means. He sometimes has an alter ego who may be a villainous henchman or a whipping boy. He is likely to be married to a good woman, whose credentials are sometimes verified by her having been a schoolteacher. In almost every instance, however, she has an opposite number too. The Southern Demagogue needs the seductive, loose-moraled sex symbol who becomes his mistress.[41] He is aggressive and ambitious. Like the Young Knight, he is apt to have Presidential aspirations. But fully half these lives end in violent death.

This violence is in harmony with the violence of the country. In some of these settings, frontier only eighty years before, the democratic processes are often carried out in an atmosphere hostile to them. Politics are almost always conducted under a one-party system. One of David Graham Phillips's protagonists, convinced that both parties were agents

[41] This pattern suggests two familiar elements in Southern cultural lore: the idealized image of Southern Womanhood whom the Southern male fanatically praised and venerated, and the seductive woman (often a colored mistress) with whom he found the satisfaction impossible with the idealized Southern Wife and Mother. For an acute analysis of these elements, see Cash, *South*, pp. 82–87 and 128.

paid from the same source, would perhaps have welcomed this simplification. But this system is, if anything, more complicated, with primary elections involving run-offs, strategies for splitting an opponent's strength, and the less subtle devices of innuendo, slander, and fraud. Issues are not uncommonly resolved by gunfire, and in these novels set in the 1930's and 1940's there are fascist overtones. Groups of returning World War II veterans band together, as in the novels of American Fascism, to combat near-totalitarian rule. An analogue of this political violence appears in sexual violence. Seduction, adultery, rape, and deviation do not exhaust it. Sadism is commonplace, and there are ingenious combinations and elaborations which can only be called sexual pathology.

Literary Ancestors

The violent passions and events of Reconstruction found violent expression in partisan fiction. Thomas Dixon, Jr., a North Carolina minister who proudly proclaimed himself a nephew of the Grand Titan of the Ku Klux Klan, was fervent and prolific. In novels such as *The Leopard's Spots* (1902), he depicted an outraged South defending itself as best it could against the hateful repression and harassment of a vindictive victor. *The Clansman* (1905) gave even wider currency to Dixon's vehement convictions, especially his anti-Negro feelings, when it was made into one of the first genuine classics of a new medium—the motion pictures. Still perennially showing nearly a half-century after its production, *The Birth of a Nation* caused riots when it was first shown. At the opposite extreme from Dixon was Albion W. Tourgée, an Ohio-born Union officer who resided in the South for fifteen years after the war. Serving as judge of the Superior Court of North Carolina, he had earned the enmity of most of his fellow citizens. In his awkward but intensely-felt novels Tourgée argued that the Federal government had blundered badly in the measures it imposed upon the South. It had failed tragically by thrusting freedom and responsibility upon uneducated masses unable fully to deal with either, then abandoning them and the decent human beings who attempted to ameliorate their lot. The South had predictably responded with repression and atrocity, and Tourgée's novels dilated upon both. In *A Fool's Errand* (1879) and *Bricks Without Straw* (1880) he had diagnosed, prescribed, and preached. "We presumed, that by the suppression of rebellion, the Southern White man had become identical with the Caucasian of the North in thought and sentiment; and that the slave, by emancipation, had become a saint and a Solomon at once," he wrote in the former volume. "So we tried to build up communities there which should be identical in thought, sentiment, growth, and development, with those of the North. It was *A Fool's Errand.*"[42] Later, in a prescription for the future, part of which was to be echoed in the next century by such leaders as Booker T. Washington, Tourgée exhorted: "Make the spelling-book the scepter of national power . . . Poor-whites, Freedmen, Ku-Klux, and Bulldozers are all alike the harvest of ignorance. The Nation can not afford to grow such a crop" (366–367). Although Tourgée's novels dealt more with political processes than did the equally wild farragoes of Dixon, neither author's work was as preponderantly concerned with these processes as the novels which follow. These violent partisans, dealing with the time of dislocation and upheaval, treated at length the larger economic and sociological aspects of the problem as well as its political manifestations. But imperfect as these works were, they enunciated themes which were to recur and sketched in the historical background against which better artists would later set their work.

Early Novels: The Righteous

In the three earliest novels of Southern politics in this century, the protagonists were neither Bosses nor demagogues although they briefly achieved both power and notoriety. Two of them emerged from the lower strata of a war-scarred society, making their appeal to an electorate predominantly composed of the impoverished, the uneducated, and the exploited. Unlike most of those to follow, they were unselfishly motivated throughout. The third protagonist was a follower rather than a leader. Although obviously intended to be amusing and even lovable, his effect is the opposite. Insensitive and boorish, he exemplifies aspects of the decadence of his culture. Ironically, in his own limited and insensitive way, he is one of the champions of the right in this culture.

Ellen Glasgow's *One Man in His Time* (1922) is apparently set in Richmond, Virginia, in the years immediately following the first World War. A young aristocrat viewing the present against the dissolution of the past perceives that "the tide of the new ideas was still rising. Democracy, relentless, disorderly, and strewn with the wreckage of finer things, had overwhelmed the world of established customs in which he lived."[43] For Stephen Culpeper the embodiment of this change is Gideon Vetch,

[42] Albion W. Tourgée, *A Fool's Errand*, p. 361.
[43] Ellen Glasgow, *One Man in His Time*, p. 2.

white trash born in a circus tent and now governor of the state of Virginia. To another aristocrat he is a demagogue who "deliberately sold his office in exchange for his election—" (148). Vetch does have shady connections. His defense—to be echoed twenty-five years later by the best embodiment of this type—is necessity: "the end for which I work seems to me vastly more important than the methods I use or the instruments that I employ" (173). His goals—new labor laws, social benefits, and eventual nationalization of mines and railroads—are to his aristocratic opponents "mere bombast . . . but the kind of thing that is dangerous in a crowd" (150).

Vetch's figure is immediately familiar, a "tall, rugged figure built of good bone and muscle and sound to the core . . ." (22). This leader of lowly birth smiles down at people "from his great height" (376), impressing even young Culpeper with "the most tremendous dignity a human being could attain—the unconscious dignity of natural forces . . ." (27). Around his story Mrs. Glasgow twists those of Culpeper and Vetch's daughter (another pair of politics-crossed lovers), two older lovers, and the secrets of Vetch's past. In the foreground of the action, he tries to find a solution to an explosive labor dispute while attempting to cleanse his Administration. At this point Mrs. Glasgow does again what she had done twenty years earlier in *The Voice of the People*: she gratuitously kills her protagonist. Again the means is mob violence. Trying to stop a fight, Vetch is shot. Later an opponent eulogizes his "humanity that is as rare as genius itself" (377).

Mrs. Glasgow's intention, as in earlier novels, was to depict another era in Virginia history. Surveying the changes wrought in social and political life by still another war, she contrasted something of the best and worst of the old order and the new. Culpeper was a familiar figure: the enervated aristocrat being thrust aside by the vigorous New Man such as Vetch. Culpeper also demonstrated the process of breakthrough from a stultifying existence to a widening and liberating one. Apart from a few gaucheries in dialogue, the novel is free from obvious awkwardness. But it never wholly succeeds in any of the author's apparent intentions. Each of the explorations is made with a combination of obviousness and insufficiency. And her greatest error, of course, which demonstrates her inability to meet the demands of her theme, is her dispatching of her hero just as he comes to grips with his basic challenges: economic reform in the face of powerful opposition, and the task of escaping contamination by the instruments and methods he has used.

A very different sort of protagonist stands at the center of Glenn

Allan's *Old Manoa* (1932). He is a tall, thin man of sixty who wears a mustache and goatee. Old Manoa serves as commissioner of Towhit County, Tennessee, only to oblige his childhood friend Jedge Warmsley, the hideously fat but benevolent Boss of the county.[44] The novel spins out the story of the revolt of Jedge's appointees. In collusion with them is the Phoenix Power Company. Aided by "mountain men" with guns, Jedge and Manoa repulse them in action culminating in arson, assault, and death. Balancing these elements are a romance, the relationship between the two old men, and the character of Manoa himself. Loving the horses he breeds and the blue-grass country where his family has lived for more than a hundred years, he is meant to be a cantankerous but lovable old gentleman. But the humor is thin and Manoa's lovableness is not convincing enough to conceal attitudes also found in some of the worst specimens in these Southern novels. To stop his Negro cook from summoning the doctor, this gallant Southern gentleman throws his whisky glass at her. He flings sticks at his old servant Bunk and refuses to allow Bunk's son Jamie to wear a hat "because Jamie understood a whack or a poke better and quicker than he did an order.[45]

This novel presents a curious kind of authorial innocence. It is meant to be humorous, but the discerning reader is much more likely to feel nausea. Towhit County politics are as much a travesty of the democratic ideal as are those in many novels of corruption, and the "good" men who win in the end (with assistance of the state Boss) are authoritarians with racist mentalities whose characters seem to rest, at least in part, upon substrata of sloth, gluttony, and brutality verging on sadism.

The last of the wholly idealistic protagonists in these novels of the Southern Politician appeared in Charles Morrow Wilson's *Rabble Rouser* (1936). A young redheaded farmhand, he rises to the governorship of Arkansas before he is beaten by the opposition and the Interests (another Power and Light Company). The most interesting aspect of this novel is not Cabe Hargis's career as such but the characteristics which make him an early representative of a common type. His home is Hemmed-in-Holler (threatened by a projected power company dam) in Izard County, and his style, strategy, and values derive ultimately from this fact. His speech is countrified, and the emotion he projects through it is genuine. Hargis turns all his emotional oratory on sympathetic juries when he acts for small litigants against the trusts. On the stump, he loves to see his

---

[44] The smart fat man becomes a familiar type of Southern politician. Usually he is villainous.

[45] Glen Allan, *Old Manoa*, p. 25.

hearers throw their black hats into the air. He is "for" men with red necks, he tells them, because he is a "redneck" too. (Robert Penn Warren's Willie Stark will later use this pejorative phrase to his own advantage.) He is folksy yet shrewd, campaigning in remote areas other candidates rarely see, sleeping under whatever roof will give him shelter, and wearing down an opponent on a grueling speaking tour. He holds his own in an environment where running a dummy candidate to split an opponent's vote is one of the subtler devices.[46]

Rabble Rouser often reads like parody, so broad do its characters and dialects become. Yet it is far from the worst of this group. Amid the overdone accents (sometimes suggesting the raftsmen of Twain's *Life on the Mississippi*) are lyric passages on the seasons, the flow of time, and the fruitfulness of nature. For this study, however, the greatest interest resides in the depiction of this young "rabble rouser" who gains power through a combination of skills. Using intelligence and country-style oratory, he allies his own interests with those of the underprivileged mass of the people from whom he himself comes. And unlike many who rise through the same methods, he does not desert his friends after gaining power.

The Southern Politician as Boss

The few Southern politicians who operate primarily as Bosses work behind the scenes rather than as dynamic leaders openly swaying the masses. They differ from their counterparts elsewhere in their manipulation of regional prejudices and resentments, their reliance upon power and intimidation more than upon favors and agreements, and—in one instance at least—readiness to resort to brutality and violence.

Robert Wilder's *Flamingo Road* (1942) dealt with not just one Boss but two. One of them, like Kevin Costello in Wilder's later *The Wine of Youth* (1955), is a wealthy construction man whose main interest in politics is protecting his investments, although he does what he can to guard Florida "against the predatory instincts of the men who shared some measure of [power] with him."[47] Dan Curtis is a kind of half-hearted Chamber of Commerce Robin Hood, for "What he took came from other men: from the stupidly conniving, the avaricious, the combi-

[46] Describing his campaign for John M. Parker in 1920, Huey Long wrote, "I took the stump for a period of approximately seventy days and went places where no other campaign orator had ever reached, traveling at times by horseback to fill appointments" (Luthin, *American Demagogues*, p. 242).
[47] Robert Wilder, *Flamingo Road*, p. 201.

nations which insisted they were smarter than he, but not from his state. If tax assessments favored his enterprises, franchises and contracts came his way, then he built good roads, operated efficient utilities, and, now and then, cut a small slice of pie for his investors." (201). His enemy is a monstrously obese county sheriff who may owe something to Faulkner's Flem Snopes, possessing as he does "a reptilian treachery and the persistence of a beaver" (237). Titus Semple builds his power carefully, assiduously cultivating both the white farmers and the Negroes. He defeats Curtis's coalition by using evidence of their own corrupt practices, but another familiar Wilder character—the intelligent and ambitious whore with a heart of gold (who also happens to have become Curtis's mistress) —murders him for past insults and injuries. Like *The Wine of Youth*, this novel is technically dextrous. Its fluent prose is almost glossy, and correspondingly, its climaxes have the ring of melodrama, as its assignations have the texture of pulp fiction.

The extremes of Southern politics show up more clearly in a novel by Franklin Coen set in Tennessee or Georgia. *Vinegar Hill* (1950) begins with the retirement of a former congressman and cabinet secretary called typical "of all of the Old Faithfuls," such as Borah, Norris, Hull, Wagner, and McAdoo.[48] He finds a struggle under way between the Boss who made him and returning World War II veterans. Finding that the organization uses intimidation and murder, Secretary Tobias remonstrates with one of Boss Tilden's men: "Red's a puny, inept Huey Long. Or tryin' to be. Long, at least, had some feelin' for people. This'll get you nothin' but trouble" (145). The reply is revealing: "Maybe, Toby. Only understand that Red's playin' for big stakes. The *South*, sir . . . The North ain't sendin' carpetbaggers down here, they're sendin' ideas— damn lousy subversive ideas!" (145). After the Secretary attempts to repudiate his indebtedness to Tilden, the veterans go further. Besieging a hundred deputized out-of-state "gorillas," they breach the courthouse wall with a kind of Bangalore torpedo, killing Tilden in the struggle. The new sheriff solemnly informs the press that "the will of the people had almost been subverted, and that this must not be allowed, even at the cost of so many dead" (308–309).[49]

---

[48] Franklin Coen, *Vinegar Hill*, p. 4.

[49] The novel's pitched battle strains credibility until one reads of the eviction by a veterans' group of the brutal machine which had for years ruled McMinn County in southeast Tennessee. In the early morning of August 1, 1946, they surrounded the county jail and successfully laid siege to it with bullets and dynamite. The local vassals of the Crump machine and their two hundred hired deputies (many out-of-town and out-of-state plug-uglies) were turned out and the GI slate

Tilden's power derives not only from a ruthless machine but also from the skillful use of economic fears and resentment against the North. Every prejudice and attitude likely to be useful is mobilized. Symptomatic of a pervasive immorality and sadism is the deputy sheriff who violates female Negro prisoners and also intimidates a respectable young Negro woman to the same purpose. As a young Congressman, Tobias had been thought a Bull Moose partisan, a trust-buster, and a radical. Although he had later been forced to compromise his principles, his long career had still maintained a fair outward aspect. Supporting it, however, had been the rotten substructure of the machine. Behind the machine's façade had been the decadence of the society which supported it. But in this particular middling novel there were signs of a resurgence of decency and responsibility in the values the veterans defend.

The Southern Demagogue

The first of the nine novels dealing with the Southern Demagogue appeared in 1941, with five of the rest following within the space of six years. Edward Kimbrough's *From Hell to Breakfast* came eleven years after the death of James K. Vardaman, six years after the demise of Huey Long, and during the lifetime of Theodore S. Bilbo. It displayed

---

of candidates installed in office. There were no deaths, but ten of the veterans were wounded and five of the deputies were hospitalized. See Theodore H. White, "The Battle of Athens, Tennessee," *Harper's Magazine*, 194 (January, 1947), 54–60. (It is somehow ironic that the final vote which decided the issue in the state legislature whose ratification made woman suffrage into law should have come from McMinn County. See National American Woman Suffrage Association, *Victory: How Women Won It*, pp. 149 and 152.) In the summer of 1946, former Marine Lieutenant Colonel Sid McMath led a movement in Arkansas which captured the mayoralty of Hot Springs by the following spring, touched off a series of similar actions throughout the state, and placed McMath in the governor's chair in 1948. However, "Not all GI leaders were white knights leading crusades against wicked local machines. The revolts picked up the usual quota of opportunists whose chief sincerity was in their wish to ride the GI band wagon into office. Nevertheless, the movement, if it could be called that, included a number of men of extraordinary idealism coupled with skill and coolness in the hard-boiled tactics of politics" (Key, *Southern Politics*, p. 204). In 1948 McMath, as governor, paid off a debt to a political supporter from a place in the Ozark Mountains called Greasy Creek. He named Orval E. Faubus state highway director. When Faubus went on to the governorship and in his second term drew world-wide attention to Arkansas during the Little Rock integration crises, McMath rued his generosity. "I wish," he lamented, "I had never built the road that led Faubus out of the hills" (*New York Times*, August 5, 1962, Section 4, p. 2E). When Faubus won the nomination for his fifth term, the man who ran third was former governor McMath.

a man and a milieu whose characteristics reappeared in the novels that followed and were to be raised to their highest power in Warren's *All the King's Men*. In his foreword Kimbrough declared he was using "the technique of satirical exaggeration," portraying "no specific Mississippi politician . . . but rather . . . satirizing a particular type of man." The object of this satire is Gus Roberts, United States senator and Boss of this state once represented by Vardaman and Bilbo. He is opposed for re-election by the son of an old friend, a pro-labor lawyer glad to argue poor men's cases. (When Roberts's daughter falls in love with the young man, the newspapers naturally enough call it a Romeo-Juliet romance.) Roberts wins easily, and his opponent is lucky to escape from Roberts-organized, white-clad "White Knights" intent on castrating him.

Roberts's perennial success is due to his organization, his conscience-less shrewdness in battle, and his sway over the electorate. Once a Methodist minister and revivalist preacher, he still orates with his old-time fervor. His denunciations of radicalism stem not so much from conviction as from their crowd appeal. Well on in years, he still enjoys his long-time association with a whore-mistress named Fanny. When his long-separated wife sues for divorce on adultery during the campaign, he counters adroitly. He declares he wants no divorce and is saved again at a revival meeting. His rule is characterized by graft and bribery, abuses such as illegal use of prison labor, and hate directed at Negroes, Jews, and outsiders. Most of the characters dilate upon the ills of the South, usually blaming them on someone or something else—Yankee-owned plants or labor organizers within them. There is the usual contempt for idealism and reform. The voters are generally regarded as dolts who can be bought with a paid-up poll tax, corn liquor, a cheap permanent for their wives, or as a last resort, cash money. The constituents most zealously protected are the rich merchants, the mill-owners, and the landowners. Throughout the novel there are references to Hitler, to Naziism, to Fascism. The similarities between their regimes and the local one, particularly in violence and corruption, are explicitly noted by the defeated candidate at the novel's end. *From Hell to Breakfast* is a tiresome novel presenting a dismal picture of its locale, but it is a picture whose details are corroborated in the novels to come.

A year later Hamilton Basso's *Sun in Capricorn* appeared, its text preceded by the epigraph, "Capricorn is said to be the sign of ambition. It looks like the horns of a goat." The cuckoldry suggested in the second sentence applies neither to Hazzard X, the narrator, nor to Governor Gilgo Slade—whose first name might well set the echoes ringing in the memories of many. Slade is campaigning for the Senate in a northern Louisiana parish, but he has his eye on the Presidency. If anyone is betrayed, it is the voter. Wooed by Slade with old-time, circus-style campaign entertainment—complete with a hillbilly band—he is bombarded from stump and radio by a Big Lie technique suggesting that of contemporary European practitioner, Dr. Joseph Goebbels. The narrator's true and passionate, but unfortunately illegal, love affair is used by Slade against his opponent, the narrator's uncle. Hazzard X's resolve to assassinate Slade is frustrated only by someone else's getting there first. The death of the nobly motivated assassin under the machine guns of Gilgo's bodyguards is another passage likely to set the echoes of memory ringing. At the novel's ironic end, Hazzard X hears two "peckerwoods" regretting Slade's demise and extolling his greatness.

In spite of a convincing narrator, this work is at bottom thin and superficial. There are many untied strands of plot and theme, and Slade, on whom much of the weight of the novel must rest, is only a cardboard ranter and raver. He is, however, another avatar of the type brought to his sinister apotheosis four years later in Warren's Willie Stark.[50]

John Dos Passos's version of the Southern Demagogue archetype, *Number One*, appeared a year after Basso's in 1943. It showed the illness which produced the Demagogue as it flourished in an oil-rich state strongly suggesting Oklahoma. (With *Adventures of a Young Man* [1939] and *The Grand Design* [1948], it formed a partially connected narrative. Following a number of characters through radicalism and corruption in the 1920's and 1930's, the Spanish Civil War, and the early days of the New Deal, the three volumes were finally published together as the trilogy, *District of Columbia*.) Texarcola-born Homer T. "Chuck" Crawford first reaches the District of Columbia as a congressman. The burden of the novel is his rise as he wins a Senate seat and goes on to enrich himself through state oil lands. And when the oil scandal breaks (suggesting a later and smaller Teapot Dome), he is still secure. His secretary, speech-writer, and public-relations man—alcoholic Toby Spotswood, the other major character in the novel—goes to jail.

Crawford is a shrewd tactician running with the hare in public and hunting with the hounds in private. The slogan he offers the people is "Every Man a Millionaire," and he demonstrates the seeming simple-

---

[50] For a discussion of Basso's rejection of the Communist variety of authoritarianism—especially as seen in interchanges with his friend Malcolm Cowley—see Daniel Aaron, *Writers on the Left: Episodes in American Literary Communism*, pp. 339–340.

heartedness that makes him one of them by such endearing mannerisms as playing the ocarina. The biography written for his campaign is entitled "Poor Boy to President." His rusticity is no more than skin deep, and like most others of this archetype, he sees the White House as an attainable prize. His relationship with a roadhouse vocalist is as pleasant as that with his Struck Oil Corporation is profitable.[51] And the latter association is disrupted only because of his exercise of his new-found power. A newspaper commentator writes: "his one man filibuster which so neatly upset one of the majority's most cherished applecarts has so angered the Administration stalwarts that they are willing to go the limit . . ."[52] Crawford differs from most of the other Southern Demagogues in that he meets no serious check. Toby's atonement for his work for Crawford (spurred by the last letter of his younger brother, Glenn, killed fighting in Spain), provides the scapegoat for the income-tax-evasion trial looming as the novel ends.

Though *Number One* is the weakest novel of the trilogy, it is by no means an ordinary novel. Using few of the experimental devices of *U.S.A.*, Dos Passos tells the story often with directness and power. His only special effects are chapter introductions forming a continuous description of "the people"—a farmer, a mechanic, a chainstore clerk, a miner, and a business executive. The concluding italicized passage, in Dos Passos's familiar hortatory manner, adjures the reader:

> weak as the weakest, strong as the strongest,
> the people are the republic,
> the people are you. (304)

The appeal was a familiar one—heard in the 1930's and earlier, though

[51] Schlesinger writes, "if within Long's limits government was benevolent and fairly efficient, it was still intricately and hopelessly corrupt. In 1934, to take an example, Long and several close associates set up the Win or Lose Corporation. The state government considerately made it possible for the new corporation to acquire properties in the natural gas fields; the corporation then persuaded natural gas companies to buy the properties by threatening to increase their taxes if they didn't. Using such persuasive sales methods, Win or Lose cleared about $350,000 in 1935" (*Roosevelt*, pp. 60–61).

[52] John Dos Passos, *Number One*, p. 228. Though bills have been talked to death by a number of legislators, the filibuster is particularly associated with the image of Senator Long. Dos Passos had seen Long and had not been well impressed. He looked, the novelist wrote, "like an overgrown small boy with very bad habits indeed" (as quoted in Schlesinger, *Roosevelt*, p. 49). Other obvious elements in this *roman à clef* include Crawford's start as county road commissioner and subsequent rise to membership on the State Utilities Commission. He manages to get his state delegation accredited over the claims of a rival faction at the national convention, as Long had done in 1932.

then warning of a different danger. This appeal sounded much the same as that of Sinclair Lewis in *It Can't Happen Here,* urging the citizen to help preserve political freedom by discharging his duty. But Dos Passos's Demagogue did not, somehow, seem as desperate and threatening as his author's tone suggested.

The sense of *déjà vu* becomes stronger as the reader goes further. And the transparent concealments of several other authors conceal nothing. The title of Adria Locke Langley's novel, *A Lion Is in the Streets* (1945), suggests the "most horrid sights seen by the watch" which Calpurnia describes to Caesar in Act II, Scene ii, of Shakespeare's *Julius Caesar*.[53] But the locale is variously Sherman, Crescent City, or Cypress Bend in Delamore Parish of the Magnolia State. The protagonist is a onetime sharecropper and traveling salesman married to a former schoolteacher. A self-educated lawyer, Hank Martin passes the state bar examination with a phenomenally high score. He rises from commissioner of public works and highways to governor of the state on the strength of his campaign theme of "Divide the Riches." His "kindlin' power" inspires his followers through speeches loaded with Biblical references and rural idiom. It is a camp-meeting technique exercised in revival-style tents. More importantly, however, he organizes a following of country people, paying a stipend to the widows among them out of a $50,000 fee he has frightened out of the Southern Light and Power Co. He insures the franchise of his illiterate followers by "Hank Martin's God-blessed Grandpappy Law," which "says that a man who voted in or before 1867, his sons or his children's children cannot be deprived a' their franchise because of failure t' pass educational or property qualifications."[54] From photostatic copies of lists of these early voters Martin assigns enfranchising ancestors to his followers.

Predictably, corruption follows power as Martin replaces his fanatical immediate followers with a bodyguard of professional "gorillas." He com-

---

[53] What the watch actually reports is that "A lioness hath whelped in the streets." Miss Langley's use of the masculine gender may perhaps suggest simply that a predatory beast is afoot rather than calling up the portents which, to Calpurnia, augur the fall of Rome's dictator.

[54] Adria Locke Langley, *A Lion Is in the Streets,* p. 247. Illiterate whites were able to evade the literacy test for voting through the so-called "grandfather clause" of the state constitution of Louisiana, put into effect without popular vote in 1898. The provisions were identical with those in the novel. Although the stratagem had been rejected in South Carolina because of its doubtful constitutionality, it was adopted by other states before it was declared unconstitutional as a result of litigation begun in Oklahoma. See Key, *Southern Politics,* pp. 538 and 556.

mits adultery, and his disillusioned wife Verity prepares to leave him.[55] She feels he has failed as a governor as well as a husband: "With all her heart she wanted . . . the things Hank planned—freedom from tax for the small cabin and the few acres; for the present taxes on the poor were exorbitant . . . she wanted to see schools, and, yes, free schoolbooks, and fine roads. Did the end justify the means? Hank declared it did. She didn't know. She only knew she hated the method" (329). Though he has built highways and a glistening capital building, an opponent likens him and his tactics to Hitler and his Saar plebiscite. His wife has sadly compared him to Mussolini, and he justifies her estimate as he plans the systematic ruination of the opposition's best men.[56] When the assassin's bullet ends his presidential aspirations, Mrs. Langley's flights of fancy transport her story beyond the bounds of reality. Discovering the assassin in a clothes closet, Verity and her friends promptly aid in his escape as a former member of Martin's staff eulogizes the killer to Martin's dry-eyed relict: "He's all the men of the Boston Tea Party; he's the men at Valley Forge . . . he's all the liberty-loving men who live by Patrick Henry's words" (479). It is here, obviously, that Mrs. Langley has departed from the life of her model in the interests of her fiction. Although Dr. Weiss may well have been concerned for democracy in Louisiana, partisan concerns seem more likely to have been uppermost in his mind.

A Lion Is in the Streets was a badly written novel crammed with clichés from the faithful mammy with the syrupy accent to the flashy gangster spectacularly exterminated. The reader is spared neither the melodramatic deathbed message nor the dollops of sex. The novel's principal interest lies in the way it amalgamates the chief characteristics of the Southern Demagogue as they had thus far evolved plus the now nearly ritualized pattern of his rise, rule, and fall. The laws of probability alone would indicate that it was now time for a treatment of this archetype that would do justice to its inherent drama, using its symbolic value to extend its meaning farther beyond the regional. Such a work would

---

[55] Although one doubts an intentional reference, one may recall the plight of Spenser's Red Cross Knight in Book I of *The Faerie Queene* after Una (Truth, among her other attributes) leaves him.

[56] Though Key does not label the Long machine a case of native Fascism, he notes Long's nearly absolute power: "He dominated the legislature. He ripped out of office mayors, parish officials, and judges who raised a voice against him. Weapons of economic coercion were employed to repress opposition. When they failed the organization did not hesitate to use more direct methods. Huey, at the height of his power, brooked no opposition and those who could not be converted were ruthlessly suppressed" (Key, *Southern Politics,* p. 156).

comment not only upon man in his political role but also in his engagement in the perennial human dilemma.

When Robert Penn Warren's *All the King's Men* appeared in 1946 it met almost immediate critical and financial success. Seven years later, Warren commented that, "the journalistic relevance of *All the King's Men* had a good deal to do with what interest it evoked. My politician hero, whose name, in the end, was Willie Stark, was quickly equated with the late Senator Huey P. Long, whose fame, even outside of Louisiana, was yet green in pious tears, anathema, and speculation."[57] Warren went on to deny that his novel was a *roman à clef*.

I do not mean to imply [he wrote] that there was no connection between Governor Stark and Senator Long. Certainly, it was the career of Long and the atmosphere of Louisiana that suggested the play that was to become the novel. But suggestion does not mean identity, and even if I had wanted to make Stark a projection of Long . . . I did not, and do not, know what Long was like, and what were the secret forces that drove him along his violent path to meet the bullet in the Capitol.[58]

As Warren said, the novel was widely construed to be the slightly fictionalized life of Senator Long, in spite of the very different and complex intent and motivation which went into its genesis. This misconception has to a large extent become a part of modern literary folklore. In the average class the student who suggests that the novel is about responsibility or self-knowledge will be outnumbered by those who reply, with the quick assurance of the young, "It's about Huey Long." To do them justice, however, there was much in the novel that *did* suggest the flamboyant personality and spectacular career of the Louisiana senator. The figure who was to become Willie Stark, Warren wrote, was first conceived as

a man whose personal motivation had been, in one sense, idealistic, who in many ways was to serve the cause of social betterment, but who was corrupted by power, even by power exercised against corruption. That is, his means defile his ends. But more than that, he was to be a man whose power was based on the fact that somehow he could vicariously fulfill some secret needs of the people about him . . . But . . . the politician was to discover, more and more, his own emptiness and his own alienation.[59]

[57] Robert Penn Warren, "A note to *All the King's Men*," *Sewanee Review*, LXI (Summer, 1953), 479.

[58] Warren, "A note to *All the King's Men*," *SR*, p. 480. Warren had taught at Louisiana State University in Baton Rouge during the Long era.

[59] *Ibid., SR*, pp. 476–477.

Vastly superior to others like it on the moral, philosophic, and symbolic levels, Warren's novel excels too in its technique and the texture
of its often poetic prose. On the narrative levels it has much in common
with the others. Willie Stark is, for instance, a farm boy who sells products door-to-door then becomes a self-taught lawyer. County treasurer
(in a state resembling Louisiana), he becomes governor and, at least
jocularly, a Presidential aspirant.[60] Guided and supported by his wife, another former schoolteacher, Willie is at first a naive idealist. Disillusionment comes after he has been tricked into running for governor by one
candidate anxious to split the "cockleburr" vote which will go to another strong in the country districts. With money earned in litigation for
independent leaseholders against an oil company, Willie campaigns
again, still "symbolically the spokesman for the tongue-tied population
of honest men."[61] Even after corruption has set in, Willie's hypnotic
oratory still expresses the idealism at first so strong.

And it is your right [he tells them] that every child shall have a complete education. That no person aged and infirm shall want or beg for bread. That the
man who produces something shall be able to carry it to market without
miring to the hub, without toll. That no poor man's house or land shall be
taxed. That the rich men and the great companies that draw wealth from this
state shall pay this state a fair share. That you shall not be deprived of hope!
(277)

He is a man of extraordinary determination and endurance. Besides
his power to fulfill the needs of others, he is a man of other remarkable
parts, possessing great shrewdness and an encyclopedic memory. But he
is a complete relativist who says that good is made from bad, that "You
just make it up as you go along" (273). And his view of the innate sin-
fulness of human nature lies behind his use of any means to gain his
ends: "You got to use what you've got. You got to use fellows like
Byram, and Tiny Duffy, and that scum down in the Legislature. You
can't make bricks without straw, and most of the time all the straw you
got is secondhand . . ."(145). Willie's actions are dictated more and
more by expediency, and both he and his methods are contaminated.
Turning to blackmail and coercion, he is forced into trafficking with the

---

[60] Goldman prints an excerpt from the *New York Times*, November 17, 1935,
quoting Long as asserting, "your Kingfish Huey, asittin' in the White House,
will know how to handle them moguls." Goldman speaks of Long "clawing his
way toward the Presidency," and discusses his potential strength and the threat
it was felt to constitute to the Administration in 1935 (*Rendezvous*, pp. 362–363).
[61] Robert Penn Warren, *All the King's Men*, p. 68.

shadiest elements of his opposition. When death comes from an outraged brother of one of Willie's mistresses, it seems in retribution for all his sins.

Warren had written that "one of the figures that stood in the shadows of imagination behind Willie Stark . . . was the scholarly and benign figure of William James." He added,

I did have some notions about the phenomenon of which Long was but one example, and I tried to put some of those notions into my book. Something about those notions and something of what I felt to be the difference between the person Huey P. Long and the fiction Willie Stark, may be indicated by the fact that in the verse play [which was the first embodiment of the idea] the name of the politician was at one time Talos—the name of the brutal, blank-eyed "iron groom" of Spenser's *Faerie Queene,* the pitiless servant of the Knight of Justice. My conception grew wider, but that element always remained, and Willie Stark remained, in one way, Willie Talos. In other words, Talos is the kind of doom that democracy may invite upon itself. The book, however, was not intended to be a book about politics. Politics merely provided the framework story in which the deeper concerns, whatever their final significance, might work themselves out.[62]

Warren's words about the character's function regarding democracy's dangers—sounding a good deal like those of Dos Passos and Lewis—are borne out in the pages crammed with political events. There is the depiction of the corrupt machine which invites its own destruction and of the kind of native dictatorship which succeeds it. And besides the study of political psychology, there is a guide, almost, to pragmatic politics: techniques for coercing legislators, quashing impeachment proceedings, and mustering support for candidates while chipping away at the opponents.

But the politics were, after all, a frame for the deeper concerns of the story. These deeper concerns and this functional use of politics were paradoxically responsible for the stature of the novel, so much larger than that of its competitors, a paradoxical situation which will be examined later. The deeper level of *All the King's Men* was indicated by the epigraph chosen from *Purgatorio,* III, of Dante's *Divine Comedy:* *"Mentre che la speranza ha fior del verde."* Together with the preceding line, it may be translated,

> . . . man is not so lost that eternal love may not return
> So long as hope retaineth ought of green.

[62] Warren, "A note to *All the King's Men,*" *SR,* p. 480.

If the epigraph pointed toward redemption, the title pointed away from it. It was immediately obvious that Warren had drawn on the child's nursery rhyme, "Humpty Dumpty." But he was using it in an anything but childish way, for the key word was "fall." The religious connotation was strongly suggested as well as the secular one. Each of the major characters fell from a state of comparative grace into sin, chiefly through an act of betrayal—of others, of self, or of both, the word "betray" occurring importantly in more than half a dozen contexts throughout the novel. Willie has first been betrayed by the agents of the Harrison machine who gain his trust and induce him to run for governor. He is later betrayed into the hands of his killer by a jealous mistress and a vengeful underling. But as he has betrayed his wife in his liaisons, so he has betrayed the electorate and the best elements in his own nature. Jack Burden, the novel's narrator, has betrayed the faith which his youthful sweetheart, Anne Stanton, had placed in him by refusing to give direction to his life. Later, by revealing her father's misconduct he shatters one of the bases on which she has constructed her scale of values. This in turn leads to her liaison with Willie, destroying one of the last illusions by which Jack has lived. As Jack puts it, "That was the Anne Stanton whom Willie Stark had picked out, who had finally betrayed me, or rather, had betrayed an idea of mine which had had more importance for me than I had ever realized" (327). Burden's real father, Judge Irwin, the friend of Jack's putative father, has betrayed his friend by the adultery with Mrs. Burden in which Jack is begotten. For Willie's political purposes, Jack betrays Judge Irwin. Uncovering evidence of his misdeeds (in which Anne's father was accessory), Jack reveals them to the Judge, precipitating his suicide.

This motif of the fall into sin pervades the novel, appearing even in secondary stories and symbolic incidents. The family story contained in the Cass Mastern papers which are to form the basis of Jack's doctoral dissertation in history—if he can ever come to terms with it and its meaning—has as its most dramatic and meaningful incident the betrayal by one friend of another with the latter's wife.[63] When Jack visits his father he finds that the latest unfortunate whom he has taken in was at one time a circus aerialist. When Jack asks his former specialty, his father informs

---

[63] An indication of the extent to which the act of betrayal permeates the novel is to be seen in the presumptive betrayal of the guilty wife to the injured husband at the hand of her slave Phebe. The wife's retaliatory act selling her down the river is described by the narrator as "the betrayal of Phebe . . ." (p. 189).

him, "He was the man who got hanged."[64] This recipient of Mr. Burden's Christian generosity now specializes in the making of angels out of stale bread masticated into a puttylike consistency. Jack learns that this sculpture is commemorative as well as decorative: his wife, Mr. Burden says, "did the angel act . . . She fell down a long way with white wings which fluttered as though she were flying." Jack completes the story: "And one day the rope broke . . ." (210).

In discussing the transmutation from play to novel, Warren described what he felt as

> the necessity for a character of a higher degree of self-consciousness than my politician, a character to serve as a kind of commentator and raisonneur and chorus . . . I wanted . . . to make him the chief character among those who were to find their vicarious fulfillment in the dynamic and brutal, yet paradoxically idealistic, drive of the politician. There was, too, my desire to avoid writing a straight naturalistic novel, the kind of novel that the material so readily invited. The impingement of that material, I thought, upon a special temperament would allow another perspective than the reportorial one, and would give a basis for some range of style. So Jack Burden entered the scene.[65]

The use of the hard-boiled newspaperman as narrator was not new, but it helped deepen the novel as Warren intended. It is Burden's probing intelligence that explores the multiple problems of identity that arise: *e.g.*, who and what is Willie Stark? And, who and what is Jack Burden? Is Willie the avenger his country partisans think him or the Fascist demagogue his rich enemies call him? Or is he a man compounded of mingled self-interest and idealism, corrupted by power and the means he feels forced to use by the imperfect world in which he lives? Is Jack a wisecracking cynic, a man concealing the scars of early wounds with braggadocio, or one slowly and painfully coming to terms with himself as he acquires belated maturity? Through Jack's eyes we see both the secular and spiritual rise and fall of Willie Stark. We see the formation of the view of human nature Willie expresses when he tells Jack, "You don't ever have to frame anybody, because the truth is always sufficient" (358). And we also hear the anguished deathbed words, "It might have been all different, Jack . . . You got to believe that . . ." (425).

It is of course through Jack Burden and his life that the motif of re-

---

[64] Thinking of the echoes of Dante in Warren, one may wonder here if he has not, like that other echoer of the Florentine, T. S. Eliot, chosen also to echo a different inscriber of myth, Sir James Fraser.

[65] Warren, "A note to *All the King's Men*," *SR*, p. 478.

demption is explored, as the reader sees what amounts to the Fall and Rise of Jack Burden. He makes progress along many lines, finally making the right marriage and changing from political hack to student of history. Learning the truth of his own paternity, he takes back the responsibility of conscience he has abrogated in Willie's favor and changes his whole conception of the human dilemma and the human obligation. He rejects the view that life is ultimately meaningless and that actions are not consequential. (This view is expressed in "the Great Twitch," a sardonic philosophical extension of the random and unrelated activity seen in the cheek of a man with a tic, a view explored from another direction in a series of comments upon a prefrontal lobotomy.) Burden makes a transition first to the position objectified in the image of life as a spider web, in which actions are consequential in the extreme. Looking back, he writes,

> I have said that Jack Burden could not put down the facts about Cass Mastern's world because he did not know Cass Mastern [who had betrayed his friend with his wife]. Jack Burden did not say definitely to himself why he did not know Cass Mastern. But I (who am what Jack Burden became) look back now, years later, and try to say why. Cass Mastern lived for a few years and in that time he learned that the world is like an enormous spider web and if you touch it, however lightly, at any point, the vibration ripples to the remotest perimeter and the drowsy spider feels the tingle and is drowsy no more but springs out to fling the gossamer coils about you who have touched the web and then inject the black, numbing poison under your hide. It does not matter whether or not you meant to brush the web of things. (200)

Jack Burden goes beyond this position, however, when he himself gives something of the eternal, redemptive love the epigraph alludes to. He marries Anne Stanton, whom he has wronged. He gives to his mother the mature understanding and love which has previously been beyond him, and he takes into his home his nominal father, now in failing health. And when the old man dictates a heretical tract, Jack finds that he too believes what he has written: "The creation of man whom God in His foreknowledge knew to be doomed to sin was the awful index of God's omnipotence. For it would have been a thing of trifling and contemptible ease for Perfection to create mere perfection . . . The creation of evil is therefore the index of God's glory and His power" (462). And in the last words of the long chronicle, Jack looks forward to the future when, his father dead and the house consumed by mortgages, "we shall go out of the house and go into the convulsion of the world, out of history into history and the awful responsibility of Time" (464).

Warren's design demanded a technique to match it. Ordinary proficiency could not have sustained it. But fortunately Warren is a poet who can combine arresting clusters of image and metaphor with the narrative drive of a novelist possessing a fine ear for accent and nuance. Occasionally these gifts led him into excess. The novel ran to 464 pages, and it could have been at once shorter and better. Warren gained force for his story through a kind of incremental repetition, a reinforcement through repeated phrase, image, and motif. But at times the returns were diminishing ones, just as the sardonic cynicism occasionally turned Jack Burden from the complex and traumatized seeker after his own identity into a plain smart aleck. Working in the tradition of Conrad and Faulkner, Warren manipulated both point of view and time sequence. The novel opens in 1936 and closes in 1939. But Warren expands this timespan by extended flashbacks in the years 1850–1864, 1914–1915, and later. Though the reader may grant him his sometimes labyrinthine method, he is not likely to be so charitable to some of the extended philosophical disquisitions in which fundamental concerns are not so much dramatized as verbalized. But Warren's stylistic resources are still, at their best, dazzling. The dense texture is enriched by subtly used imagery—the death imagery contributes throughout to the force of the dominant themes—and by a kind of epic repetition of characters' attributes, features, and habits. It is a rich prose which can combine the sharpness associated with Hemingway and O'Hara and the rolling rhetoric of that novelist to whom Warren seems much indebted, William Faulkner.

A third of the way through *All the King's Men* Jack Burden declares that "the story of Willie Stark and the story of Jack Burden are, in one sense, one story" (168). As we have seen, it is this cunning strategy that gives the novel its richness. Warren uses these entwined lives to deal with what Dostoevsky called The Eternal Questions—the nature of truth, time, and man, the perception of life as meaningful or meaningless, and the whole problem of cultural and personal values. These are among the considerations Warren designated as "the deeper concerns" which might work themselves out within the political framework of the story. And both these elements were thematically and stylistically related. Talos was "the kind of doom that democracy may invite upon itself" (480) through the refusal to realize that every act is so consequential, that man must assume responsibility and—in an extreme formulation—give love. Correspondingly, Jack shows the kind of doom the individual may invite upon himself through a refusal to recognize consequentiality, assume responsibility, and give love. It is this kind of synthesis, combined with Warren's often brilliant technique, which makes this despite occasional prolixity and obscurity, the best American political novel of this century. It helps, moreover, to make it a work of art with promise of enduring.

Hodding Carter's *Flood Crest* (1947) began with a five-page, poetic description of an oncoming Mississippi flood which suggested the catastrophic duststorm in John Steinbeck's *The Grapes of Wrath*. And like Steinbeck's novel, Carter's used the natural crisis and disaster to parallel one in the social and political realm. U.S. Senator G. Cleve Pikestaff is running for re-election from a state one takes to be Mississippi, the home of newspaper-editor Carter.[66] Pikestaff is a coarse hillman, a nose-picker and bottom-scratcher who has won his way to Congress, the governor's mansion, and the Senate. Combining shrewdness with old-style campaign tactics and oratory, he has an intuitive understanding of the most exploitable of his hearers' prejudices. Running against a young veteran (another hillman campaigning on issues such as Pikestaff's real but unprovable pardon-selling), Pikestaff shows himself as resourceful as ever in the face of changing times and tastes. Pitching his appeal for both the large and small landowners, he hits out at "FEPC. The CIO. Negro suffrage. Social equality. Yankee interference."[67] Like others before him, he makes his guide pragmatism, not principle:

Cleve laughed to himself . . . He ought to write Joe Stalin a thank-you letter, with a carbon to the American Reds. Those fellows had given him something big; something even bigger, if he worked it right, than white supremacy . . . A Red was one who disagreed with you . . . A Red was any nigger who wanted to vote and any white man who thought he ought to. The lowdown, sneaking labor organizers . . . and . . . everybody who belonged to the CIO. Reporters . . . and most college professors, and the Jews and the rest of the foreign element in New York. So were a lot of dissatisfied young no-goods who got ideas overseas, but you had to go slow about them, because they were Veterans. Some of the younger preachers were Reds too, but you mentioned them only as pinks, and sadly, not critically, on account of the Jesus angle. (144)[68]

---

[66] Key writes: "Hodding Carter's novel *Flood Crest* . . . builds on the theme of the reconciliation of Bilbo and the delta" (*Southern Politics*, p. 244). Carter knew at first hand political excesses other than those of Mississippi's "Bilbonic Plague." Writing for the *Hammond Courier* as an outspoken critic of the Long regime, Carter had been forced to carry a weapon for his own safety. See Carter, "Huey Long, American Dictator," in Isabel Leighton (ed.), *The Aspirin Age*, p. 341, and Carter's book, *Where Main Street Meets the River*, Chapter Eight.

[67] Hodding Carter, *Flood Crest*, p. 133.

[68] Writing of the strike of textile workers in Gastonia, North Carolina, in the spring of 1929, Cash asserts that it served "to clinch the matter, to fix solidly in the minds of the great mass of Southerners the equation: labor unions+strikers=

He combines accusation and innuendo. At his climactic rally, just before the crashing strains of "Dixie," he holds aloft a perjured statement supporting his baseless allegation of Communist influence: " 'Here in my hands—' he shouted. 'Here in my hands is the proof of everything Cleve Pikestaff has been warning you about.' "[69] The professor smeared by Pikestaff says of him, "It's his kind who're responsible for the hatred and suspicion. Evil little men, willing to open the floodgates to ensure their elections" (132). But though the literal flood is successfully dealt with (by the lieutenant colonel of Army Engineers who breaks off with Pikestaff's daughter), there is no shoring of the levee against the figurative one. Pikestaff is sick over his intelligent daughter's profligacy, but he has the consolation that his overwhelming re-election is assured.[70] And the lieutenant colonel's words of assurance to his new sweetheart which follow have a somewhat hollow ring. This capably done novel shows the Southern Demagogue at work again—persuasive, cynical, cunning, and adept at combining the effects of old prejudices with new. And he shows no signs whatever of losing any of his power although he undergoes experiences revealing the rottenness around him, and, indeed, very close to him.

A novel published a dozen years later showed the image of the Southern Demagogue just as it had been. Far from changing, it seemed if anything closer to the earlier pattern. In Philip Alston Stone's *No Place to Run* (1959) the setting is again Mississippi. Sixty-one-year-old Eugene C. "Gene" Massie, born into a sharecropper family but a former senator and state power for years, is running in the gubernatorial primary. He relies on personal appearances rather than television, taking off his coat

---

Communism+atheism+social equality with the Negro—and so to join the formidable list of Southern sentiments already drawn up against the strikers the great central one of racial feeling and purpose; and, in fact, to summon against them much the same great fears and hates we have already seen as giving rise to the Ku Klux Klan" (Cash, *South,* p. 353).

[69] Cash, *South,* p. 124. This same gambit, couched in the familiar phrase, "I have here in my hand," will be seen again in the novels of McCarthyism considered in Chapter Eight.

[70] Discovering the two in a compromising situation, Pikestaff struggles with the convict, who uses his pistol to inflict a scalp laceration on him. Later, speaking at a rally, Pikestaff wears the vote-getting bandage as testimonial to his valor in fighting what he calls the pro-red, anti-American forces which will stop at nothing to silence him. Key writes, "In 1934, Bilbo brought into play his genius for rough-and-tumble campaigning. He wore, from an earlier campaign, a scar won in his oratorical battles for the people. He had been rapped over the head with a pistol butt by an opponent," one he had particularly vehemently calumniated (*Southern Politics,* p. 242).

and exposing his red galluses whenever possible.[71] He delivers the only speech he has ever used. It encompasses the themes through which he has played upon his hearers' prejudices successfully for decades: retention of the white primary election and white supremacy in general, a tax policy designed to "soak the rich," and the retention of prohibition. He admits "stealing" $14,000 in a power contract transaction, but he tells his audience he did it "for you."[72] Adultery, bribery, coercion, incarceration, libel, and murder occur before Massie predictably wins the primary. His death by gunshot wounds at the hands of an outraged husband follows soon after. The nymphomania of the errant wife is a principal aspect of the sexual pathology in the novel. It is complemented by the satyriasis of Massie and the ignorance of drugstore clerk Eurene Hogroth. Unaware of the effects of her seduction, she precipitately gives birth to a child in an alley. The novel's sexual violence is complementary to its other forms of violence. The most spectacular instance is probably displayed by Massie's father. Outraged by a Negro family's arrival on the same land which he farms for shares, he locks the Negro family in the house. Then he burns it before returning to his own dwelling to shoot his family and himself.

This is a competent first novel though a derivative one which shows the influence of Faulkner, Warren, and Tennessee Williams.[73] Stone

---

[71] Describing Eugene Talmadge's first campaign for office in 1926, Key writes that his "lambasting of the corporations was reminiscent of the populists. Then and after his colloquialisms on the hustings and a pair of bright red galluses marked him as a man of the farming people" (*Southern Politics,* p. 116). Key also writes that a candidate "of Talmadge's audacity, occasional uncouthness, iconoclasm, disrespect for established processes always aligned against him a healthy number of Georgians who are usually damned with the designation 're- spectable' " (*Southern Politics,* p. 125).

[72] Philip Alston Stone, *No Place to Run,* p. 75.

[73] The author's father, Phil Stone, an Oxford lawyer, had befriended young William Faulkner when he returned to Mississippi from World War I service with the R.A.F., lending him books and providing him with free secretarial serv- ices. Like the rest of Oxford, Stone knew many of the exploits of the fabled Faulk- ner family. In *No Place to Run,* when Massie's career is threatened by accusa- tions of rape, he goes to his sometime mentor, aristocratic old Judge Rogers. When the Judge receives him coldly, Massie is daunted:

"why, I thought I'd jest come by for a little visit and see you—" "Gene," said Judge Rogers, "our relations are business and political. They are not social. Good afternoon." And he closed the door in his candidate's face and started back up the hall (240–241).

J. W. T. Falkner, the novelist's grandfather, was a supporter of the "redneck" politician, Senator James K. Vardaman. Mr. Falkner allowed a young Mississip- pian named Lee Russell to read law in his office. After he received his degree from the University, Russell practiced law for a time as an associate of Falkner.

has a good ear, and he tells a story well, a story here of the basest kind of appeal to abysmal political passions in a nearly mindless electorate. And it is a story in which death is not so much retribution as the result of a destructive drive in the protagonist not so very different from that manifested at various times by his victims.

Two novels published within roughly a half dozen years of each other both dealt with the process by which a new-style Southern Demagogue was created. The protagonists were not successful politicians in mid-career but mature men entering politics. Both stories were set in the early 1950's, and like *Flood Crest,* they showed the adaptation of the techniques and themes of McCarthyism to the milieu of the Southern Demagogue. Tom Wicker's *The Kingpin* (1953) is set in a coastal, to-bacco-raising state that suggests North Carolina. Its protagonist is Bill Tucker, campaign manager for Colonel Harvey Pollock, a banker backed by a small group of industrialists and businessmen in the primary election for the United States Senate. Tucker successfully devises a campaign based on anti-Negro and anti-Communist sentiments which discredits Pollock's courageously liberal and ethical opponent. But Tucker's power drive is frustrated when he is ousted by a faithful Pollock adherent who discredits him, using the strategy he devised to ruin Pollock's opponent. Tucker's situation is like Frankenstein's with his monster. He observes Pollock in action:

the sweat streaming from his fat face, over all of his body, he howled doggedly on, hitting and running and hitting again . . . at the jellied, quivering fear of the people who listened, howling not so cruelly as Talmadge and Bilbo and McDowell, not so piously as his Reconstruction ancestors, not so viciously as the Klan, but somewhere in between, somewhere in that dreamlike state where a Negro is not a nigger but a Nigra, where segregation is neither an evil nor the will of God but a necessity, where an opponent is not a nigger lover nor a Communist but a pink.[74]

Pollock's appeals to the hate and ignorance of a people "slow-moving, ill-fed, ill-housed, ill-clad, prey to all the dark moods and passions" (184)

He was elected to the state legislature and in 1915 ran successfully for lieutenant governor. The gubernatorial winner that year was Theodore G. Bilbo. One life-long resident of Oxford recalls that one Sunday afternoon following his victory, Russell appeared at the door of the Falkner home. When Falkner asked him what he wanted, Russell replied that he had come to pay a visit. Whereupon Falkner told him that their relations were business and political, not social, and slammed the door.

[74] Tom Wicker, *The Kingpin,* p. 287.

are made even more effective by the tactics of his opponent. He speaks of the Marshall Plan, the Atlantic Pact, Point Four, and asks for "a new evaluation of policy in the Middle East." An aide thinks to himself, "how in the name of God . . . does he expect a peanut farmer to know what even the old policy is?" (115).

The pressing economic problems involve inequitable distribution of land, violent labor-management disputes, poor transportation facilities, and preferential letting of contracts. The tax structure is shaped for the wealthy interests which control the state machine and which find it necessary to unseat Pollock's opponent—who had been appointed rather than elected to the Senate to fill out a term.[75] The political problems and strategies which grow out of this situation include the familiar one of splitting the opponent's rural vote. It is accomplished when Tucker lures an old-style demagogue out of retirement. Rooster Ed McDowell's perennial anti-Jew, anti-Yankee, anti-Negro speeches pull the votes sufficient to require the second primary which Pollock eventually wins.[76] In a newer technique, bogus postcards supporting Pollock's opponent are mailed out from "The National Society for the Advance of Colored People" (116).

The sexual pathology takes familiar forms. Mrs. Pollock's nymphomania in New York, Miami, New Orleans, and Tokyo has been documented by her foresighted husband. Elsewhere, Tucker's bed-partner conveys her contempt for his inferior status through hostile lovemaking, whereas he practices physical violence upon each of the women with whom he is intimate.[77] This combined pathology and violence runs deep in this novel which is thoroughly professional in technique and execution.

Francis Irby Gwaltney prefaced *A Step in the River* (1960) with a

[75] It has been suggested to me that this unsuccessful campaign of liberal Senator Ralph Anson owes something to the defeat of Frank P. Graham, "by all odds the South's most prominent educator and versatile public servant" (Key, *Southern Politics*, p. 206). Graham had left the presidency of the University of North Carolina in 1949 to accept appointment to the U.S. Senate. He was defeated the next year when he ran for election to the post.

[76] Names such as Rooster Ed are plentiful enough in American politics so that one need not necessarily ascribe one to a specific, not to say Southern, source. One thinks of Oklahoma's Alfalfa Bill Murray. But one thinks also of South Carolina's Cotton Ed Smith, a fruitful model for the political novelist, being, in Cash's words, "the archetype of the man who served only the planter and industrial interests in his state, while whipping up and delighting the people with attacks on the Negro, appeals to such vague shibboleths as states' rights, and heroic gasconade of every sort" (*South*, p. 422).

[77] One of these women provides an interesting perspective on the changing role of women. She is observing Pollock's campaign in order to gather material for a Ph.D. dissertation "on the effects of women's suffrage in a specific election" (Wicker, *The Kingpin*, p. 65). Her effect is to provide Tucker with a bed-mate.

conventional disclaimer, remarking, "To those who shall insist that this novel is concerned with the political structure of the author's native state: bad cess." The author's native state was Arkansas, and though the disclaimer was no more convincing than most, it was supported by the fact that the protagonist was not another Huey Long image, although he possessed certain elements in the Southern Demagogue archetype. Like *The Kingpin,* this novel showed the creation and installation of another new-style politician. Wealthy and educated like Colonel Pollock, he is also handsome and magnetic. Thirty-two-year-old John Frank Miller has genius on the platform and shrewdly employs a hillbilly band and a tattooed clown. He also uses of the power of his cousin, who fills many state contracts, and successfully buys off his opposition. The opposition is Preacher Clutts, a backwoods spellbinder who refuses his biennial $50,000 bribe for not running and finally accepts a $100,000 check for his Tabernacle Fund. In return he transfers to Miller a quarter million in cash hotly sought by tax authorities.[78]

This novel's sexual pathology runs riot as Miller and his fiancée engage in a nude orgy including his sister-in-law and the tattooed clown. "I work ten years trying to run a decent establishment," the motel owner complains, "and a candidate for governor organizes a gang bang in my place" (300). This decadence is rejected by the book's narrator, the third of the cousins who serves as their pilot during the campaign. Later to repudiate the old concept of family loyalty, he ironically comments, "I recognize the stench of decay beneath the scent of such a beautiful thing . . ." (79). That the decay is there is clear—in the individuals, the family, the state, and the culture. But it is a decay overlaid with strength which appears capable of perpetuating the rule of this new-style Southern Demagogue on the old power base supporting it. The author has chosen his point of view for reasons, one suspects, which are probably

[78] The evangelical, revivalist preaching style is often seen in these novels in rallies which have much of the prayer meeting tempo and fervor. Key gives an indication of the continuing efficacy of this technique: "In 1948 in Arkansas 'Uncle Mac' MacKrell was accompanied in his vote-getting tour by his gospel musicians and the hat was passed. 'Uncle Mac's' pastoral experience gave him exceptional skill in the extraction of contributions. Hard-boiled politicians almost wept when they saw the collections" (*Southern Politics,* pp. 479–480). Religion and politics have, of course, been more intimately connected in the South than in most other American regions, particularly during the Reconstruction and after. At the time of Al Smith's candidacy, "the ministers of the evangelical sects finally towered up to their greatest power, until almost literally nobody in the South dared criticize their pronouncements or oppose the political programs they laid out . . ." (Cash, *South,* p. 335). Though the power of the clergy does not extend so far in the more recent novels, it is still formidable.

like those of Warren in his creation of Jack Burden. That he does not derive more advantage from this strategy is partly due to the limitations imposed by this particular narrator. Most often tough-talking and taciturn, he is awkward and unconvincing in eloquent passages. Like the others, this book is pervaded by violence. It is competently done, however, and capable at times of bodying forth whole attitudes in a phrase. Preacher Clutts, a man behind "the Confederate Curtain"(107), remarks, "Well I always say . . . if you keep niggers and honest men in their place, they're all right" (287).

The Southern Demagogue and the Status Quo

Nineteenth-century political novels set in the South usually fell into three categories. Like Harriet Beecher Stowe's *Uncle Tom's Cabin* (1852)—a novel more political in effect than in content—one showed the evils of the Southern system. Like Tourgée's *A Fool's Errand* (1879), another demonstrated the baleful effects of the mismanaged Reconstruction program frustrated by resurgent Southern nationalism. Like Thomas Nelson Page's *Red Rock* (1898), another embodied the Southern view that federal policies and their results were abominations in both wartime and peacetime.

The reader is struck by the fervor and conviction which run through these novels, whether they are elicited by The Battle Cry of Freedom or The Lost Cause. The novels of the Southern Politician which appeared between 1922 and 1960 were more sophisticated in both form and content and for the most part written from an ethically and politically irreproachable point of view. But they usually depicted fervor and conviction of only the basest kind. The fervor was bred of ignorance and prejudice, and but for the idealism of a few protagonists, the conviction was mostly that of cynical men who had for years successfully made use of ignorance and prejudice. It was a conviction that these conditions were perpetual sources of power which they could continue to tap at will. Symptomatic of this shift from the old to the new is the contest in one of the most recent novels. The victorious Colonel Pollock of *The Kingpin* introduces certain modern restraints and nuances into his demagoguery, but his line of descent is still from Talmadge and Bilbo. The opponent he defeats, able newspaper publisher Ralph Anson, is a man "self-educated in the best Abe Lincoln manner"(112). The character in the tradition of self-seeking demagogue who appeals to the lowest common denominator wins out over the one suggesting the heroic leader.

Although it is patently impossible to return to the antebellum order, the impulse of most of these politicians is a profoundly conservative one aimed at maintaining the *status quo*. A minority works to remedy inequities which favor the wealthy landowner and industrialist while handicapping the impoverished small farmer and tenant farmer. More enter into alliances with the wealthy and powerful, protecting their interests and ranging themselves against organized labor and other forces of change. In one view, the complex of emotions and attitudes which creates a favorable environment for the demagogue has an economic base. His wealthy allies support him in return for preferential treatment which will maintain his state as their economic preserve. The poorer whites support him because his doctrine of White Supremacy offers them support against the economic threat posed by the Negro farmer—who can and must work with less for less. He taps prejudices in them which are both traditional and subrational. And these prejudices show no sign of diminution, at least in these novels. They are still directed with undiminished fervor against the Negro, the Jew, the Yankee, and other outsiders.

Later novels involving the Boss often assert that his very existence has been in jeopardy through the increasing influence of the federal government in local affairs. There is no evidence in any of these novels that a similar force is at work in the area of the Southern politician. When foreign concerns do intrude, they are manipulated to serve the interests of the traditional wielders of power. In these novels, the fascism of the 1930's and 1940's merely provides a new and potent weapon for ruining an opponent with greater dispatch. It is still conceived of merely as a useful political tool, however; the ideology implied by the terms used could not have a remoter significance for those who use them. When Calvin Hall, the narrator of *A Step in the River*, declares he will sue for allegations of communist sympathy made against him, Preacher Clutts, his libeller, is both hurt and aghast. "Now wait a minute!" he exclaims. "Hell! This is a damn political campaign!" (295).

If this amoral adroitness and adaptability of the Southern Politician seems to indicate anything, it is that there has been no material change in the predominant pattern demonstrated through the years of the twentieth century. And equally, there seems in these novels no indication of any fundamental change in sight.

7. American Fascism

> . . . if in a people a certain amount of energy and active force
> appears united towards one goal and thus is taken permanently
> from the inertia of the great masses, this small percentage has
> risen to be the masters of the whole number. World history is
> made by minorities whenever this numerical minority incorpo-
> rates the majority of will and determination.
>
> Adolf Hitler
> *Mein Kampf*[1]

In the years after the Fascists seized power in Italy and the National Socialists began their preparations in Germany, groups resembling them
began to appear in the United States. Never so broadly based or powerful, they nonetheless combined European techniques with American
prejudices to increase tension and aid subversion in a period of national
crises and international struggle.

In 1924 the first branch of the Teutonia Club was founded in Chicago.
It shortly "raised a platoon of storm troopers modelled directly on Hitler's
Brownshirts, and adopted the swastika."[2] With support and control from

[1] Adolf Hitler, *Mein Kampf*, p. 603.

[2] John Roy Carlson, *Under Cover*, p. 111. The book (whose author's real name
was Arthur Derounian) was subtitled, *My Four Years in the Nazi Underworld
of America—The Amazing Revelation of How Axis Agents and Our Enemies
Within Are Now Plotting to Destroy the United States*. The journalistic sensationalism of this subtitle makes one uncomfortable about such a source, and although it contains a great deal of information, it is almost always presented without documentation. The book is free, however, of the extremism and slangy vitu-
peration often found in others using a similar approach. Other works to be cited
later, such as Rollins's *I Find Treason* and Seldes's *Facts and Fascism* produce
even more uneasiness, and I have tried to use materials from such sources only
when they gave specific corroboration of generally known or accepted conditions
or when they accorded with the rather scanty materials available in scholarly histories.

the Nazi Party and later the German government, the German-American Bund grew. The storm troops and the summer camps, the swastikas and "Horst Wessel" choruses, all gave evidence of what was intended to be a fifth column in the United States. It was the only such European-directed organization that achieved any real effectiveness. But it was far from being the only one that tried.[3]

In the early 1930's two native Americans were causing the Roosevelt Administration and certain federal bureaus considerably more concern than the Fritz Kuhns and Heinz Spanknoebels of American Naziism. One was a Roman Catholic priest and the other was a senator. Of the Reverend Charles E. Coughlin, Arthur Link writes, he "fell to discussing politics and economic issues in radio sermons around 1930; soon his animadversions against bankers and the Republican leadership were more popular than his religious messages." Senator Huey P. Long, says the same historian, was a "much more dangerous menace to the American democracy . . ."[4] At the height of his power, he claimed he had enrolled ten million people in his Share Our Wealth Society. By 1935 it was demonstrating so potent an appeal outside his state that the Administration felt compelled to take counter action in which "the President launched a program frankly designed to provide larger security and incomes for the masses . . . So powerful was his hold over the lower classes," writes Link, "that in 1934–35 he established a dictatorship, organized a private army of storm troopers, and could declare, 'I am the law'."[5] H. R. Trevor-Roper calls Long's movement only "semi-fascist," however.[6] And it was true that such Fascist tenets as the corporate state and antisemitism were never a conspicuous part of Long's rather light intellectual baggage. The same could not be said of Father Coughlin's "Social Justice" movement.

By 1936 Father Coughlin was claiming nine million supporters. His activities had begun to extend beyond the Shrine of the Little Flower, in Royal Oak, Michigan, beyond the Sunday radio broadcasts and the

[3] See Carlson, *Under Cover,* pp. 108–131.

[4] Arthur Link, *American Epoch: A History of the United States since the 1890's,* pp. 401–402.

[5] Link, *American Epoch,* p. 402. Some of the trappings of this dictatorship were bizarre in their Southern context. When, for instance, Long's cadets paraded at halftime on the Baton Rouge football field of Louisiana State University, they marched to the tune of "La Giovanezza," Mussolini's Fascist anthem (James Rorty and Moshe Decter, *McCarthy and the Communists,* p. 113).

[6] H. R. Trevor-Roper, "A Rockwell Cannot Be a Hitler," *New York Times Magazine,* November 25, 1962, p. 147.

magazine, *Social Justice*. That year he endorsed the Presidential candidacy of Representative William Lemke, a North Dakota radical farm leader running on the Union Party ticket. Lemke also had the support of old-age pension advocate Dr. Francis E. Townsend and the Reverend Gerald L. K. Smith. (Upon the demise of the Kingfish, Smith had moved to Detroit, converted the "Share Our Wealth" clubs into the Committee of One Million, and begun agitating against Jews, Negroes, and Communists.[7]) Lemke polled nearly 900,000 votes—more than ten times as many as Communist Earl Browder received. By the spring of 1938 Coughlin was urging his followers to organize platoons. That summer thirty-six activists formed the antisemitic, pro-Nazi, Christian Front. It found room not only for the *Social Justice* distributors' clubs, but also for the American Nationalists, the American Patriots, the Citizens Protective League, the Crusaders for Americanism, and some members of the German-American Bund. Its gun clubs and storm troops came later.[8] The strong-arm squads of the Christian Front and other such organizations were likely to be mixed. They even included National Guardsmen, some of them aliens trained and equipped under state and federal military programs.[9] Nazi-style organizations were of course not new. William Dudley Pelley had organized his Silver Shirts of America the day after Hitler came to power. During 1935 and 1936 the Black Legion was active. A "secret, hooded, revolutionary terror-group," its membership was composed of Klansmen, strike-breakers, convicts, rapists, murderers, and variously assorted thugs and felons. Baiting Jews, Catholics, Negroes, and Labor, it perpetrated arson, flogging, and lynching "across a half dozen mid-western states. Fifteen murders were ascribed to it—many of them still unsolved."[10]

The series of mergers proceeded in strange ways. It culminated in one of the strangest of all American political weddings on the night of August 18, 1940, at Camp Nordland, New Jersey, when the German-American Bund and Ku Klux Klan were united. "To symbolize the union," wrote Richard Rollins, a Pillar of Fire minister "married a twenty-three-year-old Klansman to a forty-four-year-old Klanswoman. They burned a fifty-foot Cross, sang a few Nazi songs—in the original—and 'The Old Rug-

---

[7] Link, *American Epoch*, pp. 402 and 442.
[8] Richard Rollins, *I Find Treason: The Story of an American Anti-Nazi Agent*, pp. 161–162. See also Carlson, *Under Cover*, pp. 54–69.
[9] See Rollins, *I Find Treason*, pp. 97, 99, 157, 165, and 171.
[10] Carlson, *Under Cover*, pp. 150 and 285. See also p. 322.

ged Cross'."[11] The joyful union was also attended by representatives of the Christian Mobilizers and the Christian Front.[12]

The leadership of the fascist organizations was varied. Men like Oklahoma-born Joseph Ellsworth McWilliams—organizer of the Christian Mobilizers and later the American Destiny Party, variously known as "the Yorkville Fuehrer" and "Joe McNazi"—were not a wholly uncommon phenomenon, though few gained his prominence.[13] But there were other politicians, among them prominent congressmen, who either adopted elements of the Fascist line or took positions to the Far Right in advocating American isolationism. In 1938, Senator Robert R. Reynolds of North Carolina returned from a European trip which included visits in Germany. In subsequent Senate speeches he praised Mussolini and Hitler for the national self-interest behind the policies then incurring wide and heated criticism. In January of 1939 Reynolds formed a patriotic organization called the Vindicators. He began to draw in his speeches upon Father Coughlin's *Social Justice,* and his prescription for America's troubles was relatively straightforward: "Nationalism is the answer. The other *great* nations are realizing it."[14] At about the same time a World War I German government agent of record, George Sylvester Viereck, allegedly managed to have German propaganda inserted into speeches delivered from the floor of Congress. They were then disseminated in the *Congressional Record* or congressmen's franked envelopes.[15]

The fall of France did nothing to deter the ill-assorted fascists and isolationists such as those of the America First movement. Arthur Link writes that they included

pro-Nazi spokesmen like Father Coughlin, Gerald L. K. Smith, and William Dudley Pelley; subtle defenders of fascism like Anne Morrow Lindbergh, whose *The Wave of the Future* argued that Germany was bound to triumph; a large body of midwestern businessmen, whose main motive was hatred of the New Deal; Irish-Americans and Italian-Americans in the Northeast; old progressives like Senators Burton K. Wheeler and Gerald P. Nye, who still identified co-

[11] Rollins, *I Find Treason,* p. 192.
[12] Carlson, *Under Cover,* p. 152. See also Nathaniel Weyl, *Treason: The Story of Disloyalty and Betrayal in American History,* pp. 318–319, and Nathaniel Weyl, *The Battle against Disloyalty,* pp. 159–160.
[13] Weyl, *Treason,* pp. 322–232. See also pp. 317–328.
[14] As quoted in Allan A. Michie and Frank Rhylick, *Dixie Demagogues,* p. 229. See also pp. 221–241.
[15] See Weyl, *Treason,* pp. 329–335.

operation with England with the machinations of Wall Street; and many Protestant ministers and idealists, who had embraced a philosophy of non-resistance. The Hearst papers, the *Chicago Tribune,* the *New York Daily News,* the *Washington Times-Herald,* and other newspapers lent editorial support.[16]

In July of 1941 a grand jury was convened in Washington to investigate seditious activities of Nazi and fascist groups. Sedition trials followed only to culminate in 1946 in the release of the defendants—most of them prominent American extremists—on the grounds that they had been denied the speedy trial guaranteed under the Constitution.[17] But with American entry into the war, a speedy roundup of enemy agents and sympathizers effectively disrupted Nazi- and fascist-style activities. What remained was Axis espionage, and this would henceforward be the concern of the military and the F.B.I.

The fascists' failure in America sprang from several causes. Although they had friends in Congress, industry, and finance, "they never gained a foothold in the high policy echelons of the executive branch of the government. Their crude, garbled, and savage philosophy had little charm for the intellectuals. Instead of recruiting agents among nuclear physicists and other pure scientists, they gathered up skilled mechanics, technicians, and production engineers . . . The sort of technical man who was neat, meticulous, a worshiper of order, of strict discipline . . ."[18] They had little in the way of ideology and no intellectual class to supply it. A disaffected former foreign-service officer and banker named Lawrence Dennis for a time supplied polemics such as those in a book entitled *Is Capitalism Doomed?* He had been honored in Italy and Germany, had conferred with Mussolini, and liked what he had seen of fascism.[19] By 1936, when he published *The Coming American Fascism,* he thought the time was ripening in his own country. He felt that Long and Coughlin more nearly met the needs of the masses than any other politicians. The Kingfish needed a good brain trust, but Dennis thought he was still smarter than Hitler. As he surveyed these new forces in American politics he found them good: "I hail these movements and pressure groups . . . because they are making fascism the alternative to chaos and national disintegration."[20] But these groups were far from dynamic. They

---

[16] Link, *American Epoch,* p. 480.
[17] See Weyl, *The Battle against Disloyalty,* pp. 162–164, and *Treason,* pp. 329–331.
[18] Weyl, *The Battle against Disloyalty,* p. 154.
[19] Carlson, *Under Cover,* p. 463.
[20] Arthur M. Schlesinger, Jr., *The Age of Roosevelt: The Politics of Upheaval,* p. 77. See pp. 69–95. See also Carlson, *Under Cover,* pp. 462–468 and *passim.*

came, wrote Schlesinger, "from the old lower-middle classes, now in an unprecedented stage of frustration and fear, menaced by humiliation, dispossession, and poverty." Largely raised in evangelical denominations, they were used to "millennial solutions." If Coughlin's Catholic followers seemed different from them in some ways, they were similar in others. Now a part of the old waves of immigration, they seemed to represent— like those native-born Protestants of older immigrant stock—an "Old America in resentful revolt against both contemporary politics and contemporary economics." The leadership was less inspired than the rank and file. A venal rag-tag and bobtail—*farceurs*, as Schlesinger called them—they were "mostly local adventurers or fanatics hoping somehow to capitalize on anxiety and unrest."[21] And they failed, moreover, "because most of them were sheer money-makers instead of conspirators . . . and, above all, because practically the entire civil and religious leadership, Protestant and Catholic, recognized the rabblerousers for what they were and effectively neutralized their propaganda."[22]

But there was allegedly a very different aspect of American Fascism which ended neither with the sedition trials nor the entry into the war. It was much more pervasive and, so ran the argument, more insidious and powerful. This argument occurs more often in fiction than in nonfiction, but in 1947 George Seldes put it strongly in *1000 Americans,* using a thesis reminiscent of some as far back as Ignatius Donnelly's time. The United States was controlled by an oligarchy so powerful, he wrote, that its influence was to be seen in industry, finance, and government. And so effective was the oligarchy's control of the press that many citizens were not aware of its power. They might not even know of the charges levelled against it by men such as Harry S. Truman, speaking as chairman of the Senate Committee Investigating National Defense.

In a chapter entitled "Big Business and the War," Seldes quoted Senator Truman's charge that the oil and steel industries had hindered the war effort out of monopolistic motives, that their action "is treason . . . You cannot translate it any other way."[23] Seldes indicted "Big Business" on three principal counts: a refusal to go into war production as urged by the government in 1939 and 1941–1942, war profiteering and delivery of inferior munitions to the armed forces, and secret cartel arrangements "by which the biggest American corporations supplied nations soon to be our enemies with materials and information, and kept America

---

[21] Schlesinger, *Roosevelt,* pp. 68 and 78.
[22] Link, *American Epoch,* p. 442.
[23] George Seldes, *1000 Americans,* p. 139.

unprepared."[24] Seldes quoted from the conclusions of a Congressional Report following an extensive investigation: "In the 1940 defense crisis, business displayed much the same attitude that it had shown 23 years earlier. Business would help the government and the people, but the basis of payment therefor would have to be fixed before the wheels would begin to turn. Profits, taxes, loans, and so forth, appeared more important to business than getting guns, tanks and airplane motors into production . . ."[25] He cited the wartime and postwar investigations of the Tolan House Committee, the Mead Committee, the Bone Committee, and elements of the Justice Department exposing "monopoly, profiteering, the cartel system by which free enterprise was shown to be anti-free enterprise, and certainly anti-American . . ."[26]

In the following chapter, "DuPont, Hoover, and Hitler," Seldes alleged that the DuPont interests "had become the American member of the Big Three which divided the world for chemical exploitation," sharing this distinction with the Britain's Imperial Chemicals and Germany's I. G. Farben. They illicitly sold munitions to Germany in violation of the conditions of the Versailles Treaty as late as 1933, he asserted, munitions including "military propellants and explosives . . ."[27] On January 6, 1944, the Department of Justice indicted the DuPont Company and Imperial Chemicals "for forming a cartel with I. G. Farben of Germany and Mitsui of Japan." Furthermore, writes Seldes, quoting Assistant Attorney General Wendell Berge's testimony in September of the same year, "The DuPont Co. informed I. G. that they intend to use their good offices after the war to have the I. G. participation [in such activities as 'the division of the South American market'] restored."[28]

Most of the book's twenty-three appendices dealt with the identity and activities of the oligarchy. Appendix 22, "The Big Subsidizers of American Reaction and Fascism," drew on reports of the Senate Lobby Investigation to record the political contributions of prominent Americans. Men such as Lester Armour, Lammot DuPont, Howard J. Pew, and Alfred P. Sloan gave to groups such as the American Liberty League, the Crusaders, and the Sentinels, whose political spectrum ranged, wrote Seldes, from a dark conservative hue to black tinges of Fascist colora-

---

[24] Seldes, *1000 Americans*, p. 140.
[25] Donald C. Blaisdell, *Investigation of Concentration of Economic Power,* pp. 171–172.
[26] Seldes, *1000 Americans*, p. 142.
[27] *Ibid.,* p. 161.
[28] *Ibid.,* pp. 153 and 164–165.

tion.[29] Similar findings appeared in the reports of the House Select Committee on Lobbying Activities. It investigated a number of organizations including the National Economic Council, which received support from sources such as Armco and Bethlehem Steel, Eastman Kodak, Standard Oil, and the Santa Fe Railway. The Council, writes Schriftgiesser, "has indulged in the fascist approach in its publications for many years." According to the Committee's report, "One of its techniques is to disparage those who oppose its objectives by appeals to religious prejudice, often in ill-concealed anti-Semitism."[30]

In an earlier appendix, Seldes had quoted the man liberal Democrats had once known as "The Chief." Woodrow Wilson had said, "The real reason that the war we have just finished took place was that Germany was afraid her commercial rivals were going to get the better of her, and . . . some nations went into the war against Germany [because] they thought Germany would get the commercial advantage of them. The seed . . . of the deep-seated hatred, was hot successful commercial and industrial rivalry."[31] Underlying Seldes' arguments—and some of the novels in this chapter—is the view that segments of commerce and industry are enormously powerful and self-seeking. They will place their own interests far ahead of those of the nation, it is charged, and they will follow any course to limit government and increase their freedom even if it leads to fascism.

Historians acknowledge that one of the principal factors in turning the tide for the West in World War II was the American industrial plant. Turning out war materials in unprecedented volume, it exceeded any productive surge since the industrial revolution. But this did not change the view of some novelists and writers of nonfiction who, looking back, felt that many of the mightiest industrialists stood, when all was said and done, with the fascists, the racists, and the disloyal in their country's hour of greatest danger.

Fascist Configurations

The novel of American Fascism appeared in the mid–1930's and continued for almost exactly the same time-span as that of Hitler's Third

---

[29] Seldes, *1000 Americans*, pp. 292–298.

[30] As quoted in Karl Schriftgiesser, *The Lobbyists*, pp. 154–155.

[31] Wilson had delivered these remarks as part of a speech in St. Louis, Missouri, on September 5, 1919. See *The Congressional Record*, Vol. 58, Part 5 (August 25 to September 12, 1919), 5006.

Reich. The first of ten was published in 1933 and the last in 1947.[32] But
the phenomenon of Fascism in American literature was not an isolated
one. It was linked by common elements to the novel of corruption and
that of the Southern Demagogue. The name of Huey Long appears, for
instance, as a native model on which a would-be dictator might pattern
his career. The industrialist who had appeared in the novel of corruption, giving his highest allegiance to a cartel rather than a government,
reappeared—resisting his own government while trafficking with others.
Other novels treated the Fascist organization rather than concentrating
upon the leader or his collaborator in industry.

There were several elements common to these three approaches. Although the setting might be a city, a state, or the nation, the author was
likely to suggest that the locale was unimportant, because this phenomenon might occur anywhere. These novels were set in New London, Los
Angeles, Pittsburgh, Chicago, and Washington, D.C.; in Georgia, Ohio,
and Texas; and unless the citizenry recognized the danger and acted,
the incidents described might well take place in the reader's home town.
Often counterbalancing these irreproachable sentiments, however, was
writing heavily larded with sex and violence. Although these elements
might have been necessary to mirror Fascistic behavior, their use was
often cheap and tawdry, the kind of writing seemingly aimed at the in-
expensive reprint market.

The novel centering around the Fascist-style dictator abounds with
references to Mussolini and Hitler. In this leader the drive to power is
enormously magnified. Washington in his ultimate aim. His desire for
self-aggrandizement appears in the blazoning of his name on public
monuments and places. He also revels in the accolades of his staff and
his populace, forced though they may be.

The dominant motive behind the Fascist-style organization may be
quite different. Its leadership is often concerned more with the material
rewards of power than with the enjoyment of power for its own sake.
Fascist techniques may simply offer the most efficient way to retain control of a town or extend it further. The ostensible leader may actually
be a front, a crackpot, or a visionary used by the group or by a dominant
member who is more promoter than politician. He may closely resemble
the confidence man or the fake healer.

[32] American Fascism entered, of course, into other novels, among them Sinclair
Lewis's *It Can't Happen Here* (1936), and Hodding Carter's *Flood Crest* (1947),
treated in Chapters Four and Six respectively.

There is usually the machinery of Fascism, with the state party, and the special organizations for men, women, and youths. Special identifying devices, magazines, and other materials sold to the faithful distinguish them from the mass of men. The habit of mind of these extremists is indicated by a standard set of prejudices: they are anti-radical, anti-Semitic, anti-Negro, and anti-Catholic. This antagonism fuels the military apparatus. The storm-troop equivalents are inevitably used, often in a manufactured emergency which serves as an opportunity for a *coup* or at least for intimidation. These often satisfy the sadism of major characters. Homosexuality also appears as another parallel with the Nazi movement. (Heterosexuality is manifested in ordinary liaisons.) Other apparatus includes a stockade or other concentration camp surrogate and a corps of assassins. Fascist and Nazi terms are used in literal or equivalent form. One organization makes a "push" upon a smaller community; another merges with a similar city organization at the other end of the state in an "axis" and later sets out to force a consolidation upon a smaller neighbor. References also occur to a march on Rome and to appeasement.

The novel depicting the fascist mentality in business and industry presents few of these trappings. There are usually no storm troopers or rallies. Instead, there is violent rejection of any form of government supervision. The industrialist or businessman wants to deal with whom he chooses (especially his employees) in any way he chooses. The animus is objectified in virulent hatred of Franklin D. Roosevelt and the New Deal. The most sinister men of power operate cartels with the Axis powers. They obstruct governmental policies from within their firms and from jobs in government.[33] They may even countenance sabotage in the violence of their reaction against governmental control and prewar aid to the Allies. This extreme action links these novels with those of the Fascist organization. In both, sympathy with Fascist-Nazi aims leads to agreements, even collaboration, and, in some novels, to outright sabotage. Only in these novels of Fascism in industry is there much concern with theoretical Fascism and Naziism. In the others there is at most racism and a crude form of statism. Any theorizing is rudimentary, and it is practice not theory that matters. Here the motives involve money and a kind of power, just as they appear more nakedly in the novels of the Fascist-style dictator and the Fascist organization.

---

[33] John Dos Passos uses such a situation in *The Grand Design*.

The Shafts of Satire

In his regrettably brief career Nathanael West produced four short novels. The best, *Miss Lonelyhearts* (1933), is a near-surrealistic work showing life as cruelly macabre and gratuitously tragic. In *The Day of the Locust* (1939), he gave Hollywood a scarifyingly satiric treatment. Sympathetic to the left, West was profoundly troubled, like many of his contemporaries, by events in America and in Europe. To West, writes James F. Light, "the capitalistic system seemed to be creaking at its very foundations. Looking abroad, he could only shudder at the German solution to its economic and psychological problems . . . It might be used in America by some potential Hitler."[34] A Jew who was keenly conscious of the role of the Jew as scapegoat, West wrote to a friend, "I believe there is a place for the fellow who yells fire and indicates where some of the smoke is coming from without actually dragging the hose to the spot."[35] In *A Cool Million* (1934) West did his best to sound the alarm. But in this comic-satiric novel he directed attention to more than incipient Fascism. He lampooned American values in politics and business. His broad satire ranged over mass culture of the 1930's in which Fascism might find fertile soil. If *A Cool Million* was not completely successful, it was still an original of sorts whose satiric components—non-Fascist as well as Fascist—deserve some attention.

A novel as extravagant and hyperbolic in its way as either *Hizzoner the Mayor* or *The Old Copper Collar*, West's book was far more effective and amusing than either. He employed a unique style which depended mainly on the cliché, especially that of Horatio Alger-style fiction. As Light points out, West was satirizing the dream of success embodied in Alger narratives such as *Bound to Rise, Onward and Upward*, and *Paddle Your Own Canoe*. The novelist read extensively in Alger in preparation for *A Cool Million*. When he came to write, he had both Alger's verbal texture and his situations. Scene shifts at approaching climaxes, nick-of-time rescues opening doors of opportunity, parenthetical moralizing—West used them all.[36] The verbal clichés were the counterparts of the cultural clichés they expressed. Although this strategy bound West in a stylistic straightjacket, he brought off ironic and comic effects through the simple, primerlike style and the actions which completely contradicted them. Faith and honesty do not bring Lemuel Pitkin suc-

---

[34] James F. Light, *Nathanael West: An Interpretative Study*, p. 117.
[35] Nathanael West to Jack Conroy, as quoted by Richard Gehman in his introduction to Nathanael West, *The Day of the Locust*, p. x.
[36] See Light, *Nathanael West*, pp. 118–124.

cess; instead they help to undo him, limb by limb. A typical development follows a successful defense of his much-assaulted sweetheart:

> Lem gave his hand in return without fear that there might be craft in the bully's offer of friendship. The former was a fair-dealing lad himself and he thought that everyone was the same. However, no sooner did Baxter have a hold of his hand than he jerked the poor boy into his embrace and squeezed him insensible.
>
> Betty screamed and fainted, so great was her anxiety for Lem. Hearing her scream, Baxter dropped his victim to the ground and walked to where the young lady lay in a dead faint. He stood over her for a few minutes admiring her beauty. His little pig-like eyes shone with bestiality.[37]

The reader can savor West's tongue-in-cheek style and, if he does not find it too grisly, the macabre comedy of the misfortunes which befall Betty and Lemuel. The defenseless young maiden and the honest young man, contrary to the Alger stereotype, are victimized at every turn. Their paths separate, and before Lem reaches New York, he has not only been jailed but has lost all his teeth and an eye as well. He attempts to rescue Betty from a Mott Street brothel where she is the American representative in Wu Fong's "House of All Nations." Characteristically, Lem not only fails to rescue Betty but is himself captured by an "enormous Chinaman" who delivers him up to Wu Fong. Costumed as a sailorboy to tempt a perverted Maharaja, Lemuel is saved only when his false teeth and glass eye fall out, disgusting the customer.

The man who victimizes Lem at the beginning of his quest is a fellow townsman of Ottsville, Vermont, and president of the Rat River National Bank. Nathan "Shagpoke" Whipple is a former President of the United States who, after one term, "had beaten his silk hat, so to speak, into a plough-share and had refused to run a second time, preferring to return to his natal Ottsville and there become a simple citizen again" (146). But he does not remain a simple citizen. (Up to this point he is a broad comic caricature of Calvin Coolidge.) Horrified at the "rank socialism" of the Democratic Party, he forms the National Revolutionary Party. As he exhorts Lem to join them, Whipple tells him, "The uniform of our 'Storm Troops' is a coonskin cap like the one I am wearing, a deerskin shirt and a pair of moccasins. Our weapon is the squirrel rifle" (186). Following the Leather Shirts' banner, Lem is dismantled, as Whipple puts it, losing a thumb, his scalp, and a leg. Finally he is shot by a double agent for the Communists and the International Bankers at a Whipple

[37] Nathanael West, *A Cool Million: The Dismantling of Lemuel Pitkin,* p. 154.

rally. Whipple is then supreme in America, for "through the National Revolution its people [have been] purged of alien diseases and America became again American"(255). Shagpoke takes the review as 100,000 coonskin-hatted American boys march by. Lem has become a Leather Shirt Horst Wessel, venerated for his martyrdom, as the crowds roar

> Hail, Lemuel Pitkin!
> All hail, the American Boy! (255)

West's attack on Fascism was not surprising, though his use of Communism for comic purposes must have been for some. According to Aaron, West had clearly demonstrated his revolutionary sympathies by the middle 1930's. In 1936 he participated with 250 others in the Western Writers' Congress held in San Francisco. Speaking on "Makers of Mass Neuroses," he was, writes Aaron, "the most talented writer of them all..."[38]

West's satiric eye took in targets other than just the vulnerable in politics, commerce, and speech usage. In the episodes in which Whipple and his party, accompanied by a bizarre Indian named Chief Jake Raven, dig for gold on the Yuba River in the Sierras, West introduces a roughneck from Pike County, Missouri. Through him he extravagantly satirizes the figure of the Pike County man of literature and folklore. Similarly, when they travel south, West describes the crowd which lynches Chief Jake Raven in terms which suggest the mob cowed by Colonel Sherburn in *Huckleberry Finn*. It is the debased lynch mob of American fiction, here presented in a comic-satiric style.[39] Whipple's harangue to the crowd is little more than 250 words long, but it presents in capsule form the appeal of the Southern Demagogue to his electorate.

The spurious and tawdry in American culture of the 1930's are satirized in the description of a part of a medicine show joined by Lem and Shagpoke. It is billed as the

Chamber of American Horrors, Animate and Inanimate Hideosities:
The hall which led to the main room of the "inanimate" exhibit was lined with sculptures in plaster. Among the most striking of these was a Venus de Milo with a clock in her abdomen, a copy of Power's "Greek Slave" with elastic bandages on all her joints, a Hercules wearing a small, compact truss.
In the center of the principal salon was a gigantic haemorrhoid that was lit

[38] Daniel Aaron, *Writers on the Left: Episodes in American Literary Communism,* pp. 307 and 432.

[39] For several of these insights into the novel I am indebted to Professor James B. Colvert of the University of Virginia.

from within by electric lights. To give the effect of throbbing pain, these lights went on and off.

All was not medical, however. Along the walls were tables on which were displayed collections of objects whose distinction lay in the great skill with which their materials had been disguised. Paper had been made to look like wood, wood like rubber, rubber like steel, steel like cheese, cheese like glass, and, finally, glass like paper. (239)

These and other bogus articles reinforce the motif of fraud and sham. It is more pointedly borne out by a performance called "The Pageant of America or A Curse on Columbus"(239), which depicts Wall Street millionaires duping a widow and her orphaned grandchildren. It is a cliché like the typical Alger story, but it presumably contains more truth, for at the novel's end Whipple is in power, protecting the interests of entrepreneurs like those in the pageant.

Although this volume of approximately 40,000 words did not show West at the top of his form, as in *Miss Lonelyhearts,* it demonstrated something of his distinctive talent. Dedicated to one of the best of modern American humorists, his brother-in-law S. J. Perelman, it gave rein to West's talent for parody and comic absurdity. It also showed how, even with the self-imposed handicap of a confining style, he could use this talent to satirize contemporary concerns just as he had attempted to analyze more personal ones in the bizarre but penetrating novels by which he is better known. And it also signalled the American artist's growing concern with native Fascism.

The Fascist-Style Dictator

Two novels appearing within five years of each other treated politicians whose drive to power suggested European dictators. The first was W. R. Burnett's *King Cole* (1936), and the second was George Cronyn's *Caesar Stagg* (1941). Burnett was a member of the so-called "hard-boiled school of fiction" of which James M. Cain was the chief ornament. He was also the author of the notorious *Little Caesar* (1929), a novel of Chicago gangsters which helped create a vogue for similar fiction. Governor Read Cole of Ohio has much in common with the gangsters of Burnett's other novels. And although he is said to be a liberal Republican of advanced views, he is actually a champion of the *status quo,* acting to the advantage of the rich men who are his allies. Running for re-election, he launches a campaign of Red-baiting, provokes riots, threatens martial law, and then calls out the militia. He thus frightens enough of the electorate to insure victory and tries to purge the state of radicals.

On one occasion he is called "the Ohio Machiavelli," on another, the Mussolini of Ohio. Elsewhere he is referred to as "Hitler." Escaping an assassin's bullet, he begins to bring order into his tangled personal life. Then, in an ambiguous and unprepared-for ending, he contemplates the columns of the governor's mansion, columns which "were standing when . . . the Ohio crowds were cheering for General Grant and Old Abe; and they would still be standing when His Honor, James Read Cole, Governor of this Sovereign State, freed of all his lusts and miseries and dreams, was dust."[40] This implication of a possible change of heart has been completely undercut, however, by a long harangue near the end from Cole's opponent apparently functioning as Burnett's *raisonneur.*

The novel's epigraph comes from the passage in which Francis Bacon gives the origin of the phrase, "Pyrrhic victory." The best lines, also Bacon's, comment on Cole's career: "It is a strange desire, to seek power and to lose power over a man's self. The rising unto place is laborious; and by pains men come to greater pains; and it is sometimes base; and by indignities men come to dignities. The standing is slippery and the regress is either downfall or at least eclipse, which is a melancholy thing" (257). But Cole's portrayal never lives up to the spectacular charges made against him. Actually, none of the characters possesses the breath of life, all of them speaking in the same primer style of monotonous short sentences that also serve for narration and description.

As George Cronyn's *Caesar Stagg* (1941) was even less convincing than Burnett's *King Cole,* so Julius Caesar Stagg was even less a real man and more a caricature than Read Cole. A complete vulgarian, as well as an adulterer and murderer, he has risen from Prohibition bootlegging to the ownership of a newspaper chain and other enterprises. He completely dominates his state through repression and intimidation. One opponent refers to "Stagg and his Storm Troopers," whereas another declares, "Our Caesar is ambitious to ape certain gentlemen abroad."[41] After his thugs persecute a group of intellectuals who oppose him, the National Guard and special deputies occupy the capital until after election day. One character, in rather obvious foreshadowing, remarks, "But maybe he'll overplay his hand. Maybe he'll go too far, like Huey Long did, and get what's coming to him" (331). And sure enough, Stagg is shot to death at the Thanksgiving Day football game.

[40] W. R. Burnett, *King Cole,* pp. 8, 172, and 292.
[41] George Cronyn, *Caesar Stagg,* p. 271.

A moral is pronounced by one of Stagg's victims: "there's a sort of natural justice that catches up with fellows like that" (443). But it has the effect of a tacked-on afterthought following the brutality and murder which are the staples of the novel. Stagg is hateful but never believable. Credibility is destroyed by diction completely stereotyped and unrealistic. One suspects that this novel, like Burnett's, took advantage of the topicality of Fascist and Nazi outrages to embellish another of those familiar novels whose lowest common denominators are Bossism or corruption and violence.

The Fascist Organization

The first of four novels centering on the Fascist organization appeared in 1940. It was Samuel M. Elam's *Weevil in the Cotton,* set in the Four Square State, which apparently adjoined Georgia and was similar to Mississippi. The novel's narrator, newspaper reporter Harry Sudbury, describes the process by which a small circle within the city machine suppresses all freedom among the sixty thousand citizens of the city of Kitticum. They form an alliance with the rulers of the city of Bailsville and begin to absorb North Kitticum, which has a population of twelve thousand and is solvent.[42] The organization uses a fabricated Negro crime to declare a state of emergency, abolish elections, and install the mayor as city guardian. The white-clad Kitticum Guards are led by a drooling homosexual bully who enjoys torturing victims in a stockade. Disaster comes only when a drive on the state capital is beaten off by troops under the governor's orders.

One suspects that this novel was meant to be taken, like *It Can't Happen Here,* as a warning that European-style dictatorship could take root on North American shores. It attempted to convey something of the quality of mind of those who would be susceptible. But rather than registering as a warning, the novel—with its cheap sensationalism and near-pornography—was exactly the kind that would appeal to the sort of person personified in the leader of the Kitticum Guards. Men such as Hitler, Himmler, and Goebbels were, of course, unspeakably evil. Nevertheless, they are usually granted an ideology which, however barbaric, was capable of being distinguished from plain avarice, sadism, and lust for power, even though these qualities were amply present in Naziism. With these characters, no such differentiation is possible. There is simply

---

[42] These figures obviously are a rough approximation of the relative sizes of Germany and Austria in the 1930's.

the naked desire, first, for spoils, and second, for power. If one could imagine a group which could conceivably show members of the Nazi movement at an advantage, it would be composed of characters such as these.

Colonel Effingham's Raid (1943) dealt with the process by which a quasi-Fascist organization assumed control over the life of a Georgia city of sixty thousand people. It was also narrated in the first person by a newspaperman. But there most of the resemblance ended. The narrator was a humane and sensitive young man who told his story with gentle humor in a self-deprecating tone. At the center of his tale was a retired soldier intent on arousing the citizenry to action. Berry Fleming's protagonist is Colonel W. Seaborn Effingham. He is a tall, thin, high-nosed man and gray military mustaches and a bald pink head. Through his young cousin, the narrator, Effingham publishes a series of newspaper articles on the history of the city, his boyhood home. His tales and anecdotes are actually parables for the present, however, which arouse the mistrust of the group in control of city affairs. They are inheritors of a Boss named Pud Toolen, who years ago had

conceived the idea which was to dominate the whole of his lengthy career in the public trust: to eliminate the needless waste of having two or more political parties in Fredericksville, competing and fighting with one another, creating discord and unrest, when all this squandered time and energy could be concentrated in one great brotherhood known as the Home Folks Party, of which he himself would be the patriarchal head.

But Effingham is met by apathy in the quarters he hopes to reach. "But, floods, boy!" he exclaims to his cousin, "Are you proposing to fight dictatorship abroad and submit to one in your home town?"[43] Carrying on his battle alone, he opposes the plan to rename Monument Square "Toolen Square." Despite harassment, he urges an increased library appropriation and tries to block the condemnation of the courthouse and the graft-ridden construction of a new one which will follow. For Effingham, this problem is crucial:

He saw the courthouse now, not as just a historic old building, but as a symbol of Law and Order and Democratic Procedure (all upper case), as a symbol of what we had fought the Revolution for, as representing a heritage of free government handed down to us over the perilous years which, through our carelessness and indifference, we had allowed to deteriorate until now something had to be done about it. (176–177)

[43] Berry Fleming, *Colonel Effingham's Raid,* pp. 78 and 88.

The young narrator meets with success in the secondary, romantic plot, but Effingham loses his campaign. He meets rebuff and hypocrisy from church and business, while friends grow cool. Symbolically, when the narrator entrains for departure with a federalized National Guard unit, Effingham—at the salute in an immaculate class A uniform—is thrust aside "for the long black automobile bearing His Honor the Mayor and his Distinguished Guests" (279).

This competently done novel, written with a light touch at seeming variance with the seriousness beneath, is actually much more realistic than such heavy-handed works as *Weevil in the Cotton*. The narrator conveys a sense of place and time, adroitly suggesting the pleasant aspects of a Southern environment at the same time that he shows how things have gone wrong morally and politically. Here it is neither assassination nor carnage but fear and apathy which permit local totalitarianism. And the citizenry continues to suffer dictatorship at home even while sending men to fight it abroad.

A very different kind of Fascism was depicted by Lewis Browne in *See What I Mean?* (1944). It displayed greater avarice than the Home Folks Party and deeper fanaticism than the Kitticum Guards. The narration again came from a former newspaperman. Clem Smullet has declined from press-agentry to confidence schemes and blackmail and thence to promotion work for quasi-Nazis in Los Angeles. An amoral, ferretlike man, he tells his story from jail while awaiting trial. His style is occasionally so literary as to be out of character, but for the most part it is convincing after the manner of Ring Lardner's *You Know Me Al* and John O'Hara's *Pal Joey*. Browne's disclaimer asserts, "no character . . . is intended to be identified with any real person now either under arrest, at large, or dead." From time to time, however, Browne's characters make identifications themselves. Doc Gribble persuades Smullet to join in promoting the organization he plans to form around John Christian Power: "I'd been running into others like it all over the country on my tour. Pelley's Silver Shirts, for example . . . Then there was Winrod's Defenders of the Christian Faith, and Edmundson's Knights of the White Camelia, and maybe a dozen more."[44] Gribble has been a preacher, a pension-scheme promoter, and a bogus physician. In his clinic he has used radio broadcasts as well as cures based on electrical diagnoses, vibrations, and orange juice. Power has worked for him administering colonic irrigations. But he is a tall and commanding fanatic

[44] Lewis Browne, *See What I Mean?* p. 39.

who hypnotically harangues crowds.[45] Smullet is later able to define his attraction:

> this villain was full of hate-appeal, and the customers we catered to were the sort who couldn't respond to practically anything else. They were mostly bellyachers and soreheads, total losers in the battle of life, and the chief reason they flocked to our meetings was because they wanted to let off steam . . . It made no difference what they were sore about—unemployment, usury, flaming youth, vivisection—no matter what it was, he'd always tell them the Jew was to blame. (106)

In Smullet's expert judgment, Power is a mad egoist, and Captain Cleaver, the leader of the storm troops of Power's "Crusade," is fundamentally "a gangster who lacked the guts to admit he was one, and therefore wore a flag instead of a bullet-proof vest" (10).

The motivation of Gribble, and Smullet, is equally clear. They concentrate on contributions at meetings, subscriptions to *The Crusader,* plus fees and equipment sales to party groups such as the Rangers and the Amazons. But Gribble's ambitions link this novel with those of fascism in business and industry. He has earlier told Smullet,

> "Take a guy like Henry Ford. He's a Jew-baiter from way back, and he'll be tickled to death to support us once we've got a real movement going. So will any number of other tycoons, whether they're Jew-baiters or not. Because we'll be able to show them that in attacking the Jews we're really attacking the New Deal, and Communism, and the labor unions, and all the other things that they're scared of. Christ, there's no limit to what we can do with this racket!"[46]

The group's activities lag until its appeal is given new impetus by Hitler's successful aggressions. Thinly disguised financial contributions have by this time made the group an instrument of Nazi sabotage. Then, as a projected march on Washington fails, Pearl Harbor is attacked and the F.B.I. closes in.[47]

---

[45] John Christian Power suggests demagogues such as George W. Christians, a leader of the Crusader White Shirts convicted in the sedition trials of 1942. He had threatened to cut off the electrical power when President Roosevelt visited Chattanooga. See Weyl, *Treason,* p. 321 and Carlson, *Under Cover,* pp. 149–150.

[46] Browne, *See What I Mean?* p. 42. Allegations of Henry Ford's antisemitism and assistance to fascist groups are frequently encountered in the literature of American Fascism. See Carlson, *Under Cover,* pp. 210, 244, and *passim* and also Seldes, *1000 Americans,* pp. 292–298 and *passim.*

[47] A number of groups—apart from the so-called Bonus Expeditionary Force of veterans dispersed on the Anacostia flats outside Washington by General MacArthur—planned at one time or another to emulate Mussolini's March on Rome

In a last irony, Browne reveals that Power is actually half Jewish. Arrested for indecent exposure meant to prove he is not Jewish, he is committed to an asylum. This novel is convincing and at times adroitly done. Focusing on the lunatic fringe to which extremist movements made a consistent appeal in the 1930's, it was not a warning like Lewis's *It Can't Happen Here.* Browne did not feel that the country was in danger of subversion and conquest from within. Instead, he concentrated upon displaying the vicious and shoddy motives which found an outlet in a movement such as the John Christian Power Crusade.

The novel of American Fascism did not disappear with World War II. Charles Dwoskin's *Shadow Over the Land* (1946) even held that overt Fascism, not simply oligarchy in industry, still remained a danger. Dwoskin wrote in his introductory note, "This novel is not entirely fiction. Although the choice of New London, Connecticut, as a locale was purely arbitrary, the events described . . . might very well have taken place in . . . Rochester, Tucson, or Oakland . . . and may yet . . ."[48] The novel itself related the effects of Patriots United! upon the Fleming family after the war. This organization suggests the America First movement with greater vilification of Jews, Negroes, and Communists. An organ called *The American Hammer* pours out venom while the local leader appeals to disgruntled veterans with rather routine demagogic oratory. Because the Flemings are frustrated and baffled, defeated by life and by themselves, they are vulnerable in various degrees to the appeals of the movement and its leaders.

Ultimately a group of public-spirited citizens faces down a Patriots United! group. True to his introductory note, Dwoskin concludes with a description clearly meant symbolically: "But there were no stars. A great mass of storm clouds hid the sky, frowning at the earth" (285). Apparently the reader is meant to conclude that only one skirmish has been won and battles lie ahead. This novel is obvious but ambitious. The author tries for intensive psychological and sociological portraiture. He also attempts to use symbol and structure meaningfully, juxtaposing

---

with a March on Washington. One of the most ludicrous, a remnant of the non-fascist B.E.F., was for a while active in Philadelphia. But "General" Art. J. Smith's Khaki Shirts (he had sold his men the shirts—and boots) never made it to Washington. About the time police closed in to uncover an illegal cache of arms, the General absconded with Khaki Shirt money. He was later sentenced to six years in prison for perjury in connection with a murder committed at a party rally and thereafter dropped out of sight (Schlesinger, *Roosevelt*, pp. 79–80).

[48] Charles Dwoskin, *Shadow Over the Land*, p. 7.

scenes and characters to heighten his situations by comparison and contrast. But neither his story nor his technique creates an ultimate impression of force or credibility. One finds his characters unconvincing and his positing of this form of Fascist danger difficult to accept in the United States of 1946.

Fascist Collaboration in Business and Industry

Three novels published in the mid-1940's collectively covered a period from Pearl Harbor to the early post-war years. They were all concerned with a struggle which gave Lawrence Lipton the title for his novel, *In Secret Battle* (1944). On one side are labor, the liberals, and the Administration. The other side in the secret battle is "reaction . . . the counter-revolution from the Right, the economic overlords stepping out from behind the scenes of government to take over total state power openly or through their demagogic Fuehrers." A reporter ferreting out Nazi activities in America reflects that, since his father's time, "the *big* thing that had happened was Fascism . . ." It is camouflaged by the enemy, he says, as "Free Enterprise, God's Plan, the American Way of Life, the Wave of the Future; and the thing they feared: labor 'racketeering,' foreign ideologies, Bolshevism."[49] Love again crosses the lines through the daughter of the tyrannical oligarch, Stuart Baldwin, inheritor of the far-flung Baldwin enterprises. One of her lovers is an economist and columnist who goes further to the left as the novel progresses. The snobbish Baldwin has many hates: Roosevelt and the unions, the government and government planning. He is a proponent of what amounts to a laissez-faire economy and he has friends among the America First movement. His immediate subordinates are made in the same mold. Baldwin will not cooperate with other firms; his primary concern is for postwar use of new patents and processes. In extreme cases, firms such as Boaz Brass are hotly antigovernment, anti-Russia, and antiwar. They are honey-combed with Nazi sympathizers and even agents who, apparently with company sufferance, sabotage the war effort. These industrialists are epitomized in a Vichy manufacturer who made tanks for the Germans. The economist-turned-columnist warns against these men in the form of "the big business crowd that smuggled itself into Washington inside the Trojan Horse . . . That's the gift horse that F.D.R. forgot to look in the mouth, and now they've swarmed out of it and surrounded him . . .

---

[49] Lawrence Lipton, *In Secret Battle,* p. 217.

They're running the show now . . ." (332).[50] Others put it differently. Roosevelt makes too many concessions to these men, they say, citing a conflict between Henry Wallace and Jesse Jones allegedly decided in favor of Jones.

One of Baldwin's collaborators is a lobbyist who resembles Rudolph Hess and plays *fuehrer* in attempting to unify Nazi organizations. His activities help propel the plot to its conclusion as he moves from anti-unionism and strikebreaking to sabotage and espionage. A laggard government finally collars him as well as a German espionage chief and an American would-be Quisling. Baldwin's daughter eventually achieves a happy marriage with a correctly oriented man. The principal impression left, however, is of a milieu dominated by reactionary tycoons. Their direction is toward the extreme right—to the America First movement and beyond—and their devious policies lead to the Ku Klux Klan, anti-labor groups, and even thugs and hoodlums. These industrialists, men like Theodore Roosevelt's "malefactors of great wealth" and Franklin Roosevelt's "economic royalists," stand in the foreground of the action. Lipton seeks something of the scope of Dos Passos's pattern novels by using characters such as the newspaperman and the columnist. In other strata are a liberal manufacturer, a university economist in government service, and a neurotic amateur Mata Hari who straightens herself out by enlisting in the Navy. But the canvas is never as broad or informative as with Dos Passos, and the brushwork is nowhere near as sure.

Lester Cohen's *Coming Home* (1945) dealt with the same phenomenon as *In Secret Battle* but on a larger scale. The author noted that his story could have been told in other cities, but that it was set in Pittsburgh "because Pittsburgh is the heart of the war effort." The protagonist drives home this point. A wounded Marine returned for recuperation, Joe Drew thinks, "All over the world, in Italy, in Germany, in the islands of Japan, fascism was going down . . . What was sacred about it in Pittsburgh?"[51] The general pattern resembles that in Lipton's novel. The tycoon here is Eugene Osmond, controller of Pittsburgh's Three Mile Mill, Osmond Aeronautical, and Osmond International. Advised once by Andrew Carnegie to "play big," he had done so:

He played with the New Order, advanced credits, helped arm Germany and Japan. The Axis was nothing new to him, he knew it had existed since 1918 . . . That was the time when the Japs were big owners of industrial stock in

---

[50] This point is elaborated in John Dos Passos's *The Grand Design* through characters such as a tycoon who goes to Washington as a dollar-a-year-man.

[51] Lester Cohen, *Coming Home,* p. 204.

the United States, and the time of the making of the "flaming coffins" of
World War I that Billy Mitchell screamed about. In fact, one of the reasons he
had had to get rid of Mitchell and [the protagonist's father] was that they
spilled the beans in Congress about his arming Japan. [But] they would not
play fair with him, they would let him be *Gauleiter* for steel, but they would
take the lion's share . . . from that moment on, he was for war. (222)

Apart from shipping defective armor plate to the Navy and defective
communications wire to the Army, Osmond enterprises perform prodi-
gies for the war effort.[52] But

> at the same time he was more deeply involved than ever in German cartels,
> Japanese cartels. He was important in SKF, the Swedish ball-bearing cartel,
> which kept the German war machine rolling . . . if all of a sudden your boy in
> a B-17 was blasted by a Focke-Wulf, you put the gold star in the window and
> were the last to realize that some of the B-17 and some of the Focke-Wulf
> were made by Mr. Osmond's companies and cartels. As we said in the last war,
> *C'est La Guerre.* (223)[53]

Osmond's low-level counterpart is J. Stoneham Pike, alderman, justice
of the peace, and controller of sixteen thousand votes in whom there is
"not merely an impulse to modern fascism, but an ancient fascism,
Neroism" (31). It is chiefly his machinations which push the plot along.
His rape of the hero's sweetheart precipitates a series of battles revealing
his longtime service to Osmond and their joint injustices to the hero's
father. Pike's arranged death is seen by a wise old newspaperman as
merely "A big fascist getting rid of a little fascist" (296). The novel's improbable ending sees Joe Drew employed by Osmond on condition that

---

[52] In spite of Drew's enmity, Osmond is drawn to him in a paternal way. In a
passage approximating the situation of Arthur Miller's *All My Sons,* Drew reveals
to Osmond that the faulty wire was responsible for the death of his own son.
George Seldes refers to "Anaconda's defective wire, the Curtiss-Wright defective
airplane engines, and the U.S. Cartridge Company's defective bullets" (*1000
Americans,* p. 149). He asserts that

one of the worst cases in American history of a corporation "defrauding the government and endangering the lives of American soldiers" was exposed in Attorney
General Biddle's indictment of Anaconda Wire and Cable Company, whose Marion, Indiana, branch had sold the United States $6,000,000 worth of telephone
wire and cable for war purposes, and had previously sold the Russian government wire which was 50% defective and which no doubt resulted in the death of
many soldiers." (George Seldes, *Facts and Fascism, p.* 257).

[53] According to Seldes. such tainted profits were common. For example, "the
Krupps got one shilling on every fuse used on the Vickers hand grenades," and
"certain supplies, shipped to Denmark by the United States, were transshipped
to Germany with the connivance of the British Admiralty (as Admiral Consett
later disclosed)" (*1000 Americans,* p. 143).

none of his military inventions will ever be made available to the cartels. Through the passion and violence of the characters and the smoke and turmoil of the mill setting, one can see some of the ideas of that shaper of the American novel, Theodore Dreiser. Looking back upon the "playing" he had done, Osmond thinks, "the Meccano set of Pittsburgh, the water faucet they called Dnieprostroi, they were his arts, his enterprises" (306). His philosophy might be that of Dreiser's superman, Frank Cowperwood: "Long ago, Mr. Osmond had discovered something about human life; either you ran things or other people ran you. And he had decided to run things. And had quite a run" (219). There is this strain too in Pike. Before his trial he contemplates a Dreiserian plea to the jury: he was shaped by society, by his environment, and the ultimate responsibility for his crimes rests not with him but with those forces which molded his character and his life. Cohen's style, like those in many of the lesser novels in this study, leans heavily on overstated, overly short sentences and paragraphs. His effects, often dependent on the sordid and violent, suggest American naturalism strained through the hardboiled school of fiction. This depiction of the seamy, though presumably well-justified by the milieu, contains nothing of the compassion which gives Dreiser's work its added dimension.[54] But Cohen's scenes—set in the wards and mills, the courts and prisons, the offices and suites—do have scope and force. And through it all one feels the power of the great industrial complex and the power in these lives, perverted though some of them are. It is, in effect, on this note that the novel ends. For Drew comes to terms with the idea that the Osmonds will be with us for some time yet and that one can use what is good in them while opposing what is evil in them. The last lines depart from this equilibrium, however, with a strong affirmation of the forces of life and growth over those of evil and death.

This whole complex of ideas was carried further in Robert Rylee's *The Ring and the Cross* (1947). More intensely political than either of the other two, it implicitly stated a position much further to the left. Emerg-

[54] Cohen had been a member of the "Dreiser Committee" which in 1931 had been "sent down by the Communist-organized National Committee for the Defense of Political Prisoners to investigate conditions in the Harlan County [Kentucky] coal fields . . ." (Aaron, *Writers on the Left*, p. 178). Other members of the committee included John Dos Passos and Samuel Ornitz. With heavy irony, T. S. Eliot had referred to Cohen's work, with that of Ornitz and Granville Hicks, as the summit of Communist literary art. See Aaron, p. 249. In 1935 Cohen was a member of the organizing committee charged by the first American Writers' Congress with the job of creating the League of American Writers, "as an affiliate of the International Union of Revolutionary Writers (I. U. R. W.) and to carry out a revolutionary political program" (Aaron, p. 283).

ing both from dialogue and narrative exposition, it suggests the utterances of radicals in David Graham Phillips and John Dos Passos. The novel is set in Texas, and its central character is Senator Adam Denbow, who has brought industry and investment to his Gulf coast city of Congreave. He has brought it, however, through "permanent alliances with the financial powers of the East," having learned early that "essential differences between the Democratic and Republican parties were almost non-existent and that the publicly proclaimed differences were a mere idle fiction."[55] His prospective opponent is Vaiden MacEachern, son of the LaFollette-like man he defeated for his Senate seat through a combination of aggressive campaigning, money, rumors, and calumny. But a more dangerous threat comes from the industrialists now become his masters. One of them, Wesley Clayton, is part owner of the shipyard in which MacEachern works and in which much of the action takes place. One employee tries to tell some of the others,

How in Italy, one must not think of Mussolini and the trappings of the Black Shirts; one must look behind and see where the power was, in the hands of the three great monopolies, Fiat, Montecatini, and Snia Viscosa . . . the monopolists fearing the people . . . and turning to Mussolini and his gangsters to enforce their power and to prop up for a little while longer their dying order. And how the German industries and industrialists, I. G. Farbenindustrie, Siemens, Krupp, Thyssen, and the rest had turned to Hitler and England and the Standard Oil Company, among others, in their war against the German people. And he spoke of the Comitè des Forges and Mitsui and Mitsubishi: the feudal barons of modern medievalism. And how it was, and might be, in the United States in the years after the second World Wars with the Rockefellers and the DuPonts and the Fords, and the Silver Shirts or the Ku Klux Klan or whatever the name would be when the time came. (64)[56]

In one of his seemingly interminable lectures, MacEachern asserts that Clayton, decorated at Berchtesgaden by Hitler, wants to return to the Middle Ages. He then quickly sketches in his Marxist view of the origins of modern industrialism:

"it was monopoly capitalism that blazed the trail, for the industrialists saw early that the term 'free competition' while useful as a myth to befuddle fools, had no place in their practical vocabulary . . . And so, by means of international cartels, they organized the world market and parceled it out among themselves and brought order—their kind of order—out of chaos." (282)

[55] Robert Rylee, *The Ring and the Cross*, p. 15.
[56] For information about William Dudley Pelley's Silver Shirts of America, see Carlson, *Under Cover*, pp. 317–319 and *passim*.

What the Claytons really want, he argues, is the Nazi system. He sees the tendency to conformity in modern American life as evidence of the susceptibility of the masses to Clayton's propaganda based on racism and hate. Then, in a passage whose ideas are identical with those of Irving Silverstone, the party-line parrot of Dos Passos's *Adventures of a Young Man*, MacEachern asserts, "Hitler was the final expression of the philosophy of life and the will to power of monopoly capitalism. If you followed the trail beyond Hitler, it would finally lead across the Channel to England, and then across the Atlantic to the United States" (286). To MacEachern, Franklin Roosevelt had good intentions, but he unwittingly gave power into the hands of the business-rightists who had infiltrated the government through agencies such as the NRA, "which was nothing more than the government providing for the powerful business men of America a university education in the techniques of Fascism" (236). Later, in a passage reminiscent of Jed Farrington's remarks about "The Squire in the White House" in Dos Passos's *The Grand Design*, MacEachern declares that Roosevelt "abdicated his presidency and turned the government over to our first families, lock, stock, and barrel . . . in doing so he made possible the final entrenchment of fascism in America, and made possible, and perhaps inevitable, the third of the World Wars . . ." (292).

Like other novels, this one has a brutal, lower-level equivalent of the fascist tycoons at the top of the structure of power. He is Brame, the head guard at the shipyard, a sadist whose projected Brown Shirt-style organization will be financed by Wesley Clayton. (The Clayton-Brame relationship appears clearly modeled on the prototypal Thyssen-Hitler one.) Moved to tears by the thought of himself at the head of his singing, marching men, Brame tells his mistress, Popcorn, that the right combination of words will unlock the door to power.[57] His organization will be tied up with religion, and it might be called The Fisherman's League, "because Jesus was a fisher of men, and all the apostles" (162). MacEachern's comments on religion have a different tone: "The industrialists, and the Roman Catholic Church," he asserts, "trying to preserve their power, backed Hitler's gangsters against the people" (235). Then he remarks that the same thing may happen here. Clayton finally makes his program explicit to the horrified Denbow. When the war is over, if a general strike is called it will be suppressed by force, provided in part by organizations such as Brame's. Then,

[57] The quality of this relationship suggests elements of the Popeye-Temple Drake-Red triangle of Faulkner's *Sanctuary*.

It will be imperative that we choose a leader, one so wise and trusted that in his presence we can dispense with such unwieldy instruments as, for example, the national Congress. Surely our history has proved that the common man is unfit to rule himself. We must have a relationship in society . . . in which authority and responsibility are vertical . . . a society of unity and order . . . governed by a leader, chosen from the natural aristocracy, the leader being, shall we say, a leader of leaders, much as was the case with the Holy Roman Empire . . . (253)

The ending of this novel is not so ambiguous as that of *Coming Home*. Brame has murdered MacEachern and been killed in turn by Mac-Eachern's revolutionary disciple. Denbow is secure in his Senate seat, but as he returns to Washington in his railroad compartment he is literally the prisoner of Clayton and his party. We are apparently meant to believe that the fortunes of this party are still in the ascendant, and that what has been forecast will eventually come to pass.

The Ring and the Cross is an ambitious novel. Rylee's prose is sophisticated but voluminous. He is fond of lengthy passages of dialectics. Although his characterization runs to the wooden (rigid Wesley Clayton) and the trite (MacEachern's wonderful, Old-Southern aunt), he can draw convincing characters. His other resources include both symbolic object and symbolic action. The objects of the title apparently signify the kind of rotten autocracy of prerevolutionary France and values symbolized in wartime by the Cross of Lorraine. This particular device is not as effective as it might be, nor is the attempt to cast over the proceedings a kind of reflective glow emanating from the vision of the Old South called up by the recollections of Denbow's patron and his sister. The novel as a whole has this quality of partial success. For the student of this form, its greatest interest lies in its being one of the very few contemporary American novels of the extreme left. And though the disquisitions of MacEachern and his disciple are long, these Marxist and quasi-Marxist views are presented with some subtlety.

Some Conclusions

The novels of American Fascism in this dozen-year time span can best be seen along two spectra: the scope of the fascist phenomena depicted, and the motives of those behind them. Fascism appears in the small city, in a state organization, and in a national movement. And it is least effective on this last level. In an industrial corporate structure, however, it can become supranational through trade agreements and cartels. The impression left by these novels is that the overt Fascism of the totalitarian leader, with its apparatus and trappings of propaganda, troops, and emblems, never constituted a serious threat to the existing American political system. It constituted at most a vehicle for divisive emotions and attitudes. It also contributed to espionage and sabotage during World War II, but in no way approaching the intensity of such activities in occupied Europe. But the effect of fascism in business and industry is a far different matter. It is more powerful and effective, more to be feared then, now, and in the future. It is presented as a threat inherent in the mentality and power of this kind of tycoon. A blood brother to Phillips's villains, he might be one of Dreiser's supermen but harboring a much more deadly intent than merely surviving and conquering. In each of the three novels which deal with this subject matter, this situation goes back to the century's early years. In the last, it is one which is capable of producing—and indeed is likely to produce—a third World War.

The spectrum of motives impelling these fascists along their courses is a narrow one. And the motives themselves are shoddy. Chiefly avarice, hate, and lust for power, they only occasionally include the fanatic's conviction. The reader never sees the selfless dedication of the engaged political man with total commitment to a particular philosophy. Much less does he observe anything approximating political idealism. Instead, he sees chiefly a few forms of self-interest. He encounters individuals seeking wealth and power which can gratify motives ranging from self-aggrandizement to sadism. In some respects there are differences between the "big" and "little" fascists. The latter is overtly more coarse, brutal, and pathological than the former; he does most of the dirty work and reaps the smaller spoils. But at bottom they are closely linked by totally destructive motivations and the resulting actions, no matter how much they may say or think of purity and independence of motive and ideal.

In reading these novels one speculates about still another kind of motivation—that of the author. In the earlier of these books it is clearly suspect. The atrocities of Fascism and Naziism provided a timely equivalent of the murder and mayhem generated by the conditions of Prohibition and capitalized upon in the fiction of the late 1920's and early 1930's. Consequently, the usefulness of these works in formulating the image of the American political experience in the twentieth century is problematical. They seem to reflect at best, and rather superficially, the clichés of the political history of the times. Other novels, later ones in the brief period treated here, appear motivated by a genuine concern for the health of the body politic. They pay the price usually exacted for didacticism. If there is not the overt appeal to the reader, there is the sense of example and message. That is not to deny that this appeal can be a component of great literature; it is rather to say that it rarely is. And there is nothing approaching great literature here. Further, there appear to be no novels here which just happen to be about people engaged in political activity, or people whose lives are portrayed in a political frame of reference within which other, more fundamental concerns of their lives and destinies (as Warren put it) can work themselves out. In sum, the literary quality here is only middling. The later novels in this small group are better than the earlier ones, but the total achievement is not high. Perhaps this is a fact not too much to be wondered at, seeing that the phenomena they treat thus far appear to be substantially delimited in time, rather than being among the eternal problems of the human situation.

8. the far Right and mccarthyism

WITCHCRAFT is a most Monstrous and Horrid *Evil.* Indeed there is a vast Heap of Bloody Roaring Impieties contained in the *Bowels* of it. *Witchcraft,* is a Renouncing of *God,* and Advancing of a filthy *Devil* into the Throne of the Most High . . .

Take heed that you do not *wrongfully accuse* any other person, of this horrid and Monstrous Evil . . . What more dirty *Reproach* than that of *Witchcraft* can there be? Yet it is most readily cast upon *worthy* persons, when there is hardly a shadow of any Reason for it . . . There has been a fearful deal of injury done in this way in this Town, to the *good name* of the most credible persons in it. Persons of more Goodness and Esteem than any of their Calumnious Abusers have been defamed for *Witches* about this Country.

Cotton Mather
A Discourse on Witchcraft (1689)

The position of the Far Right is more often—and more easily—defined in terms of what it is against than what it is for. This segment of American political thought and action has consistently opposed increasing the regulatory functions of the central government, particularly as they bear on business and industry. It has opposed the increase of existing taxing powers and the creation of new ones. The Federal income tax is still regarded by some rightist leaders as one of the chief sources of twentieth-century ills they deplore. Much government spending they equally deplore. Economy—particularly a balanced budget—is high on the scale of positive values, and anything that increases appropriations, such as social benefits, is to be avoided. Most alarming to the militant segments of the right have been the labor movement, legislation increasing federal power, and radical philosophies and movements such as Communism. Less prominent but nonetheless present have been fear and distrust of foreigners coupled with occasionally virulent anti-intellectualism.[1]

The presence of the Far Right is most obvious in its unrelenting anti-Communism and opposition to any kind of accommodation with Russia. It has also consistently advocated withdrawal from the United Nations and from programs involving international cooperation and aid. It has supported limitations upon immigration. Zealously advocating congressional investigations, it has opposed extension of federal social and medical benefits.[2] Despite its up-to-the-minute opposition to controversial contemporary measures such as fluoridation, the militant right is a segment of the American political spectrum whose manifestations, though they took other forms, go back more than a century. But through these manifestations certain continuing attitudes, values, and hostilities, can be seen.

The Know-Nothing Party of the 1850's characterized itself in a way that certain of its descendants were to emulate. It advertised its patriotism; it was the American Party by name, and its sentiments were America for Americans. Behind its formation were a combined hostility toward and fear of foreign immigrant masses. To a large extent uneducated and predominantly Roman Catholic, they appeared likely to constitute an economic burden if not a threat. The Know-Nothing Party polled one-fourth of the total popular vote for President in 1856, but virtually ceased to exist during the depression of the following year. Its successor appeared thirty years later, still opposing Catholics and still attempting to cloak itself in righteous patriotism. The American Protective Association did not become as considerable a political force as the American Party had been, but the A.P.A. further inflamed prejudice, slowed down the absorption of new national and cultural strains in American life, and provided a kind of continuity in rightist thought and action in the second half of the nineteenth century. It also supplied an organized and vocal outlet for these complex attitudes and feelings which have increased rather than abated—among the extremists of the militant right—with the passage of time.

The Populist and progressive movements also had their anti-immi-

---

[1] For a definition of the American Right Wing with examples of its activities, see *The American Right Wing: A Report to the Fund for the Republic, Inc.,* by Ralph E. Ellsworth and Sarah M. Harris.

[2] See Ellsworth and Harris, *American Right Wing,* p. 31.

grant feelings. To many native sons in the rank and file, these waves of immigration constituted crucial threats to American institutions. Not only were these masses of immigrants apt to be uneducated, conditioned to civil and ecclesiastical authority, and used to a highly rigid and stratified society, they were likely material for the big-city bosses who would organize them in the rabbit warrens in which they took up their new lives.[3] Thus the political radicalism of nineteenth-century Populism and twentieth-century progressivism was tempered by a conservatism in racial and ethnic matters. It appeared in one of the proposals of President Ephraim Benezet in Ignatius Donnelly's *The Golden Bottle* (1892) : halt the immigration from Europe of the indigent masses who, as they flood the labor market, will be used by employers to lower native workingmen's wages. This conservatism was to reappear in later rightist movements.[4]

It is axiomatic among liberal American historians that reform inevitably suffers under the rigors of wartime. This was true as the energies which had gone into Woodrow Wilson's New Freedom program were channeled into mounting the A.E.F. and converting the United States to a wartime footing. But matters went further than simply bringing the reform movement to a standstill. Under wartime pressures rioting erupted and certain civil liberties were suspended altogether. Early in 1916 investigations of Bolshevik activities led to the arrest of alien Communists for deportation. Later that year Victor Berger, a Socialist congressman from Milwaukee, was tried under the Sedition Act for conspiracy. A moderate Socialist, Berger was convicted and sentenced to a twenty-year jail term, being denied his seat in 1918 when he was free on bail and again in 1920 after he had been re-elected in a special election.[5] The discovery in April, 1919, of a large-scale Communist bomb plot to assassinate cabinet members, governors, and other officials led to large-scale repressive measures. State legislatures outlawed membership in organizations advocating the use of violence. A mob invaded the offices of the Socialist New York *Call* on May Day, while on the other coast

[3] For a close examination of this view and its accompanying hostility, see Richard Hofstadter, *The Age of Reform: From Bryan to F. D. R.*, pp. 173–184.

[4] Hofstadter, *Reform*, pp. 8–9, and 20.

[5] By 1917 it had become risky to criticize the Y.M.C.A. or the Red Cross, for the Espionage Act passed in June of that year, "became a tool to stamp out dissent and radical, but never conservative, criticism" (Arthur Link, *American Epoch: A History of the United States since the 1890's*, p. 215). Eleven months later the Sedition Act extended government control to printed and spoken opinions without regard to their effect.

murder and lynching followed an invasion of I.W.W. headquarters by American Legionnaires in Centralia, Washington.[6] Near the end of that violent year, Attorney General Palmer embarked upon a personal deportation campaign after Congress had refused to enact his Sedition Bill. On New Year's Day, 1920, 6,000 persons were taken into custody all over the country by federal and local agents acting under his direction. A third were released for lack of evidence, and eventually, when Secretary of Labor William B. Wilson took charge of the proceedings, only 556 aliens, all members of the Communist Party, were finally deported.[7]

It was but a short step from official governmental action to the violent, unofficial action of self-constituted defenders of the "American Way." Eric Goldman notes that radical labor leaders "were tarred and feathered, ministers were unfrocked for emphasizing the Sermon on the Mount, clubs expelled members who questioned the omniscience of the Administration, college professors were dismissed or bludgeoned into resigning for pacifist leaning or for ardent prowar statements that also criticized the home front." And Outagamie County, Wisconsin, provided the case of a patriotic German-American farmer nearly lynched for his failure to buy more Liberty Bonds at the time and pleasure of a mob.[8] Paradoxically and ironically, these same conditions had the effect of drawing into government service some young intellectuals who combined ambition with the reform impulse. In what Goldman calls hyperbole, Harold Stearns wrote, "The bold critics were committed to prison; the more amenable ones were taken into the government and committed to keeping their mouths shut."[9] Then, in 1920, Nicola Sacco and Bartolomeo Vanzetti were arrested for the murder of the paymaster of a South Braintree, Massachusetts, shoe factory. The trials which followed constituted the most celebrated *cause célèbre* in American juridical history. Most of the American liberal community was convinced that the execution of Sacco and Vanzetti in 1927 came not for robbery and murder (which most students of the case now feel they did not commit), but because they were anarchists who were also aliens, draft-dodgers, and labor men. The fervor and bitterness expended in their behalf extended far beyond the end of the decade. It was one of the most striking results of the postwar era which, writes Arthur Link, "bequeathed to the 1920's a heritage of

[6] John Dos Passos dramatized these events in the "Wesley Everest" section of *1919*.

[7] See Link, *American Epoch*, p. 244.

[8] Eric F. Goldman, *Rendezvous with Destiny: A History of Modern American Reform*, p. 256.

[9] Harold W. Stearns, *Liberalism in America*, p. 110.

hatred and hysteria that permeated and disturbed every aspect of life and thought."[10] This persecution of the left was by no means the exclusive responsibility of the radical right. It was performed by the center as well. But this activity, though not restricted to the radical right, was in keeping with its characteristic pattern of action and attitude.

At this time an instrument of violent political action and reaction which had flourished more than a half century earlier reappeared. The white-sheeted terrorists of the Ku Klux Klan were again riding, beating, and burning, but their area of influence was no longer confined principally to the states which had formed the Confederacy. Most of the 5,000,000 members enrolled by 1925 lived in the Midwest,[11] the Southwest, and on the Pacific Coast. The Klan dominated the Republican state organization of Indiana and exercised formidable power in the governments of Ohio, Oklahoma, Arkansas, Texas, and California as well. And even when its membership had declined by the end of the decade to a mere tenth of that at its peak, it still served as a focus for bigotry and hatred. It was also to be a ready supply for the organizations of American Fascism.[12]

Although a number of Ku Klux Klan leaders were, like their later native Fascist counterparts, exposed as greedy charlatans rather than potential American embodiments of the Man on a Horse, the base of resentments which they used was real and massive enough. It consisted chiefly of rural or small-town Americans of native stock who suspected the hyphenated-American and often felt their security and status threatened by the aggressive and successful among the new groups. Seymour Lipset wrote that groups such as the Know-Nothings, A.P.A.'s, Progressives, and Ku Klux Klan showed how—contrary to common assumption—American society produces protest movements in times of prosperity and not mainly in periods of economic depression.[13] Lipset goes on to conclude that, if this is assumed to be a pattern in American politics, the affluence of the decade following World War II should have produced another such movement. And, like the earlier ones, McCarthy-

---

[10] Link, *American Epoch,* p. 244. See also pp. 241–244.

[11] For a discussion of the metamorphosis of the Midwest of the early Bryan and Progressivism to the Midwest of McCarthy and reaction, see Hofstadter, *Reform,* pp. 285–287.

[12] See Link, *American Epoch,* pp. 339–343. For full-length studies see William Peirce Randel, *The Ku Klux Klan: A Century of Infamy;* and David M. Chalmers, *Hooded Americanism: The First Century of the Ku Klux Klan, 1865–1965.*

[13] Seymour Martin Lipset, "The Sources of the 'Radical Right'," in Daniel Bell (ed.), *The New American Right,* p. 172.

ism "is characterized by an attack on a convenient scapegoat, which is defined as a threat to American institutions, and also involves an attempt to link 'cosmopolitan' changes in the society to a foreign plot."[14]

Although Joseph Raymond McCarthy showed himself resourceful from his first emergence into public life, it was ten years before he found the issue with which he was to seize the leadership of the militant right and make himself the most powerful demagogue since Huey Long and the most influential one in American foreign policy. He was, wrote Richard Rovere, "our first and only national demagogue."[15] After a false start in 1936 with the Democratic Party organization of Shawano County, Wisconsin, he won a place in 1939 on the Republican ticket as candidate for circuit judge of the Tenth Judicial District. Barely thirty, he was inexperienced and undistinguished. But his office staff sent out thousands of handwritten postcard appeals while he stumped the three-county area, campaigning door-to-door, folksily and indefatigably. Asserting that his 66-year-old veteran opponent was 73 and falsely crediting him with a suspiciously high income during his judgeship, he won the election. As a judge, McCarthy became known for the number of his cases and the speed with which he tried them. But his greatest legal celebrity—in the notorious Quaker Dairy case—was subsequently cited by the Wisconsin State Supreme Court as an egregious example of judicial misbehavior.[16]

But McCarthy was apparently little concerned. He had procured a first lieutenant's commission (though he was later to assert that he "enlisted as a buck private"), and he would shortly be serving as a Marine Air Intelligence officer in the Pacific. In June of 1943 he sustained a fractured foot in the "Shellback" ceremonies aboard a seaplane tender crossing the equator. Subsequent campaign literature presented him as "Tail-gunner Joe," and he later declared he wore an elevator shoe because, "I carry ten pounds of shrapnel in this leg!"[17] After returning briefly to Wisconsin in 1944 and losing an unconstitutional primary campaign (he was still a judge), he resigned from the war five months before

---

[14] Lipset, in Bell (ed.), *New American Right*, p. 173. See also pp. 167–173 and Lipset's note on p. 221 citing "earlier extremist agitation [which] also dealt with supposed plots of foreign agents" such as "the agitation leading to the Alien and Sedition Acts before 1800, the anti-Catholic movements, [which] all involved claims that agents of a foreign power or of the Pope sought to subvert American life and institutions."

[15] Richard H. Rovere, *Senator Joe McCarthy*, p. 259.

[16] Jack Anderson and Ronald W. May, *McCarthy: The Man, the Senator, the 'Ism'*, pp. 48–49.

[17] Anderson and May, *McCarthy*, p. 66.

V-J day. He came home to win re-election as Judge Joe McCarthy, but he had bigger things in mind.

By the end of the war, the Progressive Party had run its course in Wisconsin, and Senator Robert M. LaFollette, Jr., had led its members, many of them reluctant, into the Republican Party. LaFollette further stacked the odds against himself by spending a relative pittance in time and money on his campaign. McCarthy charged that LaFollette spent too little time in Washington on Wisconsin business and intimated that the Senator had turned into an internationalist playing into the hands of the Communists. He also charged that LaFollette had made an illegal wartime profit out of the share of a radio station he had purchased. McCarthy won the primary by 4,500 of the 410,000 votes cast and went on to defeat his Democratic opponent with ease. Thus the man to be voted the "worst Senator" by the Washington Press Gallery replaced the one who had earlier been voted the "best Senator." Later, when his successor was at the height of his power, Senator LaFollette, who had represented Wisconsin with honor and distinction for twenty-one years, put a bullet through his head.

Wisconsin's new junior senator kept an eye to the welfare of McCarthy as well as that of Wisconsin. In 1947 he helped end wartime sugar controls five months earlier than scheduled, earning the name, "The Pepsi-Cola Kid." Five weeks later, when he was being pressed to cover a $20,000 note back home in Wisconsin, a friend came forward to do it for him. He was Russell M. Arundel, lobbyist, sugar-interest spokesman, Pepsi-Cola bottling-plant owner, and friend of Pepsi-Cola president Walter Mack.[18] In 1948 McCarthy interested himself in the public-housing issue and helped defeat the government bill opposed by the housing lobby. He also found time to earn a fee of $10,000 from the Lustron Corporation for a 7,000-word pamphlet on housing.[19] But this was

[18] Anderson and May, *McCarthy*, pp. 128–137.
[19] Anderson and May, *McCarthy*, p. 152. See also Rovere, *Senator Joe McCarthy*, pp. 183–184. Both these studies are critical of McCarthy, as is James Rorty and Moshe Decter, *McCarthy and the Communists*. Sympathetic is *McCarthy and his Enemies*, by William F. Buckley and L. Brent Bozell. Covering early 1950 to early 1953, Buckley and Bozell deplore the liberties McCarthy took with truth but in effect condone them in the light of his declared objectives. They assert that McCarthy plunged into a crucial area of the anti-Communist struggle at a crucial time. Despite their disapproval of McCarthy's most egregious offenses, the end result is something like the familiar end-means proposition, made apropos of him, that you can't fight skunks and come out smelling of roses. Messrs. Buckley and Bozell conclude their "afterword" with a statement of their belief "that on McCarthyism hang the hopes of America for effective resistance to Communist infiltration" and the hope that "his spirit may infuse American foreign policy with

not the extent of his concern for his friends' interests. Later, writes Schriftgiesser, he "was to become notorious as a tool of the so-called 'China Lobby'."[20]

It was a year afterwards in 1949, however, that signs of McCarthy's propensity for controversial issues, his disregard for facts, and his technique of slashing attack began to appear. Affidavits from SS troops under sentence of death for the massacre at Malmedy of 250 Americans and Belgians captured during the Battle of the Bulge alleged that their confessions had been obtained by torture. McCarthy charged the United States Army with atrocities and helped save the SS men from death. (The charges had been supplied him by "a man named Rudolph Aschenauer, a Communist agitator who evidently saw in the Malmedy affair a means of spreading anti-Americanism.")[21] Later that year he attacked Francis Matthews, the Secretary of the Navy, secured national headlines, and helped muddy the waters in which the battle over carrier-based aircraft versus long-range bombers was being fought. But suddenly it was 1950, and he would be up for re-election in two years. Under attack in the press at home, he had no issue which would supply the leverage to propel him back into his Senate seat. But before the first week of the New Year was out he had found it.

For a perspective on the extraordinary events which were to follow, it is necessary to go back seventeen months to a far-reaching *cause célèbre* which then seemed not to concern Joe McCarthy directly at all. It had begun to break in the first week of August, 1948, as two Congressional committees conducted the first public hearings of disloyalty charges which, during the previous eight years, had been investigated by the F.B.I. and federal grand juries without any indictments being returned. Acrimonious controversy had swirled up after President Truman had called the hearings a "red herring" dragged across the trail of con-

---

the sinews and purpose to crush the Communist conspiracy. Only then can we afford to do without McCarthy" (p. 340). Buckley has in recent years constituted himself a spokesman for the far right, less erudite than Russell Kirk, for instance, but about the only figure on the Far Right having any of the credentials of an intellectual. For a consideration of Buckley and his role, see Mark Sherwin, *The Extremists,* pp. 14–25.

[20] Karl Schriftgiesser, *The Lobbyists: The Art and Business of Influencing Lawmakers,* p. 210.

[21] Rovere, *Senator Joe McCarthy,* p. 112. See also pp. 113–118, for Rovere's talk with McCarthy about this subject, in which McCarthy demonstrated his propensity for interpreting adverse evidence as fraudulent. See also Anderson and May, *McCarthy,* pp. 158–164. See Seymour Lipset on isolationism and Midwestern pro-German ethnic groups, in Bell (ed.), *New American Right,* pp. 199–201.

gressional shortcomings. He had refused to give up naval and civil service records of persons under investigation, and partisans of the committees' work had threatened impeachment proceedings.

The hearings before the two committees were interrelated. Former Communist Elizabeth Bentley described a Communist espionage system in America to a Senate Committee on Expenditures in the Executive Departments. Louis Budenz, a Fordham economics professor and former editor of the New York *Daily Worker* who had renounced Communism and joined the Roman Catholic Church, corroborated part of her testimony. On August 3, former Communist Whittaker Chambers testified before the House Un-American Activities Committee on a pre-war Communist underground in Washington. He named ten he said were members. The response was most shocked at a single one of the names: Alger Hiss. A former director of special political affairs in the State Department, he was now at forty-three the $20,000-a-year president of the Carnegie Endowment for International Peace. His record had been brilliant. A *cum laude* graduate of Harvard Law School where he had studied under Felix Frankfurter, he had served for a year as secretary to Justice Oliver Wendell Holmes. After his work in Henry Wallace's A.A.A. his star rose higher during the war. He was secretary of an international conference at Dumbarton Oaks. He accompanied Roosevelt to Yalta. He was secretary of the conference at San Francisco. In 1946 he went to London as adviser to the U.S. delegation to the first U.N. General Assembly session. Now he was accused of treason.

The accuser was an equivocal figure. At forty-seven Whittaker Chambers was making $30,000 a year as senior editor of *Time* magazine. But his boyhood had been vagrant and uncertain. He had put in two years at Columbia University and then joined the Communist Party in 1924. Like Budenz, he had been on the *Daily Worker*, serving as editor until 1929. He turned to writing fiction which appeared in *The New Masses* until he went underground in 1932 on Party orders. Three years later he met Alger Hiss. Shortly thereafter, he declared, Hiss began feeding him State Department documents. But by 1937 he had become disillusioned and renounced the Party, trying unsuccessfully to persuade Hiss and his wife to leave with him. In fear of reprisals he went into hiding for a year. Now this highly-paid journalist, a Quaker, a man who spoke five languages, was revealing his past under the bright glare generated by the Committee hearings.

On August 5 Hiss went before the Committee and emphatically denied knowing Chambers, belonging to the Communist Party, or sympathizing with it. Two weeks later he admitted knowing Chambers in 1934–1935, but as George Crosley. That was wrong, Chambers said, he knew him as Carl. Faced with this contradiction, the Committee brought the two men together in a New York hotel on August 17. Afterwards Representative Richard M. Nixon announced that Hiss had admitted that Chambers, as Crosley, had occupied his apartment in Washington in 1935, but denied the charges of Communism and espionage. The next morning brought a dramatic public confrontation before television cameras in the jam-packed caucus room of the old House Office Building. When Chairman J. Parnell Thomas concluded the hearings at eight o'clock that night, the two men's stories were still radically at odds on more than half a dozen key points. One of the two witnesses, Thomas declared, would certainly be tried for perjury. When the Committee issued its report, it declared itself unable to say who was the perjurer but commented that Chambers' account had been partly corroborated whereas Hiss' had not, and that Hiss was often "evasive."

Accusation led to litigation. When Hiss dared Chambers to make his charges where he could be sued for libel, Chambers obliged on August 27 on a New York radio program. In six weeks' time Hiss had replied with two suits totalling $75,000. During a pre-trial deposition Chambers produced more than sixty documents as evidence of State Department materials transmitted to him. Representative Nixon thereupon had a subpoena issued calling for any further evidence Whittaker Chambers might have. It came in the early hours of December 3 when he led Committee investigators to a spot on his Westminster, Maryland, farm where he had hidden rolls of microfilm in a pumpkin, in fear of a Communist search in his absence, he said. When developed, the "pumpkin papers" turned out to be copies of secret State, War, and Navy Department documents dated in 1937 and 1938. Senator Karl E. Mundt, chairman of the Senate subcommittee investigating Communist espionage, said that they had a direct bearing on the Chambers-Hiss case.

On December 15, nine days after Chambers told the Committee that Hiss and two other government employees had passed documents to him, a New York grand jury indicted Alger Hiss. The statute of limitations on espionage had run out, so he was charged with perjury when he denied giving State Department documents to Chambers in 1937–1938 and seeing him after entering the Department in September, 1936. The trial was set for January 24, 1949. But in one of the choicest of political ironies, the Committee chairman was to go on trial before his witness.

Representative Thomas was up on charges of defrauding the government—charges that were going to stick.

After six postponements, the Hiss trial began in federal court in New York on May 31. In the account which Chambers now gave, he had met Hiss in 1934. While he was serving as a Communist courier in May, 1935, he had lived rent-free in Hiss' Washington apartment. Chambers said that in early 1937 he had introduced Hiss to Colonel Boris Bykov in a Brooklyn movie house. The Colonel, head of Soviet espionage in the United States, asked Hiss to provide State Department documents and Hiss agreed, Chambers alleged. From early 1937 until his break with the Party in April, 1938, said Chambers, he would visit Hiss nightly to pick up documents for photographing, after which Hiss would return them to their files. Sometimes, he said, they would be copied on Mrs. Hiss' typewriter. He would then deliver the copies to Bykov in New York. Under cross-examination Chambers admitted that he had lied on half a dozen occasions when he hadn't told all about the espionage, but he explained that he had held out to give Hiss a chance to quit the Communist Party. On June 23 Hiss took the stand in his defense, denying Chambers' charges and reiterating his earlier version of their relationship. Two of the character witnesses in his behalf had impressive credentials: they were Supreme Court Justices Felix Frankfurter and Stanley F. Reed.

The six weeks' trial ended on July 8 with a hung jury. After twenty-eight hours they had split eight–four for conviction—the four dissenters refusing to accept evidence based on the Hiss typewriter. Representative Nixon wanted the Committee to investigate what he considered Judge Samuel H. Kaufman's prejudicial handling of the trial. This the Committee did not do, however, and a new trial began under a new judge on November 2. Judge Henry W. Goddard admitted the testimony of two prosecution witnesses whom Judge Kaufman had excluded. This was mid–December. In early January, 1950, he also admitted the testimony of a defense witness, a psychiatrist who declared Chambers to be in his judgment a liar and a scoundrel, completely unreliable and immoral. On January 17, testimony ended.

This time the jury was out for twenty-three hours, and on January 21 it brought in a verdict of guilty. Four days later the defendant was sentenced to five years' imprisonment. He was once again freed on bail, but on December 7 the verdict was upheld by the United States Court of Appeals in New York. Three months later the United States Supreme

Court refused to review the conviction. On March 29, 1951, nearly two years and eight months since that day when Whittaker Chambers had testified before the House Committee, the doors of the Federal Penitentiary at Lewisburg, Pennsylvania, closed behind Alger Hiss.

The impact of these events had been profound and, for many, traumatic. A brilliant man, seemingly one of the brightest of the government's servants, a man who had been a State Department official for ten of his forty-five years, had been found guilty of perjury and, by implication, of espionage on behalf of a foreign power—the Russian Communists. It was understandable if some people now gave more credence than they had in 1948 to the charge of Louis Budenz—another of Hiss's accusers—that possibly thousands of Communists had worked their way onto federal payrolls.[22]

On February 9, 1950, Senator McCarthy gave the speech in Wheeling, West Virginia, in which he charged that the State Department was still infested with policy-making Communists. Whether he said 205, or 81, or 57 of them has never been quite clear, and—as in the Quaker Dairy case—the record has disappeared. McCarthy's talent for making headlines began to flower. Privately he was more disarming. Asked in the early spring when he had discovered Communism, he answered unhesitatingly, "Two and a half months ago."[23] He had sought the advice of friends for a re-election issue. Finally Father Edmund Walsh of Georgetown University raised the question of Communism. McCarthy seized on it immediately but agreed that such a campaign would have to be based on probable facts rather than sensational charges. His friends little realized, wrote Jack Anderson and Ronald May, "that a day would come when they would all have to repudiate the young man who started his Big Show with their basic idea."[24] McCarthy repeated his charges in March before a specially-constituted subcommittee of the Foreign Relations Committee. Four months later the committee's majority, under its chairman, Senator Millard Tydings, concluded that McCarthy's charges were "a fraud and a hoax," but the Republican minority issued

[22] For much of this account I have used *Facts on File: Weekly World News Digest,* Volumes VIII–XI, *passim.* Two journalistic studies of the case appeared in 1950: *Seeds of Treason: The True Story of the Hiss-Chambers Tragedy,* by Ralph de Toledano and Victor Lasky, and *A Generation on Trial: U.S.A. v. Alger Hiss,* by Alistair Cooke. The principals' own accounts came later: Chambers' *Witness* in 1952 and Hiss' *In the Court of Public Opinion* in 1957.

[23] For slightly different versions of this interchange see Rovere, *Senator Joe McCarthy,* p. 55; Rorty and Decter, *McCarthy and the Communists,* p. 153; and Eric F. Goldman, *The Crucial Decade and After: America, 1945–1960,* p. 145.

[24] Anderson and May, *McCarthy,* p. 173.

its dissenting report, amid general dissatisfaction.[25] McCarthy had distorted evidence and failed to turn up any on-the-job security risks, but if no spies had been uncovered, a certain laxness of security measures seemingly had. It was, wrote Leslie Fiedler, a dubious report.[26]

One sequel transpired when Senator Tydings came up for re-election in the fall of 1950. McCarthy went to Maryland to campaign against him. His staff contributed a pamphlet containing a composite photograph of Tydings and Earl Browder, chairman of the American Communist Party.[27] Tydings was one of the Democrats who lost in a Republican election year, but few questioned the proposition that McCarthy had helped beat him. The next year McCarthy campaigned against the re-election of Senator William Benton of Connecticut, who had offered the Senate a resolution calling for McCarthy's impeachment. Benton lost. McCarthy also campaigned against Scott Lucas of Illinois and Ernest MacFarland of Arizona. They lost too. It was true that Senators James P. Kem of Missouri and Harry Cain of Washington lost in spite of McCarthy's help, and that in 1952 he was the poorest vote-getter of all the Republican nominees for major office in Wisconsin. But nonetheless, in the wake of the elections of 1952, "it was believed in the Senate that McCarthy was responsible for the presence there of eight men— which meant that he was responsible for the absence of eight others."[28]

With the advent of the Eisenhower administration in 1953, McCarthy began a two-pronged movement. One was a series of spectacular allegations and investigations of Communism in government; the other was an attack upon the Administration construed by many as an attempt to win control of the Republican Party and eventually the Presidency, even if it was necessary to form a third party to do it. A onetime friend later recalled that McCarthy had once told her, "I'll end up either in the White House or in jail."[29]

[25] See Rovere, *Senator Joe McCarthy*, p. 156, and Richard Luthin, *American Demagogues*, p. 282.

[26] Leslie A. Fiedler, "McCarthy and the Intellectuals," in *An End to Innocence: Essays on Culture and Politics*, p. 52. Fiedler's essay is a healthy corrective to studies such as those of Rovere and Anderson and May. While perceiving McCarthy's abuses, Fiedler also explores McCarthy's adversaries' use of some of his techniques. He suggests that they acted out of complex attitudes, often mixed with guilt, arising out of their roles and convictions in political affairs two decades earlier. "McCarthyism," he writes, "the psychological disorder compounded of the sour dregs of populism, the fear of excellence, difference, and culture, remains still a chronic disease of our polity . . ." (p. 87).

[27] See Anderson and May, *McCarthy*, pp. 297–298.

[28] Rovere, *Senator Joe McCarthy*, p. 37.

[29] Anderson and May, *McCarthy*, p. 373.

As new chairman of the Government Operations Committee and its permanent Subcommittee on Investigations, he began with an investigation of the International Information Administration. James Wechsler, once-Communist but for fifteen years anti-Communist and now vigorous editor of the New York *Post*, took the witness chair in April to endure a long ordeal. He had been summoned ostensibly because of allegedly subversive books he had written. They had been discovered in overseas libraries of the United States Information Service by twenty-six-year-old Roy M. Cohn, the Committee's chief counsel, "Short and short-tempered, sullen in expression and manner, brutal in speech," and by his friend, the Committee's "chief consultant," G. David Schine, also twenty-six, and "a good-looking young man in the sallow, sleekly coiffed, and somnolent-eyed style that one used to associate with male orchestra singers. . . ."[30] These allegations were among the fruits of an eleven-day trip the two had made through U.S. Information Agency branches in Europe—an investigation that had supplied material for a good deal of ridicule directed at America. It turned out that Cohn and Schine were unable to state which of Wechsler's four books had been found. This gambit had proved less spectacular and no more successful than McCarthy's earlier allegations before the Tydings Committee that Owen Lattimore was the "top Russian espionage agent" in the United States, when Lattimore had earlier espoused a policy close to that of the Soviet view of Asia, but had not been a spy, a Communist Party member, or an employee of the State Department.[31] Wechsler charged that the real purpose of the investigation was to intimidate him as a newspaper editor who had been eloquently critical of McCarthy and his activities. At the hearings McCarthy acted, he said, "like the gangster in a B-movie who faces the unpleasant necessity of rubbing out someone who has gotten in his way . . ."[32]

McCarthy's challenge became even clearer. He opposed Charles E. Bohlen's confirmation as ambassador to the Soviet Union and criticized State Department personnel and security procedures. ("You wait," he told a reporter, "we're going to get Dulles' head."[33]) He announced that he had gotten Greek ship owners to stop trading with Red China—when the State Department had negotiated such an agreement a short time

[30] Rovere, *Senator Joe McCarthy,* p. 191.
[31] See Fiedler on Wechsler as demonstrating the dilemma of the liberal versus McCarthy (*End to Innocence,* pp. 53–54 and 71–75).
[32] See James A. Wechsler, *The Age of Suspicion,* p. 283.
[33] Luthin, *American Demagogues,* p. 290.

before. Continuing his attack on the International Information Administration, he threatened to investigate the Central Intelligence Agency. The Administration was still ready to compromise. In the matter of the Greek shipping agreement, the President failed to support Mutual Security Director Harold Stassen when he charged that McCarthy was undermining American foreign policy. More crucially, the President had permitted the appointment of Mr. Scott McLeod, a man totally committed to McCarthy, as personnel *and* security officer for the State Department.

In the fall of 1953 McCarthy suddenly began an investigation of the Army Signal Corps at Fort Monmouth, New Jersey. When President Truman defended his Administration, McCarthy demanded equal television and radio time. Granted it, he turned instead on the current Republican Administration, implying it was lax in security measures and asserting that the main issue of the 1954 elections was the McCarthy-style Communists-in-government issue. But Secretary Dulles's counterattack, like the failure of the investigation to turn up anything striking at Fort Monmouth, did not seem appreciably to slow him down.

Something else was brewing, however, that would do more. It had begun some time earlier, according to Richard Rovere, when G. David Schine received a draft notice in July of 1953. Special Counsel Roy Cohn "liked Schine enormously," Rovere wrote, and "began fretting himself about Schine's Army life and giving more and more time to it ..."[34] Unavailing efforts had been made to secure a place for Schine as special assistant to the Secretary of the Army or within the C.I.A. (McCarthy himself actually hoped that Schine would not be reassigned to his Committee.) McCarthy had placed considerable reliance on Cohn in working up material to be investigated. But here his aide led him into more treacherous waters than anyone had foreseen. "It was Cohn's rage," continued Rovere, "that led to the affairs of Major Peress and General Zwicker and the Fort Monmouth investigation and the Army-McCarthy hearings in which the whole series of messes was disclosed. It was Cohn's loyalty to Schine and McCarthy's to Cohn that led to decline and eventual fall."[35]

In January of 1954 McCarthy charged that Major Irving Peress had not only been inducted in the Army despite Communist affiliations but had even been promoted. He went on to allege "coddling" of Communists and to vilify combat veteran, Brigadier General Ralph Zwicker,

[34] Rovere, *Senator Joe McCarthy,* p. 206.
[35] *Ibid.,* pp. 206–207 and p. 211.

commandant of Camp Kilmer, where Peress was stationed.[36] Things came to a head when the Army charged that the Senator and members of his Committee had employed improper methods to secure favored treatment for Schine. McCarthy countercharged that the Army had been using Schine as a kind of captive to force him to abandon his investigations. The Fort Monmouth hearings were suspended, and the Chairman stepped down temporarily while Senator Karl Mundt, of South Dakota, took the gavel as the Subcommittee investigated its own chairman.

The Army-McCarthy hearings ran for thirty-five days, occupying 187 television hours before an audience that at times exceeded 20,000,000.[37] Photographs in the press and Herbert Block's caricatures in the Washington *Post* of a scowling, unshaven McCarthy had already made his countenance one of the best known in the Senate. He had been described as "a big barrel-chested man with a large head, huge hands, and short, restless, muscular arms; a man who is so aware of his stock resemblance to Pat O'Brien that he keeps the movie star's autograph picture on his office wall."[38] Television made the image larger and firmer, but it was that of the B-movie gangster Wechsler had described. The effect was devastating. It became clear, wrote Fiedler, "that no one could join McCarthy's ranks or even combat him on issues of his own choosing without being degraded. The dignity of the nation and the government seemed at stake."[39] And the camera also brought McCarthy's staff into the living room: "Roy Cohn . . . obviously tremendously attached to Schine, obviously tremendously attached to Roy Cohn; Cohn and Schine, endlessly Cohn and Schine."[40]

The reports which the Subcommittee finally issued were no more conclusive than those of the Tydings Committee four years before. The majority and minority divided along party lines. But there were significant practical effects. The Fort Monmouth hearings were not resumed, Roy Cohn departed from the Committee, and Senator McCarthy's popularity—as measured by the polls and sensed in the press—had begun to slip badly. Under the glaring lights and the great television camera eyes, McCarthy had displayed more than his self-interest and fundamentally anarchistic tactics. He had also revealed some of their effects as embodied

[36] See Rorty and Decter, *McCarthy and the Communists,* pp. 48–50.
[37] Rovere, *Senator Joe McCarthy,* p. 207.
[38] Anderson and May, *McCarthy,* p. 4.
[39] Fiedler, *End to Innocence,* p. 86.
[40] Goldman, *The Crucial Decade,* pp. 271–272.

in the "Loyal American Underground" from which he received pilfered classified material from a number of Federal agencies. He had also demonstrated his unwillingness—in argumentation and testimony as well as decorum—to abide by anyone's rules but his own. Army Counsel Joseph Welch carried out his duties with skill and intelligence. But he had been assisted by his chief adversary: "the fact that he was a seditionist was made manifest to the entire country, so that only those tolerant of sedition (a very considerable number of Americans) could remain tolerant toward him."[41]

In July Senator Ralph Flanders of Vermont had introduced a resolution of censure on McCarthy for his contempt not only of the Senate, but of truth and "people" as well. When the Senate finally voted 67–22 to "Condemn" him on December 2, 1954, the Zwicker count had been dropped and for it had been substituted the contempt and obloquy which he had visited on the Subcommittee on Privileges and Elections. The offenses to truth and to people had been disposed of, but those to the Senate, its apparatus, and its members remained. It seemed to Leslie Fiedler "a little like the case of the gangster whose kidnapings, assaults, and murders cannot for one reason or another be proved against him, and who is finally jailed for income-tax evasion."[42]

Even McCarthy's outspoken opposition to the President could not regain much of the space he had once commanded in the press. There were financial troubles and ill health. Then, after acute hepatitis, he resumed the heavy drinking he had briefly given up. He died on May 2, 1957, as one member of the self-styled "goon squad" of reporters once assigned to him put it, "just in time for the seven o'clock news . . ."[43]

---

[41] Rovere, *Senator Joe McCarthy*, pp. 213 and 217–218. Peter Viereck observed that "the reason why emotional McCarthyism, more by instinct than design, simply *must* be against traditionalists, conservatives and government-by-law is explained by its unadmitted but basic revolutionary nature. It is a radical movement trying to overthrow an old ruling class and replace it from below by a new ruling class" ("The Revolt Against the Elite," in Bell [ed.], *The New American Right,* p. 111).

[42] Fiedler, *End to Innocence,* p. 86.

[43] Rovere, *Senator Joe McCarthy,* p. 47. Weisberger writes that

He knew how to . . . [make] his accusations at an hour which would make it impossible for the denials of his victims to reach the same edition as the charges, and he had an instinct for spreading his "revelations" over several days so as to . . . [leave] an impression of massive wrongdoing, when in fact there was virtually no evidence to support him. The newspapers . . . were caught in the toils of an "objectivity" which forbade them to evaluate their news sources and forced them into an irresponsible pattern of stressing "hot" items, which made Monday's charge a front-page matter and Wednesday's denial a back-page story. The blame

An assessment of McCarthy and McCarthyism involves a number of complex questions. What conditions made the time ripe for him and what talents helped him seize it? What were his inner convictions and intentions, and what were the final consequences of the actions they set in motion?

Besides inheriting many extremists and crackpots from organizations such as the Ku Klux Klan and the Christian Front, McCarthy found a ready response among those who felt their status threatened in a fast-changing world.[44] There had been the sacrifices and dislocations of World War II. Then came the sickening realization that the West was engaged in another war, cold though it might be. More than this, revelations of past treacheries were matched by descriptions of present catastrophes. The activities of Julius and Ethel Rosenberg and others in "a far-flung Communist espionage network in the United States"[45] were seen in the context of a world picture:

> the fall of China, the Berlin blockade, the Hiss case, the Communist coup in Czechoslovakia and the murder of Jan Masaryk, the Gouzenko case in Canada, the Fuchs case in England, the Judy Coplon case, the trial of the eleven top American Communist leaders, the leap to freedom of the Russian schoolteacher Kasenkina from the Soviet Consulate in New York, the revelations about Soviet espionage and slave-labor camps...[46]

And then came the military action in Korea. Frustrating and agonizing because of the bitter war it was, it also infuriated many because it engaged America in far-off conflict, subordinating American troops, in theory at least, to an international authority. For many, these nightmarish events demanded a straightforward and palatable, all-in-one explanation. The ability to provide just such an answer was one of McCarthy's skills.

Jacques Barzun observes that the theories of Darwin and Marx were attractive because they provided unified systems with complete explanations for a whole range of phenomena yet were based on principles at

---

for McCarthyism belongs not only to national neuroses but to the press . . . (Bernard A. Weisberger, *The American Newspaperman*, pp. 167–170).

See also Rovere, *Senator Joe McCarthy*, pp. 162–167 and Fiedler, *End to Innocence, passim,* who feel the press had a more limited choice than does Weisberger.

[44] See Daniel Bell on "status politics" in "Interpretations of American Politics," in Bell (ed.), *New American Right,* pp. 13–14.

[45] Link, *American Epoch,* p. 619.

[46] Rorty and Decter, *McCarthy and the Communists,* p. 149.

once simple and profound.[47] In a simpler all-in-one explanation, Hitler blamed Germany's defeat in World War I primarily on the Jews. So McCarthy also offered an omnibus solution: a conspiracy within the U.S. government to betray the country to world Communism had been carried out so effectively that China had been "lost," and that both the State Department and the Army had been so infiltrated that they were not only ineffective but dangerous.

But McCarthy had other things to offer, and assessments of his skills varied. One emphasized his "furious physical energy and capacity for work," another his use of a simple formula: "attack, attack, attack; never defense."[48] Some were self-contradictory; he was "a poolroom politician grandly seized with an urge to glory," and "the ultimate fool, a paragon of ignorance and innocence and irresponsibility," but at the same time "a fertile innovator, a first-rate organizer and galvanizer of mobs, a skilled manipulator of public opinion, and something like a genius at that essential American strategy: publicity."[49] One analysis listed ten "easily discernible . . . consistent patterns" in his methods including the multiple untruth, the abuse of documents, the slander amalgam, contempt for the law, and the unfounded charge of treason.[50] Also, "McCarthy was surely the champion liar. He lied with wild abandon; he lied without evident fear . . . he lied often, with very little pretense to be telling the truth."[51] Fiedler attempted to put the lying in context. It was tempting, he wrote, to compare it with the Big Lie of Hitler, "but it seems more closely related to the multiple little lies of our daily political forum . . . McCarthyism is, in part, the price we pay for conniving at or ignoring the alderman's deal with the contractor . . . McCarthy's distortion of the truth . . . is also the courtroom lawyer's unchallenged device for 'making a case' rather than establishing a fact."[52]

But underlying all the tactical skill and shrewdness, the instinct for the jugular, was something curiously different. "McCarthyism was," writes Rovere, "among other things, but perhaps foremost among them, a headlong flight from reality."[53] Wechsler describes the way each successive

---

[47] Jacques Barzun, *Darwin, Marx, Wagner: Critique of a Heritage*, pp. 321–327.

[48] See Anderson and May, *McCarthy*, p. 4, and Luthin, *American Demagogues*, p. 298.

[49] Rovere, *Senator Joe McCarthy*, pp. 148, 135, and 10–11.

[50] Rorty and Decter, *McCarthy and the Communists*, pp. 50–85.

[51] Rovere, *Senator Joe McCarthy*, p. 53.

[52] Fiedler, *End to Innocence*, p. 64.

[53] Rovere, *Senator Joe McCarthy*, p. 40.

exhibit of his anti-Communism was simply construed as additional evidence that he had led a double life. "Here indeed was a daring new concept in which the existence of evidence of innocence becomes the damning proof of guilt," he wrote.[54] These analyses are sometimes carried to the point that McCarthy is seen as embodying other antithetical qualities: paranoia and the most complete matter-of-fact cynicism about his whole campaign.

Richard Rovere asserts that he was a classic demagogue, that there "has never been the slightest reason to suppose that he took what he said seriously or that he believed any of the nonsense he spread." He concedes that it is "conceivable that in his later days he began to believe what he was saying and to imagine himself truly persecuted by his enemies," but at bottom he was "a prospector who drilled Communism and saw it come up a gusher. He liked his gusher, but he would have liked any other just as well."[55] What was true of the man, was, to Peter Viereck, true of the whole movement: "McCarthyism tends to be more a racket than a conspiracy, more a cruel publicity hoax (played on Fort Monmouth, the Voice of America, the State Department) than a serious 'fascist' or war party."[56] Unsurprisingly, this too is Wechsler's view: "McCarthy is a poker player, not a zealot, a cold-blooded operator in a big game. There were a few off-the-record asides when he almost seemed to be saying: 'Look, don't get excited, old man, we've all got our rackets'."[57]

It is not easy to gauge the permanent effect of Senator McCarthy and McCarthyism upon the United States. During the height of his career, he wielded great power in affairs of the State Department, the Army, and the nation as a whole. Almost singlehandedly, he succeeded in creating a climate of fear, suspicion, and distrust in large areas of national life. Abroad, the efforts of Cohn and Schine gave more aid and comfort to the generators of anti-Americanism than any other single series of events since the end of the war. Assessing the potential of the radical right, Richard Hofstadter wrote, "it is at least conceivable that a highly organized, vocal, active and well-financed minority could create a poli-

---

[54] Wechsler, *Age of Suspicion*, p. 272. This technique is carried to its logical conclusion in Robert Welch's "principle of reversal"—in the area of Communism and anti-Communism, everything is the reverse of what it seems. See Sherwin, *Extremists*, pp. 44 and 74.

[55] Rovere, *Senator Joe McCarthy*, pp. 46, 58, and 72.

[56] Peter Viereck, "The Revolt Against the Elite," p. 111, in Bell (ed.), *New American Right*.

[57] Wechsler, *Age of Suspicion*, pp. 283–284.

tical climate in which the rational pursuit of our well-being and safety would become impossible."[58] Seymour Lipset commented that McCarthy helped in the emergence and solidification of the radical right chiefly through providing symbols under which its many potential adherents could unite.[59]

Opinions vary about McCarthy's precise relationship to other elements of the Far Right. To one he was the rallying point of the "extreme anti-communists."[60] To another he wasn't even a conservative.[61] A further view saw him as both the inheritor and superior of Huey Long and Father Charles E. Coughlin, for "neither of them had anything like McCarthy's influence on American life and institutions."[62] A unique eulogistic comment had emanated from the Shrine of the Little Flower upon the Senator's demise. It was, said the Reverend Charles E. Coughlin, "the most regrettable thing in modern history."[63] Coughlin's role in modern American politics has interested a number of commentators. Peter Viereck asks the question, "What figure represents the transition, the missing link, between the often noble, idealistic Populist-Progressives (like that truly noble idealist, LaFollette) and the degeneration of that movement into something so different, so bigoted as McCarthyism?" And the answer, in his hypothesis, is Father Coughlin.[64]

McCarthy's decline and fall—together with the departure of such figures as Senators Knowland, Jenner, Bricker, and Welker—did not presage the disappearance of the Far Right. This became abundantly clear in the five years following his death. It was estimated in 1960 that there were approximately a thousand active rightist organizations in the United States.[65] The spectrum was as varied as ever, extending from Senator Barry Goldwater—taxed with having an eighteenth-century mind—to Robert Welch, former candy manufacturer turned leader of the extremist John Birch Society. And there was also George Lincoln Rockwell, organizer and fuehrer of the New American Nazi Party.[66] Seymour Lipset noted a few years earlier that the decline in McCarthy's power had probably begun when he and the radical rightists began to battle the

[58] Richard Hofstadter, "The Pseudo-Conservative Revolt," p. 54 in Bell (ed.), *New American Right.*
[59] Lipset, in Bell (ed.), *New American Right,* p. 210. See also note 57, p. 231.
[60] Robert Welch as quoted by Sherwin, *Extremists,* p. 52.
[61] L. Brent Bozell, as quoted by Rovere, *Senator Joe McCarthy,* p. 241.
[62] Rovere, *Senator Joe McCarthy,* p. 20.
[63] As quoted by Luthin, *American Demagogues,* p. 270.
[64] Viereck, *New American Right,* p. 94.
[65] See Ellsworth and Harris, *American Right Wing,* p. 3.
[66] See Sherwin, *Extremists, passim.*

Republican moderates and powerful business groups. The Ku Klux Klan had been badly mauled earlier when it roused the traditional power groups to action. "Today as in 1923–24," Lipset wrote, "the moderate conservative upper-class community has finally been aroused to the threat to its position and values represented by the radical right."[67] If, as Lipset asserts, the radical right is in a decline, McCarthyism will have been the greatest convulsion of the Far Right since the Red Scare of World War I. And Joseph R. McCarthy seems certain to stand forth as its most dramatic and powerful single figure in this century, if not in American history.

General Configurations

The voice of the militant right had been heard early in the twentieth-century from among those usually arrayed against the Young Knight. Conservative politicians, as well as the Interests and the Lobby, feared and detested him. He represented a threat not only to their influence and lucrative enterprises, but to the very society which made them possible. And when the Young Knight happened to be a champion such as David Graham Phillips's young men were, these apprehensions were justified. The case was not like that of seasoned politicians hotly contesting each campaign yet feeling for each other occasional admiration and even, at times, something near affection. Here the antagonist was an enemy to be destroyed, and the means were likely to reflect the intensity of feeling.

Conservatism and reaction were of course to be seen in most novels dealing with the Southern Politician and American Fascism. As the years of the century wore on, however, the views of the extreme right took still another fictional manifestation. They appeared in a special political climate and a characteristic set of techniques. The climate was one of unreason, fear, and persecution. The fear was twofold: that of the persecutors who dreaded the destruction of the old order for a radical new one, and that of some of the persecuted (although most were represented as heroic)—intimidated, hounded, and sometimes deprived of constitutional rights. As before, the forces of the right were made up of conservative politicians, the wealthy, the financiers, the business men, and those under their control. These included lobbyists and members of law-enforcement agencies.

Three of the eleven novels in this chapter came in the 1940's. In them

[67] Lipset, *New American Right,* pp. 216–217.

the air of Washington is heavy with apprehension and suspicion. The days of the New Deal are over. The atmosphere of participation in a great experiment has been replaced by that of survival in a witch hunt. Disillusionment with the aftermath of World War II in Europe and shock at the "loss of China" (plus chagrin later at reverses in Korea) have combined to wound the national ego. And one usually sees the easier of two possible responses: search for a scapegoat rather than realistic appraisal of deficiencies in American foreign policy which were in part responsible for the reverses (apart from the massive geopolitical changes). This milieu is one in which emotions are so strong that, for many, proof may take the form of guilt by association. In this weather most men ride out the storm. They speak and act circumspectly. But many are overwhelmed. Some are Quixotes who speak out at the wrong time. Others become sacrificial victims, like passengers dropped from the sledge to delay the pursuing wolves.[68] The strategy of the Administration is to cut its losses, while that of the opposition is to attack. But the motives behind the attack involve both party concerns and personal concerns. Congress seems in a mood to seek sacrificial victims. But the persecution (as distinct from prosecution for espionage or other traitorous activities little treated in these novels) also satisfies the less rationalizable motives of personal ambition and even sadism.

Between 1954 and 1960 the views and actions of segments of the extreme right were presented in sharpest focus in the half dozen novels of McCarthyism. Some are *romans à clef* in which one easily identifies not only the Senator but also members of his Committee. One recognizes Messrs. Cohn and Schine as well as repentant defectors from Communism. There are such other facets of that era as the whirlwind, evidence-gathering trips through American installations in Europe and the censure motion introduced in the Senate. Some of the plots closely follow only Senator McCarthy's career and phenomena associated with it. One deals primarily with an organization's techniques for discrediting public figures. But in all these novels there is the permeating aura of suspicion—in its extreme forms, hysteria and persecution—that marked the periodic

---

[68] Irwin Shaw's *The Troubled Air* (1951) related the effect of these political conditions upon the radio broadcasting industry in New York City. A theatrical agent addressing a meeting of workers in the entertainment field advises them, "Resign, Dis-affiliate, Quit, Entertain" (p. 290). This powerful and convincing novel reveals equally the excesses of the right and the left, *e.g.*: the blacklist which makes it impossible for its victims to find work; the conspiracy by which a Communist cell implicates the protagonist because he will most conveniently serve as a vehicle for their propaganda and counterattack.

upsurges of the forces of the Far Right in the years of World War I, and periods in the 1920's, the 1930's, and the decade following World War II.

Anarchy and Repression

The time lag between the end of the Sacco-Vanzetti case and the publication of *Boston* was even shorter than that between the Teapot Dome scandal and *Oil!* Upton Sinclair published *Boston* in 1928, a year after the execution of Bartolomeo Vanzetti and Nicola Sacco. Although *Boston* did not present as many politicians and as much party politics as did *Oil!*, nearly all of its principal characters acted from motives that were profoundly political as well as economic.

The execution of the two Italians had been preceded by a series of appeals from their conviction in 1921 for a holdup-murder allegedly committed in 1920. The long–drawn-out defense and the execution had engaged the sympathies of members of the intellectual classes as few other events of the century had done. It had both political and literary sequels. In a frequently quoted passage, Malcolm Cowley wrote of this swing to the left among the intelligentsia: "whatever else it might be, it was also a sequel to the Sacco-Vanzetti case, a return to united political action."[69] John Dos Passos, one of the most deeply engaged writers in this cause, commemorated the martyrs in *The Big Money* (1936). Plays and poems also followed. But the best literary uses of these events, as Walter Rideout notes, were made by Dos Passos and Upton Sinclair, where "the dignity of the event is matched by the author's passion and understanding."[70]

Sinclair had decided to write his novel the night the two men died. For it he carried out exhaustive research in many sources, not the least of which was the 3,900 pages of testimony taken in the Dedham trial of Sacco and Vanzetti. The published novel spanned a dozen years in its recreation of the circumstances preceding the trial, the trial itself, and its aftermath. "There is one simple rule for guidance in reading the novel," he wrote in his preface; "the characters who are real persons bear real names, while those who bear fictitious names are fictitious charac-

---

[69] Malcolm Cowley, "Echoes of a Crime," *New Republic*, LXXIV (August 28, 1935), 79, quoted in Walter B. Rideout, *The Radical Novel in the United States 1900–1954: Some Interrelations of Literature and Society*, p. 134 and Daniel Aaron, *Writers on the Left: Episodes in American Literary Communism*, p. 173.

[70] Rideout, *Radical Novel*, p. 133. For discussions of the engagement of writers in the Sacco-Vanzetti case, see Rideout, pp. 131–134; Aaron, *Writers on the Left*, pp. 168–173 and 418–419; and G. Louis Joughin and Edmund M. Morgan, *The Legacy of Sacco and Vanzetti*, pp. 233–234.

ters."[71] Sinclair had visited Bartolomeo Vanzetti in prison. He found him "one of the wisest and kindest persons I ever knew, and I thought him as incapable of murder as I was." Sinclair renamed one real person. She was, he recalled more than thirty years later,

an elderly lady, socially prominent in Boston; Mrs. Burton was her name, and she enjoyed telling me odd stories about the tight little group of self-determined aristocrats who ruled the social life of the proud old city. Governor Alvan T. Fuller and President A. Lawrence Lowell of Harvard belonged to that group—and Bartolomeo Vanzetti didn't. Mrs. Burton had come to California, seeking a new life, and I delighted her by saying that she would be my heroine—"the runaway grandmother," I would call her.[72]

Sinclair declared that he had not "written a brief for the Sacco-Vanzetti Defense." Instead, he asserted, "I have tried to be a historian"(vi). But no matter what his intentions, the book was a spirited defense of the two men and a passionate attack on the forces arrayed against them. Once again, as in *Oil!*, the malefactors act to perpetuate a system inimical to the welfare of the great majority of the American people. This book's two principal and complementary characteristics quickly emerge as an attack upon the Interests in a capitalistic system and a defense of radicalism. An important component of the political milieu in which this dialectic is set is the strong antiradical sentiment of the war years, intensified, as Sinclair describes it, by war hysteria against Bolshevism. In a passage only a little more extreme than similar ones in novels of McCarthyism in the 1950's, Sinclair describes the excesses of the Far Right: "City policemen, federal secret agents, and an army of spies and informers in the pay of wealthy patriots, would break into offices and homes at any hour of the day or night, and spirit people away and hold them for as long as they saw fit; in short they would commit all the crimes they were trying to prevent, and destroy beyond repair the Constitution they professed to worship" (149). Later, describing protests against war with the Bolsheviks and the resulting countermeasures, he states simply, "It was the White Terror" (176).

Sinclair's principal character is Cornelia Thornwell, the "runaway grandmother" whose conversion to radicalism constitutes the principal fictional portion of the novel. A gentle but courageous woman, she has been released from a loveless marriage by the death of her husband, a mill owner and former governor of Massachusetts. Sinclair immediately

---

[71] Upton Sinclair, *Boston,* p. v.
[72] Upton Sinclair, *The Autobiography of Upton Sinclair,* pp. 240–242.

introduces a theme upon which he will play throughout when he relates the fate of the two anarchists to Governor Thornwell's loss of money through the New York financiers' looting of a New England railroad. Sinclair had been quite explicit about it in his preface. "Paralleling the Sacco-Vanzetti case throughout the book," he wrote, "is a story of business and high finance which will be recognized as a famous law case recently carried to the United States Supreme Court" (v). The charge of interference in New England affairs by New York bankers had been made twenty years before in *Mr. Crewe's Career*, but Sinclair goes on to describe depredations that dwarf those in Churchill's novels. For a case history he uses the experience of Jerry Walker, who controls the New England felt industry. He is regarded as an unreliable parvenu, however, by the oldline bankers and manufacturers who systematically pirate his companies, using the legal process to destroy him as it destroys Sacco and Vanzetti. The reader sees that Walker's recourse to law is just as futile as that of the two Italians, for he does not belong to the class which controls it. Growing impatient with literary devices, Sinclair writes,

To drop metaphors, it was a fact that a small group of bankers had to decide, during the Panic, which industries of the community were to be saved and which were to go to the wall. And needless to say, in a place like Boston, it was not a question of vulgar material efficiency, it was a question of social status. Who was who, and who was married to whom, and what was the relative blueness of this blood and that? (270)

Sinclair puts the kernel of his interpretation of the Sacco-Vanzetti case just as succinctly:

The cruelty of the dilemma lay here, that what was supposed to be justice was really class-greed. Bart and Nick were not going to be tried because they had held up a payroll; they were going to be tried because they were dangerous leaders of social revolt. That would be the real motive power behind the prosecutor, judge and jury; that would be the thought in the minds of every one of them, at every stage of the trial. (365)

The accused are not thieves, much less murderers; they are anarchists. Nor are they violent men; Vanzetti is a vegetarian out of reluctance to contribute to the killing of living things. Christlike in gentleness, he is thirty-three at the time of his arrest. He is, however, a dedicated anarchist who feels toward socialists as Victor Dorn does toward David Hull in *The Conflict:* anything aimed at ameliorating conditions is bad, for the system should not be patched up but swept away.

The two men are tried before Judge Webster Thayer, who has a pathological hatred and fear of radicals. It is a proceeding in which the chief defense lawyer, Lee Swenson, declares that he must resort to bribery, false swearing, and subornation of perjury in order to counter the tactics of the prosecution. Swenson has gained experience in this kind of "miniature war" (330) through the Ettore-Giovanni case seven years before, which he calls "as perfect a frame-up as ever came under my eyes . . . the whole case prepared and the indictments drawn up by the lawyers of great corporations. The victims were Italians, I.W.W. leaders, efficient and dangerous—the more so because one of them was a fine poet" (295). Sinclair describes in detail a series of fruitless appeals from the conviction of Sacco and Vanzetti. He quotes at length from an article by Felix Frankfurter charging Judge Thayer with misconduct. Committees of prominent citizens are appointed to pass on the fairness of the trial. Of one which confirms it Sinclair writes,

There they stood, the three intellectual and spiritual guides of Boston: the Cardinal of the Holy Roman Catholic Church, the Bishop of the Protestant Episcopal Church, and the President of Harvard University. When a stranger inquired concerning them, he was struck by a curious fact: the first statement about any one of the three would be that he was an efficient administrator of enormous properties . . . if you were to go to any of the three administrators, and make a remark suggesting that he should act upon the creed he taught, he would begin to watch you to see whether you were the dangerous kind. (677) [73]

Sinclair devotes long passages to the plight of exploited workers, the activities of strikebreaking police, the role of the capitalist press, and the career of Calvin Coolidge. He writes of Coolidge's "political and financial boss . . . a great lord of cotton-mills in New England, soon to be made a United States senator" (498), who leads the fight against an amendment prohibiting child labor. It was he, says Sinclair, "who led this campaign, and rallied the business men and bankers, the criminals, the hierarchy of the Catholic Church" (498). The last portion of the book returns to the Sacco-Vanzetti case. Sinclair concludes it with a description of world-wide riots following the executions, and of the 200,-

---

[73] John Dos Passos agreed with Sinclair about the locus of power, but he was a shade less pessimistic, for he granted at least the possibility of improvement when he wrote to President A. L. Lowell of Harvard: "It is upon men of your class and position that will rest the inevitable decision as to whether the coming struggle for the reorganization of society shall be bloodless and fertile or inconceivably bloody and destructive" (John Dos Passos, in *The Nation,* CXXV, p. 7).

000 people who watch the funeral cortege of 50,000 despite police brutality intended to disperse it.

Sinclair's fictional characters are only a secondary concern to him, and their insubstantial quality shows it. He duly relates their histories, writing, as it were, with his left hand. Early in the novel, Mrs. Thornwell has gone to live with her granddaughter Betty, a vigorous suffragette like herself. Together they gradually sever their connections with the rest of the family. By the time they travel to Russia for the First Congress of the Third Internationale, they have left their class as Bunny Ross did his in *Oil!* Like him, Betty even helps to found a labor college. But, like the fictional characters in *Oil!*, Betty and the others in *Boston* are pale beside the historical ones. This novel, for all its length and ponderous recounting of events and evidence, is the more effective of the two. Partly through the length and the massive, often excessive, use of detail, Sinclair builds up convincing and moving portraits of Sacco and Vanzetti. The reader comes to know them as living men, capable of being prosaic as well as heroic, rather than remote tableaulike figures in the greatest *cause célèbre* of American jurisprudence in the twentieth century. The novel gives a convincing sense of the long struggle of the trial, the cruel ordeal of the appeals, and the passionate dignity of the deaths. And serving for background is the panoramic view of the times and currents which, the author argues, made the end of these events inevitably tragic once their course was begun. For all its shortcomings, this passionate, deeply-felt novel shows why, according to the well-known radical writer Michael Gold, no one else in the early 1920's "had such influence with young thinkers as Sinclair; no one combined the artist and the revolutionary so admirably."[74]

The 1940's and the Gathering Storm

Three novels published within a three-year period gave a sense of the gathering anew of the forces of reaction a quarter of a century after the Sacco-Vanzetti trial. They showed the ebbing of the ideals which mark the New Deal in these novels. They depicted the cutbacks in authority and appropriations, and they portrayed the men who were forced out of government. The last of the three introduced the McCarthy-figure, adding the further elements necessary for the half-dozen full-fledged novels of McCarthyism to appear in the following decade.

Benjamin Appel's *But Not Yet Slain* (1947) and Merle Miller's *The*

[74] Aaron, *Writers on the Left*, p. 98.

Sure Thing (1949) both had young protagonists who had come to Washington in the 1930's but were to leave it in the 1940's. Both worked under liberal chiefs progressively less powerful as the climate of the Roosevelt administrations faded further into the past. In Miller's book, a departmental assistant secretary remarks, "The dream seems to have died. With the Boss, I suppose."[75] The truest notes in Appel's book are struck in similar chords evoked by the figure of Roosevelt and the idea of a new society conceived in a spirit of liberalism. His protagonist, like Miller's, is vulnerable through causes he has espoused in the 1930's. But unlike Miller's Bradley Douglas, Appel's Matthew Wells is a basically weak man. Throughout most of the period spanned by the novel he cannot bring himself to resign. Instead, he tailors the speeches he writes to the strictures of a reactionary superior placed in the chain of command between him and the director of the agency. His abortive suicide attempt is unconvincingly turned into a liberation reminiscent of the last lines of Lawrence's *Sons and Lovers,* and there is slim justification for the import of the novel's title. Appel takes it from a fragment of a variant version of the ballad, "Johnnie Armstrong":

> A little I'm hurt but not yet slain,
> I'll but lie down and bleed awhile,
> And then I'll rise and fight again.

Appel ambitiously uses flashbacks, interior monologue, and a conflict apparently meant to signify a kind of split personality. But the novel's strongest point is its creation of the atmosphere of tension and fear in the federal agency. It is an atmosphere intensified by the deputy director whose conversation is heavy with references to "Pinks" and "Reds," by the intimidating congressmen, and by the citizens' committees protesting activities such as governmental planning.

Early in *The Sure Thing* economist Bradley Douglas's State Department superior tells him, "This is not a happy time . . . It never is after the war's end after the illusions are gone. A kind of madness sets in . . . It's happening now, and it probably won't last . . . But meantime, I fear, some exceedingly unpretty things may occur" (20). The fulfillment of this fear constitutes most of the action of the novel. F.B.I. agents shadow Douglas and interrogate him and his wife. They also secure evidence on which he is finally dismissed from the Department. But Douglas's case is more complicated than that of Wells. Though now a dedicated anti-Communist civil servant, he has actually been a member of the Com-

---

[75] Merle Miller, *The Sure Thing,* p. 265.

munist Party for a year prior to the Russo-German Pact of August, 1939.
More than this, he has concealed this fact in joining the Department.
The reader's sympathies still center upon Douglas, however, as his career is destroyed and with it the likelihood, in the existing climate, of
decently supporting himself and his family.

One of this novel's virtues is the fact that solidly though it presents
the plight of the protagonist, it also depicts its effects upon a varied group.
The friends range from Douglas's boss, a father-figure who loves him,
to a lawyer who wants to help but is constantly reminded of his own
moral failure in New Deal days. There is also the colleague expelled
earlier and the well-intentioned columnist. When she writes a friendly,
retrospective column, the newspaper syndicate manager warns her,
"You'd be tarred with the same brush, only twice as bad. These days a
little thing like this could ruin you, Millicent. Could ruin anybody"
(324). Douglas's enemies include the F.B.I. agents who telephone him
at 7:30 A.M. and hang up without speaking: "preparation, for our visit.
Psychological, you might say" (61). The junior investigator laughs tri-
umphantly after Douglas finally signs their prepared statement. "Good
luck," he calls out after him. "You'll need it" (263). His senior colleague
(whose compulsive hand-washing suggests Jaggers in Dickens's *Great
Expectations*), reflects that his junior is "the perfect man for his job . . .
he hates them all, and, oddly, he hates me too" (239). He also realizes
that "the time would come when he would no longer be able to continue
with his job" (238).[76] Douglas is also an object of hate and envy for the
chief security officer of his department. He is sure that Douglas is subversive no matter what his present affiliations or lack of them. He wishes
only "that Douglas were a little better known; Congress was demanding
action, and Congress would get action, and the more spectacular it was,
the more pleased Congress would be. Congress had an election coming
up" (99). Douglas's experience with congressmen is far from happy. In
1941 he had called one of them a member of the "unholy alliance of isolationists" (137). When the investigation is completed, the same congressman informs the press that Douglas leads the "Russian Wing" of
the State Department (128).

Miller follows the widening ripples even further as a senior colleague
tongue-lashes the informant:

---

[76] The reader may recall here the relationship in Arthur Koestler's *Darkness
at Noon* between N. S. Rubashov's two interrogators: Ivanov, his classmate and
war comrade, and Gletkin, the cold, mechanical new Soviet man who triumphant-
ly succeeds him and breaks Rubashov.

We've been working on this Red business for more than a year, and we weren't ready to break it yet. You come up with the name of one piddling $8,500-a-year clerk. They're all going to run for cover . . . and the Administration's going to take the ball right out from under us . . . Do you realize, Jensen, that your goddam foolishness might cost us next year's election?" (221–222)

Douglas's plight is made clearer in the reply of the assistant secretary to the former New Deal lawyer when he pleads Douglas's case: "you can't fight history, Hal . . . We have to sacrifice the future of one man to save the future of thousands . . . The pagans had the right idea. They sacrificed an occasional virgin to avert the anger of the gods. Douglas isn't exactly a political virgin, except for the purpose of the analogy. He must be sacrificed" (268).

For all the care and craft with which Miller reveals the many ramifications of the case of Bradley Douglas, he never lets the story of the man himself drift out of focus. He suffers both private and public tragedies. In one, a passionate love has brought about a heartbreaking divorce. In the other, he is one of the last of the young men "who had come in the thirties when there was a dream and who stayed on, dedicated to obscurity," but who now "were going away or being sent away, hounded away" (310). Leaving his office for the last time he realizes, "He had plenty of time. He had all the time there was or ever would be" (341).

Miller's technique is sure. If the novel is rather heavily loaded with flashbacks it is also true that they are functional. They are not there merely to show authorial dexterity or to convey information with the maximum of doing. They provide the substance that make Douglas and his wives believable and sympathetic. They show how Brad Douglas, the liberal college boy who "loved *all* Jews and *all* Negroes, without exception" (207), became the young union economist who "had to change the world by tomorrow afternoon at three o'clock or he wasn't happy" (200). They trace the way he reached the conclusion that "American and British capital, the capital of all the world, was strengthening Adolf Hitler and Benito Mussolini for the inevitable war" (243), and how, reviewing the action to which that conviction led, he could reflect, "You check your intellect at the door . . . when you're in the Party" (258). They show him, like Irwin Shaw's Clement Archer in *The Troubled Air,* a man doubly victimized. Innocent yet suspicious-looking documents are filched from his desk to incriminate him. At the same time, his secretary, a dutiful Communist Party member, takes advantage of his trust to carry out espionage.

In this novel, the best in this chapter, Miller portrays attitudes as well as people and events. They vary from those of the defeated idealist to those of the police agent. Like *All the King's Men,* the story turns on moral problems. And like Warren's novel, it deals with a series of betrayals: the lawyer who forsook the Administration in pique and turned to rich clients, the envious ones who contribute to Douglas's downfall, Douglas himself in forsaking his first wife and in concealing from his superior his onetime Communist affiliation. Miller is so successful in enlisting the reader's sympathies for Douglas's that the reader only belatedly asks, "But *weren't* security checks necessary? Didn't the cases of Hiss and Fuchs, of the Greenspans and the Rosenbergs prove at least that?" And then one concludes that perhaps such a question is irrelevant, that what Miller is dealing with is the effect of excessive zeal—combined with human malice and an unpropitious time in American history—upon the innocent, or at least the substantially innocent. For this young man, self-purged of whatever in him may have been subversive, zealous in advocacy of humane and democratic values, is sacrificed to ambition, revenge and hypocrisy.

Merle Colby's *The Big Secret* (1949) was set sometime in advance of its date of publication. There was not enough emphasis on this element, however, to make the book a futurist novel. It follows a young mathematical physicist who bumblingly frustrates efforts to clamp down a rigid secrecy on scientific research. Colby delineates several kinds of politics: White House, Pentagon, and intradepartmental. He uses familiar types: the violently militaristic general, the empire-building bureaucrat, the right-wing extremist, the veteran lobbyist, and the prehensile utilities magnate. But Colby introduces one character new to American political fiction. He is Senator J. Skimmerhoff, of the Senate Temporary Committee on Subversive Associations and Disloyal Thoughts. SCAT has its own staff of investigators, one inept member being used for comedy. But Skimmerhoff's tactics are not comic. Distortion and misrepresentation are his staples, and he is expert at asking loaded questions to which Yes and No answers produce seemingly damaging admissions. And the Senator's concern with press coverage and press time indicate that his main interest is not so much national security as personal publicity. In an improbable ending, the young physicist unmasks the Senator as a tool of the utilities interests. He then returns to his college with a victory over the proposed executive order if not over "the system."

This ambitious and knowledgeable novel presents a wide range of characters against the background of a Washington which is bureaucratic, hard, and cynical. It includes opinion-molding experts, ghost writers, and versatile cab drivers. But for all its variety, neither its humor nor its satire is very effective, and often it seems not quite a seriously adult novel. For the purposes of this study, its greatest interest lies in the way in which it provides a transition between the novels in which the militant right asserts its power in investigations and dismissals and those in which the McCarthy-figure emerges as the central concern.

McCarthyism

Six novels using McCarthy-figures as major characters were published between 1954 and 1960. In two they provided the generating forces for the action. William L. Shirer's *Stranger Come Home* (1954) described the process by which Senator O'Brien forces a diplomat and a news commentator out of public life, whereas Ernest Frankel's *Tongue of Fire* (1960) gave a straight chronological treatment of the rise and fall of unscrupulous Congressman Kane O'Connor. Though the time-spans differ, both show the same characteristics at work: cynical opportunism combined with utter unconcern for justice, and sensitivity to opinion coupled with genius for publicity. A dozen of Shirer's major characters are clearly portraits from life. They include members of the Senate Committee, a former Communist now a professional informer, the controller of a yellow-press empire, and a syndicated columnist specializing in scandal. Whereas Shirer is preoccupied with O'Brien's victims, Frankel's attention never shifts for very long from O'Connor. Providing him with family, sweethearts, and friends, he charts his transition from war hero to national figure. But he too uses models from life in the former Communist turned informer and the television commentator whose documentary program helps start the tide turning against O'Connor.[77]

Shirer's book suffers from being clearly a *roman à clef* only a step away from the very thinly fictionalized journalism of Upton Sinclair's Lanny Budd novels. It also suffers from the defects of its style, a rather wooden account transmitted through the journal of the journalist-commentator, Raymond Whitehead. But for all this, the novel had immediacy and impact when it appeared. The 114-page segment dramatizing Whitehead's appearance before Senator O'Brien's Committee on Security and Americanism creates suspense and secures the reader's sympathy

---

[77] Goldman mentions Edward R. Murrow's treatment of McCarthy on "See It Now" in February, 1954 (*The Crucial Decade*, p. 270). Murrow receives more attention in the fictional than in the nonfictional treatment of McCarthy.

for Whitehead as he is badgered with accusation and innuendo. His words are misconstrued and the statement he is grudgingly allowed to make is interrupted by O'Brien as he conducts the hearing with a constant eye to press coverage and newspaper deadlines. The Committee finds against Whitehead, in effect branding him a Soviet agent, just as the State Department Loyalty Board finds against his closest friend. At the novel's close both the innocent victims are making new lives on their joint farm. But O'Brien goes on undeterred. The Korean War serves his ends as he contemplates carrying his investigations into other fields, one of which will probably involve a prominent American physicist. If there is anything in the novel beyond the depiction of some of the "exceedingly unpretty things" feared by Bradley Douglas's boss, it is apparently the conclusion that evil must be fought no matter what the cost. The principle is demonstrated by Whitehead's hazardous voluntary testimony before O'Brien's committee in the hope of helping clear his friend's name. It also appears that it is possible to survive such a course (although two of O'Brien's victims commit suicide) and to ride out the storm until, in the phrase of Douglas's father-figure, the madness subsides.

Early in *Tongue of Fire*, Kane O'Connor displays the technique which becomes his trademark. Finding an element of truth in a situation, he distorts it to serve his own ends. Once a congressman, he spreads himself, accepting $7,500 for writing a pamphlet for a manufacturer. Hypocritically battling the Navy, he alleges failure to safeguard the morals of Naval personnel abroad. He ingratiates himself with a "Lincolnesque" senior congressman who one day mentions a three-year-old report about screening out undesirable government employees in the war's-end shuffle of personnel. With this O'Connor finds his metier, proclaiming that, "these traitors in our midst are planning the actions of our State Department! They are handling the codes and war plans in the Department of Defense! . . . They stand before the test tubes in our top-secret laboratories!"[78] Building a fanatical staff, O'Connor attacks alleged subversion in the State Department. In the televised hearings of his special subcommittee of the Committee on Government Administration, his technique of using innuendo, old opinions, and former memberships becomes notorious. Engaging in character assassination on the floor of the House, he also goes into the Lincolnesque congressman's district to help defeat him for re-election. O'Connor's investigation of the National Experimental Center vies with the Korean War for headlines. His slaughter of

[78] Ernest Frankel, *Tongue of Fire,* p. 226.

the innocent and the reformed is impeded only by appointment of a special committee "to investigate O'Connor's activities and to report to the House if they find cause to expel him" (407). The television documentary increases his feelings of persecution, which lead to excesses causing his richly deserved but rather improbable death.

Obviously, *Tongue of Fire* is as much a *roman à clef* as *Stranger Come Home*. But while the latter is closer to history in its characters, the former is closer in events. Frankel's book, like Shirer's, offers a moral as well as fictionalized current history. It is the pronouncement, printed as the book's epigraph, of Shepherd Reade, the Lincolnesque congressman: "The lying tongue is like a fire that consumes everything around it, and then, in the end, must consume itself." Like Shirer's novel, this one has its distinct drawbacks. Its excessive length carries a cargo of detail which blunts the story rather than sharpening it. Much of the writing is awkward. And there are many highly erotic scenes which are not so much functional as decorative. The work as a whole is rather heavy and, in the end, unimpressive. A fatal difficulty here is that art has followed nature too closely; the work grew not organically but imitatively.

In two novels of 1959 the McCarthy-figure appeared without dominating the story. One, Allen Drury's *Advise and Consent*, dealt with the personal and partisan struggles involved in naming a Secretary of State.[79] The other, Richard Condon's *The Manchurian Candidate*, was in part a thriller involving Communist espionage. Drury's novel was dedicated to "The Senate of the United States," and it contained expository passages freighted with devotion to it. Four of its five books are told from the point of view of the four Senators most involved in the struggle over the confirmation of the appointment. The novel does not focus on McCarthyism, but it is instructive to note the pervasiveness of its aura and the use of the McCarthy-figure to move the plot along. A wily old Southern Senator opposes the nominee for an aspersion cast years before. Maneuvering the chairman of the Foreign Affairs Committee into setting up an examining subcommittee, he produces a witness who claims that he and the nominee were once members of a four-man Communist cell at the University of Chicago. When the President decides that he must apply pressure to the subcommittee chairman to report favorably on the nominee, he gives to Senator Fred Van Ackerman evidence of the chairman's wartime homosexual affair. The senator from Wyoming is a militant whose tenets, unlike those of McCarthy, include

[79] The treatment of this generating circumstance can be compared with that in Frederick Buechner's *The Return of Ansel Gibbs* in Chapter Nine.

appeasement of Russia. He is the extremists' darling, however, and his campaign of vilification against Anderson uses tactics associated with "O'Brienism" in Shirer's book and the methods of O'Connor in Frankel's. Like O'Connor, Van Ackerman is censured, but Anderson has committed suicide, and the nominee has been defeated.[80] Although the novel is set in future time after the Eisenhower administration, there is much of the *roman à clef* about it, as characters demonstrate attributes which suggest Franklin Roosevelt, Harry Truman, and Robert Taft, among others.[81] It is on verisimilitude, however, that the novel has been most roundly criticized. Douglass Cater writes,

> Why not accept as realistic that Presidents use their power callously and cruelly to destroy those who stand in their way, that Supreme Court Justices filch damaging documents; that high Cabinet officers lie under oath; that Senators play the hero by committing suicide . . .? The most obvious answer, it seems to me, is that these things do not happen . . . Creating hyperbolic plots merely serves to stretch the moral dilemma of politics all out of proportion. It results in caricature rather than convincing commentary.[82]

[80] The Washington *Post* reported on June 19, 1954, that the Special Subcommittee on Investigations of the Committee on Government Operations of the U.S. Senate had met in closed session the previous morning. Senator McCarthy had temporarily relinquished the chair and his committee membership as well because the meeting had been called by the Democratic senators to carry out "a housecleaning of the staff of the Subcommittee" (p. 4). A story in the *New York Times* on the same day but datelined Washington, June 18, reported that "Senator McCarthy denounced the Democratic plan of action, and countered with the declaration that he was investigating 'very serious charges' against a Democratic Senator unconnected with the committee." The story also included a report that McCarthy had contended in a television interview that his colleagues' real intent was to delay his investigation both of Communists in general and of the unidentified senator in particular. He added that he did not know at that time whether there was any merit in the charges against the senator or not. The *Post's* coverage of these charges quoted McCarthy as saying that the allegations had nothing to do with communism. On the next day, June 20, 1954, both newspapers reported in headlines the suicide of Senator Lester C. Hunt, Democrat of Wyoming, on the 19th. In the obituary, the *Times* reported that "Senator Karl E. Mundt of South Dakota said he wanted it understood that Mr. Hunt 'positively' was not the Senator referred to last night by Senator Joseph R. McCarthy as under investigation by the staff of the Permanent Subcommittee on Investigation" (p. 72).

[81] Compare the situation of Drury's new President with that of Harry S. Truman and his predecessor: "His shadow was always over your shoulder. You had been let in so little on really important affairs that you had to keep summoning Roosevelt intimates, Harry Hopkins, Admiral Leahy, or Jimmy Byrnes, merely to get the basic facts" (Goldman, *The Crucial Decade,* pp. 18–19).

[82] Douglass Cater, "Advice and Dissent about the Best Man," *New York Times Magazine,* May 22, 1960, p. 27.

One of the novel's principal aesthetic flaws is that it is too long by at least one third. The story—realistic or not—is often compelling, although it tends to lose momentum late in the book and is related in a style which is easy but prone to gaucherie. For the purposes of this study, it provides an instructive instance of the McCarthy-figure becoming assimilated into the genre. Used now as a secondary character, he is rather like the earlier historical personages made into fictional ones and thence into stock characters.

As with *Advise and Consent,* the McCarthy-figure in Richard Condon's *The Manchurian Candidate* (1959) was an ancillary one who nonetheless functioned as a mainspring of the novel's wild plot. The principal character was a bogus hero, a Congressional Medal of Honor winner fabricated in a complex operation by the Communist Chinese. Captured in Korea, Raymond Shaw and his patrol are flown to China for four days' intensive brainwashing. Surreptitiously returned, the patrol believes in Shaw's heroism. He is now a conditioned killer with access to high places through the Congressional Medal to come. The insecurities which made him psychologically vulnerable are largely due to his attractive and vicious mother, who had divorced his father to marry the governor of a Northern state with a large Scandinavian population. John Iselin is not particularly intelligent, and she has directed his senatorial career with great skill. Between 1951 and 1960 Iselin is chairman of the Committee on Federal Operations and chairman of its Permanent Subcommittee on Investigations. One analyst writes, "Iselinism has developed a process for compounding a lie, then squaring it . . . He has bellowed out so many accusations about so many different people . . . that no one can keep the records of these horrendous charges straight."[83] By 1957 he has become an international figure. Condon assesses his strong points:

His very looks: that meaty nose, the nearly total absence of forehead, the perpetual unshaveness, the piggish eyes, red from being dipped in bourbon, the sickeningly monotonous voice, whining and grating,—all of it together made Johnny one of the greatest demagogues in American history, even if, as Ray-

---

[83] Richard Condon, *The Manchurian Candidate,* p. 154. Rovere quotes Elmer Davis as writing, "I have a stack of McCarthy's speeches two feet thick on my office shelf; but when he says something that stirs a vague recollection that he once said something very different, I seldom have time to run through his speeches. I can't afford to hire a full-time specialist to keep up with what McCarthy has said" (Rovere, *Senator Joe McCarthy,* p. 170).

mond's mother often said to friends, he was essentially a lighthearted and un-serious one. Nonetheless, her Johnny had become the only American in the country's history of political villains, studding folk song and story, to inspire concomitant fear and hatred in foreigners, resident in their native countries. He blew his nose in the Constitution, he thumbed his nose at the party system or any other version of governmental chain of command. He personally charted the zigs and zags of American foreign policy at a time when the American policy was a monstrously heavy weight upon world history. To the people of Iceland, Peru, France, and Pitcairn Island the label of Iselinism stood for anything and everything that was dirty, backward, ignorant, repressive, offen-sive, anti-progressive, or rotten ... (154)

Raymond's mother directs tactics as well as strategy. She advises her husband on leaving committee hearings to go to the bathroom, to shout, "Point of Order," declare that he will not dignify the proceedings with his presence, and then stalk out of the room.[84] She also makes an investi-gative trip through Europe, ostensibly for her husband, antagonizing vir-tually everyone she meets. Shaw's assignments include murder, and his "operator" is finally revealed as his mother. Working to run the United States through Iselin, she has asked for a perfect assassin only to find that the Communists have made him out of her son to bind her closer to them. Then, after obtaining the Vice Presidential nomination for Iselin, she plots an assassination of the Presidential nominee so as to sweep Ise-lin into his place and into the Presidency. The scheme is barely foiled in the bloody ending.

This fast-paced, broadly-written novel is ingenious and fantastic. Con-don offers varied violence and sex: death by strangling and death by shooting; light-hearted sex, romantic sex, and perverted sex (Shaw's mother is a drug addict who recaptures the ectasy of paternal incest through filial incest). Obviously, there is little of the concern here that presumably contributed to the genesis of *Stranger Come Home* or *Tongue of Fire*. One has the feeling that Iselin, like the Korean War and brainwashing, appealed to Condon as part of what some reviewers are prone to call "a rattling good yarn." This is another novel which must be treated carefully in assessing the image of modern American politics in fiction. But Condon's phrase placing Iselin in the gallery of "the coun-try's history of political villains" (154) is significant. In this novel the McCarthy-figure has become a stock character, like the Lincoln-figure or the Long-figure. And though he is still a stench in the nostrils, he has

[84] See Rovere, *Senator Joe McCarthy,* p. 58.

become the butt of a kind of contemptuous humor. It is as though the voice had finally announced that the emperor was, in fact, naked, and the spectators could now substitute laughter for hate and fear.

McCarthyism in Other Concerns

The last two novels in the group appeared in 1960, and as if to emphasize the waning literary appeal of McCarthyism, the authors used it no more centrally than had Drury and Condon. In *Men of Career* John Lorraine(the pen name of an American Foreign Service officer) used the atmosphere of McCarthyism—as generated by Congressional "investigators"—as a contributory theme in a neatly constructed novel of men and ideas in the American Embassy in occupied Austria. William R. Reardon's *The Big Smear* centered on character-assassination as practiced on a liberal senator by a firm serving those familiar clients, the Interests.

Lorraine's protagonist is intelligent, compassionate Policy Liaison Officer Crane Marek of the American Embassy in Vienna. The reader comes to know him through chapters written from his point of view, that of his chief, and that of a Foreign Service inspector. The inspector's investigation of the suicide of a disturbed man who has opposed Marek and his chief in a policy dispute involves Marek's professional life and personal life as well. The complementary theme is the impact upon these Foreign Service officers of another series of events. An order directs all United States Information Service Libraries to check all magazines and other media for Anti-American material. The volume of material makes it impossible to comply with the directive, the work of "the Senator." A list of banned authors is followed by the arrival of "the twin investigators" whom the press attaché calls "the Gold Dust Twins."[85] Rude and contemptuous, they sweep into the embassy with notes from informers, hoping to induce members of this embassy to inform on still others. They check the library for sensational material to be used later, out of context, or to prove guilt by association. The press attaché resigns to fight abuses he cannot combat as a Foreign Service officer: "There's the enemy outside, and that's the Soviet one we're fighting out here; and there's the enemy inside, and that's our friend the legislator and all he stands for," he says. It is a "colossal historic irony, because it's the State Department that made Americans conscious of the enemy outside; and

[85] John Lorraine, *Men of Career,* pp. 93–94.

now the fear has boomeranged and it's the State Department that's taking a beating from the enemy inside" (125).[86] Marek submits his resignation too. In this climate symbolized by sinister-appearing security officers, he feels vulnerable because of his Slavic origins and past history (he has published a volume of poetry). He is finally persuaded, however, to accept reassignment instead.

This novel is persuasively written. Its journal-style chapters are much more adroit than those in *Stranger Come Home,* and although the mysterious element of the suicide is stretched rather thin, it is convincingly related. Marek's romantic triangle constitutes a relationship which could stand further exploration, but he himself is a complete and convincing character, as is the inspector. The book as a whole just misses the extra insight and sureness which would make it a really fine novel. It succeeds, however, in performing a double task: it explores the problems of individuals and of an organization. And the depiction of the climate of Mc-Carthyism—hampering the Embassy's functions and undercutting its influence—is sharp and effective.

After the conventional disclaimer which precedes *The Big Smear,* William R. Reardon adds, "The author wishes he could say that nothing described in the following pages could happen here; unfortunately, campaigns differing in specific detail but similar in substance have happened here." The campaign of the public-relations division of the Associated Research Institute against Senator Guy Morrison of Michigan has some similarities with that of Kane O'Connor against Shepherd Reade in *Tongue of Fire.* This in turn suggests the Maryland senatorial campaign to which *Tongue of Fire* seems indebted. It appears more elaborate than either, however. It includes not only rumors, defamatory stories, and a brochure, but plots as well. (Morrison is tricked into meeting an old friend—discredited as a Communist and a homosexual—to provide suspicious-seeming photographs.) Morrison is narrowly re-elected, but the destruction of his Presidential hopes earns the Institute its $300,000 fee. The narrator is a newspaperman duped into working for the Institute. His eyes opened, he concludes that its head "would go on, circumscribed only temporarily. There would be others to join him . . . The ranks were heavy with potentials . . . David no longer kills Goliath. It takes a man

---

[86] This picture of American activities abroad should be compared with the cynical version given by Hans Habe in *Off Limits* and *The Devil's Agent,* considered in Chapter Ten.

of Morrison's size to destroy a Carson. If nothing more, he had helped keep Morrison alive for that day."[87]

Although this novel has a superficial, spurious kind of gloss, it is actually badly written. The prose is often awkward, with both dialogue and exposition containing many irrelevancies. In some ways it suggests novels of the hard-boiled school of fiction. Like them, it leans heavily toward the sensational. Its primary relevance for this study is that it shows the perfection of techniques associated in these novels with McCarthyism. And their end purpose is now not personal political aggrandizement, but merely money.

There was, fortunately, one literary result of McCarthyism which was not only satiric but also witty and urbane. Warren Miller's *The Sleep of Reason* was published in the United States in a paperback edition in 1960. In his introduction, Miller wrote, "This novel was published in England four years ago. It had been written a year or two before that. As I recall, the manuscript was still making the rounds of New York publishers while the Army-McCarthy hearings were in progress. It was rejected everywhere, usually with a pleasant note from the editor."[88] The author's strategy is engaging: he uses an early Henry Jamesian style to render a spectacular period. Peopling his *roman à clef* are not only McCarthy, Cohn, and Schine figures, but also the journalistic Alsop brothers and others equally well-known. Among the stable of inventive informers (used to implicate on demand witnesses before congressional committees) are Webster Calhoun (who has a farm as well as doubly-familiar initials) and talented women named Hilde Meinschaft and Anne Marie Peritonitis. Miller also uses organizational names for comedy. One character mentions "the second annual victory banquet of the Interim Committee for the Deportation of Charlie Chaplin, the I.C.D. C.C. as we call it here . . . I missed the reading of congratulatory messages from the Attorney-General and the Let's Get Einstein Committee" (45). But the prevailing humorous tone derives from the gentle ridiculousness of the protagonist, Evans Howells, newly graduated from Harvard and secretary to a right-wing congressman. Talking constantly, aphoristically, and epigrammatically in a Jamesian style, he and his friends make their way through the dangerous political mazes of Washington of the early 1950's. When a high-school boy remonstrates with Evans that innocent men are going to jail, Evans replies, "It's the only

[87] William R. Reardon, *The Big Smear*, p. 292.
[88] Warren Miller, *The Sleep of Reason*, p. xi.

place for the innocent to be, these days . . ." (154).[89] Evans and his coevals conceal education and intellect in order to survive. Being careful from the outset, he fabricates answers for an employment form. To the question, how many books does he read a year, he answers, "more than twelve, but with slackening interest" (48). And this is not a needless precaution. Ann Derringer, a seductive federal employee, is careless for one moment. At a picnic, momentarily carried away, she sings "I am a Bennington Girl" to the tune of "I Love a Parade." The others immediately stand apart from her, for, having revealed her college antecedents, she is doomed. She leaves Washington one week later.

Miller's sharpest satire is reserved for Senator Mugonnigle, his assistants Burke and Hare, and the Senator's whole organization.[90] Occasionally, the humorous tone vanishes: "In the Committee's offices the typists had been working overtime for a week, preparing copies of confidential and top-secret memoranda stolen from various departments, and typing long lists of quotations painfully wrenched from context. In the darkroom, quite ordinary men in rubber aprons made photostatic copies of forged letters, and cropped photographs in a meaningful way" (90). The Senator's appearance is familiar, and so are the implications about his assistants: "Burke sat back and smiled at his assistant, G. Duncan Hare, who returned a shy smile. They had an almost brotherly pride in each other's accomplishments" (112). Miller mixes comedy and satire in the *gaffe* which precedes Evans' exposure of Mugonnigle's methods. A new Committee victim-to-be is Tom Paine. He is asked in open session if he wrote *Common Sense* and *The Rights of Man* before the Committee realizes he is not the right Tom Paine for their purposes. The witness is a 70-year-old rugged individualist who has six times run for governor of Montana under the Freedom and Glory Party. He has been brought under the Committee's scrutiny by the president of the Montana Women Minute Men. Miller's range of comic devices is wide, including parody, caricature, epigram, aphorism, and a talent for the restrained use of the ridiculous. Like John Steinbeck's *The Short Reign of Pippin IV* (1957), a gently satiric novel built on French political crises, *The Sleep of Reason* depends on the topical for much of its humor. But something of the au-

[89] For a similar Washington atmosphere forty years earlier, see Goldman, *Rendezvous*, p. 277.

[90] Miller's use of the names of these infamous grave robbers of early nineteenth-century Edinburgh obviously equates Mugonnigle with their equally infamous employer, Dr. Knox, who dissected the corpses from the graves they robbed and the bodies of the more than sixteen victims they murdered.

thor's seriousness is indicated in the epigraph he identifies as an old Spanish proverb: "The Sleep of reason breeds monsters."

McCarthyism in Literary Perspective

The phenomenon which came to be called McCarthyism was one manifestation of widespread rightist sentiment which has appeared in the United States for over a century. Its earlier expressions came in the antiradical measures of the first World War and the 1920's—as seen in the fiction of Upton Sinclair and John Dos Passos. Other related manifestations formed important components of novels dealing with extremist Southern politicians, particularly the Southern Demagogue, and with American Fascism. Novels of McCarthyism differ from these other varieties in that they are occupied to a much greater extent with the exposure of specifically Communist activities and affiliations. Apart from the election of the McCarthy-figure, they are also usually more concerned with the discrediting of suspects than with the drive to power characteristic of the Southern Demagogue, the American Fascist, and the organizations within which they function. And although the novel of McCarthyism has no monopoly on the use of false and distorted charges, it is more often found there than in the other two varieties of American political novels. It is only in a book such as *See What I Mean?* that one finds the same degree of cynical self-seeking.

In more than half the contests which dominate these novels, the force represented by the extreme right is successful. The McCarthy-figure himself, however, ultimately loses in four of his five appearances. This is a record substantially less successful than that of the Southern Demagogue and one matched only by the American Fascist. The phenomenon of McCarthyism is, of course, much closer to the present than that of the fascist and the old-style Southern Demagogue. For a time it has held interest as compelling as either of the others, judging by the number of works it has inspired. Five appeared in 1959 and 1960. One is inclined to suspect that this cycle of appearance and reappearance of the forces of the militant right will continue in American political novels. One can only speculate whether the McCarthy-figure will recur as those of the reactionary magnate, the lobbyist, and others have done. The Huey Long-figure has displayed considerable vitality and staying power. One cannot say whether the McCarthy-figure will have for the artistic imagination the continuing appeal of its Southern predecessor, but it already has a good start and appears to be developing into a stock type.

9. Disillusionment and the intellectual

There was a time when meadow, grove, and stream,
The earth, and every common sight,
  To me did seem
 Appareled in celestial light,
The glory and the freshness of a dream.
It is not now as it hath been of yore;
  Turn wheresoe'er I may,
  By night or day,
The things which I have seen I now can see no more.

   · · ·

Whither is fled the visionary gleam?
Where is it now, the glory and the dream?

> William Wordsworth
> "Ode: Intimations of Immortality from
> Recollections of Early Childhood"

The subjects of this chapter are separate yet related. The first concerns the individual's gradual disillusionment with a revolutionary movement—usually Communism—and his attempts to make a new life for himself outside it. In the second area, the fictional protagonists are not so much pragmatic professsional politicians as men who are first intellectuals and second involved in politics. And this involvement comes from a specific set of ethical values rather than from chance, a taste for politics, or pursuit of the quickest avenue to affluence and power.

The Progressive movement provided a striking example of the intellectual in politics. Henry George's *Progress and Poverty* almost had the status of holy writ, but its author was more than a prophet. On one occasion when he went down into the arena he nearly won the guerdon: "In 1886, single-taxers, socialists, union members, and thousands of citizens who were just plain irritated supported Henry George with such fervor that he barely missed winning the mayorship of New York; a rising young liberal named Theodore Roosevelt ran third."[1] Fifty years later Upton Sinclair won the California Democratic gubernatorial nomination in 1934 on a radical tax and pension program. But a marked influx of intellectuals into government had been in the making just before the turn of the century. It was presaged by the ferment of Reform Darwinism stirring at Johns Hopkins, Columbia, Chicago, Wisconsin, Washington, and elsewhere. And in 1912, of course, an advocate of Reform Darwinism and former Princeton president would be occupying the White House.[2] The first big transition from campus to capitol was made in Wisconsin, where "before the turn of the century there was an intimate union between the La Follette regime and the state university at Madison that foreshadowed all later brain trusts."[3] The theoretical and the practical became intimately connected as the sizable group of Reform Darwinians on the faculty became deeply involved in research leading to the formulation of legislation. The first Legislative Reference Bureau was located in the university library. It was so effective the "conservatives were soon furious at the imposing array of facts that were always at hand to support a La Follette bill."[4]

Theodore Roosevelt's intellectual credentials were considerable. Eclectically responsive to elements in the thought of men as different as Henry George and Herbert Croly, T. R. wrote introductions to dissident books and elevated that questioner of accepted values, Oliver Wendell Holmes, to the Supreme Court. The intellectual figured in the New Freedom of Woodrow Wilson as he had in the New Nationalism of Theodore Roosevelt. Hofstadter notes that "National recognition of the importance of the academic scholar came in 1918 . . . when the President took with him as counselors to Paris that grand conclave of expert advisers from several fields of knowledge which was known to contemporaries as The Inquiry."[5]

In the years after the war, the great conflict seemed to have damped

[1] Eric F. Goldman, *Rendezvous with Destiny: A History of Modern American Reform*, p. 43.
[2] Goldman, *Rendezvous*, pp. 102–104.
[3] Richard Hofstadter, *The Age of Reform: From Bryan to F. D. R.*, p. 155.
[4] Goldman, *Rendezvous*, pp. 170–171.
[5] Hofstadter, *Reform*, p. 155.

any residue of the reform movement's energy. A withdrawal among the intellectuals, marked a "retreat from politics and public values toward the private and personal sphere . . ."[6] But with the national emergency of the Depression, Roosevelt and the first New Deal brought a resurgence of intellectuals into government. Columbia's Professor Raymond Moley headed a brain trust whose economic planning was designed to set the economy again in working order. Other men, as disparate as erudite Professor Rexford Tugwell of Columbia and blustering General Hugh S. Johnson of West Point, bent their dissimilar talents and radically different personalities to the same ends.[7] Later a new group of brain trusters began to arrive. Harold Ickes and Harry Hopkins were still key figures, but there were many new faces, among them "a half-dozen or more brilliant young graduates of Harvard Law School who had been placed in New Deal posts through the influence of the day's leading Jeffersonian legalist, Felix Frankfurter."[8] Two of them quickly rose to special eminence. Thomas G. Corcoran became a leader in "the second Brain Trust." With the brilliant Benjamin V. Cohen, he studied problems, wrote directives, and drafted legislation. The most dramatic of this legislation helped counterattack political foes and the recession of 1937. The second World War found intellectuals in government bureaus and federal agencies, in military training programs and the OSS, in grey-painted hulls and new slit trenches—like everybody else. But some felt a special sense of community in the loss of the President shortly before the conflict ended: "Liberals were not only stunned. Suddenly they realized to what extent their confidence in the postwar had rested on one man. Suddenly all their long-running fears of another debacle swirled back."[9]

The fears of an immediate debacle proved unjustified as the Fair Deal Years produced much legislation liberals could approve. By then, too, the place of the intellectual, including the professional academic, seemed secure in the world of government rather than being a kind of informal, somewhat indefinite arrangement. But then, with the Eisenhower years, a new era began. And for many, the electorate's decisive rejection of Adlai Stevenson was symptomatic as well as heartbreaking. He had lost to a national leader who had defined an intellectual as "a man who takes

---

[6] Hofstadter, *Reform,* p. 284.
[7] See Goldman, *Rendezvous,* pp. 333–342.
[8] *Ibid.,* p. 363.
[9] *Ibid.,* p. 405.

more words than is [*sic*] necessary to say more than he knows."[10] As one partisan put it, "It's not just that a great man has been defeated. It's that a whole era is ended, is totally repudiated, a whole era of brains and literacy and exciting thinking."[11] Then, as the realities of Russian conquest and espionage became better recognized, some detected a dangerous swing of the pendulum. Professor Owen Lattimore, standing accused, became a symbol as well as a man—for both adherents and detractors. The intellectual became the "egghead," a term more opprobrious than ever "brain trust" had been. Critics such as Leslie Fiedler carefully analyzed the ambiguous and uneasy situation of the intellectual. Other writers put it more bluntly. "The real kings (the cultural elite that would rank first in any traditional hierarchy of the Hellenic-Roman West)," wrote Peter Viereck, "are now becoming declassed scapegoats: the eggheads." And though this was in part retribution for their ineptness with the Communist issue, the retribution deplorably would endanger the civil liberties of everyone.[12]

But perhaps the intellectual had been undercut in an even more fundamental way. Through the successful reform legislation of the New Deal, the old issues around which the liberal intellectuals rallied had died. So influential a commentator as David Riesman postulated a paradox: while the intellectuals have fallen silent, chiefly out of "feelings of inadequacy and failure" many spoke who had been voiceless until their transformation by "an unacknowledged social revolution." Riesman wrote of them: "Rejecting the liberal intellectuals as guides, they have echoed and reinforced the stridency of right-wing demi-intellectuals—themselves often arising from those we shall . . . call the ex-masses."[13]

With the advent of the New Frontier the pendulum swung back, and the influx of intellectuals—many of them swapping classroom for office —recalled this pattern in the New Deal, the New Freedom, and the New Nationalism. But the New Frontier is beyond this study's bounds, and the novels within it are set in a time when the barometric readings for the intellectuals were falling.

Nine novels gave fictional expression to disillusionment or the intel-

---

[10] As quoted in Eric F. Goldman, *The Crucial Decade and After: America 1945–1960*, p. 291.

[11] Professor Val Jamison, quoted in Goldman, *The Crucial Decade*, p. 234.

[12] Peter Viereck, "The Revolt Against the Elite," in Daniel Bell (ed.), *The New American Right*, p. 96. See also Richard Hofstadter, *Anti-intellectualism in American Life*.

[13] Nathan Glazer and David Riesman, "The Intellectuals and the Discontented Classes," in Bell (ed.), *New American Right*, pp. 59–60.

lectual in politics within a twenty-year time-span. Between 1938 and 1951—in the first four—disillusionment and estrangement were primary. But in five novels published between 1952 and 1958 the emphasis shifted to the intellectual—as such—in his often precarious role as a political person.

One of the four, John Dos Passos's *The Grand Design* (1948), has as its protagonist a businessman who joins the first Roosevelt Administration. But during World War II he resigns, convinced that New Deal aims have been nullified by wartime necessity, political expediency, and government infiltration by conservatives. The other three are fictional embodiments of the commitment and estrangement presented strikingly in *The God That Failed*. The editor, Richard Crossman, collected essays by four Europeans: Arthur Koestler, Ignazio Silone, André Gide, and Stephen Spender; and two Americans: Richard Wright and Louis Fischer. In his introduction Crossman wrote, "The only link, indeed, between these six very different personalities is that all of them—after tortured struggles of conscience—chose Communism because they had lost faith in democracy and were willing to sacrifice 'bourgeois liberties' in order to defeat Fascism." Marxism attracted them, he writes, in exposing fallacies of the liberal position and teaching that "progress is not automatic, that boom and slump are inherent in capitalism, that social injustice and racial discrimination are not cured merely by the passage of time, and that power politics cannot be 'abolished,' but only used for good or bad ends."[14] He describes their renunciation of intellectual freedom which followed the acceptance of Communist dogma, an act performed in the faith that achievement of the ultimate aims of the movement justified such renunciation. He notes the combination of factors—rejection of fundamental values of Western culture, rejection of human freedom and dignity, as well as such events as the Moscow trials and the Russo-German pact—which in each case brought about the break with the Communist movement as led by the Soviet Union. It was a break of such severity, Crossman wrote, that in the case of the "true ex-Communist" (the man who had been a party member working for a long period under party discipline with full commitment to its aims, as opposed to the sympathizer or relatively new member), he could never again be a whole personality.[15]

Two of the essayists treated aspects of this experience in fiction as well as autobiography. Arthur Koestler's classic *Darkness at Noon* (1941)

[14] Richard Crossman (ed.), *The God That Failed*, pp. 4–5.
[15] Crossman (ed.), *The God That Failed*, p. 11.

dealt with the destruction of N. S. Rubashov, one of the Bolshevik Old Guard, and Stephen Spender's *Engaged in Writing* (1958) portrayed a step in the deterioration of Olim Asphalt, former writer and Communist sympathizer.[16] The varieties of experience in the other three novels of disillusionment are just as varied. John Dos Passos's *Adventures of a Young Man* (1939) related a career which might almost have come from *The God that Failed* but for the death of the protagonist. Lionel Trilling's *The Middle of the Journey* (1947) was as subtle and complex in its dialectics as any of Crossman's six essays, and Trilling's Gifford Maxim had renounced his activist Communist past as clearly as the essayists had. In *Barbary Shore* (1951) Norman Mailer's protagonist was distinctly different in being a Trotzkyist. But he too rejected Soviet Communism as a betrayal of Marxism. None of these novels has the emotional power of *Darkness at Noon,* and only *The Middle of the Journey* can match the ease and languid grace of *Engaged in Writing.* However, like the novels of the intellectual to follow, they achieved a generally higher level of art than those in any of the other chapters of this study.

Crossman characterizes the intellectual in politics as

always "unbalanced," in the estimation of his colleagues. He peers round the next corner while they keep their eyes on the road, and he risks his faith on unrealized ideas, instead of confining it prudently to humdrum loyalties. He is "in advance," and, in this sense, an extremist. If history justifies his premonitions, well and good. But if, on the contrary, history takes the other turning, he must either march forward into the dead end, or ignominiously turn back, repudiating ideas which have become part of his personality.[17]

This generalization about the intellectual's precarious position—and the concomitant suspicion of those who keep their eyes on the road—is borne out in the five novels where an intellectual is the protagonist. When he is able to keep his eyes on the road and peer round the next corner, he may find himself charged with self-seeking and cynicism. Four of these protagonists are even further set apart by being not only intellectuals but—now or formerly—college professors as well. And though they do not adopt the security measures of Evans Howells and his friends in *The*

---

[16] The fullest fictional treatment of the American literary left is probably James T. Farrell's trilogy: *Bernard Clare* (1946), *The Road Between* (1949), and *Yet Other Waters* (1952). Walter Rideout writes, "The latter two make up a detailed and thinly disguised history of the 'proletarian movement' of the thirties, and belong in outlook to the growing body of anti-Communist fiction" (Walter B. Rideout, *The Radical Novel in the United States 1900–1954: Some Interrelations of Literature and Society,* p. 323).

[17] Crossman (ed.), *God that Failed,* p. 3.

Sleep of Reason, they do nothing to flaunt their academic backgrounds. The precarious situation of one of them is increased by disillusionment with the idea of collaboration between various elements of the left. It is further complicated by a corollary personal block: an inability to break through and communicate in his relations with other human beings.

The experience of these protagonists forms a less distinct pattern than that of the disillusioned. There are, however, recurrent elements. If they are ivory tower men at all, they learn that they must descend and become committed, like the men who keep their eyes on the road. They may also realize that they have a good deal to learn from these men, practical rather than theoretical though it may be. And they understand they must do more than become committed; they must become engaged in a conflict often bitter and fought without rules.

The Loss of Illusions

When Ernest Hemingway's hero joins the guerrilla band in *For Whom the Bell Tolls,* their leader, now intent only on survival, speaks cynically of "the Illusioned ones." More eloquently, a former Marxist in Arthur Koestler's *The Age of Longing* (1951) asks, "Do you remember 'The Possessed'? They were an enviable crowd of maniacs. We are the dispossessed—the dispossessed of faith; the physically or spiritually homeless. A burning fanatic is dangerous; a burnt-out fanatic is abject."[18] John Dos Passos's protagonists are not fanatics, but we see them in both their illusioned and disillusioned phases. The motives of Glenn Spotswood in *Adventures of a Young Man* (1939) and Millard Carroll in *The Grand Design* (1949) are fundamentally different. As a boy, Spotswood identifies himself with the oppressed, and later he commits himself as an active member of the Communist Party. A middle-aged executive, Carroll departs for Washington to help in the social revolution as a planner in the New Deal Farm Economy Administration. One wants to sweep away the old to bring in the new, whereas the other, though dedicated to change, is willing to work within the framework of the old order. But both come to the same conclusion: the organization has been diverted from its original purpose, and ultimately, they can no longer remain within it. Glenn works as a labor organizer (in an area like Harlan County, Kentucky), becoming deeply involved with the miners. Explaining the Party's failure to aid imprisoned workers, Elmer Weeks—its American head—declares, "Our function is to educate the

[18] Arthur Koestler, *The Age of Longing,* p. 28.

American workingclass in revolutionary Marxism. We are not interested in the fates of individuals."[19] Glenn accepts the view of a rival organizer that the imprisoned miners are being exploited for propaganda, fund-raising, and proselyting. He knowingly becomes a deviationist expelled because, he says, he "couldn't swallow the party line" (297). Carroll rises high, becoming at one point, "next to the President about the most powerful man in Washington."[20] Even so, he retains the old idealistic devotion that marks Glenn. An intimate says of him, "Millard's absolutely determined that this money we're spending on war contracts all over the world is going to be spent in such a way as to encourage a decent wage level, collective bargaining and all the basic New Deal objectives." And then, in a phrase which suggests he is the kind of "dangerous visionary" his opponents would like him to be thought, the speaker adds, "It was all in that speech about a bottle of milk for every headhunter . . ." (404).[21] Finally, sacrifice of reform to wartime expediency combines with the death of his son to produce Carroll's resignation. In the pattern of the disillusioned revolutionary, Glenn refuses to pursue an ordinary career. "Got too many commitments," he tells his friend, Paul Graves, "comrades who've gotten in jams on account of me . . . workers who been framed and put in jail" (298).[22] He follows his convictions to their logical end—the Loyalists ranks in the Spanish Civil War. But even there the Party is his nemesis. "First time I get a guy who's a mechanic and not a muledriver," his boss complains, "the bastard turns out to be a Trotzkyist" (329). Imprisoned and interrogated by political officers, he is then intentionally sent on a fatal mission.

[19] John Dos Passos, *Adventures of a Young Man*, p. 253. Together with *Number One* and *The Grand Design*, *Adventures of a Young Man* was published as part of a trilogy in 1952 entitled *District of Columbia*. Several historical figures, among them Franklin D. Roosevelt, are mentioned by name. As Elmer Weeks suggests Earl Browder both in position and appearance, many others are given the disguise—heavy or thin—of the average *roman à clef*.

[20] John Dos Passos, *The Grand Design*, p. 294.

[21] Henry Wallace wrote, "Half in fun and half seriously, I said the other day to Madame Litvinoff: 'The object of this war is to make sure that everybody in the world has the privilege of drinking a quart of milk a day' " (Henry Wallace, *The Price of Free World Victory*, p. 14, as cited in Goldman, *Rendezvous*, p. 393).

[22] Graves is a secondary character appearing in both novels who also embodies the theme of disillusionment. He returns from a year's work in a Soviet Agricultural Experiment Station completely distrusting the Russians for their conspiratorial habit of mind which eventually gets them "so tangled up all they know how to do is shoot everybody they can lay their hands on . . ." (Dos Passos, *Grand Design*, p. 405).

In both these novels, Dos Passos endorses the views of his protagonists. In the last lines of *The Grand Design,* he writes, "Today we must learn to found again in freedom our republic" (446). He sums up similarly, but with more fervor, at the end of *Adventures of a Young Man*:

In America the Communist Party grew powerful and remarkably rich out of the ruin of freedom in Europe and the sacrifice of righteous men. Agents of the Kremlin plan were able to play on the benevolence of busybodies, the blindness of charitable dogooders and the vanity of well-to-do young men with windy brains. Stalin, the schoolmaster of fascism, could become in the editorials in liberal newspapers the grand antifascist: because the American people had little preparation in world affairs, because the American people had forgotten our primer of liberties: that every right entails a duty, that free institutions cost high in vigilance, self-denial, and the canny weighing of political prospects; and that the freedom of one class of people cannot be gained at the expense of the enslavement of another; and that means are more important than ends . . . and that only a people suspicious of selfserving exhortations, willing to risk decisions, each man making his own, dare call themselves free, and that when we say the people we don't mean the proletariat or the salariat or the managerial class or the members of a fraternal order or a political party, or the right-thinking readers of editorials in liberal or reactionary newspapers; we mean every suffering citizen, and more particularly you and me. (341)

The critical responses to *Adventures of a Young Man* were colored as much by politics as aesthetics. Malcolm Cowley called it Dos Passos's weakest book in nearly twenty years, a verdict which he admitted might have been influenced by his disagreement with Dos Passos's ideas.[23] In another review, James T. Farrell called the unfavorable criticism "a warning to writers not to stray off the reservations of the Stalinist-controlled League of American Writers to which more than one of the critics belong."[24] In general, however, these two novels and the third, *Number One,* which together formed *District of Columbia,* were regarded as a falling off from the earlier trilogy, *U.S.A. The Grand Design* was felt to lack the vitality of the other works, and *Adventures of a Young Man,* conventional in technique, disappointed those who expected the kind of experimentation that furnished *U.S.A.* with devices such as the Biography, the Newsreel, and the Camera Eye. Actually, both were solid achievements. Although the passages of description and

[23] Daniel Aaron, *Writers on the Left: Episodes in American Literary Communism,* p. 343.
[24] James T. Farrell in *The New Republic,* XCIX, p. 163, as quoted in Aaron, *Writers on the Left,* p. 440.

analysis of contemporary history could be intrusive rather than unifying, and though the author handicapped himself by putting much of his dialogue in awkward indirect discourse, the books were enlivened by vivid characters and events. There were memorable and often traumatic happenings of the time. There were also patterns of experience, which, like Glenn's, had an archetypal quality. Although the range might not be as wide as in *U.S.A.,* Dos Passos gained a greater unity by making his many characters function chiefly in one predominant narrative. He also subordinated their life-lines to that of the central character more than he had done earlier. And even though the tenor of these novels reflected the tragic lives of the protagonists—producing an effect which to some seemed sapped of vitality—there were passages of passionate commitment to Marxist revolution or democratic reform. Pungent satire of the monolithic mentality or bureaucratic intrigue showed Dos Passos very close to the top of his bent in *U.S.A.* And the novels had the added merit, for this genre, of being more closely concerned with overt political acts than with the social and economic factors shaping political attitudes. Moreover, they were a welcome relief from mediocrity, for however they might compare with their earlier embodiments, they bore the impress of a major twentieth-century novelist.

In 1947, two years before the appearance of *The Grand Design,* the eminent critic, Lionel Trilling, had published *The Middle of the Journey.* It was a carefully wrought novel, and though vulnerable to the charge of being static and at times prolix, it was one of the most ambitious and intellectually complex of all those in this study. It was one of the few so profoundly serious and skillfully composed as to be ranked near *All the King's Men.* As Dos Passos's two novels could be read against each other, so Trilling's book could be juxtaposed with one equally ambitious but not nearly so well executed. It was Norman Mailer's *Barbary Shore* which, appearing in 1951, was the last of these novels of disillusionment. They are complex not only in their political sophistication, but also in the changing relationships between characters. Sharing the forefront with each ostensible protagonist was a communist revolutionary. In Trilling's novel he was in flight from persecution for leaving the movement, in Mailer's, a fugitive from the F.B.I. But juxtaposed to each of these disillusioned activists was a younger person, still fervently committed to revolutionary aims and reacting therefore with ambivalence or hostility.

The disillusioned revolutionary of *The Middle of the Journey* is Gifford Maxim, long one of the dedicated core in the American Communist

Party. He has broken with the Party after vanishing underground for a
year of secret work. Fearing for his life, he seeks to re-establish his identity and secure a job with enough status to make assassination more difficult.[25] To his younger friends Maxim's defection from the party is un-
forgivable, for he has fulfilled a special function for them. "After all,"
says economist John Laskell, "we've been nothing but liberals and perhaps that's all we'll ever be . . . When we act, if we can call it action,
it's only in a peripheral way. We do have sympathies with the Party,
and even, in a way, with its revolutionary aims. But maybe, sympathetic
as we are, we prefer not to think about what the realities of such a party
are."[26] When Laskell accuses him of having lied in defending actions in
the Moscow Trials and the Spanish Civil War, Maxim replies,

"I was a professional . . . What mattered to me were results. I always knew
what the means were. They are not delicate or charming. They are even brutal.
Please understand that I never had any of the liberal illusions about that . . .
As a revolutionary I was wholly professional. But now the results do not
please me. The present results and the inevitable later results. It's not what
I bargained for." (128)

---

[25] If Maxim's fear seems implausible, one might note the situation of the American writer, Max Eastman, in 1938, long after he had moderated his radicalism.
In the Moscow trials of that year, Eastman's old friend, Christian Rakovsky,
testified that it was Eastman who had made the contact for him with British Intelligence which led to his betrayal of Russia. Eastman was also an accomplice
of Trotsky, he charged. On the advice of Carlo Tresca, Eastman thereupon sued
the *Daily Worker* for libel,
. . . not because he wanted a retraction of this ridiculous story, but to protect himself. Tresca had advised this move, Eastman says, to circumvent any assassination
attempt by the vindictive Stalin's gunmen. By calling attention to himself as an
anti-Stalinist, he could use the publicity as a shield. The newspaper settled for
$1,500, and Stalin, having already assassinated his character, was content to leave
his body unriddled (Aaron, *Writers on the Left*, pp. 320–321).
See also p. 435.
[26] Lionel Trilling, *The Middle of the Journey*, p. 144. Eight years before the
publication of the novel, Trilling had written that the left literary movement gave
"a large and important part of the intellectual middle class . . . 'something to live
for,' a point of view, an object for contempt, a direction for anger, a code of excited humanitarianism" which could not be "wholly reprobated" (Lionel Trilling in *The Partisan Review*, VI, p. 109, as quoted in Aaron, *Writers on the
Left*, pp. 391–392). It is tempting to make a partial equation between Maxim's
function and that of the movement to which Trilling referred. Like Maxim, Trilling had himself been regarded as a renegade by some for his affiliation in 1937
with the American Committee for the Defense of Leon Trotsky (see Aaron, pp.
359 and 443). It has also been suggested that the character of Maxim was at least
partially based on Whitaker Chambers, whose role in the Hiss case was discussed
in the preceding chapter.

In her bitterness, Nancy Croom accuses Maxim of first trying to draw them into the movement and now trying to undo his work. His reply indicates the depth of his disillusionment and cynicism:

"The dialectic of the situation . . . mind you, *The Dialectic of the Situation* detached certain disaffected portions of the middle class from their natural class interests and connections, and attached them to the interests of the oppressed classes . . . And in the logic of the situation—it is called the *Inexorable* logic of the situation—you were drawn only to the ideational aspects of the movement, to the emotional superstructure of the movement, not to its base in reality." (216)

In a concluding jibe, which arouses in Laskell only feelings of pity and disgust, Maxim adds, "In a short time I will be known as Maxim & Co. Perhaps you yourself can see the froth of the counterrevolutionary maddog on my mouth. As for you, you will, I hope, go a nobler way" (217).

Maxim's path has been tortuous. He had been led into the Party by a sense of guilt, he tells them, presumably for his share of the responsibility for society's inequities. But after performing the secret work to which his sense of guilt ultimately had driven him, he had discovered that, "We are all of us, all of us, the little children of the Grand Inquisitor. The more we talk of welfare, the crueller we become" (219). His new course suggests that of men such as Ignazio Silone: social and political action based on religious faith. "My community with men," he declares, "is that we are children of God" (221). In an essay on Melville's *Billy Budd,* Maxim has argued that not only are Captain Vere and Billy symbolically pure Spirit and Law in the world of Necessity, respectively, but also God the Father and both Christ and Christ in Adam. And later, uncontradicted by Maxim, Laskell says, "You said that this world was the field of Law and Necessity not of Justice and Freedom. You denied in effect the possibility of the ultimate social aims of revolution" (228). Maxim tells Arthur Croom that he has no trouble believing in the unseen: "I am practiced in believing doctrine that is full of mysteries. I have, you know been dealing with free-will and predestination and fore-knowledge, in original sin and redemption, all under different names and with a different outcome for a good many years now" (291).

Trilling's novel is rich not only in its investigation of these four characters and their relationships, but also in the use of other characters to obtain a kind of spectrum of political belief. Besides Maxim, with his several political identities, there is Laskell, whom Maxim calls a bourgeois intellectual, and the Crooms, who are aggressive liberals and fellow-travelers. Kermit Simpson, on whose magazine masthead Maxim re-establishes his identity, is a wealthy liberal who wishes to assume social responsibility. But he feels neither passion nor necessity strongly, displaying an utter blandness "fatal to his character" (208). Mr. Folger, who lives where Laskell boards, reads a paper published by "an isolate socialist group in Hartford . . . with [an] insistence on the honesty of the workingman and its flavor of William Morris and of meetings held on Sunday afternoons, its appearance of having discovered socialism for the first time and its implied refusals to mix itself with extravagant foreigners, the red-revolutionaries of Paris and the Second International" (70). The Crooms' handyman represents another shade in the spectrum. Duck Caldwell is proud and individualistic but lazy and dishonest. The Crooms' reaction to him and to his wife, Emily, tells more about the Crooms than it does about the Caldwells. Emily is to Nancy, "cheap Village, cheap Provincetown, quaint tearoom," and to Arthur, "an historical monument, like a castle overgrown by time . . . " (78). Duck, say the Crooms, has played Mellors to Emily's Lady Chatterley. Emily is also a poseur to them, whereas Duck is idealized into a rebellious rustic proletarian. But Laskell places the correct valuation upon them. (Trilling uses him as a kind of limited central intelligence, as James does Lambert Strether in *The Ambassadors,* though Laskell is no Strether.) To him, Duck rightly suggests anarchy and evasion. Emily is beautiful in her person and in her mythic attributes. Laskell sees her with her daughter drawing water at dusk. In prophetic if obvious foreshadowing, "it was inevitable," writes Trilling, that he should think of "Demeter and Persephone . . . of violence and sorrow" (16).

Often the terms are more specifically political. To Maxim, Duck is "the criminal personality with the strong, narrow streak of intellect . . . It's a modern type and extremely useful in making revolutions . . . It has to be liquidated eventually, either by changing its character or by—or in other ways" (226). And Laskell, contemplating Croom and Maxim early in the novel, sees them as "the administrator and the revolutionary who might eventually kill each other" but who now "complemented each other to make up the world of politics" (55).

Each of the four major characters illustrates degrees of illusion or disillusion, engagement or disengagement. Laskell's case is the one Trilling presents with greatest thoroughness. On one level genuinely shocked with a profound sense of loss by Maxim's apostasy, Laskell is on a deeper level even more disengaged himself. Laskell's friends would have called his recent illness "the mechanism of escape" (31). As he steps into a flower bed, Nancy says, "I'll thank you, John, to step out of the cosmos" (73). Her remark, which becomes a family joke, is innocent of any deliberate double entendre, yet his pattern *is* one of evasion of the responsibilities of this world. Trilling repeatedly uses imagery suggesting a difficult re-birth. Shopping in an old-fashioned drugstore, Laskell recalls the smells of the drugstores of his childhood. Then, as he leaves, "the striking force of the sunlight reminded him of the sudden light he had always exper-ienced, in his childhood, on emerging from the special darkness of the drugstore" (104). Whereas Maxim has disengaged himself from the party, Laskell has disengaged himself from life, and the process which he undergoes in the book is really a triple one. He recuperates from a near-fatal case of scarlet fever; he begins to regain his capacity for emo-tional engagement with life (severely depleted by his mistress's death); and he begins to understand something of the forces causing Maxim's defection and profoundly changing his world and the Crooms'. His own change is variously marked. Emerging from a Keatsian fascination with beauty and death, he is nourished briefly by becoming Emily's lover. With his return to reality and a measure of health, he disposes of his medical equipment and his illusions. In one of many symbolic passages, he throws away the test tube in which he had boiled his urine to test for kidney infection. Then he packs his rod and creel, the latter having held no fish during all his sojourn with the Crooms.

Both statement and symbol serve Trilling's purposes. The whole tenor of the novel is intellectual. Conversational references to Dostoevsky and Spengler operate functionally. *Billy Budd* bears its share of ideo-logical weight, and the poem which Emily's daughter recites at the Church Bazaar is a reinforcing detail: it is Blake's famous stanzas ("Till we have built Jerusalem . . .") from his "Milton." When a scene from *The Marriage of Figaro* is heard from the radio, it serves as a commen-tary on the novel. Listening, Laskell visualizes it, with "the cloaked fig-ures searching with lanterns in the dark shrubbery, the plots and dis-guises of the garden, everyone deceiving, no one being the person he or she is taken for, and then all the discoveries . . ." (68).

At the end each of the characters has reached a kind of equilibrium. There has even been something like a *rapprochement,* as Maxim tells the Crooms that, however much they may detest him, they must go hand in hand, preaching the law for the "leaders" and the "masses" as they make the new world. After that, "maybe we will resurrect John Las-kell" (305). Earlier, Laskell has himself tried to sum up. Looking back-ward rather than forward, he has concluded, the idealism of Nancy and Arthur, which raised to a higher degree, had once been the idealism of Maxim himself, had served for some years now the people who demanded ideas on which to build their lives. It had presented the world as in movement and drama, had offered the possibility of heroism or martyrdom, made available the gift of commitment and virtue to those who chose to grasp it. But Laskell saw that the intellectual power had gone from that system of idealism, and much of its power of drama had gone. The time was getting ripe for a competing system. And it would be brought by the swing of the pendulum, not by the motion of growth. Maxim was riding the pendulum. (300)

Despite Maxim's dramatic appearance and the intellectual combats he fights, despite Emily's lovemaking, her daughter's death, and Duck's violence, the novel does have a static quality its richness in statement and symbol cannot counterbalance. But it is pre-eminently a novel of ideas, and this static quality is probably inevitable in all but greatest of such novels. On balance, the novel constitutes a fine achievement, accomplished in technique and profound in its exploration of the phenomenon of disillusionment in several embodiments. At its end Trilling has taken the character who serves as his central intelligence through half of his journey.[27] He has shown the reader where Laskell has been, how his crisis in direction arose, and how it was resolved. Then he leaves him free to strike out anew, where and how he will.

Like *The Middle of the Journey,* Norman Mailer's *Barbary Shore* (1951) employs a limited group of characters. Chief among them are a disillusioned, disengaged revolutionary and a disapproving younger one. There are significant differences, however, in that these two finally achieve a kind of union as the younger carries on the revolutionary tradition. William McLeod had joined the Communist Party at the age of twenty-one, studying Marxist classics by night and leading a strike by day. Working in agit-prop, serving a jail term, he had risen to membership on the American Central Committee. He has made many trips to Moscow, only to break with the Party in 1941, after "Nineteen years with the wrong woman," as he puts it.[28] He describes the discovery one day that "an object of some sort or other" was gone from the enormous organism of the Soviet state, with the result that, "cysts broke, pus spread, the blood became infected and carried the fever with it. You should have seen the giant stagger . . . The organism was not the same" (184).

---

[27] Whereas Robert Penn Warren's epigraph quotes Dante, Trilling's title only suggests him.
[28] Norman Mailer, *Barbary Shore,* p. 121.

After a year in a federal agency, he resigns to live in idleness, convinced that he is destroyed as a person. A lodger in the same rooming house, Mikey Lovett suffers from amnesia pierced by flashes of memory:

"I was an adolescent again, and it was before the war, and I belonged to a small organization dedicated to a worker's revolution, although that dedication already tempered by a series of reverses was about to spawn its opposite and create a functionary for each large segment of the masses we had failed to arouse . . . There was a great man who led us, and I read almost every word he had written, and listened with the passion of the novitiate to each message he sent from the magical center in Mexico." (125)

In spite of the betrayal of the revolution and the persecution of his leader, Lovett anticipates eventual success. McLeod agrees, but he argues that it will come only after the United States and Russia have destroyed each other in a third World War. "That there be theorists at such a time is of incalculable importance," he declares. "The culture of a revolutionary socialist is not created in a day, and not too many of us will be alive" (285). It is precisely as another Lenin that Lovett sees himself, though he is an aspiring novelist who takes odd jobs to accumulate enough money for prolonged periods of writing. Throughout the novel McLeod is hounded by the sinister Leroy Hollingsworth for an unnamed possession. At the novel's end when Hollingsworth—finally revealed as a government investigator—kills McLeod, an envelope reveals that McLeod has passed it on to Lovett. This mysterious object of Hollingsworth's search is very likely the same one whose disappearance caused the illness in the Soviet organism. It is also the sole bequest of his will: "To Michael Lovett . . . I bequeath in heritage the remnants of my socialist culture . . . And may he be alive to see the rising of the Phoenix" (311). Although himself injured by Hollingsworth, Lovett escapes to guard his heritage and wait in wariness. In spite of the implication that Lovett may well find fulfillment at some time in the future, the novel reflects, as Rideout says, "the unhappiness that may come over the independent radical when he fully realizes that he must depend for emotional sustenance, not on a sense of community in an organization of like-minded comrades, but solely on a faith in the purity of his own individual beliefs."[29]

Each of Mailer's characters is clearly intended to be symbolic. But unfortunately, they are not very convincing on the symbolic level and not at all on the literal one. The landlady, a blowsy trollop called Guini-

[29] Rideout, *Radical Novel*, p. 342.

vere, is secretly married to McLeod but seduced by Hollingsworth. She is easily seen as a symbol of American amplitude corrupted by the Hollingsworths and unfaithful to the McLeods.[30] Guinivere's goal for her daughter, Monina, who speaks an atrocious kind of baby talk, is stardom in the studios of Hollywood.[31] Another roomer, Lannie Madison, is a bisexual Trotskyist. Having denied herself everything for the cause, she is now a timorous masochist.

Mailer handles Marxian dialectics with as much familiarity as any novelist in this study, but he covers pages with doctrinal arguments which simply cannot sustain dramatic interest. The result is the preachment of the novel of ideas at its worst. Combined with the strangeness and repulsiveness of characters such as Hollingsworth and Guinivere, these interminable harangues give an effect as of Kafka gone garrulous and sour.

This novel is unique, presenting as it does a *rapprochement* between a disillusioned Bolshevik and an illusioned Trotskyist who hopes to carry the heritage bequeathed him through holocaust to utopia. But the book is further unique as the only one of this group infused with revolutionary zeal. Its appearance in 1951—given the American political climate of the early 1950's—makes it still more unusual. Ambitious but unsuccessful, intense but contorted, it carries to extremity the political views in the fine war novel, *The Naked and the Dead* (1948), which first brought Norman Mailer to literary prominence.[32]

The Learning Process and the Individual

A bridge between the novel of disillusionment and that of the intellectual in politics is provided by May Sarton's *Faithful Are the Wounds,* which appeared in 1955. The protagonist is dead at the novel's opening. Like Glenn Spotswood and Gifford Maxim, he had been committed to the left. His death had been caused by a combination of factors: failure to be effectual, despair over factionalism, the constricting climate of the late 1940's, and his failure to overcome his emotional isolation. But unlike Glenn Spotswood, Edward Cavan dies at his own volition beneath

[30] For this and other insights into *Barbary Shore,* I am indebted to Professor Louis H. Leiter, of the University of the Pacific.

[31] Compare with child star Adore Loomis in Nathanael West's *The Day of the Locust.*

[32] For an analysis of *The Naked and the Dead* as a radical novel exposing a sick society through a military microcosm, and for a discussion of Mailer's indebtedness to John Dos Passos's *U.S.A.,* see Rideout, *Radical Novel,* pp. 271 and ff.

the wheels of an elevated train. As he is not precisely in the mold of the disillusioned, so neither is he identical with the other intellectuals, most of them professors too. He makes the force of his mind and convictions felt, but he is ineffectual—until after his death. The others commit themselves to action, learning as they go, but it is only in death that Edward Cavan strikes any effective blow.

Faithful Are the Wounds is set at Harvard University in October, 1949. When Cavan's sister flies there after the suicide of this outstanding specialist in American literature,[33] his crisis is posthumously reconstructed. He had broken with his chairman for refusing to protest the firing of a Nebraska economics professor who had campaigned for Henry Wallace. He had broken with his old friend for leaving the Progressive Party to vote for Truman and agreeing that the national office of the Civil Liberties Union should receive "written assurance that the executive committee of its Boston affiliate contained no Communists or fascists."[34] But these have been only the immediate precipitating factors. His chairman comments,

"There were two things Edward couldn't accept. For one, that his idea of socialism was old fashioned . . . It's as rigid as the statism Edward so feared and hated in Nazi Germany . . . But Edward simply couldn't admit this. What he saw when he was over there was the fervor, the struggle, the hope . . . that was one thing; the other was his sentimentality about the working man and about the unions, and his refusal to admit that in American democracy as it is, the intellectual *is* isolated, suspected and never an organic part of political life, at best an amateur, at worst a dupe as Wallace proved to be." (197)

Another friend says much the same thing:

"Now we are facing an enemy from the Left . . . all our loyalties and faith have been bound up with the Left. This shift makes deep psychological wounds— we have to admit things that we do not want to admit . . . For some of us . . . the failure of the Czechoslovakian Socialists to hold out against communism was the final illuminating thing." (206)[35]

[33] Cavan has published a major work on American literature and at the time of his death was working on a book on Wallace Stevens. It seems agreed that Cavan bears a strong resemblance to Professor F. O. Matthiessen, author of *American Renaissance* and *The Achievement of T. S. Eliot,* who committed suicide in 1950. Cavan's colleague and chairman, Ivan Goldberg, probably owes something to one of the three men mentioned by Professor Matthiessen as "the kind of audience I wanted most to satisfy . . ." (F. O. Matthiessen, *American Renaissance: Art and Expression in the Age of Emerson and Whitman,* p. xviii).

[34] May Sarton, *Faithful Are the Wounds,* p. 51.

[35] See Crossman (ed.), *God that Failed, passim,* and Leslie A. Fiedler, *An End to Innocence: Essays on Culture and Politics,* pp. 3–87.

Miss Sarton also provides psychological insights into Cavan's suicide. His sister reflects that he was unable to establish intimate relationships, that he was doomed "to be the witness always, the one who is aware and can do nothing . . ." (46). This pattern had been ingrained, the reader learns, by an Oedipal situation intensified by a deep incompatibility between his parents. From early childhood, it had "made his loyalty intransigent and narrow, deepened him, tightened him, matured him— and, in the end, murdered him. It was the wall before which he sat, in his fifties" (246).

In an epilogue Cavan's spirit—like that of E. M. Forster's Mrs. Moore or Virginia Woolf's Mrs. Ramsay—fosters noble action and a drawing together of disparate persons. Five years later, his friend spiritedly defends Cavan before a congressional committee investigating Communism at Harvard, and a militant old Socialist is able to speak well and conciliatingly of liberals such as the speaker.[36] There are other suggestions of Virginia Woolf, chiefly in the texture of the prose—which has a tendency to go soft and feminine at the wrong times in the context of the revealed political and psychological motivations. Passages revealing one character's ambivalent feelings toward her husband and Isabel Cavan Ferrier's invocation of her brother's spirit suggest the concerns, phrases, and cadences of Mrs. Woolf. But lacking her poetic intensity, and placed in their particular context, these passages produce incongruity rather than insight.

Much of the interest lies in the characters' shades of liberal and radical opinion. They range from a gentlewoman of "the generation of Darwinians and Socialists for whom Debs, Huxley and Shaw were heroes" to Cavan, "of the Eliot era," who "called himself a Christian Socialist," to Cavan's young protégé, who with time moves toward the positions Cavan himself would have taken (43). It must be added that Miss Sarton brings off her challenging task of recreating her dead protagonist. And though the style seems often effete and imitative, this is more than counterbalanced by the detailed portrayal of an intellectual who, deeply troubled and disillusioned, is ultimately destroyed by his political experience rather than being able, like those who follow after him, to come to terms with it.

The varieties of political experience in the remaining four novels in this group differ from those in the four novels of disillusionment in two

[36] For examples of the radical's contemptuous attitude toward "liberal tigers," see Aaron's quotations from Michael Gold and the youthful Dos Passos. Aaron, *Writers on the Left*, pp. 317, 325, and 347.

prominent ways. Whereas Glenn Spotswood, Paul Graves, Gifford Maxim, and Bill McLeod enter politics on the lower levels, acquiring theoretical knowledge as they go, Ellery Hodder of *There Was a Man in Our Town* (1952), Jack Trimble of *The Children of Light* (1955), and William Clelland of *The Experts* (1955), meet the realities of practical politics only after extensive experience of political and economic theory. It is true that Trimble, like the protagonist of *The Return of Ansel Gibbs* (1958) has held high appointive office. But both find their new political activity a vastly different pursuit from what they have known on higher levels. It is one requiring much quicker reflexes and highly specialized techniques. Although Paul Graves apparently succeeds in making a fruitful and satisfying life for himself after his experience of disillusionment, the careers of Spotswood and McLeod end in sacrificial death, whereas Maxim seems what Spotswood described himself as being—a one-man splinter party. Trimble is very nearly destroyed in his ordeal, but at its end he tenaciously makes plans and takes action. Hodder has enjoyed some moderate success, whereas Gibbs's confirmation for a cabinet post seems assured and Clelland has a chance at a Presidential nomination. In the small number of books treated in this chapter, the American radical works wholeheartedly for the extreme left but one day reaches his breaking point. Conversely, the American intellectual, usually a liberal of academic background, comes to his active political role with a strong theoretical background, learns to adjust to the realities of practical politics, and then goes forward, most often with a measure of success after testing under fire.

Behind *There Was a Man in Our Town* stood experience of the literary left that could be matched by few American writers. A New Hampshireman educated at Harvard, Granville Hicks taught English at Smith College and then at the Rensselaer Polytechnic Institute until his contract was allowed to lapse in 1935. By 1933 he had become one of the most articulate of Communist literary spokesmen although not yet a Party member. A thoroughgoing Marxist, he was increasingly influential among many intellectuals as literary editor of *The New Masses* after its reorganization in 1933. Hicks was one of the most active of leftist writers, publishing *The Great Tradition,* a Marxist survey of American literature in 1933, and *John Reed: The Making of a Revolutionary,* a biography of the American Communist saint, in 1936. After literary warfare with individuals and journals such as the *Partisan Review,* he resigned from the Party and left *The New Masses* on September 26, 1939. He declared that much left criticism had been invalidated by the events of

1939. He summed up his experience with the hard-won knowledge, "Politics is no game for a person whose attention is mostly directed elsewhere."[37]

As in *The Middle of the Journey*, contrasting degrees of commitment figure largely in *There Was a Man in Our Town*. It is not commitment to the left or to the Communist Party, however, but to small-town New England politics instead.[38] Playwright and narrator Bert Shattuck fulfills the function of Trilling's John Laskell (like him a temporarily transplanted New Yorker), while Ellery Hodder, former sociology professor and dean, has much of the intensity of Maxim and the Crooms. He tells Shattuck that he is not an impractical theorist, that he has been an administrator and consultant, but that here, in a small, northern New England town, he sees what is for him a new opportunity: "Just for once I want to make my influence felt where I can measure the results. I was going to write a book on what was wrong with the world. Well, to hell with that. Let's find out whether what I've learned in fifty-odd years can be applied to Colchester."[39] Enjoying himself enormously, he helps plan strategy for gaining Democratic control of the township council. He is fascinated with such practical matters as the protocol of the candidate's traditional call at the home of the voter. Shattuck believes, however, that Hodder's interest goes far deeper than he professes. In one of his letters (which Hicks uses for unobtrusive analysis), he writes,

"Ellery is seeking a faith. What he has believed in . . . is the comprehensibility of human behavior . . . Lately he has had his doubts . . . It's not so much an experiment he's engaged in as a gamble. He's betting that he, with his good will and his knowledge, can make a recognizable difference in the life of this particular town. Because if he can, you see, it proves to him that society is amenable to intelligent human control, even if he and his blessed sociologists haven't quite got the hang of it." (166)

Before the experiment is concluded, he has been wrongly charged with Communist sympathies, and his own failure of tact has seriously jeop-

[37] Granville Hicks, "The Failure of Left Criticism," *The New Republic*, CIII, p. 346, as quoted in Rideout, *Radical Novel*, p. 354. See pp. 225–229 and *passim*. See also Aaron, *Writers on the Left*, pp. 354–364 and *passim*.

[38] The interested reader may want to compare the novel with Hicks's *Small Town*, a nonfictional book on American small town life in a place the author calls Roxborough, N.Y. In his autobiographical *Part of the Truth*, he describes his life in the village of Grafton, New York, after his break with the Communist Party. His efforts were largely responsible for the building of a new school, a library, and a fire house in Grafton.

[39] Granville Hicks, *There Was a Man in Our Town*, p. 32.

ardized the Democrats' chances. But he has helped more than he has hurt, and he looks forward to an even deeper involvement in the life of the town as one of its people rather than as a manipulator and measurer. As he assesses his experience, he asserts that his failures were due to his methods because he simply did not know people. He is determined now to work so effectively that his ideas will be adopted. He further demonstrated his devotion to Colchester by declining to join a committee appointed to inform the world about the workings of democracy. He has decided that he doesn't know enough about the subject and that he will stay right where he is. And Shattuck quite rightly adds, he "was really committed to the town now, in a way that he hadn't been before" (272). What had begun with a combination of the enthusiasm and detachment brought to an experiment ends with the passion of engagement.

Hicks's novel has a surprising amount in common with *The Middle of the Journey*. It sets off city intellectuals against practical—often sly and dishonest—country people, playing a special variation on the old theme of the country mouse and the city mouse. At the end of this novel Shattuck, like Laskell, has been in a measure drawn out of himself. And although he does not approach anything like the commitment of Hodder, he prepares to take a job rather than continue as an unsuccessful writer and to that extent at least to rejoining the world of men. More than Trilling, Hicks creates a whole community and peoples it with varied and convincing characters. So well does he project their personalities that all of their actions, both political and personal, follow logically from them. *There Was a Man in Our Town* is written with grace and skill. Shattuck is quite as articulate as Laskell, though not nearly so much the aesthete. And using him as a first-person narrator rather than a kind of Jamesian central intelligence, Hicks manages him well, not only manipulating such devices as his epistolary analyses expertly, but making Shattuck a convincing character too. This novel has apparently been little remembered in the past dozen years, but it is a substantial piece of work on what is likely to become an increasingly familiar phenomenon. The action come full circle finally returns to the New York apartment in which it started. A pretentious young anthropologist asks Shattuck, "what are these trained, cultured men and women going to do to the small towns?" And he answers, "And what are the small towns going to do to them?" (281).

The protagonist of Gerald Sykes's *The Children of Light* (1955) is at work on a book one of whose chapters has appeared as a magazine article entitled, "The Intellectual in Politics." Like Hodder and Clelland, he has an academic background. He also has more practical experience of high governmental office, but some of his skills have atrophied. John Peyton Trimble—former geology and "psychopolitics" teacher, former roving ambassador in Asia, and former president of Trimble College, waits in Trimble, Ohio, for the maturing of a plan set afoot by his older brother. Collecting on prudent campaign contributions, the latter hopes to dispose of his younger brother by securing his appointment as director of the Administration's new Point Four program. This plan is frustrated, however, when John Trimble's refusal to endorse the Congressional candidacy of his son—who hates him for "deserting" his mother—provokes the young psychopath to innuendoes of homosexuality and Communist sympathy. Trimble's present wife has tried to help him gauge his situation:

He tended to imagine that he was still as clever at politics as he had once been, before an increasing habit of scholarly withdrawal had overtaken him. He tended to imagine that he could hold his own with Hank. This was a gross self-delusion, she had already told him, and he needed her to protect him from some remembered image of himself which he still treasured from more active and less scrupulous days.[40]

His son's demagoguery is direct and damaging: "Let us get up petitions to remove these namby-pamby professors . . . and get some good hard-headed business-men in our colleges to teach us what we have to know to be a success" (117). His instinct is demonstrated in a situation which suggests the Presidential election campaign of 1952. Rightly taxed with possessing sums which make his common-man claims ridiculous, he takes to television to explain his situation. With an emotional appeal he turns the whole incident to his advantage.[41] The State Department representative who comes to talk with Trimble feels as though he "was a visitor in Salem" (48). It is another case, Trimble decides, in which "an American demagogue was imitating, with equal disregard for truth, the best German, Italian, and Russian masters" (140). He adjudges himself the victim of having read too many books, a fighter who had lost his punch. "His new intellectual habits had dried up his political skills," he reflects. "He had lost them while developing an occupational detachment. No man can serve two masters. No man can serve both his will and his mind" (150). Trimble is neither broken like Millard Carroll nor destroyed like Edward Cavan. And when his Point Four job and a lucra-

---

[40] Gerald Sykes, *The Children of Light*, p. 92.
[41] See Goldman, *Crucial Decade*, pp. 227–230.

tive professorship on the West Coast go glimmering, he grimly digs in to make his stand in Trimble, Ohio. It will be a stand against people like his son, for "If he's not checked, and others like him, there will be no such thing as democracy. He's the end product of one of the main currents in American life today" (222–223). He begins his campaign as he delivers the convocation address. His wife hears him, "plunging them once more, surely, into ostracism and sore disappointment . . . She leaned forward eagerly to catch every word . . . to make suggestions later on, to join up too in a necessary war that never came to an end" (303).

Sykes uses not only obvious villains such as Trimble's brother and son for counterpoint, but two other characters as well who have basely sold out whatever talents they had. Both are writers, one a reporter and the other, called only Rudenko, a former magazine editor. One bows subserviently to the elder Trimble and the other curries favor. Rudenko's career as editor of *The Scythian Review* introduces literary politics. Trimble calls Rudenko's method "intellectual terrorism." During his editorial career, "by skillful seamanship in all kinds of intellectual weather, during one of the most changeable periods in history, [the magazine] had been guided safely from Stalinism to Trotskyism, to Freudianism, to Henry Jamesism, to Sartrean Existentialism, to Kafkan symbolism, to Eliot's royalism, to Scythian Scythianism, until it was generally recognized as the leader in its broken field" (18, 12). Actually, this thread of the novel is not dissociated from the political as it might seem, dealing as it does with conscienceless expediency. And, as the magazine strongly suggests one still-extant review of literature, so does another character— even more literary than Rudenko—suggest a still-extant playwright. He is Cairo Thornton, whose first name is assumed, but whose blatantly homosexual air is not. Sykes uses Thornton to advance his plot in the discrediting of Trimble, but he is rather a risk as a character. So is Rudenko, who leads Sykes into excesses such as the passage in which, writing of Rudenko, he says, "The caged circular shaft of a gashouse evoked the tender, memorable day when he refused to play handball with the morgue attendant who had raped his sister—because he had just discovered *The Waste Land*" (16).

The Children of Light is dedicated "To our new Bilinguals," and they, presumably, are not children of darkness such as Hank Trimble and Rudenko, but rather those whose bilingualism equips them to speak not only the language of the ethical and idealistic intellectual but also that of the man who can go down into the market place and speak words which will move the hearts and minds of his fellow citizens. If the identity of the new bilinguals is not certain, that of the Children of Light is. They are the John Trimbles, matched in seemingly unequal contest with the Children of this World who, in the Parable of the Unjust Steward in Luke, XVI:8, "are in their generation wiser than the children of light." This novel is in many places slow, overwritten, and even rather precious. But like all the other novels in this chapter, it is the work of a sophisticated and cultivated mind. Shaped with craft, it reveals another aspect— here a rather somber one—of the experience of the intellectual in merciless political combat.

Martin Mayer in *The Experts* (1955) and Frederick Buechner in *The Return of Ansel Gibbs* (1958) treated different aspects of the same question: in what manner should a man undertake and discharge the responsibilities of power? Through Governor William Clelland, Mayer explored the problem of purity of motive in a good man whose actions will affect his chances for the Presidency. Through the character of cabinet member-to-be Ansel Gibbs, Buechner dealt with the familiar problem of commitment, but exemplified in a man unsure of whether he is sufficiently engaged to accept the trials involved in confirmation of his appointment. Both are men of affairs. Clelland, a teacher and scholar before becoming a politician, has natural genius for political action combined with considerable experience. A former wartime administrator, Gibbs has never actually been in academic life, but much in his habit of mind and attitudes makes him very like Cavan, Hodder, Trimble, and Clelland.

A popular professor of political science before his midwestern governorship, Clelland is the author of a biography of Edmund Burke and another study entitled, *Peel and Disraeli: The Ethics of Tory Revolution*. His interest in intellectual and scholarly matters continues, but now he must manage them differently when they cross his desk. When he is asked to provide an introduction for Professor Gottfreund's new book, *The Intellectual in Politics,* he quickly reacts, "Jesus, no . . ."[42] Similarly, he is thankful that no voter, so far as he knows, has ever read his book on Peel and Disraeli. But at the annual press club satire he suddenly realizes that a number of people have seen through his scholarly appearance to the hard reality of the expert politician beneath. He has consistently chosen what seems the right course, believing it will also be the popular course. His crisis comes over the sentence of a feeble-minded holdup-murderer. He is urged to commute it by his young assistant who is in a measure the keeper of his conscience. In answer Clelland asks him,

[42] Martin Mayer, *The Experts,* p. 116.

"Why? What are we running here, a high-school civics class? I think it might be politically unwise to let Mancioni out of the chair. It leaves too big an opening, brings back the October scandals . . . If I'm going to get to be president I can't be politically unwise. I've got a complicated case here, and you want me to let my emotional bias against capital punishment fly me over the clouds into an action that isn't dictated by the facts and would almost certainly hurt me politically . . ." (249)

These words may sound to the reader much like those of the corrupted senator in George Garrett's *The Finished Man*. That this is more than a case of rationalized expediency appears in Clelland's Dostoevskyan argument:

"My God, how long does this poor country have to be misgoverned? What's important? That one idiot murderer should live or that the world should be led with some intelligence for the next four years? . . . Nothing valuable has ever got done . . . without the most painful labor, and damage to almost everybody involved . . . Intelligence, a sense of perspective, a sense of proportion—they're what's needed. Principles without these qualities are worse than worthless—they're dangerous, like Calvin's principles, or Lenin's principles, or the principles of those early Christian idiots who destroyed Mediterranean civilization." (250–251)

To no very great surprise on the reader's part, Clelland does commute the sentence, reassuring himself that either his Presidential chances will be uninjured or he will be able to retire to private life and a marriage which will be adequate recompense for the lost public life. And the reader feels that handsome Billy Clelland will somehow eventually have both.

The Return of Ansel Gibbs (1958) was Frederick Buechner's second novel. Whereas his first, *A Long Day's Dying* (1950), was a subtle, mythic, and Jamesian tale in a university setting, this story was played out in part in a television studio and transmitted further by newspaper columns. What first promises to be simply brisk interrogation before confirmation for a cabinet post becomes for Ansel Gibbs a personal crisis. He is a man who was capable of replying, during the war, to the question, "What are you doing to save civilization?" with the answer, "I am civilization."[43] Goaded by his chief congressional critic, Gibbs becomes increasingly troubled by the extent of his responsibility. He even begins to question his fitness for the post because of his sense of disengagement, the weakness of his drive toward involvement in the problems he will have to

[43] Frederick Buechner, *The Return of Ansel Gibbs*, p. 5.

meet. His predatory opponent (who suggests aspects of McCarthyism),
turns the television appearance into a kind of trial, labelling him the
"worst kind of cynic" (120). Though his chances for confirmation appear little damaged, he decides to withdraw because he "fall[s] short of
common humanity . . . What else can it mean to have a friend and not
to save him, to have a daughter and not to know her, to meet a friend's
son and not to trust him, to have had a wife and hardly to remember
her?" (245). But it is no real surprise when he and his daughter both become engaged—he to the demanding job and she to the son of the friend
Gibbs did not save. He is toasted by an old mentor and spiritual guide:
"I drink this to you, Ansel, whoever you are, whoever you turn out to be.
And to your involvement. It was bound to happen. We are all involved,
Mesdames, Messieurs. God have mercy on us" (307). This novel has
greater subtlety than power, more thought than emotion. Like *The Experts*, it demonstrates the sophistication of technique and idea now
brought to the best political novels.

Similar in exploring relationships between morality and power, Mayer
and Buechner differ in technique. In *The Experts* structure is emphasized through two sets of characters. Remote from each other in every
way, they draw gradually closer until their fates are in large measure
interlocked. One group includes Clelland, his friends, and his staff. The
other group includes the murderer, his wife, and his partners. The element of chronology is strong as Mayer forcefully conveys the sense of
ongoing, interlocked events. The two major groups—together with that
of a newspaper publisher bent on ruining Clelland and those keeping the
watch around the death cell—converge and finally meet, producing a
strong dramatic effect in an altogether professional novel. It is vivid and
convincing, presenting a broader range than Buechner's novel, with
both the deadly journalist (much like Sykes's Rudenko) and the mo-
ronic murderer equally well rendered.

Although *The Return of Ansel Gibbs* lacks the dramatic force of *The
Experts*, it attempts to explore more issues more profoundly. The principal concerns are those of political engagement, Christian commitment
(together with the nature of one's responsibility to and for others), and
the problem of identity. It also considers three different kinds of power:
the spiritual power invested in Henry Kuykendall by his episcopal priesthood, with which he hopes to galvanize that latent in Gibbs; the temporal power craved by loyal Porter Hoye, who will go to Washington
with Gibbs if he accepts; and the frightening power conferred upon
Rudy Tripp by his television program, which he hopes initially to turn

upon Gibbs in revenge. Buechner, himself a clergyman, compares the world of Gibbs and the world of Kuykendall. The old man speaks of Gibbs as one who would have made "The kind of priest I think God dreams of. A man who profoundly knows the world, renouncing it" (87). A famous Old Testament scholar who had left Harvard for the East Harlem Puerto Rican Church of the Holy Innocents, Kuykendall ponders Gibbs's identity: "There was a time that I thought it might be you who were going to speak the word of judgement to this generation. I even looked for another Jeremiah, another Isaiah . . ." (196). Buechner contrasts the faith of Kuykendall with the doubt of Gibbs, and also the worlds which they will inhabit: the worlds of Harlem and of Washington. In technique, the novel is suggestive and allusive. There is a consistent motif of Biblical references. For Dr. Kuykendall's congregation, the sermons must be acted out, and the one Buechner chooses involves the story of Saul and David. Even the language is at times Biblical. When Kuykendall finally tells Gibbs, "Go . . . I speak with authority" (286), one thinks of Samuel addressing Saul or David.[44] Gibbs is almost obsessed by the old specter of guilt which Tripp's appearance raises. It is generalized into the problem of responsibility—to what extent was he his brother's keeper? The estates of fatherhood and sonship are likewise involved, and many of the psychological undercurrents are expressed in symbolic action. In the climactic scene, Gibbs orders Tripp away. When Tripp leans forward in defiance to kiss Anne Gibbs, her father shoves him so that he falls, cutting his right temple on a coffee table. Not only does this suggest Gibbs's sin against Tripp's father, it also suggests an Old Testament-style sign from Heaven, for unity follows division, leading to harmony and commitment. *The Return of Ansel Gibbs* is a political novel with religious concerns or, one might say equally, a religious novel with political concerns.

In May of 1959 the American Academy of Arts and Letters awarded Buechner a prize of $1,000, intended to go "to a novel of outstanding excellence published during the previous year that has happened not to

[44] Kuykendall suggests Walter Rauschenbusch, leader of Reform Darwinism in American Protestantism. His first pastorate, on the edge of New York's Hell's Kitchen, had led Rauschenbusch to a reading of George, Bellamy, Ruskin, and others. After study in Germany and England (where he stayed with Beatrice and Sidney Webb), he returned to the United States and in 1897 accepted a professorship at the Rochester Theological Seminary. He published *Christianity and the Social Crisis* in 1907 and *Christianizing the Social Order* in 1912. In the latter he wrote, "Translate the evolutionary themes into religious faith, and you have the doctrine of the Kingdom of God" (as quoted in Goldman, *Rendezvous,* p. 107). See also pp. 106 and 108.

attract as much attention or to sell as well as it deserved."[45] It is not surprising that the novel did not "sell as well as it deserved," for it was complex and thoughtful rather than straightforward and spectacular. What is surprising was that it should have appeared at all in a genre where the tawdry and violent were commonplace and where craft and integrity came all too seldom in such unusual books as *All the King's Men, The Middle of the Journey,* or *The Grand Design.*

Ends and Beginnings

The characters in these novels differ from those in the preceding chapters as much by their capacity for faith and zeal as anything else. As Gifford Maxim remarks, he has for years believed in a doctrine whose cardinal points might, with different terminology, seem identical with tenets of Christian belief. These men often possess a curious kind of purity: none is self-seeking like the Bosses or demagogues. The impure drive to power is present, but never as the major motive. Some commit acts abhorrent under the Christian code. But always these actions have been prompted by faith and zeal, and never for motives of personal gain or the satisfactions of sadism. Those the reader is likely to find the most admirable suggest Christian analogues. If McLeod and Maxim are children of the Grand Inquisitor, Lovett and Spotswood are secularized children of the Apostles. And in their searching examinations of conscience, and their willingness to assume roles carrying sacrificial elements in them, Clelland and Gibbs appear chosen of God.

It is also worth noting that unlike other areas, here one finds the tone becoming brighter rather than darker. Apart from *Faithful Are the Wounds,* which falls into both groups, the novels of disillusionment appeared in a twelve-year period ending in 1951. The related novels of the intellectual in politics have come since 1955. This would be cold comfort, one would guess, to people such as Norman Mailer, who would probably construe the nonappearance of other novels of disillusionment to mean only that the phenomenon which is to Lovett the betrayal of the revolutionary movement has been absorbed, that the death of the God That Failed had lost power to shock, not that conditions had emerged which gave rise to faith and hope. But these novels of the intellectual in politics are interesting and even remarkable for the underlying affirmation to be found in different degrees in all of them. The protagonists are all good men, in all the senses in which this term is usually under-

[45] *New York Times,* May 21, 1959.

stood. And though as political persons they must encounter active evil, they show that the ethically motivated intellectual cannot only survive but perhaps even triumph if he has the courage and endurance to match his faith.

The novels in this chapter are further marked by their general level of craftsmanship and by the particular excellence of individual ones. *The Middle of the Journey* is close to *All the King's Men* in quality and certainly among the half dozen best of all those included in this study. If *Adventures of a Young Man* does not have as much subtlety, it has more raw power and dramatic force. *The Grand Design* is more diffuse, but it is also more comprehensive. All of the others possess some admirable qualities, and if there are relatively few such qualities in *Barbary Shore*, there are a number in *The Experts, There Was a Man in Our Town*, and *The Return of Ansel Gibbs*. Gradual improvement in quality marks the novel of the Young Knight and the novel of McCarthyism. In neither group, however, is there such clear announcement as there is here that the American political novel has reached a level that would have seemed unlikely fifteen years before.

10. American politics abroad

For so hath the Lord commanded us, saying, I have set thee to
be a light of the Gentiles, that thou shouldest be for salvation
unto the ends of the earth.

The Acts of the Apostles, XIII: 47

If isolationism has been one dominant strain in American national attitudes since Washington's Farewell Address, there has been another,
curiously contradictory, which sometimes expressed itself in a kind of
moralistic interventionism. In analyzing patterns of American reactions
to the rest of the world, Cecil V. Crabb, Jr., notes five related attitudes.
Americans have usually deprecated the role of power in international
affairs, he asserts, and emphasized moralism in relations with other countries. They have insisted that moral behavior be demonstrated in international relations but have been slow to recognize some responsibilities to
colonies and possessions that go with power. Americans have regarded
the United States as totally unique and separate from the European
sources of its origins, he argues. This has given rise to a sense of special
purpose and leadership in a self-styled country of progress and hope. As
seen in pronouncements of statesmen from the time of Lincoln to that of
Wilson and on into the present, this has run counter to the equally deep-
seated and emotional isolationist attitudes.[1] An America which could endorse avoidance of foreign entanglements could still applaud Commo-
dore Perry's opening Japan to the West. It could approve the Open
Door policy in China (in large part to check expanding Russian influence), and the acquisition of the Philippines and other Pacific possessions.[2] It could begin planning for the independence of the Philippines

[1] Cecil V. Crabb, Jr., *American Foreign Policy in the Nuclear Age: Principles,
Problems, and Prospects*, pp. 27, 32–33, 36–37, 40, and 44.
[2] Crabb, *American Foreign Policy*, pp. 333 and 359.

even before establishing its rule. Unlike other colonial powers, it would assume many of the expenses generally the lot of colonial peoples instead of exploiting the colony for economic gain.[3] These attitudes could also lead to fevered exhortations like that of Senator Kenneth Wherry, who in 1940 told an emotionally wrought-up audience, "With God's help, we will lift Shanghai up and up, ever up, until it is just like Kansas City."[4]

By 1940 the interventionist aspect was again in the ascendant after two decades of eclipse. The first of the sums which would eventually total forty-one billion dollars were soon to be spent for lend-lease aid to our allies-to-be. Then, while the war was raging, the American government entered into its first agreement to render postwar aid when it pledged its participation in the United Nations Relief and Rehabilitation program.[5] With the war's end, assistance entered an unanticipated second phase as a means of meeting the Russian and Communist Chinese campaigns of subversion. In the spring of 1947, when Russian pressure threatened to topple Greek and Turkish regimes oriented toward the West, the United States made its commitment. Its policy, President Truman declared on March 12, 1947, must be "to support free people who are resisting subjection by armed minorities or outside pressures . . ."[6] Then, three months later, Secretary of State George C. Marshall made the speech proposing long-range economic assistance to Europe. By June of 1950 twelve billion dollars had been dispensed in loans and grants in the European recovery program. By the time the Marshall Plan expired in 1951, the Mutual Defense Assistance Program was supplying military aid, bolstering the North Atlantic Treaty which had been signed two years earlier.

Although nearly four billion dollars had been spent in Asian aid programs in the five years after the war, the tide there was running in the opposite direction. The Chinese Communists had driven Chiang Kaishek's Koumintang armies to the Taiwan bastion, and an uneasy truce acknowledged the Korean stalemate which was the only alternative to major warfare. In French Indochina, the Viet Minh and the Pathet Lao —again with Chinese assistance—threatened to carry Vietnam, Laos, and Cambodia into the Communist camp. And it was a complex situa-

---

[3] Lucian W. Pye, "The Politics of Southeast Asia," in Gabriel A. Almond and James S. Coleman (eds.), *The Politics of the Developing Areas*, p. 96.

[4] As quoted in Eric F. Goldman, *The Crucial Decade and After: America, 1945–1960*, p. 117.

[5] See "The Objectives of United States Economic Assistance Programs," *The Foreign Aid Program*, Sec. I, pp. 4–15, as cited in DeVere E. Pentony (ed.), *United States Foreign Aid: Readings in the Problem Area of Wealth*, pp. 12–24.

[6] *Congressional Record*, Volume 93, pp. 1980–1981.

tion which could not be blamed exclusively upon Communist aggression and the war. Nationalist and anticolonialist movements were strong— forces set in motion by the West, ironically, in a number of ways. Crabb suggests that Wilsonian idealism was a revolutionary force for Southeast Asia. In asserting the effect of Wilson's Fourteen Points in politically backward areas, one writer argues that "It may not be an exaggeration to say that in modern times only the Communist Manifesto of Karl Marx was more subversive. Indeed, in the relations of empires and colonies Marx was probably less subversive than Wilson." Moreover, in Asia, "he prepared the ground for Lenin and Stalin."[7]

In the years after World War II, the hottest conflict spot in Asia was the great Southern peninsula. There, to the east of Thailand and the north of the Indonesian archipelago, Laos, Cambodia, and Vietnam emerged from what had been French Indochina. During the Japanese occupation (which enjoyed Vichy's cooperation), Viet Minh guerilla cadres had been organized by Ho Chi Minh with Chinese and Allied support. When the French, with British assistance, tried to reassert control in 1946, open warfare broke out. It continued undiminished in 1949 when the French granted nominal independence to the Vietnamese under the rule of Bao Dai, the emperor of Annam. Four years later bitter fighting was still draining French resources despite substantial American aid. It was not until July of 1954, after the fall of besieged Dien Bien Phu, when Pierre Mendes-France signed a truce agreement in Geneva, that the struggle abated with the country divided at the 17th parallel.

In November of 1955 Bao Dai was ousted as a national referendum established the Republic of Vietnam, with the strongly anticommunist Ngo Dinh Diem as its president. Between 1950 and 1954 the United States spent an estimated $3.5 billion on Indochina, with $2.6 billion of that amount being administered by the French for military operations. Thereafter, assistance took the form of grants made through the Foreign Operations Administration and its successor, the International Cooperation Administration. In actual outlay, these grants "came to $322 million in fiscal year 1955 and then tapered off somewhat, though the figure never fell below $170 million until 1961. The total by mid-1960 was $1,311 million in grants, in addition to $82.4 million in loans."[8] This aid underwrote the settling of a million refugees from the north, a land re-

[7] Nathaniel Peffer, *The Far East*, pp. 272–273, as cited in Crabb, *American Foreign Policy*, p. 362.

[8] John D. Montgomery, *The Politics of Foreign Aid: American Experience in Southeast Asia*, pp. 22–23.

form program, and efforts to increase the efficiency of the administration, the army, and internal security forces. With the bettering of economic conditions and the lessening effectiveness of propaganda, the Communist forces in 1958 followed a familiar pattern. Graduated military aggression began with infiltration and standard guerilla tactics meant to increase until full military units could complete the conquest. Guerilla forces carried on a war of assassination and sabotage, infiltrating South Vietnam by way of Cambodia and Laos, which was itself the scene of similar activities by the Communist Pathet Lao. Hostilities were soon to grow more intense, gradually engaging the United States in deeper commitment involving American uniformed troops as well as a continuation of earlier measures on an increased scale.[9]

If Vietnam and Taiwan were the most directly threatened, peril was next greatest in Burma and Thailand, particularly with the penetration of Laos by Communist guerilla forces. Whereas Burma's response was one of neutralism in spite of moral sympathy for the West, Thailand placed itself unequivocally in the Western camp. Thailand had outlawed the Communist Party and had given "strong support to the United States' position in the United Nations and elsewhere, being the first UN member to send troops to support the 'police action' in Korea."[10] Because Thailand's economy was better off than her neighbors' and because she was spared the crises of Vietnam and Taiwan, the pace of American aid was different. Thai officials jokingly suggested fiscal mismanagement or flirtation with Communism as a means of receiving aid in something like the proportions accorded to neutralist India and Cambodia. It was, however, substantial. Economic and technical aid for the ten years beginning in September, 1950, was set at $265 million, and in the same period $285 million were disbursed for military assistance.[11] The total effect of the program was in strong contrast to that in Burma, where aid was for a considerable period discontinued, and in Vietnam, where the need seemed endless and the goal not in sight. Without American aid to Thailand, writes Montgomery, "the costs of her participation in the Korean War, her restrictions on trade with China, and her solid support of the Southeast Asia Treaty arrangement could have endangered her domestic and international position. As it was, the government maintained its

---

[9] For accounts of deepening American involvement in Vietnam see David Halberstam, *The Making of a Quagmire*, and Malcolm W. Browne, *The New Face of War.*
[10] Montgomery, *Politics of Foreign Aid*, p. 28.
[11] *Ibid.*, pp. 28, 30–31.

pro-Western alignment with no sacrifice of public support or evidence of economic hardship."[12]

Two questions are frequently raised about this unparalleled effort—Why did the United States do it? and, Is it worth it? In a summary paragraph, Montgomery writes,

a substantial American involvement in the modernization of other nations was . . . part of its commitment to world peace. Two great wars had shattered the possibility of returning to the old system . . . and the United States had assumed its uncomfortable role as restorer of Europe, chief Western protagonist in the cold war, and protector of weak and inexperienced nations from involuntary subjection to communism.[13]

Edward S. Mason isolated three motivating factors in American aid. They were the humanitarian factor, the economic factor, and what was to him the dominant factor—political and security interests: "the furtherance of the kind of world in which we can live and prosper under institutions chosen by and not for us."[14]

Whether or not foreign assistance, as constituted in the recent past and presently, is worth it, remains a vexed question. The official spokesman of the successive administrations have strongly defended it. Criticism has covered a wide spectrum. Six articles entitled "Our Hidden Scandal in Viet Nam" were published in eighteen newspapers of the Scripps-Howard chain. Appearing in July, 1959, their charges of mismanagement led to hearings before the Subcommittee on State Department Organization and Public Affairs of the Senate Committee on Foreign Relations.

Arising out of a sensational journalistic attack and conducted in an atmosphere of cynicism and suspicion [writes Montgomery], the hearings left a trail of unresolved innuendoes, indecisive charges and countercharges, and administrative paralysis. Almost every congressional misgiving about foreign aid appeared to be confirmed; but, at least the need for a new and stronger leadership in American aid diplomacy was irrefutably established.[15]

Another widely read article, with the catchy title "Living It Up In

---

[12] Montgomery, *Politics of Foreign Aid*, p. 51.

[13] *Ibid.*, p. 243.

[14] Edward A. Mason, "United States Interests in Foreign Economic Assistance," in *International Stability and Progress*, pp. 63–91, reprinted in Pentony (ed.), *United States Foreign Aid*, pp. 65–66.

[15] Montgomery, *Politics of Foreign Aid*, pp. 224–225. See also pp. 226–235 and 304–313.

Laos," claimed that "Laos has been ecstatically drowning in American aid ever since 1955 . . ."[16] Senator Mike Mansfield interested himself in Vietnam. Having personally explored some of the problems there, he made specific recommendations to the Administration. His advice was ignored, and he eventually recommended "the virtual abandonment of ICA and Defense Department missions and the merger of their functions with those of the permanent diplomatic agencies."[17] Economist James R. Schlesinger argued that the almost infinite capacity for absorbing aid, the real limits of economic resources, and intelligent self-interest should lead to an emphasis on trade over aid. He concluded, "The claims of realism may appear cheap and tawdry to those who would have us dedicate ourselves anew to the ideals of Woodrow Wilson, but in the end there is no alternative, and the costs of undiluted idealism generally run high."[18]

American aid to Europe seemed by the 1960's to have been successful by almost any standard. It was true that Yugoslavia had entered into a *rapprochement* with Russia, and some taxpayers wondered if that aid hadn't been money down the drain. But many realized that moderation in some satellites, such as Poland, probably owed something to Tito's refusal to capitulate to Stalin. And the Yugoslavs had made this refusal stick with U.S. aid. Western Europe was thriving—to the extent that the Common Market was clearly giving America and Britain increasingly stiffer trading competition. But the balance sheet in Asia was, after nearly two decades, very difficult to add up. Without American assistance, South Korea, Taiwan, Thailand, and South Vietnam would clearly have been drawn behind the Bamboo Curtain. SEATO, the area counterpart to NATO, was still in effect. It was still hoped that continuing aid would contribute to the stability of the individual countries of Southeast Asia, and ideally, to a detente there between East and West. However, as Crabb noted, "by the early 1960's the growing strength of communism in countries like Indonesia and Laos argued against drawing too many optimistic conclusions about the relationship between American military assistance programs and peace and security in Asia."[19]

[16] Igor Oganesoff, *The Wall Street Journal* (Pacific Coast Edition), April 9, 1958, p. 1., reprinted in Pentony (ed.), *United States Foreign Aid*, pp. 130–138.
[17] Montgomery, *Politics of Foreign Aid*, p. 224.
[18] James R. Schlesinger, "Foreign Aid: A Plea for Realism," *The Virginia Quarterly Review*, 35 (Spring, 1959), p. 239.
[19] Crabb, *American Foreign Policy*, p. 364.

National Characteristics in Fiction

The most recent group of political novels to cluster about a particular subject is understandably the smallest. Five novels appeared during the 1950's which dealt with American policy abroad as embodied in governmental programs and in the individual Americans who helped or hindered them. A political scientist analyzed seven novels set in Southeast Asia in terms of five "crucial" elements used in a research project "aimed at uncovering factors involved in effective overseas performance by Americans." The factors included cultural empathy, technical skill, belief in mission, a sense of politics, and organizational ability.[20] These novels show Americans and others both as national representatives and as individual human beings in personal situations. A few generalizations can be hazarded. If the Russians appear Machiavellian and efficient, the Americans are likely to be boorishly materialistic or dangerously naive. The good ones are always outnumbered by the bad or the stupid. The French are usually fatigued and decadent, whereas the natives divide roughly into materialists corrupted by foreign overlords, semi-tragic and ill-fated fighters for democracy, or fanatically dedicated Communist insurgents. These novels can be seen to advantage against the background provided by other contemporary fiction. A brief detour to glance at some European works will be useful in outlining a familiar image of the American abroad.

Complementary Views

Four novels—one by an American, one by an Englishman, and two by a German—represent American prewar and wartime foreign policy as fundamentally isolationist and money-oriented. American postwar efforts appear at once simple-minded and economically aggressive. *The Crack in the Column* (1949), by George Weller, is set in Greece in the summer of 1944. Armed forces of several political persuasions struggle for power in the postwar period to come. An American flier hidden by partisans hears most of the comments on American policy, made more often by British soldiers in charge of underground nets there than by Greeks. The major commanding tells him, "Americans are the only people who try to buy their way out of things instead of into them. You think yourself in and then buy yourself out. Let your conscience black-

[20] Donn V. Hart, "Overseas Americans in Southeast Asia: Fact in Fiction," *Far Eastern Survey*, 30 (January, 1961), pp. 1–15.

mail you and then pay ransom."[21] This inexpertness is in part temperamental, because "You wander around the world led by thwarted theologians who dislike double-entry bookkeeping" (331) The Americans think principally in terms of disbursements so that the Greek response to a future under American "proconsuls" is, "it will not be so bad. Each nation must accept the Americans it gets. You cannot expect the money without any Americans, can you? Greece has not the worst Americans . . ." (259). In his final harangue, the major declares, "You Americans . . . forget that war is continuous and this everlasting series of visits to the strategic pawnshop a wasteful streak of postponements of the eventual showdown" (365).[22] *The Crack in the Column* skillfully mixes warfare, politics, and love. Most importantly for present purposes, it presents the familiar stereotype of American participation in foreign power politics as reluctant, ignorant, vacillating, and primarily financial.

The treatment of Americans in *The Crack in the Column* is solicitous compared with that in Graham Greene's *The Quiet American* (1956). This novel, with Burdick and Lederer's *The Ugly American* (1958), has probably contributed most to shaping the literary stereotype of the American abroad. Weller's American is young and naive, but he is decent, educable, and potentially useful. His government is stupid and mercenary, but the huge sums it is ready to expend may be put to some good, if only accidentally. Greene's Alden Pyle, of the United States Economic Aid Mission to Vietnam, has a curious makeup. He has an impeccable background, but he is misguidedly idealistic, strangely unfeeling, and dangerously zealous. Like the other Americans, he is an impossible caricature matched only by the more horrifying demonstration pieces of Burdick and Lederer. Pyle wears a crew cut and Hawaiian sport shirts. He goes into the field provisioned with a thermos of lime juice laced with vitamins. His sandwiches are made with a new spread called Vit-Health sent from the States by his mother. He wants to marry his native mistress, Phuong, and take her home with him. Thomas Fowler, the English correspondent he has supplanted in her affections, is Greene's narrator. He knows Pyle is trying with undercover military and financial

[21] George Weller, *The Crack in the Column*, p. 315.

[22] Commenting on the search for peace in the 1920's, Arthur Link writes that "the American peace sentiment was conceived in naiveté concerning European affairs and born of a romantic delusion as to the manner in which the United States could best serve mankind. Americans wanted peace, to be sure, but they were unwilling to assume obligations to enforce an international system" (*American Epoch: A History of the United States since the 1890's*, p. 288).

aid to turn the Caodists into a "Third Force" which, committed neither
to Communists nor colonialists, will democratize the country. Fowler
tells him, "You and your like are trying to make a war with the help
of people who just aren't interested." He brushes off the evils of colonial-
ism: "the French are dying every day—that's not a mental concept. They
aren't leading these people on with half-lies like your politicians—and
ours. I've been in India, Pyle, and I know the harm liberals do . . . I'd
rather be an exploiter who fights for what he exploits and dies with it."[23]
Fowler becomes convinced that the plastic explosive Pyle has given the
Caodists has cost fifty innocent lives. Before he helps the Vietminh assassinate Pyle (who has saved him under Vietminh attack) he remonstrates with him again: "We are old colonial peoples, Pyle, but we've
learnt a bit of reality, we've learned not to play with matches" (205).

More complex and interesting than Pyle, of course, is Fowler. He is
another characteristically "seedy" Greene creation, although his spiritual
malaise is not nearly so central to the novel as those in *The Heart of the
Matter* and *The End of the Affair*. Although Fowler asserts that he
genuinely likes Pyle and considers him a better man than himself, he is
a focus for Fowler's paranoid anti-Americanism. It is sprayed over obvious targets such as money, power, unconcern, hygienic cleanliness, air
conditioning, sewing machines ("for starving seamstresses"), ice cream,
Coca Cola, and chewing gum. But it pervades his thoughts. Taunting
Pyle about the prizes he will offer Phuong, he mentions "children . . .
Bright young American citizens ready to testify" (173). In what is probably a deliberate strategy, Greene attempts to undercut the virulence
of his portrait of Pyle by Fowler's attributes: atheism, opium smoking,
adultery, lechery, lying, necrophilia, and assassination. And until he
acquires the last attribute, he is as politically disengaged as a man can be.

The picture is quite clear. Stuffed with twisted idealistic notions—
gleaned chiefly from journalistic volumes on countries hurriedly visited—
and equipped with enough money, weapons, ignorance, and callous-
ness to make him dangerous, the seemingly decent young American med-
dles in an already agonizingly troubled country. Responsible for indis-
criminate killing, he makes harder the work of the dedicated military
of the previously ruling European power. Although a colonial power,
it was at least realistic, being materialistic and venal only in old, familiar
ways. Graham Greene is a gifted if obsessed and idiosyncratic novelist.

[23] Graham Greene, *The Quiet American*, p. 121.

Consequently this novel, even with its familiar bias, stands out over most of the rest.

The setting was not Southeast Asia but Europe in two novels by Hans Habe. But the image of the American abroad, once allowances were made for military personnel and postwar behavior, was much the same.[24] *Off Limits* (1957) employed a large cast, both American and German, to explore postwar tensions and jockeying for power from January, 1945, to January, 1949, in Munich, Berlin, and Nuremberg. *The Devil's Agent* (1958) was told through the memoirs of a deceased double agent for the Americans and Russians (and briefly Vatican intelligence as well) from May, 1947, through the early spring of 1955. Although there is an attempt at a kind of panoramic novel in the first book and a familiar example of the rogue's-memoir genre in the second, both turn out primarily to be adventure stories told with a certain flair. The good Germans and Americans and the bad Germans and Americans are instantly identifiable, and often the resemblance to historical figures is close enough to suggest Upton Sinclair's mildly fictionalized journalism of the Lanny Budd series.[25]

Thomas Fowler's American PX Culture has its counterpart here in pronouncements of the omniscient narrator and German staff officers of *Off Limits* and the memoirist in *The Devil's Agent*. In both novels the Americans are gullible victims of German intelligence officers who obtain enormous sums (fifteen million and twenty-five million dollars, respectively) ostensibly to reconstruct German intelligence networks to be put at the service of the West but actually intended for personal and German aggrandizement.[26] The American military is stupid and wasteful. Unable to sort out "good" Germans and "bad" Germans, they come as conquerors rather than liberators. Operating luxuriously and partly

[24] Hans Habe is the nom de plume of Jean Bekessy, Hungarian-born writer who rose to rank of colonel in American Army Intelligence during the war and has since engaged in journalism and publishing in Austria.

[25] It takes little imagination to see the resemblance between concentration camp tyrants Irene Gruss and Ilse Koch, between political entertainers Walter Wedemeyer and Putzi Haenfstangl.

[26] Reports of testimony in the treason trial of Swedish Air Force Colonel Stig Winnerstroem noted that he had been listed as a "valuable contact" by "the Gehlen Organization." This intelligence agency, it was reported, had been formed at the end of the war by former Wehrmacht general Reinhard Gehlen, who financed it with American money, it was said, before it was taken over by the West German government in 1956 (Reuters dispatch, *New York Herald Tribune*, April 23, 1964).

at the expense of Germany's slim resources, they waste a whole series
of opportunities and seriously jeopardize the future.[27] As General Stap-
penhorst prepares to organize his intelligence system, he explains to his
subordinates, "America is a democracy ruled by the mob. That mob is
at present urging the destruction of the German military machine . . .
Thus, by smashing the German Wehrmacht the Americans who won
the war only because of their material superiority, can at a pinch afford
the luxury of being the stupidest nation on earth—as in fact they are.
We, gentlemen, must look ahead."[28] The few decent, intelligent, sensitive Germans (who are almost, but not quite, as few as the comparable
Americans) are naturally not in positions from which their moderate
pronouncements can be heard.

Habe's novels are entertaining thrillers which have no claims to quali-
fying as lasting literature. But no matter how biased and unreliable parts
of them may be, they are interesting for their corroboration in another
theater of the stereotype of the American abroad as a naive and dangerous materialist whose appearance, far from being a blessing, is a curse.

American Views

The five of these novels by Americans are set in Southeast Asia. The
countries are Vietnam and Thailand, although fictitious place names
are used in two of the five. By and large, Americans fare somewhat better in them than at the hands of Greene and Habe. Their strength is no
greater but their hearts are often purer. Though there are characters in
The Ugly American quite as inept and even more objectionable than
Alden Pyle, there are considerably more who are honest, attractive, and
intelligent. The first of these five novels appeared in 1952 and the last in
1958. Each achieved a greater total effect than its predecessor.

James Ramsey Ullman's *Windom's Way* (1952) dealt with a Schweit-
zerlike physician who rejected a Park Avenue practice to build a small
thatch-roofed hospital amid the rubber plantations of Papaan. In contrast to this one-man force for good and goodwill are an unsympathetic
American military attaché; Windom's alcoholic wife; corrupted native
businessmen, officials, and soldiers; and the good natives who become
cruel and violent once they have submitted themselves to Communist

---

[27] Denazification and other aspects of American policy in postwar Germany are
viewed similarly in *Fragebogen*, by Ernst Von Solomon.
[28] Hans Habe, *Off Limits*, pp. 232–233.

discipline. Predictably, Windom is at the novel's end steadfastly preparing to go on with his work in the face of personal tragedy and ominous events. The novel's craftsmanship is professional. It does not—unlike some others—embarrass the reader, but it is thin, magazine-style fiction studded with clichés of both character and event. It reminds the reader of the more compressed case-histories in *The Ugly American* while lacking their stinging-power.

Like Lorraine's *Men of Career*, two of the remaining novels are set largely within American embassies, and much of the generating action of two more begins there. The reader comes to recognize character types: the good, intelligent American who will be undercut by the stupid or craven superiors to whom he is disturbing, and the seductive Eurasian spy who works for the Americans and serves as mistress to at least one before defecting to the Communists. Others include the rough-hewn American technical expert, the wily French merchant or official, and the deadly, dedicated native turned Communist. In each novel, American aims and prestige suffer blows. And the future seems no more promising than the past.

Both Kathryn Grondahl's *The Mango Season* (1954) and Robert Shaplen's *A Forest of Tigers* (1955) are set at about the same time, the first in May, 1949, and the second perhaps a year later. Miss Grondahl is more concerned with the texture of life and the personal relationships which shape it within the American embassy in Bangkok than with the kind of dramatic events which reflect the large movements which figure so prominently in *Men of Career*, *A Forest of Tigers*, and *The Ugly American*. The good American ambassador and his complex wife, the Ivy League third secretary and his Radcliffe wife, the alcoholic political officer and his fragile wife who is actually the novel's protagonist—these are the characters whose concerns give the novel its primary impress. Wily Simonetta Murphy, tough General Bahti, comfortable agriculturalist Ben Kovich, and charming Madame Chanchanachatra help make the plot go round. But Miss Grondahl's real focus is the fine, Jamesian central intelligence of frail and faded but still lovely Leonora Shepperd. Through her eyes the lives around her are revealed. One gathers that the native democracy and Western interests are not likely to fare much better here than in corollary settings, but the dominant impression the reader is likely to retain is in some ways like that created by a work of Virginia Woolf or E. M. Forster. Mrs. Shepperd often suggests Mrs. Woolf's Clarissa Dalloway. She has her sensitivity to shifting light and shadow in human lives. The inner consciousness is a primary concern, and many of the novel's moods and nuances suggest Mrs. Woolf's concerns.

The kindly, spiritually advanced teacher Dr. Rajendra Chand, the complex Hindu familial relationships, the spiritual presence of an intuitive woman remaining after death, all make one think of Forster's *A Passage to India*. Miss Grondahl's novel deals with political people and events, reflecting the same attitudes of novelists more engaged than herself, but it is fundamentally a study in human relationships, a novel of feminine nuances and perceptions.

A Forest of Tigers might, with major modifications, be *The Quiet American* by a different author. The situation in Saigon is one of frustrating inactivity punctuated by political homicide. Negotiations drag into their fourth month in Paris as the French in Saigon try to carry on business as usual. The Vietminh quietly build up their strength as they carry on guerilla infiltration tactics, and the position of the Americans, to protagonist Adam Patch, gradually becomes untenable.[29] "The position was untenable in various ways, of course—most dangerously . . . in the effect it had of frittering away the vestiges of prestige and almost divine good will the Americans had enjoyed when the war had ended in Asia. If one looked far enough ahead, one could already see the possibility of complete Communist victory, and the loss of considerably more than prestige alone."[30] Superficially like Pyle in that he is a clean-cut young American, Patch is actually radically different. An official with consular status in Saigon, he has intelligence, imagination, and compassion. These qualities, together with courage and independence of mind, earn him a junior colleague's hatred and the minister's disapproval. The minister, previously assigned to a Soviet satellite, responds keenly to the McCarthy-era atmosphere within the State Department. The eventual result is a request that Patch be recalled to Washington. When French officials falsely implicate him in a political assassination, the senatorial attention this draws from Washington insures the minister's recall request. M. Paul Remy paradoxically has twinges of regret, just as Fowler does at Pyle's death. But he is an official in the French High Commissioner's colonial administration of

---

[29] It is apparently coincidental that Shaplen's protagonist bears the name given a quite dissimilar character in F. Scott Fitzgerald's *The Beautiful and Damned* (1922).

[30] Robert Shaplen, *A Forest of Tigers*, p. 17.

Vietnam, and his deepest feelings are ranged against the government Patch serves. Remy ruminates,

The Americans, wide-eyed, harping on the shibboleths of their own distant revolution, were at least as difficult if not as implacable an enemy as the Communists themselves. In fact, Remy had concluded, since one had to deal on a daily bureaucratic level with the Americans, they presented a far more serious problem. It became exacerbated when their peculiar romantic mixture of blandishment and infantile enthusiasm was regarded as a kind of clarion call. (336)

Remy has recognized Patch as his most dangerous American antagonist, not because of naiveté but because of practical anticolonialism. "The one thing we can still do is dissociate ourselves as much as possible from the French," Patch has told the minister. "We have our own social-welfare and economic experts. They should be welded together into effective working parties and be allowed to make their own contribution in the villages. Immediately" (19). But this advice serves only further to alienate the minister, whose inclination is not to suggest policy but always to await its promulgation in Washington.

Shaplen uses his subordinate characters well, if predictably. One gives her attractive Eurasian body to Patch before her mind compels her final allegiance to the head of Vietminh terror squads operating in Vietnam. Through her the Vietnamese physician defecting from the Communists meets death as he waits for employment the minister will not authorize. Shaplen manipulates another by-now-familiar character type equally well. He is Irving Lockman of the United States Economic Cooperation Administration. (His counterpart in *The Mango Season* is agricultural expert Dr. Ben Kovich. There is more than one character of this sort in *The Ugly American*, but the best exemplar is the rough-hewn, true-blue, down-to-earth, man with a heart of gold who gives the novel its name: ugly American Homer Atkins, a retired self-made-man worth three million dollars.)

In some ways *A Forest of Tigers* is the most satisfactory novel of this group. It lacks the vivid intensity of *The Quiet American*, the fine perceptions of *The Mango Season,* and the forceful if propagandistically emotional impact of *The Ugly American*. But for all its failing to equal these individual qualities, it creates the Southeast Asian milieu with a completeness superior to that of the other novels. This quality does not reside only in the evocation of city scenes and river scenes, of cold terrorists and sleazy merchants, but of the complex international structure of the classes in power and those struggling to wrest it from them. The characters have depth and body, and they project conflicts which go beyond the personal to the national, political, and racial. Adam Patch is related to the Young Knights who battle Dragons of corruption on native fields. Dragons appear—a sketch of two with tails entwined serves as the novel's chapter-heading device—but they inhabit more sinister lairs and possess more lethal powers than ever they did on the Knight's far distant native soil.

Like corruption and McCarthyism, American involvement in the tragic recent history of Southeast Asia provided material for satiric comedy. Thomas Streissguth prefaced *Tigers in the House: A Satirical Novel of American Do-Good-Ism in Indochina* (1958) with an unconvincing disclaimer. He noted the work of the United States International Cooperation Administration in Indochina since 1954 and declared, "The author spent more than two years in Indochina with the United States Information Service . . . In all sincerity he has not attempted to ridicule, in any way, the Foreign Service of our government or American non-government organizations overseas." He went on to add that, "The majority of overseas Americans are doing—and have been doing—an excellent job, working with great dedication and effectiveness. And with far too little thanks." There is very little dedication or effectiveness in the work of Streissguth's fictitious Americans, however. Nor could there well be, in a novel written to extract the maximum of farcical comedy from characters so broadly sketched as to go beyond both parody and caricature. The book is closest to burlesque, depicting private armies and revolutionary factions in comic-opera style warfare. For instructive contrast one may compare it with the warfare in *The Quiet American*. The author's protagonist joins USCREAM (United States Commission on Rehabilitation, Economic and Military) only to be virtually dropped from the narrative once it shifts to Saigon. Thereafter two principal comic lines are exploited: the attempted rehabilitation of two thousand prostitutes thrown out of work in the campaign against vice following the end of French domination, and the capture of an American government documentary film unit by the forces of the Pope of the Cao Cao faction. (The program's failure is disclosed when the girls are discovered acting in pornographic motion pictures thereafter distributed by local native officials using USCREAM resources.) Improbability is piled on improbability before the happy ending. Reading this novel illustrated with caricaturelike drawings by the author, one is reminded of nothing so much as the kind of humor of extravagance which seems amusing in the college magazine but belongs without promise to that genre.

The most spectacular political novel of Americans abroad set in Southeast Asia was in a great tradition. Like Disraeli's *Coningsby* and Dostoevsky's *The Possessed,* it was written first of all as a political instrument. As Disraeli tried to advance the "Young England" Party and Dostoevsky attempted to transmit his alarm and contempt for revolutionaries, so William Lederer and Eugene Burdick indicted what they felt was tragic mismanagement in American aid programs. *The Ugly American* (1958) also had a "Factual Epilogue." "We have the material, and above all the human resources, to change our methods and to win," they wrote. "We must, while helping Asia toward self-sufficiency, show by example that America is still the America of freedom and hope and knowledge and law. If we succeed, we cannot lose the struggle."[31] This novel is in the tradition of Turgenev's *A Sportsman's Sketches* and Harriet Beecher Stowe's *Uncle Tom's Cabin.* Though no one liberated serfs over it, it has aroused more controversy than any other modern American political novel. Branded in reviews and essays as inaccurate, propagandistic, and awkward, it has sold well over a million copies and has been made into a motion picture. A year after its publication, the dust still had not settled. On May 21, 1959, Senator J. W. Fulbright, chairman of the Senate Foreign Relations Committee, was quoted by the United Press as saying the novel contained gross exaggerations and was based on the assumption "that any American loyal and devoted enough to serve his nation overseas is a boob or worse, but somehow the Russian diplomats are all talented, dedicated servants of communism." Moreover, he added, it had "misled a number of gullible Americans, including a few Senators" into believing it was an accurate portrayal.[32] But two months later Senator Mike Mansfield, assistant Senate majority leader, was quoted by the Associated Press as declaring that American foreign aid officials in Vietnam were living "a supercilious 19th-century colonial existence." They were receiving too much money, he said, and he called for a full Congressional inquiry into the entire aid program for Southeast Asia to de-

[31] William J. Lederer and Eugene Burdick, *The Ugly American*, p. 285.
[32] *The New York Times*, May 20, 1959.

termine the extent of alleged waste and mismanagement.³³ Although the controversy has cooled, belated reverberations of the original blasts are still heard from time to time.

In this novel the lines are drawn much the same as they are in *A Forest of Tigers*. The villains are the bad Americans and the French, abetted by the native Communists and the Russians. The good Americans far outnumber the bad ones, and though some are tricked or defeated, contributions are made to Sarkhanese welfare and to American prestige. The American ambassador is a stupid and self-seeking political hack. Like a junketing senator fatigued and duped by economic and military officials, he unwittingly serves the interests of the enemy in Sarkhan, Vietnam, and Washington.³⁴

The ambassador's successor is career man Gilbert MacWhite, whose expertness on Soviet matters suggests George Kennan or Charles Bohlen. The Secretary of State, "a deeply religious and profoundly dedicated . . . man who traveled endlessly and relentlessly" (266), of course suggests John Foster Dulles. Studying anti-Communist tactics in the Philippines, MacWhite is given authoritative answers by President Ramon Magsaysay:

average Americans . . . are the best ambassadors a country can have . . . They are not suspicious, they are eager to share their skills, they are generous. But something happens to most Americans when they go abroad. Many of them are not average . . . they are second-raters . . . But get an unaffected American, sir, and you have an asset . . . keep him out of the cocktail circuit, away from bureaucrats, and let him work in his own way. (109)

A series of illustrative case histories forms the body of the novel. One such man is so effective in disseminating information and promising agricultural aid that the Communists nearly manage his assassination. Rather than protecting him, Ambassador Sears gives credence to the charge of attempted rape against him. A poultry expert does great good among the people until he is out-maneuvered by French and Cambodians competing with him for aid dollars. By the time he has reached home, delay and French luxury treatment have deadened his resolve to

---

³³ *The New York Herald Tribune*, July 22, 1959. See Montgomery, *Politics of Foreign Aid*, pp. 44–45, 221–224, 226–233, and 271 for Senator Mansfield's activities bearing on foreign aid in Southeast Asia.

³⁴ The persistence of the Lincoln image is attested to in *The Ugly American*. Honest and well-intentioned in later life, Senator Brown had been aided early in his career by money from corrupt sources and "a craggy face that reminded people of Lincoln's . . ." (p. 239).

take his case to Congress. An American major and his gallant French comrade, both veterans of Dien Bien Phu, devise successful tactics to counter Vietminh guerillas. The result is a reprimand from an American general and a refusal by French generals and two admirals to adopt them. An American Air Force colonel—a one-man harmonica band, information service, and aid mission—has helped win a Communist province for Magsaysay. Loved by Filipinos, he is called "that crazy bastard" in the American embassy. Even more successful than the colonel are Father John X. Finian, overseer of Catholic Missions and advocate for the general of the Society of Jesus, and Homer Atkins, retired construction man. Just as Gifford Maxim declares, in *The Middle of the Journey,* that it is not difficult for him to turn from Communism to religion, so Father Finian perceives that, "The Communists had duplicated the ritual, faith, dedication, zeal, and enthusiasm of the Church. There was the same emphasis upon training, the same apostolic energy, the necessity to see beyond facts to a greater truth. The only difference was that the Communists served evil" (46). Learning Burmese, suffering dysentery, and integrating himself into village life, he organizes devout native Catholics and with them wages devastatingly successful propaganda warfare against native Communists and their Russian helpers. Frustrated in Vietnam as the poultry expert is to be frustrated in Sarkhan, Homer Atkins—the ugly American—speaks his mind about the local status of the French, who with their native vassals have just defeated him in an Aid allocation meeting conducted by an American official. "They hate 'em, mister. Even the Anti-Communists hate the French," he tells MacWhite. "I've had enough of these damned French. Every time they bring anything into a country there has to be a trade agreement and a patent and a royalty. The result is that no one can afford their things" (211–212). Journeying to Sarkhan with MacWhite, Atkins helps set up a simple native pump manufacturing industry while his wife grows a new strain of long broom reeds which prompt the local Sarkhanese to build a shrine to her. Its altar is inscribed, "In memory of the woman who unbent the backs of our people" (238).

MacWhite's tenure as ambassador is marked by a number of successes. The major has established an indoctrination camp for guerillas, and Father Finian's station has developed into a small nondenominational college for 250 Sarkhanese. Atkins's early efforts have matured into a tiny industrial complex, and a herd of imported American cattle has flourished. But material from a confidential report on the peril in Southeast Asia is read on the Senate floor and MacWhite is identified as its author. The duped Senator Brown refutes it from his bogus experience there, and as a sequel, MacWhite is recalled to Washington. He is to be replaced in Sarkhan by Joe Bing, an information officer of the International Cooperation Administration, a man clearly worse than MacWhite's predecessor.

The Ugly American has the disadvantages of propaganda. And though it is not slapdash, the result of this collaboration is episodic, with a good deal of reliance on dossierlike blocks of facts on individual characters, rapidly if vividly sketched incidents, and an inevitable dispersion of energy from rapid and frequent scene-shifting. The novel is not art, but as a political document—which is precisely what its authors meant it to be—it is an extremely effective work. In Burma, where the results of the aid program were generally unsatisfactory,

criticisms implied in *The Ugly American* were subjects of special comment among Burmese officials, [according to Montgomery]. As a member of the national planning staff pointed out to the author, the Burmese government wanted to approve every proposed American technician in advance in order to get "decent chaps" instead of "the other kind." The general preference for using American companies that had no experience in the Far East was based on the desire to avoid those who had "learned how to bribe government officials."[35]

The novel's enormous sales gave wide circulation to the authors' clear and unequivocal message. American Foreign Aid programs were reviewed closely before the appearance of this book in 1958. The added scrutiny they have since received (in finances, general aims, and specific implementation) has in some measure reflected the influence of this most controversial American political novel of recent years.

Diagnosis and Prognosis

It is easier here than elsewhere to sum up the fictional picture of American politics. The total view is clearly as somber as in the novels of corruption. But here the authors deal with extremes that beggar even those in the novel of domestic politics—in terms of the money and power, the amount of human misery, and the size of the ultimate stakes involved.

Nonmilitary American influence abroad before and during World War II is generally represented as negligible. When it appears it takes the form of conscience-salving blood-money and ineffectual meddling.

[35] Montgomery, *Politics of Foreign Aid*, p. 43.

It serves only to make more difficult the task of allies in protecting their interests—which somehow eventually become the interests of the West. From the time of growing recognition of the Cold War, American efforts increase enormously, but the results are disappointing. Huge sums are injudiciously spent and much of the equipment supplied is often too advanced for the areas which receive it. On the human level, American representatives show their worst side. They arrogantly flaunt lush living in the face of low standards while self-righteously preaching credos their actions no longer exemplify. And they either harass and impede allies spending their blood and treasure in bitter warfare or become easy dupes of those allies who fleece them as, in a different way, they have fleeced the natives of the countries the Americans misguidedly try to assist.

These works sometimes strike the reader as part of the orgy of self-criticism that American novelists present elsewhere in this study and in much of the nonfiction appearing in American books, magazines, and newspapers over the last twenty years. There is little attention given to the very substantial good intentions, the enormous amount of giving, and the considerable good accomplished through the foreign aid program. But here as elsewhere, it is generally the abnormal and the parlous rather than the optimistic or constructive which the author is likely to emphasize.

Like the socialist fiction of David Graham Phillips and others, that of Burdick and Lederer prescribes as well diagnoses. Ambassador Mac-White writes the Secretary of State that he believes Sarkhan can still be saved from Communism by a six-point program providing that, (1) all appointees read and speak Sarkhanese; (2) none bring dependents unless they are willing to stay two years, living in normal local housing on local foods; (3) the commissary and PX be eliminated and specially imported supplies restricted to baby food and a few other key items; (4) no private automobiles be allowed; (5) the classics of communist literature be made required reading for all appointees; and (6) recruiting be made honest and clear (268). Burdick and Lederer declare in their "Factual Epilogue" that actually, "the state in which we find ourselves is far from hopeless. We have the material, and above all the human resources, to change our methods and win" (284). This constitutes an encouraging statement in an otherwise grim book, but the list of measures needed to produce success shows how fundamental they feel the failures of the past to have been.

In the convocation speech Jack Trimble makes at the end of *The*

Children of Light, he courageously resumes his teaching and tries to bring his internationally oriented gospel to Midwestern Trimble College. Metaphorically he poses the problem at the heart of this chapter. "We are a boy king," he tells his audience, "in a murderous palace, whose father has died unexpectedly. Either we are going to learn how to rule— and learn very soon—or we are going to lose almost as quickly as we got it the power that we did not seek, did not want, and yet must keep if we are to keep life itself" (302). In these novels the boy king has made many mistakes and been served ill more often than well by those in his service. He is learning, but time is pressing, and he does not know how much of it he has.

CONCLUSION

It remains now to attempt some last generalizations about the view of the American political experience offered by these authors. An assessment of the general quality of these novels as art will lead us to some estimate—so far as past evidence and present indication will permit—of where this form is likely to go from here.

The assertion that the United States is fundamentally moralistic, if not a moral nation, is supported in the work of these American writers. Just as the greatest American novels—*The Scarlet Letter* and *Moby Dick, Huckleberry Finn* and *The Ambassadors, The Sun also Rises* and *The Sound and the Fury*—are written from implicit moral bases of judgment, so these lesser novels render verdicts as well as scenes. The reader seldom finds in their pages the Flaubertian detachment that marks *Madame Bovary* or the determined effort at objectivity in the work of the brothers Goncourt. Just as Norris and Dreiser—for all their naturalistic practice—render judgments, so do most of these novelists. The work of a few of them is in the main descriptive and dispassionate, but most are engaged writers, though their intensity may range from violent commitment to the subtle indication of a position.

For the sake of generalization, these views can be stated in a somewhat oversimplified way. The Young Knight *should* attempt to slay the Dragon, and even though he may be defeated or corrupted more often than victorious, his Quest, for all the odds against him and the Quixotism into which it sometimes leads him, remains a consecrated action. The Boss reaps his own reward; like Midas, like Faustus, like Dorian Gray, he pays for what he receives, and it proves always to have been a bad bargain. Similarly, pitch defileth, and those who profit by corruption are eventually tainted and spoiled utterly by it. In the novel of the future, as in *Hamlet*, two portraits are presented—one of the blasted ear and one of the whole. They signify that man's dual nature, alternately corruptible and perfectable, makes possible the kind of new Jerusalem Blake visualized if he will only give rein to the angelic in him and, failing that, makes likely the kind of Inferno Orwell foresaw if the demonic prevails. The role of Woman should call on her higher nature; it is not

Eve who will suppress the Old Adam but the guiding angel who will lead on to higher things, even though she may have to slay the Angel in the House and become a militant leader to do it. The Southern politician most often plays on ignorance and prejudice for his own selfish ends. If there is retribution, it does not serve to bring appreciably closer to an end an historical era which for this region was a tragic one. American Fascism, nourished on sinister strains in national history and temperament, was an evil plant which bloomed briefly. Though its roots have not been killed, it is unlikely to flourish again. Although McCarthyism tapped some of the sources of strength which nourished American Fascism, its growth was stimulated by America's precipitation into a major role in a peril-fraught world. The accompanying tensions and frustrations prepared the way for the demagogue. Though eventually self-defeating, at the height of his power he could jeopardize the most fundamental American guarantees. The disillusioned radical learned the old lesson that the end does not justify the means. The newly activist intellectual found that he had to learn new skills to achieve his goals. But they justified the hard knocks he took in the attempt. And finally, a peculiarly American kind of schizophrenia seemed to be resolved as American messianic impulses overcame isolationist prejudices. Americans were at times meddlesome and bureaucratic, naive and dangerous. Fundamentally, they were both potent and benevolent, however, where tired European powers had played their last cards—if only the best Americans, pragmatic as James and selfless as Johnny Appleseed, were sent into the field while the materialists and organization men were kept out of the way.

To repeat, the view is a moral one. Indeed, it is almost Manichaean, for evil is ubiquitous. And even when the forces of right triumph, the triumph is but one engagement in a most uncertain conflict, one more like the conflict on Matthew Arnold's darkling plain than the crusade of the Templars to roll back the Infidel and liberate the Holy Sepulcher. It is true that the power of trusts is not so great as it once was, and the old-style Boss no longer cuts the swath he once did. The Machine finances no trainloads of floaters, and municipal Rings gut no treasuries with carnival abandon. But the change is not so much an unqualified improvement as an exchange of new evils for old. The Mafia-dominated underworld insinuates its way into legitimate commerce and into government. And the functions of that government proliferate while the huge shadow of the state looms larger over the diminishing one of the individual. New methods in psychology and technology combine to transform parts of the political process. Subliminal suggestion becomes a reality and thought control is not quite so fantastic as it once seemed.

But perhaps this Manichaean-seeming view is not simply a direct response to experience of contemporary history. It is probably in large part a reflection of the fact that the artist is far more often sensitive to what is wrong with society than what is right with it. Swift's imagination reacted far more strongly in terms of Yahoos than Houyhnhmns, and Pope wrote much more trenchantly about fops and flirts than he ever did about forests and fields. Beyond this, the dramatic possibilities inherent in conflict and in evil are usually more compelling to the artistic imagination than their opposites. As William Faulkner expressed it when he commented on the role of the Old General in *A Fable*, "to me he was the dark, splendid, fallen angel. The good shining cherubim to me are not very interesting, it's the dark, gallant, fallen one that is moving to me."[1]

In one of young Stephen Dedalus's disquisitions on his aesthetic in James Joyce's *Stephen Hero*, he defines poetry as the perfect coincidence of the artist's selective and reproductive faculties. The domain of art Stephen imagined

to be cone-shaped. The term "literature" now seemed to him a term of contempt and he used it to designate the vast middle region which lies between apex and base, between poetry and the chaos of unremembered writing. Its merit lay in its portrayal of externals; the realm of its prince was the realm of the manners and customs of societies—a spacious realm. But society is itself, he conceived, the complex body in which certain laws are involved and overwrapped and he therefore proclaimed as the realm of the poet the realm of these unalterable laws.[2]

Most of the novels in this study will have little claim on posterity. And in the point of the cone which they form, to use Stephen's figure, there is a small enough number distinguished from those in the two lower areas. But this is not remarkable; it is no more than the result of any such evaluation, whether on the "curve of normal distribution" or a simpler illustration, such as the relatively small number of books we choose to keep by us during most of our adult lives out of the great number which pass through our hands.

In spite of this, however, one is likely to feel more than a twinge of

---

[1] Frederick L. Gwynn and Joseph L. Blotner (eds.), *Faulkner in the University*, p. 62.
[2] James Joyce, *Stephen Hero*, edited by Theodore Spencer, pp. 82–83.

misgiving when one compares American political novels with Joseph
Conrad's *Nostromo, The Secret Agent,* or *Under Western Eyes,* with
Aldous Huxley's *Brave New World,* or George Orwell's *1984.* These
misgivings are in no wise abated if one substitutes titles such as Ignazio
Silone's *Bread and Wine* or Arthur Koestler's *Darkness at Noon.* One
can compare with these only a few American novels of the contemporary
period, perhaps only *All the King's Men, Adventures of a Young Man,
The Grand Design,* and possibly *The Middle of the Journey.* Other
European novels such as Joyce Cary's *To be a Pilgrim* and Andre Malraux's *Man's Fate* achieve levels challenging for American authors. To
extend the perspective of comparison, perhaps one should see them all
against the standard provided by such classics of the genre as Stendhal's
The Charterhouse of Parma and Dostoevsky's *The Possessed.*

Daniel Aaron considers one aspect of this problem in its twofold nature: the writer who cared too much about politics and the writer who
didn't care enough. Quoting Philip Rahv to the effect that the crux of
the relationship was "How does his political faith affect him as a craftsman, what influence does it exercise on the moral qualities and on the
sensibility of his work?" he notes that the strongest writers of the 1930's
—Dos Passos, Hemingway, Lewis, Dreiser, Steinbeck, Wolfe—used politics rather than being used by it. He notes the case of the left writer who
subordinated his craft to his politics: "He willingly enrolled or inadvertently found himself in the corps of literary shock troops . . . He became a spokesman or a partisan in the literary wars . . ."[3] And then there
were their opposites, writers who withdrew from the radical movement
but were unable to analyze their experiences "in autobiography or fiction
with the philosophic insight of a Silone, a Koestler, or a Malraux, a
Mannes Sperber or a Victor Serge." Was it possible Aaron asks, quoting
one conference report, that "American writers were not 'close' to situations in which the ideological conflict makes for genuine human tragedy?
Were these 'ideological matters' entertained as abstractions merely and
not passionately felt?"[4]

Irving Howe argues that the American political novelist has suffered
from the lack both of ideology itself and of the passion for it which he
ascribes to the French. This has resulted not only from the failure of
political ideas to crystallize and impinge upon "sensitive minds" here as
they have in Europe. It also has been due to an overwhelming set of cir-

[3] Daniel Aaron, *Writers on the Left: Episodes in American Literary Communism,* pp. 392–393.

[4] Aaron, *Writers on the Left,* p. 365.

cumstances: "The uniqueness of our history, the freshness of our land, the plenitude of our resources—all these have made possible, and rendered plausible, a style of political improvisation and intellectual freewheeling." He goes on to assert that here "serious political appetites and impulses . . . have generally remained diffuse, eccentric and fluid." The result has been that politics has not seemed a "natural" subject to American novelists, and so very few of them "have tried to see politics as a distinctive mode of social existence, with values and manners of its own."[5] The reader is likely to feel that many of them fail precisely because they see politics too much as a distinctive mode of social existence, that the action of the novel is removed from the context of life and set down in another where the governing elements are not so much the constants in human experience as parliamentary procedure, the tactics of the back room, or the milieu of the campaign. It is certainly true, however, that except for the work of Dos Passos, Trilling, and a few others, there is little sense of ideology as found in Koestler, Silone, and Malraux. And clearly, America's riches, its oceanic insulation, and its political history marked by only two great domestic upheavals have spared it much. If a kind of political sophistication has been absent, so have many of the agonies the older continent has known.

The views of major modern novelists suggest other reasons for the shortcomings of most modern political novels. For William Faulkner, the material for enduring fiction was "man in his predicament." The novelist's subject should be "the conflicts of the human heart," man's conflicts with "himself, his fellows, and his environment." When he concentrated on political events he risked treating the ephemeral and creating not literature but "journalism."[6] To John Dos Passos, the impulse which produced a political novel might be worked out in the treatment of other areas, with a focus more diffuse than in the primary political novel. Although Dos Passos did not suggest it, *U.S.A.* provides just such an example. This trilogy is intensely political. Yet ranging over a wide area of American life, these books cannot be thought of as strictly political novels.[7]

When Albert Camus was asked if much of his fiction came to any large extent from political attitudes, he replied, "If so, the less good they." It would be wrong, for instance, to overemphasize political concerns in *The Plague*. "There are three levels in *The Plague*," he said.

[5] Irving Howe, *Politics and the Novel*, pp. 159, 160, 161, and 162.
[6] Conversation with the writer, April 26, 1962.
[7] Conversation with the writer, February 21, 1963.

"The first is that of people in action with and against each other; the second is that of the German occupation; the third is that of evil in the world." The overtly political level, he explained, is the simplest. Although he liked the political fiction of Silone and Koestler, he reserved his highest praise for Melville's *Moby Dick, Billy Budd,* and *Mardi.* He also felt that *The Possessed* (which he had dramatized) was a great book. Dostoevsky began it as a doctrinaire work, Camus said, "and then the people got hold of him. He began with old Stepan Trofimovich as a bad example, and then he forgave him. He became a tragic figure who touches us in his suffering. From that moment the novel became great." It was interesting to see how people interpreted novels. Balzac's had been used by the Communists when Balzac himself was actually to the right of center. One could only speculate about the causes of any falling off in the modern political novel. One thought of such novels as Stendhal's *The Red and the Black.* One might say that now, with more people, there is more mediocrity. "The center of the novel should be the passions of men," said Camus. "Before it was the passions of individuals, now it is the passions of the mass."[8]

Vasco Pratolini remarked that in *A Hero of Our Time,* he had demonstrated the consequences of Fascism after twenty years for a generation that had known nothing else. But the reviewers were wrong who had called it only a polemical novel. It was, he said, more than that, "it was a treatment of the human condition." No book, he added, was only political. The story came first. Some books were at the moment of writing political like Dostoevsky's *The House of the Dead.* Or they were personal interpretations of history, as with Tolstoy's *War and Peace.* But being great books, they were more than this. The scarcity of Italian novels about politics came from a number of causes, he said. The Italian author had a limited audience. The cost of books was high. Most writers had to supplement their incomes by doing other things, and the political novel was not often likely to reach the widest audience and sell the most copies.[9]

One practical consideration for the British novelist who dealt with political subjects, said Stephen Spender, was the libel laws. One had to be extremely careful if he worked from life, as most British political novelists in the century have rather clearly done. There were other areas

---

[8] Conversation with the writer, June 8, 1959.
[9] Conversation with the writer, June 22, 1959.

he could treat which would probably interest him just as keenly and involve considerably smaller risk of expensive litigation.[10]

Even if one concludes that there is a disappointingly small number of modern American political novels of any excellence, and that there are more in European fiction, one can still take some comfort from two factors. The quality of American political novels in this century has shown a steady improvement in technical competence. The amateur writing propaganda fiction rarely appears. An acceptable level of professionalism is the rule, and the proportion of novels offering more is increasing. Finally, there is the number of novels considered here. With less than 140, perhaps it is not so exceptional that only a few should show real excellence and that only one seems likely to become a classic. In any fixed group of such size and time span, it is perhaps not so bad a showing when distinction is attained by the number which have clearly earned it here.

Brief Review of Political Novels, 1961–1965

During the last six years of the period covered by this study, about a half dozen new political novels came out each year. Then, in 1961, there were five. In 1962 fifteen appeared, more than twice as many as for any year but 1959. It is interesting to speculate about the causes of this increase. With the use of television as a major campaigning instrument— the decisive one, many said, in 1960—certain aspects of politics had been felt by numbers of people as never before. In its national and international aspects, politics came home to many with much more force. The novelist's audience was likely to be more receptive, and *The Ugly American* and *Advise and Consent* showed the kind of rewards that were possible if he rang the bell. In 1963 the number of political novels published dropped off surprisingly to a mere two. But in 1964, a Presidential election year, the number rose to eleven. In 1965, five had come out by mid-spring.

The thirty-eight political novels which were published from the beginning of 1961 through the first third of 1965 showed evidence of changing trends. During the period between 1900 and 1960 the novel of the Young Knight had appeared regularly. Since then there have been none.

Novels dealing with the Boss had appeared almost as early as those

[10] Conversation with the writer, March 15, 1962.

about the Knight, and though there was one long period when there were few, interest in that figure continued generally greater than in most others. But latterly his case appears like that of his opposite: only one novel since 1960, and that in 1962. Thomas J. Fleming's *All Good Men* focused on a Boss in his declining years whose son, briefly standing in for him, displays aspects of the Knight.

The first novel of corruption had come out in 1904. It was not until the early 1920's that another appeared, but more followed until the late 1930's. Then there were none until the early 1950's. Interest in this kind of political novel continued unbroken through the rest of that decade and into the first years of the next. In *The Grand Parade* Julian Mayfield portrayed violence and corruption in the political and racial struggles within a border city. This novel of 1961 was followed a year later by another permeated with corruption, Andrew Tully's *Capitol Hill*. There were two more in the same year. Walter Ross's *Coast to Coast: A Novel about Corruption in High Places* used the 1959 television quiz scandals as a basis and combined them with a congressional inquiry. *Noon on the Third Day,* by James Hulbert, showed a liberal senator caught between two sets of interests in a labor-legislation crisis and finally losing his seat after casting his vote on the basis of morality as well as politics.

The novel of the future had appeared before the first World War but not again until a half-dozen year period in the 1930's. It reappeared during a seven-year time span beginning in 1958. In the 1961–1965 period, it became the most popular of forms. There were twelve in all. Two came in 1961. Tristram Coffin's *Not to the Swift* was a *roman à clef* which used many recognizable elements of the Eisenhower era to give an ominous view of the future. Marquis Childs's *The Peacemakers* depicted a twenty-four-hour crisis in which an American Secretary of State tried to steer a moderate course while America, Britain, and Russia sought a detente in a crisis provoked by a French invasion of Tunisia. Three more such novels came out in 1962. One, Edward A. Rogers's *Face to Face,* dealt with an attempt to rig electronically the television debate between two Presidential candidates. The other two novels were frightening. In *Seven Days in May* Fletcher Knebel and Charles W. Bailey II followed an attempted coup by elements of the military. In *Fail-Safe,* Eugene Burdick, collaborating with Harvey Wheeler, frightened large numbers of people just as profitably as he had outraged and alarmed them in *The Ugly American.* This time the topic was accidental atomic warfare. A year later, in 1963, Mark Rascovitch similarly treated Cold War tensions (on Arctic seas) in *The Bedford Incident*. That same year Earl Conrad published *The Premier*. He portrayed a Negro state—its boundaries shaped like those of Africa—covering Wyoming and parts of seven other states. The novel ended with its leader's death in the late 1960's and used Jeremiah to predict dire events to come. Four novels of the future were published in 1964. Eugene Burdick was back in the lists with *The 480*, wherein he showed the electorate being fed into computers which analyzed and predicted their political attitudes and habits. Irving Wallace's *The Man* reflected the racial crisis in a way different from *The Grand Parade* and *The Premier*. (One feels it also owed an obvious debt to the assassination of President John F. Kennedy.) In *The Man* a Negro succeeds to the office upon the accidental death of the President, and the book follows the aftermath. Fletcher Knebel and Charles W. Bailey II were back with *Convention*, but it was a very ordinary novel despite a large cast in which many of the fictional faces were familiar. In *'68: A Novel of Presidential Politics*, Peter Scaevola went back to an old formula, the attempt of rightist groups to seize power in a time of desperate national and international conditions. This Presidential convention and ensuing campaign has as much of the *roman à clef* as Knebel's and Bailey's. 1965 saw the appearance of Ed McBain's *The Sentries*, in which a band of Far Right fanatics takes over a Florida town preparatory to starting a hot war over Cuba. Like familiar fictional Minute Men of the right, the Sentries of Freedom combine violence and sadism with a sense of the absolute rightness of their purpose.

There were no novels on the role of Woman, but the hardy figure of the Southern politician reappeared. He had first held the stage by himself through a few novels in the 1920's and 1930's then generated increasing interest through the 1940's and into the 1950's. There were four more in the period 1961–1965. William Brammer's *The Gay Place* was actually composed of three interlocking novels. The author, a former member of the Senatorial staff of Lyndon B. Johnson, set the first two in a Southern state much like Texas. Although the third shifted to a desert movie set, a wily governor dominates it too. Also published in 1961 was David Halberstam's *The Noblest Roman*, which had a familiar odor of corruption. Much like it was Don Tracy's *The Hated One* of 1962, in which the principal characters were despicable. Borden Deal's *The Loser*, published in 1964, also presented familiar themes: the sucker who is run only to split the vote of a front-runner, the poor boy clawing his way to the top, and sexual encounters running as counterpoint and obbligato to the political ones.

There were no novels of American Fascism. Apparently the transition of the late 1940's, in which such novels gave way to those centering on McCarthyism and the Far Right, had become permanent. But in another interesting transition, the novels which dealt with the Far Right were novels of the future: Scaevola's *'68* and McBain's *The Sentries.*

Novels of disillusionment and the intellectual in politics were primarily products of the late 1940's and the 1950's. There were five more of them in the 1961–1965 period. The first, coming in 1961, was William Manchester's *The Long Gainer,* which followed a New England college president's entry into politics and the threat posed to his campaign by scandal. The first of two published the next year was *Hornstein's Boy,* in which Robert Traver focused on an embattled but unsuccessful intellectual. In the other, Richard Dougherty's *Duggan,* a well-meaning Manhattan liberal plunges into politics, working his way downward, in the eyes of his friend, while, familiarly, cuckoldry is counterpoint for the politics. The last two appeared in 1964. In *The Big Man,* Henry J. Taylor followed the fortunes of a protagonist who seemed clearly indebted to Wendell L. Willkie. The decline of Taylor's big man is attributable, however, to a falling away from early ideals and later moral lapses. Doris Grumbach's novel, *The Short Throat, the Tender Mouth,* was actually on the periphery of this class of works, displaying a group portrait of devoted leftists at New York University in 1939.

Although the novel of American politics abroad had only appeared in the 1950's it was represented by more volumes in 1961–1965 than any of the other types except the novel of the future and fantasy. There were seven in all. The first three were novels of 1962. In *A Gift for Gomala* John Baxter satirically examined a developing country's pursuit of American foreign aid. John Baxter was a pseudonym (as John Lorraine had been for the author of *Men of Career*) for another former member of the United States Foreign Service. American politics abroad and American foreign relations also served in large part as the subject matter of Paul Hyde Bonner's *Ambassador Extraordinary* and Allen Drury's *A Shade of Difference.* Leonard Wibberly mixed broad comedy and sharp satire in *A Feast of Freedom* (1964). There American anticolonialism dislodges two British South Sea islands, whose natives solve postfreedom depression by a return to cannibalism. Familiar trouble spots provided the settings for the last three novels of this kind, all of them published in 1965. In *A Certain Evil,* David Kraslow and Robert Boyd followed an American President as he plots a revolution to save a Caribbean island from Communism. Politicians' ethical dilemmas, CIA machinations, and newspaper exposés all season the mixture. Jack Hoffenberg's *A Thunder at Dawn* shared the same semihypothetical geography as well as the same geopolitical environment. CIA agents' capers suggest the James Bond influence, whereas the use of a Negro Foreign Service officer indicates awareness of sociological changes and pressures. In *The Ambassador,* Morris L. West's protagonist plans and executes a coup very like the one which felled President Ngo Dinh Diem in Vietnam in 1963. The novel suggested elements of *The Ugly American* in its study of disaster far away, though here there were fewer Europeans and the cast was almost exclusively Asiastic-American.

Five novels appearing in the period 1961–1965 were hard to classify. Phyllis Moore Gallagher's *All Is Not Quiet on the Potomac* (1962) was advertised as "a panorama that has never been done before!" Georg Mann's *The Blind Ballots* of the same year employed heavy-handed comedy and satire in describing campaigns and elections on both the statewide and suburban school-board levels. Two very different novels came out in 1964. Thomas B. Dewey's *Don't Cry for Long* dealt with a private eye, a congressman, and murder. *A Flag Full of Stars,* by Don Robertson, was set on election day 1948, and while Truman defeats Dewey, the author splashes his panoramic representation of the nation's politics with splotches of comedy and sex. Patricia McGerr's *Is There a Traitor in the House* (1965) testified to the influence both of Ian Fleming and television adventure serials as—one blenches to write the words down—Section Q of U.S. Intelligence assigns girl journalist and aristocrat Selena Mead the job of tracking down a congressman suspected of treason. The adman's copy left no doubt that a television series and sequels would follow. Ending this review on this note points up once more the vast amount of dross appearing in a genre which produced *Nostromo* and *All the King's Men.*

One is struck again by the closeness of the political novel to the events of its time. This would appear to lessen the chances of lasting achievement. It would seem that the impact of new communication technology on politics will become just as dated—and perhaps sooner—as the rapacious trusts did as a subject for serious fiction. But the unexpected does happen. When that rare chance brings a deeply engaged genius to grips with highly topical materials, the result can be a work such as Dostoevsky's *The Possessed.* And for the artist who can see beyond present phenomena to those common denominators in human experience which link them with the concerns of men in other times and places, he too may reach the permanent and general. He may choose to say, with a number of these authors, *plus ça change, plus c'est la même chose*.

For the artist who does take this view, the conclusion reached may be a bitter one. Nearly a century ago, that most American of poets, Walt Whitman, expressed in *Democratic Vistas* what was for him a deeply disturbing, paradoxical situation. "Sole among nationalities, these States have assumed the task to put in forms of lasting power and practicality, on areas of amplitude rivaling the operations of the physical kosmos, the moral political speculations of the ages, long, long deferred, the democratic republican principle, and the theory of development and perfection by voluntary standards, and self-reliance." The greatness of the New World still lay ahead. "Who else, indeed," he asked, "except the United States, in history, so far, have accepted in unwitting faith, and, as we now see, stand, act upon, and go security for, these things?" But when he looked about him he saw a terrible contradiction of the dream: "The depravity of the business classes of our country is not less than has been supposed but infinitely greater. The official services of America, national, state, and municipal, in all their branches and departments, except the judiciary, are saturated in corruption, bribery, falsehood, maladministration; and the judiciary is tainted. The great cities reek with respectable as much as non-respectable robbery and scoundrelism." This spectacle was repeated on a grand scale. "It is as if," Whitman wrote, "we were somehow being endow'd with a vast and more and more thoroughly appointed body, and then left with little or no soul."[11] Whitman hoped for a "literatus," a great national poet, and a cluster of "national expressers" who would give expression to the true nature and promise of this country. In giving it its nature, they would also give it its laws and culture as well.

Great artists, in Whitman's own time and since, have certainly expressed and interpreted the American experience. None of the novels in this study has done what Whitman hoped for. It is, of course, too much to expect that of one book, perhaps even of a considerable number of books, though Whitman credits the Greek and Roman classics with this function. It seems rather in these novels that the balance of sentiment lies with Whitman's view of contemporary reality rather than with the potential greatness he envisioned. For most of the novelists in this study, it does not seem too much to say, the Great Experiment, as Whitman understood it, has failed.

[11] *Walt Whitman: Complete Poetry and Selected Prose*, edited by James E. Miller, Jr., pp. 455, and 461–462.

Archetypal figures in the American political experience dominate and enrich a number of these novels. Some are more nearly unique than those of the Knight and the Boss. Most conspicuous among them are the Lincoln-figure, more recently the Southern politician as embodied in the Long-figure, and the McCarthy-figure. The attributes of the Lincoln-figure have not changed, but the figure itself appears less often. It is as though it no longer symbolized a constant in American national experience but was rather distinctly of the past—great and poignant, but somehow very dated and a little naive. The Long-figure and the McCarthy-figure are of too recent date, perhaps, wholly to be compared with this most national of the archetypes. But they show signs of persisting, dramatizing potentially deadly threats to fundamental parts of the American political system. They do not, in this fiction, dominate current democratic vistas. But there are currently no others which have their force and persistence, however brief they may prove in a relative scale. If any measure of truth reposes in this art, as critics such as Aristotle have asserted, one can only hope that the dominating figures which will appear in the future will have in them something more of light, even though shadowed with tragedy, and less of darkness.

BIBLIOGRAPHY

I. Primary Sources

A. The Novels Discussed in This Study

1902

Whitlock, Brand. *The 13th District*. Indianapolis: Bowen-Merrill.

1903

Flower, Elliott. *The Spoilsmen*. Boston: L. C. Page & Company.
Lewis, Alfred Henry. *The Boss: And How He Came to Rule New York*. New York: A. S. Barnes and Company.

1904

Lewis, Alfred Henry. *The President*. New York: A. S. Barnes and Company.

1905

Phillips, David Graham. *The Plum Tree*. Indianapolis: The Bobbs-Merrill Company, Inc.

1907

Friedman, I. K. *The Radical*. New York: D. Appleton & Company, Inc.

1908

Churchill, Winston. *Mr. Crewe's Career*. New York: The Macmillan Company.
London, Jack. *The Iron Heel*. New York: The Macmillan Company.
Steere, C. A. *When Things Were Doing*. Chicago: Charles H. Kerr & Company.

1909

Phillips, David Graham. *The Fashionable Adventures of Joshua Craig*. New York: D. Appleton & Company, Inc.

1911

Phillips, David Graham. *The Conflict*. New York: D. Appleton & Company, Inc.

1912

House, Edward M. *Philip Dru, Administrator: A Story of Tomorrow, 1920–1935*. New York: B. W. Huebsch.

Merwin, Samuel. *The Citadel: A Romance of Unrest.* New York: Century Company.

Phillips, David Graham. *George Helm.* New York: D. Appleton & Company, Inc.

1914

Blythe, Samuel G. *The Fakers.* New York: George H. Doran Company.

1922

Banning, Margaret Culkin. *The Spellbinders.* New York: George H. Doran Company.

Glasgow, Ellen. *One Man in His Time.* New York: Doubleday, Page & Company.

1923

Curran, Henry H. *Van Tassell and Big Bill.* New York: Charles Scribner's Sons.

Fergusson, Harvey. *Capitol Hill: A Novel of Washington Life.* New York: Alfred A. Knopf, Inc.

1926

Adams, Samuel Hopkins. *Revelry.* New York: Boni & Liveright.

1927

Brennan, Frederick Hazlitt. *God Got One Vote.* New York: Simon and Schuster, Inc.

Hedges, M. H. *Dan Minturn.* New York: Vanguard Press, Inc.

Mitchell, Ruth Comfort. *Call of the House.* New York: D. Appleton & Company, Inc.

Sinclair, Upton. *Oil!* New York: Grossett & Dunlap, Inc.

1928

Cavanagh, Dermot. *Tammany Boy: A Romance and a Political Career.* New York: J. H. Sears & Company.

Huston, McCready. *Dear Senator.* Indianapolis: The Bobbs-Merrill Company, Inc.

Sinclair, Upton. *Boston.* New York: Albert & Charles Boni, Inc.

Whitlock, Brand. *Big Matt: A Story.* New York: D. Appleton & Company, Inc.

1929

Coe, Charles Francis. *Triumph: The Undoing of Rafferty, Ward Heeler.* New York: J. H. Sears & Company.

Davis, Clare Ogden. *The Woman of It.* New York: J. H. Sears & Company.

1930

Crowell, Chester T. *Liquor Loot and Ladies.* New York: Alfred A. Knopf, Inc.

Fairbank, Janet Ayer. *The Lion's Den.* Indianapolis: The Bobbs-Merrill Company, Inc.

Paul, Elliot. *The Governor of Massachusetts.* New York: Liveright Publishing Corporation.

1931

Brier, Royce. *Crusade.* New York: D. Appleton & Company, Inc.

Endicott, Stephen. *Mayor Harding of New York.* New York: The Mohawk Press.

1932

Allan, Glenn. *Old Manoa.* New York: D. Appleton & Company, Inc.

Mellett, Berthe K. *Wife to Caesar: A Novel of Washington,* New York: Brewer, Warren & Putnam.

Palmer, Frederick. *So a Leader Came.* New York: Ray Long & Richard R. Smith.

1933

Gilkyson, Walter. *Tomorrow Never Comes.* New York: J. H. Sears & Company.

Sayre, Joel A. *Hizzoner the Mayor.* New York: The John Day Company, Inc.

[Tweed, Thomas Frederic.] *Gabriel over the White House: A Novel of the Presidency.* New York: Farrar & Rinehart.

1934

Anonymous. *The President Vanishes.* New York: Farrar & Rinehart, Inc.

Hackenburg, Frederick L. *This Best Possible World.* New York: Robert O. Ballou.

Hart, Henry. *The Great One: A Novel of American Life.* The John Day Company, Inc.

West, Nathanael. *A Cool Million: The Dismantling of Lemuel Pitkin.* New York: Covici, Friede, Inc.

1935

Goldsmith, John Francis. *President Randolph as I Knew Him: An Account of the Historic Events of the 1950's and 1960's Written from the Personal Experience of the Secretary to the President.* Philadelphia: Dorrance & Company, Inc.

Lewis, Sinclair. *It Can't Happen Here.* New York: Doubleday, Doran & Company, Inc.

Stribling, Thomas S. *The Sound Wagon.* New York: Doubleday, Doran & Company, Inc.

1936

Burnett, W. R. *King Cole.* New York: Harper & Brothers.

Dineen, Joseph F. *Ward Eight.* New York: Harper & Brothers.

↘Fairbank, Janet Ayer. *Rich Man Poor Man.* Boston: Houghton Mifflin Company.

France, Royal Wilbur. *Compromise.* Philadelphia: Dorrance & Company, Inc.

Trumbo, Dalton. *The Washington Jitters.* New York: Alfred A. Knopf, Inc.

Warshawsky, Samuel Jesse. *The Woman of Destiny.* New York: Julian Messner, Inc.

Wilson, Charles Morrow. *The Rabble Rouser.* New York: Longmans, Green & Co., Inc.

1937

Appel, Benjamin. *Runaround.* New York: E. P. Dutton & Co., Inc.

Childs, Marquis W. *Washington Calling.* New York: William Morrow & Company, Inc.

Kerr, Sophie. *Fine to Look at.* New York: Farrar & Rinehart, Inc.

Vanderbilt, Cornelius, Jr. *A Woman of Washington.* New York: E. P. Dutton & Co., Inc.

Zara, Louis. *Some for the Glory.* Indianapolis: The Bobbs-Merrill Company, Inc.

1938

Adams, Samuel Hopkins. *The World Goes Smash.* Boston: Houghton Mifflin Company.

1939

Dos Passos, John. *Adventures of a Young Man.* Boston: Houghton Mifflin Company.

Hueston, Ethel. *The Honorable Uncle Lancy.* Indianapolis: The Bobbs-Merrill Company, Inc.

1940

Elam, Samuel. *Weevil in the Cotton.* New York: Frederick A. Stokes Company.

1941

Cronyn, George. *Caesar Stagg.* New York: The Greystone Press.

Kimbrough, Edward. *From Hell to Breakfast.* Philadelphia: J. B. Lippincott Company.

1942

Basso, Hamilton. *Sun in Capricorn.* New York: Charles Scribner's Sons.

Jordan, Elizabeth. *Young John Takes Over.* New York: D. Appleton-Century Company, Inc.

Wilder, Robert. *Flamingo Road.* New York: G. P. Putnam's Sons.

1943

Dos Passos, John. *Number One.* Boston: Houghton Mifflin Company.

Fleming, Berry. *Colonel Effingham's Raid.* New York: Duell, Sloan & Pearce, Inc.

1944

Browne, Lewis. *See What I Mean?* Cleveland: The World Publishing Company.
Kaup, Elizabeth Dewing. *Seed of the Puritan.* New York: The Dial Press, Inc.
Lipton, Lawrence. *In Secret Battle.* New York: D. Appleton-Century Company, Inc.

1945

Cohen, Lester. *Coming Home.* New York: The Viking Press, Inc.
Langley, Adria Locke. *A Lion Is in the Streets.* New York: McGraw-Hill Book Company, Inc.

1946

Dwoskin, Charles. *Shadow Over the Land.* New York: The Beechhurst Press.
Raymond, Clifford. *The Honorable John Hale: A Comedy of American Politics.* Indianapolis: The Bobbs-Merrill Company, Inc.
⟩Warren, Robert Penn. *All the King's Men.* New York: Harcourt, Brace and Company, Inc.

1947

Appel, Benjamin. *But Not Yet Slain.* New York: A. A. Wyn, Inc.
Carter, Hodding. *Flood Crest.* New York: Rinehart & Company, Inc.
Rylee, Robert. *The Ring and the Cross.* New York: Alfred A. Knopf, Inc.
Sylvester, Harry. *Moon Gaffney.* New York: Henry Holt and Company, Inc.
Trilling, Lionel. *The Middle of the Journey.* New York: The Viking Press, Inc.
Wellman, Paul I. *The Walls of Jericho.* Philadelphia: J. B. Lippincott Company.

1948

Adams, Samuel Hopkins. *Plunder.* New York: Random House, Inc.

1949

Colby, Merle. *The Big Secret.* New York: The Viking Press, Inc.
Dos Passos, John. *The Grand Design.* Boston: Houghton Mifflin Company.
McCarthy, Mary. *The Oasis.* New York: Random House, Inc.
Miller, Merle. *The Sure Thing.* New York: William Sloane Associates.

1950

Coen, Franklin. *Vinegar Hill.* New York: Rinehart & Company, Inc.

1951

Field, Francis T. *McDonough.* New York: Duell, Sloan & Pearce, Inc.

Mailer, Norman. *Barbary Shore.* New York: Rinehart & Company, Inc.

1952

Amsbarry, Mary Anne. *Caesar's Angel.* Cleveland: The World Publishing Company.

Caldwell, Taylor. *The Devil's Advocate.* New York: Crown Publishers, Inc.

Coe, Charles Francis. *Ashes.* New York: Random House, Inc.

Hicks, Granville. *There Was a Man in Our Town.* New York: The Viking Press, Inc.

Ullman, James Ramsey. *Windom's Way.* Philadelphia: J. B. Lippincott Company.

1953

Manchester, William. *City of Anger.* New York: Ballantine Books.

Wicker, Tom. *The Kingpin.* New York: William Sloane Associates.

1954

Grondahl, Kathryn. *The Mango Season.* New York: William Morrow & Company, Inc.

Guinn, Jack. *The Caperberry Bush.* Boston: Little, Brown & Company.

Shirer, William L. *Stranger Come Home.* Boston: Little, Brown & Company.

1955

Deasy, Mary. *The Boy Who Made Good.* Boston: Little, Brown & Company.

Mayer, Martin. *The Experts.* New York: Harper & Brothers.

Sarton, May. *Faithful Are the Wounds.* New York: Rinehart & Company.

Shaplen, Robert. *A Forest of Tigers.* New York: Alfred A. Knopf, Inc.

Sykes, Gerald. *The Children of Light.* New York: Farrar, Straus & Young, Inc.

Wilder, Robert. *The Wine of Youth.* New York: G. P. Putnam's Sons.

1956

Burdick, Eugene. *The Ninth Wave.* Boston: Houghton Mifflin Company.

Clune, Henry W. *The Big Fella.* New York: The Macmillan Company.

O'Connor, Edwin. *The Last Hurrah.* Boston: Little, Brown & Company.

Schneider, John G. *The Golden Kazoo.* New York: Rinehart & Company, Inc.

1957

Cushman, Dan. *The Old Copper Collar.* New York: Ballantine Books.

Deasy, Mary. *O'Shaughnessy's Day.* New York: Doubleday & Company, Inc.

Foster, John. *Let George Do It!* New York: Harcourt, Brace and Company, Inc.

Haines, William Wister. *The Hon. Rocky Slade.* Boston: Little, Brown & Company.

Reichley, James. *The Burying of Kingsmith.* Boston: Houghton Mifflin Company.

1958

Buechner, Frederick. *The Return of Ansel Gibbs*. New York: Alfred A. Knopf, Inc.

Dineen, Joseph. *Queen Midas*. Boston: Little, Brown & Company.

Farrar, Larston D. *The Sins of Sandra Shaw*. New York: Signet Editions.

Hadley, Arthur T. *The Joy Wagon*. New York: The Viking Press, Inc.

Lederer, William J., and Eugene Burdick. *The Ugly American*. New York: W. W. Norton & Company, Inc.

Streissguth, Thomas. *Tigers in the House: A Satirical Novel of American Do-Good-Ism in Indochina*. New York: Exposition Press.

1959

Condon, Richard. *The Manchurian Candidate*. New York: McGraw-Hill Book Company, Inc.

Drury, Allen. *Advise and Consent*. New York: Doubleday & Company, Inc.

Garrett, George. *The Finished Man*. New York: Charles Scribner's Sons.

Longstreet, Stephen and Ethel. *The Politician*. New York: Funk and Wagnalls Company.

Pearson, William. *A Fever in the Blood*. New York: St. Martin's Press, Inc.

Selby, John. *A Few Short Blocks Between*. New York: Thomas Y. Crowell Company.

Stone, Philip Alston. *No Place to Run*. New York: The Viking Press, Inc.

Williams, Wirt. *Ada Dallas*. New York: McGraw-Hill Book Company, Inc.

1960

Frankel, Ernest. *Tongue of Fire*. New York: The Dial Press, Inc.

Gwaltney, Francis Irby. *A Step in the River*. New York: Random House, Inc.

Lorraine, John. *Men of Career*. New York: Crown Publishers, Inc.

Miller, Warren. *The Sleep of Reason*. Boston: Little, Brown & Company. First published in London in 1956 by Secker & Warburg.

Reardon, William R. *The Big Smear*. New York: Crown Publishers, Inc.

Reichley, James. *Hail to the Chief*. Boston: Houghton Mifflin Company.

B. Related Novels

1844

Disraeli, Benjamin. *Coningsby: or, The New Generation*. London: Henry Colburn.

1852

Stowe, Harriet Beecher. *Uncle Tom's Cabin: or, Life among the Lowly*. Boston: John P. Jewett & Company.

1867

DeForest, John W. *Miss Ravenel's Conversion from Secession to Loyalty*. New York: Harper & Brothers.

1873

Twain, Mark, and Charles Dudley Warner. *The Gilded Age: A Tale of To-Day*. Hartford: American Publishing Company.

1875

DeForest, John W. *Honest John Vane*. New Haven: Richmond & Patten.
———. *Playing the Mischief*. New York: Harper & Brothers.

1877

James, Henry. *The American*. Boston: Houghton Mifflin Company.

1879

Tourgée, Albion W. *A Fool's Errand*. Cincinnati: Forshee & McMakin.

1880

Adams, Henry. *Democracy: An American Novel*. New York: Henry Holt and Company, Inc.
Tourgée, Albion W. *Bricks Without Straw*. New York: Fords, Howard & Hulbert.

1881

Shapley, Rufus E. *Solid for Mulhooly: A Political Satire*. New York: G. W. Carlton & Company. Citations in the text are from the second edition, Philadelphia: Gebbie & Company, 1889.

1883

Burnett, Frances Hodgson. *Through One Administration*. New York: Charles Scribner's Sons.

1885

Crawford, F. Marion. *An American Politician: A Novel*. Boston, New York: Houghton Mifflin Company.

1886

James, Henry. *The Princess Casamassima: A Novel*. London and New York: Macmillan & Co., Ltd.

1888

Bellamy, Edward. *Looking Backward: 2000–1887*. Boston: Ticknor and Company.

1890

Donnelly, Ignatius. *Caesar's Column: A Story of the Twentieth Century*. Chicago: F. J. Schulte & Company. (Edited by Walter B. Rideout. Cambridge, Massachusetts: Harvard University Press, 1960)

1892

Donnelly, Ignatius. *The Golden Bottle: or, The Story of Ephraim Benezet of Kansas*. New York and St. Paul: D. D. Merrill Company.

Garland, Hamlin. *A Spoil of Office: A Story of the Modern West*. Boston: Arena Publishing Company.

1894

Ford, Paul Leicester. *The Honorable Peter Stirling and What People Thought of Him*. New York: Henry Holt and Company, Inc.

Howells, William Dean. *A Traveler from Altruria*. New York: Harper & Brothers.

1898

Page, Thomas Nelson. *Red Rock: A Chronicle of Reconstruction*. New York: Charles Scribner's Sons.

1900

Glasgow, Ellen. *The Voice of the People*. New York: Doubleday, Page & Company.

1901

Friedman, I. K. *By Bread Alone: A Novel*. New York: McClure, Phillips & Company.

Williams, Francis Churchill. *J. Devlin—Boss: A Romance of American Politics*. Boston: Lothrop, Lee & Shepard Co.

1902

Dixon, Thomas, Jr. *The Leopard's Spots: A Romance of the White Man's Burden, 1865–1900*. New York: Doubleday, Page & Company.

1904

Conrad, Joseph. *Nostromo: A Tale of the Seaboard*. New York and London: Harper & Brothers.

1905

Dixon, Thomas, Jr. *The Clansman: An Historical Romance of the Ku Klux Klan*. New York: Doubleday, Page & Company.

1906

Churchill, Winston. *Coniston*. New York: The Macmillan Company.

Sinclair, Upton. *The Jungle*. New York: Doubleday, Page & Company.

1907

Conrad, Joseph. *The Secret Agent: A Simple Tale*. London: Methuen & Co., Ltd.

1911

Conrad, Joseph. *Under Western Eyes: A Novel*. London: Methuen & Co., Ltd.

1913

Dostoevsky, Feodor. *The Possessed*. New York: The Macmillan Company.

1916

Joyce, James. *A Portrait of the Artist as a Young Man.* New York: B. W. Huebsch.

1917

Phillips, David Graham. *Susan Lenox: Her Fall and Rise.* New York: D. Appleton & Company, Inc.

Sinclair, Upton. *King Coal: A Novel.* New York: The Macmillan Company.

1920

Fitzgerald, F. Scott. *This Side of Paradise.* New York: Charles Scribner's Sons.

Lewis, Sinclair. *Main Street: The Story of Carol Kennicott.* New York: Harcourt, Brace and Howe.

1922

Lewis, Sinclair. *Babbitt.* New York: Harcourt, Brace and Company, Inc.

1923

Ford, James L. *Hot Corn Ike.* New York: E. P. Dutton & Co., Inc.

1925

Fitzgerald, F. Scott. *The Great Gatsby.* New York: Charles Scribner's Sons.

1927

Lewis, Sinclair. *Elmer Gantry.* New York: Harcourt, Brace and Company, Inc.

1928

Lawrence, D. H. *Lady Chatterley's Lover.* Florence, Italy: Privately Printed.

1929

Burnett, W. R. *Little Caesar.* New York: The Dial Press, Inc.

Lewis, Sinclair. *Dodsworth.* New York: Harcourt, Brace and Company, Inc.

1932

Don Passos, John, *1919.* New York: Harcourt, Brace and Company, Inc.

Huxley, Aldous. *Brave New World.* London: Chatto & Windus.

1936

Dos Passos, John. *The Big Money.* New York: Harcourt, Brace and Company, Inc.

Faulkner, William. *Absalom, Absalom!* New York: Random House, Inc.

Steinbeck, John. *In Dubious Battle.* New York: Covici, Friede.

1937

Dos Passos, John. *U.S.A.* New York: Harcourt, Brace and Company, Inc.

Hemingway, Ernest. *To Have and Have Not.* New York: Charles Scribner's Sons.

Silone, Ignazio. *Bread and Wine.* New York and London: Harper & Brothers.

1939

Steinbeck, John. *The Grapes of Wrath.* New York: The Viking Press, Inc.
West, Nathanael. *The Day of the Locust.* New York: Random House, Inc.
  (Also published by New Directions [New York, 1950], with an Introduction
  by Richard B. Gehman.)

1940

Hemingway, Ernest. *For Whom the Bell Tolls.* New York: Charles Scribner's
  Sons.

1941

Koestler, Arthur. *Darkness at Noon.* New York: The Macmillan Company.

1942

Cary, Joyce. *To Be a Pilgrim.* London: Michael Joseph.

1946

Farrell, James T. *Bernard Clare.* New York: Vanguard Press, Inc.

1948

Mailer, Norman. *The Naked and the Dead.* New York: Rinehart & Company,
  Inc.

1949

Farrell, James T. *The Road Between.* New York: Vanguard Press, Inc.
Orwell, George. *Nineteen Eighty-Four: A Novel.* London: Martin Secker &
  Warburg, Ltd.
Weller, George. *The Crack in the Column.* New York: Random House, Inc.

1951

Koestler, Arthur. *The Age of Longing.* New York: The Macmillan Company.
Shaw, Irwin. *The Troubled Air.* New York: Random House, Inc.

1952

Cary, Joyce. *Prisoner of Grace.* London: Michael Joseph.
Farrell, James T. *Yet Other Waters.* New York: Vanguard Press, Inc.

1953

Bradbury, Ray. *Fahrenheit 451.* New York: Ballantine Books.
Cary, Joyce. *Except the Lord.* London: Michael Joseph.
Karp, David. *One: A Novel.* New York: Vanguard Press, Inc.

1954

Basso, Hamilton. *The View from Pompey's Head.* New York: Doubleday &
  Company, Inc.

1956

Greene, Graham. *The Quiet American.* London: William Heinemann, Ltd.

1957

Habe, Hans. *Off Limits*. New York: Frederick Fell.
Shute, Nevil. *On the Beach*. London: William Heinemann, Ltd.
Steinbeck, John. *The Short Reign of Pippin IV: A Fabrication*. New York: The Viking Press, Inc.

1958

Habe, Hans. *The Devil's Agent*. New York: Frederick Fell.
Kauffman, Lane. *A Lesser Lion*. Philadelphia: J. B. Lippincott Company.
Spender, Stephen. *Engaged in Writing: and, The Fool and the Princess*. New York: Farrar, Straus and Cudahy, Inc.

1960

Chase, Ilka. *Three Men on the Left Hand*. New York: Doubleday & Company, Inc.

1961

Dos Passos, John. *Midcentury*. Boston: Houghton Mifflin Company.

C. *Novels Published between 1961 and April, 1965.*

1961

Brammer, William. *The Gay Place*. Boston: Houghton Mifflin Company.
Childs, Marquis W. *The Peacemakers*. New York: Harcourt, Brace and World, Inc.
Coffin, Tristram. *Not to the Swift*. New York: W. W. Norton & Company, Inc.
Halberstam, David. *The Noblest Roman*. Boston: Houghton Mifflin Company.
Manchester, William. *The Long Gainer*. Boston: Little, Brown & Company.
Mayfield, Julian. *The Grand Parade*. New York: Vanguard Press, Inc.

1962

Baxter, John. *A Gift for Gomala*. Philadelphia: J. B. Lippincott Company.
Bonner, Paul Hyde. *Ambassador Extraordinary*. New York: Charles Scribner's Sons.
Burdick, Eugene, and Harvey Wheeler. *Fail-Safe*. New York: McGraw-Hill Book Company, Inc.
Dougherty, Richard. *Duggan*. New York: Doubleday & Company, Inc.
Drury, Allen. *A Shade of Difference*. New York: Doubleday & Company, Inc.
Fleming, Thomas J. *All Good Men*. New York: Doubleday & Company, Inc.
Gallagher, Phyllis Moore. *All Is Not Quiet on the Potomac*. Baltimore: Reid, Alton.
Hulbert, James. *Noon on the Third Day*. New York: Holt, Rinehart and Winston, Inc.
Knebel, Fletcher, and Charles W. Bailey II. *Seven Days in May*. New York: Harper & Row.

Mann, Georg. *The Blind Ballots*. New York: The Macmillan Company.

Rogers, Edward A. *Face to Face*. New York: William Morrow & Company, Inc.

Ross, Walter. *Coast to Coast: A Novel about Corruption in High Places*. New York: Simon and Schuster.

Tracy, Don. *The Hated One*. New York: Pocket Books.

Traver, Robert. *Hornstein's Boy*. New York: St. Martin's Press, Inc.

Tully, Andrew. *Capitol Hill*. New York: Simon and Schuster, Inc.

1963

Conrad, Earl. *The Premier*. New York: Doubleday & Company, Inc.

Rascovich, Mark. *The Bedford Incident*. New York: Atheneum Press.

1964

Burdick, Eugene. *The 480*. New York: McGraw-Hill Book Company, Inc.

Deal, Borden. *The Loser*. New York: Doubleday & Company, Inc.

Dewey, Thomas B. *Don't Cry for Long*. New York: Simon and Schuster, Inc.

Grumbach, Doris. *The Short Throat, the Tender Mouth*. New York: Doubleday & Company, Inc.

Knebel, Fletcher, and Charles W. Bailey II. *Convention*. New York and Evanston: Harper & Row.

Robertson, Don. *A Flag Full of Stars*. New York: G. P. Putnam's Sons.

Scaevola, Peter. *'68: A Novel of Presidential Politics*. New York: W. W. Norton & Company, Inc.

Taylor, Henry J. *The Big Man*. New York: Random House, Inc.

Wallace, Irving. *The Man*. New York: Simon and Schuster, Inc.

Wibberly, Leonard. *A Feast of Freedom*. New York: William Morrow & Company, Inc.

1965

Hoffenberg, Jack. *A Thunder at Dawn*. New York: E. P. Dutton & Co., Inc.

Kraslow, David, and Robert Boyd. *A Certain Evil*. Boston: Little, Brown & Company.

McBain, Ed. *The Sentries*. New York: Simon and Schuster, Inc.

McGerr, Patricia. *Is There a Traitor in the House?* New York: Doubleday & Company, Inc.

West, Morris L. *The Ambassador*. New York: William Morrow & Company, Inc.

II. Secondary Sources

A. Books and Monographs

Aaron, Daniel. *Writers on the Left: Episodes in American Literary Communism*. New York: Harcourt, Brace & World, Inc., 1961.

Adams, Samuel Hopkins. *The Incredible Era: The Life and Times of Warren Gamaliel Harding.* Boston: Houghton Mifflin Company, 1939.

Almond, Gabriel A., and James R. Coleman (eds.). *The Politics of the Developing Areas.* Princeton, New Jersey: Princeton University Press, 1960.

Anderson, Jack, and Ronald W. May. *McCarthy: The Man, the Senator, the 'Ism.* Boston: The Beacon Press, 1952.

Arnold, Thurman. *The Symbols of Government.* New Haven, Connecticut: Yale University Press, 1935.

Barzun, Jacques. *Darwin, Marx, Wagner: Critique of a Heritage.* Revised edition. New York: Anchor Books, 1958.

Beard, Charles A. *An Economic Interpretation of the Constitution.* New York: The Macmillan Company, 1913.

————.*Jefferson, Corporations and the Constitution.* Washington, D.C.: National Home Library Foundation, 1936.

Bell, Daniel (ed.). *The New American Right.* New York: Criterion Books, 1955.

Blaisdell, Donald C. *Investigation of Concentration of Economic Power.* Washington, D.C.: U.S. Government Printing Office, 1941. A study made for the Temporary National Economic Committee, 76th Congress, 3rd Session.

Blotner, Joseph. *The Political Novel.* New York: Doubleday & Company, Inc., 1955.

Bodkin, Maud. *Archetypal Patterns in Poetry: Psychological Studies of Imagination.* New York: Vintage Books, 1958.

Browne, Malcolm W. *The New Face of War.* Indianapolis: The Bobbs-Merrill Company, Inc., 1965.

Buckley, William F., and L. Brent Bozell. *McCarthy and His Enemies.* Chicago: Henry Regnery Company, 1954.

Campbell, Joseph. *The Hero with a Thousand Faces.* Cleveland and New York: The World Publishing Company, 1956.

Carlson, John Roy. *Under Cover: My Four Years in the Nazi Underworld of America—The Amazing Revelation of How Axis Agents and Our Enemies Within Are Now Plotting to Destroy the United States.* New York: E. P. Dutton & Co., Inc., 1943.

Carter, Hodding. *Where Main Street Meets the River.* New York: Rinehart & Company, Inc., 1953.

Cash, W. J. *The Mind of the South.* New York: Alfred A. Knopf, Inc., 1941.

Chalmers, D. M. *The Social and Political Ideas of the Muckrakers.* New York: The Citadel Press, 1964.

Chalmers, David M. *Hooded Americanism: The First Century of the Ku Klux Klan, 1865–1965.* New York: Doubleday & Company, Inc., 1965.

Chambers, Whittaker. *Witness.* New York: Random House, Inc., 1952.

The Congressional Record. Volumes 58 and 93.

Cooke, Alistair. *A Generation on Trial: U.S.A. v. Alger Hiss.* New York: Alfred A. Knopf, Inc., 1950.

Crabb, Cecil V., Jr. *American Foreign Policy in the Nuclear Age: Principles, Problems, and Prospects.* Evanston, Illinois: Row, Peterson & Company, 1960.

Crawford, Kenneth. *The Pressure Boys: The Inside Story of Lobbying in America.* New York: Julian Messner, Inc., 1939.

Croly, Herbert. *The Promise of American Life.* New York: The Macmillan Company, 1909.

Crossman, Richard (ed.) *The God That Failed.* New York: Harper and Brothers, 1949.

Curley, James Michael. *I'd Do It Again: A Record of All My Uproarious Years.* New York: Prentice-Hall, Inc., 1957.

de Beauvoir, Simone. *The Second Sex.* Translated by H. M. Parshley. New York: Alfred A. Knopf, Inc., 1953.

Dineen, Joseph F. *The Purple Shamrock: The Hon. James Michael Curley of Boston.* New York: W. W. Norton & Company, Inc., 1949.

Duffield, Marcus. *King Legion.* New York: Jonathan Cape and Harrison Smith, 1931.

Dunne, Finley Peter. *Mr. Dooley in Peace and in War.* Boston: Small, Maynard & Company, 1898.

—. *Mr. Dooley in the Hearts of His Countrymen.* Boston: Small, Maynard & Company, 1899.

—. *Mr. Dooley Remembers: The Informal Memoirs of Finley Peter Dunne.* Edited by Philip Dunne. Boston: Atlantic-Little, Brown, 1963.

Ellsworth, Ralph E., and Sarah M. Harris. *The American Right Wing: A Report to the Fund for the Republic, Inc.*, University of Illinois Library School, Occasional Papers, Number 59, November 1960.

Facts on File: Weekly World News Digest, VIII–XI (1948–1951).

Federal Trade Commission. *Summary Report.* Document 92, Part 71A. Seventieth Congress, first session.

Fiedler, Leslie A. *An End to Innocence: Essays on Culture and Politics.* Boston: The Beacon Press, 1955.

Filler, Louis. *Crusaders for American Liberalism.* New York: Harcourt, Brace and Company, Inc., 1939.

Foner, Philip S. *Jack London: American Rebel.* New York: The Citadel Press, 1947.

Frazer, Sir James George. *The Golden Bough: A Study in Magic and Religion.* New York: The Macmillan Company, 1943. (One volume abridged edition.)

—. *The New Golden Bough: A New Abridgment of the Classic Work.* Edited with notes and foreword by Dr. Theodore H. Gaster. New York: Criterion Books, 1959.

Frye, Northrup. *Anatomy of Criticism: Four Essays*, Princeton, New Jersey: Princeton University Press, 1957.

Goldman, Eric F. *The Crucial Decade and After: America, 1945–1960*. New York: Vintage Books, 1960.

—. *Rendezvous with Destiny: A History of Modern American Reform*. New York: Alfred A. Knopf, Inc., 1952.

Gwynn, Frederick L., and Joseph L. Blotner (eds.) *Faulkner in the University*. Charlottesville: University of Virginia Press, 1959.

Halberstam, David. *The Making of a Quagmire*. New York: Random House, Inc., 1965.

Harris, Thomas O. *The Kingfish: Huey P. Long, Dictator*. New Orleans: The Pelican Press, 1938.

Hicks, Granville. *Part of the Truth*. New York: Harcourt, Brace & World, 1965.

Hiss, Alger. *In the Court of Public Opinion*. New York: Alfred A. Knopf, Inc., 1957.

Hitler, Adolf. *Mein Kampf*. New York: Reynal & Hitchcock, Inc., 1939.

Hoffman, Frederick J. *Freudianism and the Literary Mind*. Baton Rouge: Louisiana State University Press, 1945.

Hofstadter, Richard. *The Age of Reform: From Bryan to F. D. R.* New York: Alfred A. Knopf, Inc., 1955.

—. *Anti-intellectualism in American Life*. New York: Alfred A. Knopf, Inc., 1963.

Howe, Irving. *Politics and the Novel*. New York: Horizon, 1957.

Josephson, Matthew. *The Politicos, 1865–1896*. New York: Harcourt, Brace and Company, Inc., 1938.

Joughin, G. Louis, and Edmund M. Morgan. *The Legacy of Sacco and Vanzetti*. New York: Harcourt, Brace and Company, Inc., 1948.

Joyce, James. *Stephen Hero: A Part of the First Draft of a Portrait of the Artist as a Young Man*. Edited by Theodore Spencer. New York: New Directions, 1944.

Jung, C. G. *The Archetypes and the Collective Unconscious*. London: Routledge & Kegan Paul, Ltd., 1959.

Kane, Hartnett T. *Louisiana Hayride: The American Rehearsal for Dictatorship*. New York: William Morrow & Company, Inc., 1941.

Kefauver, Estes. *Crime in America*. Edited by Sidney Shallett. New York: Doubleday & Company, Inc., 1951.

—. *In a Few Hands: Monopoly Power in America*. With the assistance of Irene Till. New York: Pantheon Books, Inc., 1965.

Key, V. O., Jr. *Southern Politics*. New York: Alfred A. Knopf, Inc., 1949.

Leighton, Isabel (ed.). *The Aspirin Age*. New York: Simon and Schuster, Inc., 1949.

Lewis, R. W. B. *The American Adam: Innocence, Tragedy and Tradition in the Nineteenth Century.* Chicago: Phoenix Books, 1955.

Light, James F. *Nathanael West: An Interpretive Study.* [Evanston, Illinois]: Northwestern University Press, 1961.

Link, Arthur. *American Epoch: A History of the United States since the 1890's.* New York: Alfred A. Knopf, Inc., 1955.

Lippmann, Walter. *A Preface to Morals.* New York: The Macmillan Company, 1929.

—. *A Preface to Politics.* New York and London: M. Kennerly, 1913.

Long, Huey P., Jr. *Every Man a King: The Autobiography of Huey P. Long.* New Orleans: National Book Company, 1933.

Luthin, Reinhard H. *American Demagogues: Twentieth Century.* Introduction by Allan Nevins. Gloucester, Massachusetts: Peter Smith, 1959.

Lynch, Denis Tilden. *Criminals and Politicians.* New York: The Macmillan Company, 1932.

Matthiessen, F. O. *American Renaissance: Art and Expression in the Age of Emerson and Whitman.* London, New York: Oxford University Press, 1941.

McClellan, John L. *Crime without Punishment.* New York: Duell, Sloan, & Pearce, Inc., 1962.

Michie, Allan A., and Frank Rhylick. *Dixie Demagogues.* New York: Vanguard Press, Inc., 1939.

Milbrath, Lester W. *The Washington Lobbyists.* Chicago: Rand McNally & Company, 1963.

Montgomery, John D. *The Politics of Foreign Aid: American Experience in Southeast Asia.* New York: Frederick A. Praeger, 1962.

National American Woman Suffrage Association. *Victory—How Women Won It: A Centennial Symposium.* New York: The H. W. Wilson Company, 1940.

New York State Legislature. *Report and Proceedings of the Senate Committee to Investigate the Police Department of the City of New York.* Five volumes. Albany: New York State Legislature, 1900.

Patmore, Coventry. *The Poems of Coventry Patmore.* Edited by Frederick Page. London: Oxford University Press, 1949.

Pentony, DeVere E. (ed.). *United States Foreign Aid: Readings in the Problem Area of Wealth.* San Francisco: Howard Chandler, 1960.

Peffer, Nathaniel. *The Far East.* Ann Arbor: Michigan University Press, 1958.

Phillips, David Graham. *The Treason of the Senate.* New York: Monthly Review Press, 1953. [Reprinted from *Cosmopolitan*, March–November, 1906.]

Plunkitt, George Washington. *Plunkitt of Tammany Hall.* Edited by William L. Riordan, with an introduction by Roy V. Peel. New York: Alfred A. Knopf, Inc., 1948.

Raglan, Fitzroy Richard Somerset, Lord. *The Hero: A Study in Tradition, Myth, and Drama.* New York: Vintage Books, 1956.

Randel, William Peirce. *The Ku Klux Klan: A Century of Infamy.* Philadelphia and New York: Chilton Books, 1965.

Regier, C. C. *The Era of the Muckrakers.* Chapel Hill: University of North Carolina Press, 1932.

Rideout, Walter B. *The Radical Novel in the United States 1900–1954: Some Interrelations of Literature and Society.* Cambridge, Massachusetts: Harvard University Press, 1956.

Rollins, Richard. *I Find Treason: The Story of an American Anti-Nazi Agent.* New York: William Morrow & Company, Inc., 1941.

Roosevelt, Theodore. *The Letters of Theodore Roosevelt.* Selected and edited by Elting E. Morison. Cambridge, Massachusetts: Harvard University Press, 1951.

Root, Jonathan. *One Night in July: The True Story of the Rosenthal-Becker Murder Case.* New York: Coward-McCann, Inc., 1961.

Rorty, James, and Moshe Decter. *McCarthy and the Communists.* Boston: The Beacon Press, 1954.

Rovere, Richard H. *Senator Joe McCarthy.* New York: Harcourt, Brace and Company, Inc., 1959.

Sandburg, Carl. *Abraham Lincoln: The Prairie Years.* Two volumes. New York: Harcourt, Brace and Company, Inc., 1926.

Schlesinger, Arthur M., Jr. *The Age of Roosevelt: The Politics of Upheaval.* Boston: Houghton Mifflin Company, 1960.

Schorer, Mark. *Sinclair Lewis: An American Life.* New York: McGraw-Hill Book Company, Inc., 1961.

Schriftgiesser, Karl. *The Lobbyists: The Art and Business of Influencing Lawmakers.* Boston: Little, Brown & Company, 1951.

Seldes, George. *Facts and Fascism.* New York: In Fact, 1943.

—. *1000 Americans.* New York: Boni & Gaer, 1947.

Sherwin, Mark. *The Extremists.* New York: St. Martin's Press, Inc., 1963.

Sinclair, Andrew. *The Available Man: Warren Gamaliel Harding.* New York: The Macmillan Company, 1965.

Sinclair, Upton. *American Outpost: A Book of Reminiscences.* New York: Farrar & Rinehart, Inc., 1932.

—. *The Autobiography of Upton Sinclair.* New York: Harcourt, Brace & World, Inc., 1962.

Speare, Morris Edmund. *The Political Novel: Its Development in England and America.* New York: Oxford University Press, 1924.

Stearns, Harold W. *Liberalism in America.* New York: Boni & Liveright, 1919.

Steffens, Lincoln. *The Shame of the Cities.* New York: McClure, Phillips & Company, 1904.

—. *The Autobiography of Lincoln Steffens.* Two volumes. New York: Harcourt, Brace and Company, Inc., 1931.

Sullivan, Mark. *Our Times.* Six volumes. New York: Charles Scribner's Sons, 1926–1935.

Toledano, Ralph de, and Victor Lasky. *Seeds of Treason: The True Story of the Hiss-Chambers Tragedy.* New York: Published for *Newsweek* by Funk & Wagnalls, 1950.

Van Devander, Charles W. *The Big Bosses.* n.p.: Howell, Soskin, 1944.

Von Salomon, Ernst. *Fragebogen. The Questionnaire.* New York: Doubleday & Company, Inc., 1954.

Wallace, Henry. *The Price of Free World Victory.* New York: L. B. Fischer, 1942.

Wechsler, James A. *The Age of Suspicion.* New York: Random House, Inc., 1953.

Weisberger, Bernard A. *The American Newspaperman.* Chicago: University of Chicago Press, 1961.

Weyl, Nathaniel. *The Battle against Disloyalty.* New York: Thomas Y. Crowell Company, 1951.

—. *Treason: The Story of Disloyalty and Betrayal in American History.* Washington, D.C.: Public Affairs Press, 1950.

White, William Allen. *The Autobiography of William Allen White.* New York: The Macmillan Company, 1946.

Whitman, Walt. *Walt Whitman: Complete Poetry and Selected Prose.* Edited by James E. Miller, Jr. Boston: Houghton Mifflin Company, 1959.

Wilson, Woodrow. *The New Freedom.* Edited by W. B. Hale. New York: Doubleday, Page & Company. 1913.

Woolf, Virginia. *The Death of the Moth and Other Essays.* New York: Harcourt, Brace and Company, Inc., 1942.

Zink, Harold. *City Bosses in the United States: A Study of Twenty Municipal Bosses.* Durham, North Carolina: Duke University Press, 1930.

B. Articles in Journals and Books

Cater, Douglass. "Advice and Dissent about the Best Man," *New York Times Magazine,* May 22, 1960, pp. 27, 89.

Cowley, Malcolm. "Echoes of a Crime," *New Republic,* LXXIV (August 28, 1935), 79.

Davidson, James F. "Political Science and Political Fiction," *American Political Science Review,* LV (December, 1961), 851–860.

Dos Passos, John. "An Open Letter to President Lowell," *The Nation,* Vol. 125 (August 24, 1927), p. 176.

Goldman, Eric F. "David Graham Phillips: Victorian Critic of Victorianism," in *The Lives of Eighteen from Princeton.* Edited by Willard Thorp. Princeton, New Jersey: Princeton University Press, pp. 318–332.

Hart, Donn V. "Overseas Americans in Southeast Asia: Fact in Fiction," *Far Eastern Survey,* Vol. 30 (January, 1961), pp. 1–15.

Hart, Henry. "Contemporary Publishing and the Revolutionary Writer," in *American Writers' Congress.* New York: International Publishers, 1935.

Hicks, Granville. "The Failure of the Left Criticism," *New Republic,* CIII (September 9, 1940), 345–347.

Hofstadter, Richard and Beatrice. "Winston Churchill: A Study in the Popular Novel," *American Quarterly,* 2 (Spring, 1950), 12–28.

Mason, Edward A. "United States Interests in Foreign Economic Assistance," in *International Stability and Progress.* New York: Columbia University Press, 1957.

Moore, Richmond. "John Dos Passos Gives Views in Interview," *The Cavalier Daily* (University of Virginia), February 20, 1963.

Schlesinger, James R. "Foreign Aid: A Plea for Realism," *The Virginia Quarterly Review,* Vol. 35 (Spring, 1959), pp. 221–239.

T. R. B. "Neanderthal Men," *New Republic,* CXVII (August 4, 1947), 3–4.

Tarbell, Ida. "History of the Standard Oil Company," *McClure's Magazine,* Vol. 20 (November, 1902–April, 1903), 3–16, 115–128, 248–260, 390–403, 493–508, 606–621; Vol. 21 (May–October, 1903), 73–88, 202–215, 312–327; Vol. 22 (November, 1903–April, 1904), 108–112, 127–140, 294–306, 435–448, 492–504, 638–652; Vol. 23 (May–October, 1904), 186–203, 532–548, 660–672.

Trevor-Roper, H. R. "A Rockwell Cannot Be a Hitler," *New York Times Magazine,* November 25, 1962, pp. 32–33, 146–148.

U.S. Senate. "The Objectives of United States Economic Assistance Programs," *The Foreign Aid Program.* U.S. Senate, The Special Committee to study the Foreign Aid Program, 85th Congress, 1st Session, 1957, Sec. 1, pp. 4–15.

Warren, Robert Penn. "A Note to *All the King's Men,*" *Sewanee Review,* LXI (Summer, 1953), 476–480.

White, Theodore H. "The Battle of Athens, Tennessee," *Harper's Magazine,* Vol. 194 (January, 1947), pp. 54–60.

White, William Allen. "Roosevelt: A Force for Righteousness," *McClure's,* XXVIII (January, 1907), 386–394.

INDEX

Aaron, Daniel: 10, 246, 360
abolition: 167, 177
Absalom, Absalom!: 204
Ada Dallas: 180–185
Adams, Henry: 10 n., 110, 111
Adams, Mildred: 167
Adams, Samuel: 125
Adams, Samuel Hopkins: 113–117 *passim*; 131, 156
Addams, Jane: 171
Adonis, Joe: 102, 103
adultery: in fiction, 45, 214, 218, 222, 228, 248, 344, 366
Adventures of a Young Man: 9, 45 n., 215, 311, 312–315, 335, 360
advertising: 22, 159, 160–161
Advise and Consent: 297–299, 363
Africa: 158, 365
agencies, diplomatic: 341
—, gov't: 235, 291, 321, 341; corruption in, 108, 279; intellectuals in, 308
Age of Longing, The: 163, 312
Agricultural Adj. Admin.: 271
agriculture: 24, 144–145
Alabama: 191 n., 192, 202
alcoholism: 181, 215, 346
aldermen, city: 31, 70, 256, 281
Alger, Horatio: 41, 73, 244–245, 247
aliens: 167, 236, 265, 266, 268 n.
Allan, Glenn: 209–210
allegory, novels of: 8
Allen, O. K.: 199
Allies, the: 155 n., 338
All Is Not Quiet on the Potomac: 367
All My Sons: 256 n.
All the King's Men: 74 n., 294; and other novels, 181–184; quality of, 204, 214, 315, 334, 335, 360, 367; discussion of, 219–226
Alsop brothers, the: 303
Ambassador, The: 367
Ambassador Extraordinary: 366
Ambassadors, The: 34 n., 82, 318, 357
ambition: 77, 285, 294
America First: 237, 253–255
American, The: 34 n.

Am. Destiny Party: 236, 237
Am. Electric Railway Ass'n: 105
Am. Expeditionary Force: 265
Am. Gas Ass'n: 105
Am. Legion: 106, 118 n., 158, 266
Am. Liberty League: 240
Am. Medical Ass'n: 106
Am. Nationalists: 236
Am. Party: 264, 267
Am. Patriots: 236
American Politician, An: 27
American Progress: 198
Am. Protective Ass'n: 264, 267
Am. Railway Union: 95 n.
Am. Writers' Congress: 44, 257 n.
Ames, Albert A.: 61
Amsbarry, Mary Anne: 135, 136
Anaconda Copper Co.: 70, 134 n., 256 n.
anarchy: 21, 149, 266, 278, 288, 318
Anderson, Jack: 274
Angel in the House, The: 164–165, 170, 358
angels: 147, 165, 223, 357, 359
Anna Karenina: 189
Anthony, Susan B.: 166, 167
anthropology: 55 n.–56 n., 327
anti-Americanism: 277 n., 270, 282, 301, 344
anti-Communism: and the Minutemen, 154 n.; in fiction, 229, 352, 353; Weschler and, 276; Farrell and, 311 n.; and Ngo Dinh Diem, 338.
Anti-Saloon League: 44, 99
antitrust laws: 25, 27, 53, 95
apocalyptic novels: 140, 145, 150–159 *passim*
Appel, Benjamin: 128–129, 290–291
Appleseed, Johnny: 358
archetypes: 11–12, 13, 315, 369
Argentina: 184 n.–185 n.
aristocrats: 158, 314; and Young Knight, 41, 44–45, 51, 52; nature of, 260; and McCarthy, 279 n.
—, Boston, 287
—, Southern, 205, 208, 209